Creative Writer's Handbook

FOURTH EDITION

PHILIP K. JASON

*Emeritus Professor of English, United States Naval Academy; Director,
The Writing Program, Naples Center of Florida Gulf Coast University*

ALLAN B. LEFCOWITZ

*Artistic Director Emeritus, The Writer's Center; Emeritus Professor
of English, United States Naval Academy*

PEARSON
Prentice
Hall

Upper Saddle River, NJ 07458

Library of Congress Cataloging-in-Publication Data

Jason, Philip K. (date)
  Creative writer's handbook / Philip K. Jason, Allan B. Lefcowitz.—4th ed.
    p. cm.
  Includes bibliographical references and index.
  ISBN 0-13-189371-8
  1. Authorship. 2. Creative writing. I. Lefcowitz, Allan B. II. Title.

PN145.J37 2004
808'.02—dc22

2004013035

Editor-in-Chief: Leah Jewell
Acquisitions Editor: Vivian Garcia
Editorial Assistant: Melissa Casciano
Executive Marketing Manager: Brandy Dawson
Marketing Assistant: Allison Peck
Production Liaison: Marianne Peters-Riordan
Manufacturing Buyer: Brian Mackey
Cover Designer: Robert Farrar-Wagner
Permissions Specialist: Mary Dalton-Hoffman
Composition/Full-Service Project Management: Anita Ananda/Integra Software Services
Printing and Binding: Phoenix Color Corp.

Pearson Education LTD
Pearson Education Singapore, Pte. Ltd
Pearson Education, Canada, Ltd
Pearson Education–Japan
Pearson Education Australia PTY, Limited

Pearson Education North Asia Ltd
Pearson Educación de Mexico, S.A. de C.V.
Pearson Education Malaysia, Pte. Ltd
Pearson Education, Upper Saddle River, New Jersey

10 9 8 7 6 5 4 3 2 1
ISBN 0-13-189371-8

Contents

Part III   The Concerns of the Storyteller

Anthology of Poems

Because the many illustrative poems in this text are not found in a single chapter, we provide the following list for convenience.

See also excerpts from works by A. R. Ammons, Robert Browning, John Ciardi, Margaret Gibson, Richard Hugo, Philip Levine, Audre Lorde, Andrew Marvell, Marianne Moore, Alexander Pope, Wyatt Prunty, John W. Saxe, William Shakespeare, Dave Smith, Andrien Stoutenburg, Dylan Thomas, Walt Whitman, and many student poets (page references in index).

Preface

The *Creative Writer's Handbook* is designed to help beginners. While creativity itself cannot be taught, our premise is that you can learn to tap and shape your creative energies. We do not hold with that popular image of the creative artist as a solitary, inspired soul who spins out a sublime work without sweat and labor. Paradoxically, you need to be "practical" about creative writing.

Just as people with physical gifts can be coached so that these gifts are perfected, people with creative imaginations can be led to exercise and develop that creativity. They can be "coached" in the intricacies of language and literary structure. Though abilities will differ, our experience with hundreds of students in creative writing classes and workshops has shown us that most people have more creative talent than they realize. When they first begin to practice the craft, however, they need some direction about conventions, forms, and procedures. Each writer does not need to invent the game for him or herself.

This book began because we felt that the texts available to us, though admirable, were too advanced *for beginners*. They were like calculus to those who need algebra. We wanted a text that responded to the issues we faced in the classroom and the workshop with novice writers who needed to know everything from the rules of the game, to the proper formats, to the professional lingo. We had in mind a text that students could refer to for specific information and help on basic issues and problems.

In each chapter, we have combined the most useful theory, practical advice, and examples. The many questions and exercises are designed to involve you in the issues and practice of literary craft. Some of them may even spark results worth developing into poems, stories, or plays.

Although your creative energies can be directed to produce successful results, not every writer can or deserves to make it into print, just as not every athlete can make it to the Olympics. Still, with hard work in a sport, craft, or art, you can improve, learn from experience and from authority, and find ways of making any such activity pleasurable and useful. Our first premise is rooted in the idea that doing creative writing is valuable in itself, if only to increase one's understanding of just how hard it is to write successfully.

Another premise is that *any* successful writing is, finally, the result of rigorous editing. As important as it is to get something down on paper in the first place—and we have given that problem much of our attention—it is even more important to learn how to shape and reshape, how to spot your problems, and how to work out your solutions. Every writer must learn how to take and use criticism and, at some point, every successful writer must take on the role of self-editor.

In the *Creative Writer's Handbook* we have provided a series of occasions for you to think, read, investigate, *write*, write again, and rewrite—and also to imitate, invent, respond, discover, and surprise yourself. However, even though we have given the order of presentation considerable thought, there can be as many paths through the book as there are readers. While this text is aimed at the student in the creative writing course, we have kept in mind the needs of the writer who wants to go at it solo.

The five chapters of "Part I: A Writer's Concerns" take up issues of importance to every creative writer; the next ten chapters—Parts II, III, and IV— focus on specific issues in the major genres; the final two chapters, Part V, contain reference materials for writers.

Chapter 1 provides an opportunity for you to assess your motives and attitudes as a student of writing. We suggest ways that will help you to become assertive, disciplined, and ready for work. We encourage you to be serious, but not sour. Once you are "Working like a Writer," you have a fighting chance of doing the work of a writer.

Chapter 2, "Keeping a Journal," aims to show one way that a writer forces commitment. Writers write. We provide a full box of suggestions to keep you working, but the goal is for you to strike off on your own. The journal is your lab, your practice field, where you can make false starts, mistakes, and discoveries.

Chapter 3 contains the broad, somewhat technical subject of "Point of View." In the journal, a person very close to the intimate "I" does almost all of the recording. Literary creations, however, often involve a less literally autobiographical "I." Who is the speaker in the story or poem? What difference does it make? Exploring these key questions requires careful reading and a number of exercises—occasions—to help you become confident in handling this complex, unavoidable issue.

In Chapter 4, "Language Is Your Medium," you have an opportunity to exercise all the muscles in the body of words that you need to command, and to get them working in harmony. You don't expect a landscape painter to succeed without knowing anything about lines, shapes, and colors, and about brushes, pigments, and canvas. The writer too must master the materials, in this case the materials of language. Most of us take language for granted—it's something we're born to. Remember, however, that just as the demands put upon your language skills are now heightened, your concern for language must be similarly heightened. We think you will enjoy these jumping jacks, push-ups, and other language calisthenics.

Chapter 5 takes up the interplay between imagination and fact. In "Invention and Research" we share ideas and techniques, collected in many places over many years, that will enable you to access your creative energies. This chapter includes suggestions on how to find the facts you need to build the worlds your imagination will create. It also provides exercises that show how to use facts to stimulate creativity. In these exercises we show how writers can create their own games.

These first five chapters are grounded in general issues, so you can come to understand the ways in which any writing task can be "creative." In the next ten chapters, you will explore the specific conventions and special concerns of the major genres: poetry, prose narrative, and drama. These chapters, the next three parts of the book, are, of course, the heart of the book; they are substantially more detailed than the preliminary chapters and require a slower pace.

The genre chapters combine information, examples, and exercises and contain both professional and student work to show various levels of achievement. We have isolated the major problems that beginners have and examined the nature and causes of those problems. Often we suggest solutions. We are convinced that effective creative writing is a network of solved problems.

Each of the three parts devoted to genre exploration begins with a chapter focusing on the conventions through which that genre defines itself. Our bias here is that without coming to grips with the conventions, you cannot reach an audience, nor can you ever become effectively unconventional.

In this book, "conventional" refers to the customs or protocols of a literary type. Just as religious groups have set patterns of observance, just as a meeting of foreign ministers has its established courtesies, just as a formal meeting has its way of getting things done (following, for instance, Robert's Rules of Order), so literary types have their conventional—customary—methods of expression. Conventions enable everyone to start off with an agreement about the ground rules, and so, it is *through* these conventions, not *despite* them, that creative expression takes place. Through them, you meet the audience halfway.

Part V provides a writer's toolbox. Chapter 16, "From Revision to Submission," aims at further development of editorial skills. It also explains and illustrates the conventions of manuscript form and discusses strategies for submitting work to editors. The lists in "Tools and Resources," Chapter 17, are not meant to be definitive but suggestive, illustrating the kinds of books a creative writer wants to know about or own. The book concludes with a glossary of key terms.

As much as possible we have followed our own classroom practice. We have tried to provide occasions for writing. Our approach is more like that of editors and writers than of critics. We have tried to give a realistic picture of the processes, demands, and rewards of the game. We cannot, of course, touch on everything. You will need someone—a teacher, workshop leader, or editor—to deal with the exceptions and complications.

For a Teacher or Workshop Leader

We have included many more examples and exercises than anyone could use, even in a year-long course or workshop, so that both you and your students might have a variety from which to choose.

We invite you, as we do all our readers, to send us the results of these exercises for possible inclusion in future editions, as well as exercises of your own. We would also like to hear about aspects of craft you would like to see treated more fully. On the other hand, where do you think we could cut back? Remembering that this text is for beginning creative writers, please let us know what elements we missed completely. As editor out in the field, you become our best source for improving the book.

Philip K. Jason
Allan B. Lefcowitz

Preface to the Fourth Edition

In this edition we have given more attention to the interrelationships among genres. Though techniques of character development or dialogue may appear irrelevant to writing poetry or nonfiction, they are not. Nor are the techniques of sound patterns beside the point when one comes to write a play or a story. As we tell students in our workshops, what makes writing both fascinating and difficult is the fact that everything counts.

Almost everywhere, we have added and replaced examples, expanded sections, deleted some material and added other material. We have tried to make the book more readable, and we have added tools like the "scam sheet" and "Proofreading Check List" in Chapter 16. Chapter 2 has new material on the journal as a literary form. Chapter 4 includes an enhanced discussion of style. Chapter 5 attends more fully to electronic research. We have added new stories to Chapter 12 as well as a creative nonfiction essay that is not a memoir. In Chapter 15, two ten-minute plays have replaced *Trifles* because we felt shorter plays would be more helpful models for beginning writers. We have deleted and added exercises. In short, we have tried to do what a revision ought to do.

If you are coming to *The Creative Writer's Handbook* for the first time, you may be overwhelmed by both the amount of detail and the number of questions we ask you to consider as well as the sizeable number of exercises.

Don't be. Our idea was to provide you with a smorgasbord from which to choose what tempts your palate.

We wish to thank the following reviewers for their valuable contribution: Joan Connor, Ohis University, and Juliet W. Kincaid, Johnson County Comunity College.

We want to stress again that this book is about useful techniques for the beginner. No book teaches; practice does.

Finally, we want to thank those students, colleagues, and friends who have helped us to improve the work.

PKJ
ABL

1

Working like a Writer

PLEASURE AND PASSION

Throughout this book, we offer ideas, illustrations, and exercises having to do with the *craft* of writing. We emphasize work habits, conventions, and techniques. If you are crafty, you will be able to write something that will please and move a reader. What we do not say much about are the pleasures a writer receives from writing. These are many and varied.

Some of you will find pleasure in writing to express an emotion or idea. You will have built up such a head of steam about a feeling or thought that only a poem or play will be sufficient to release that energy. Some of you will write to wrestle with personal demons. Others will write because of the pleasure it gives you to make people laugh or to amaze them. Most of you, we hope, will write for the sheer delight of playing/working with words and forms. You will find joy in those moments of "getting it right," of solving the series of problems that each writing challenge presents. Most of you will write to enjoy a mixture of these pleasures, and a few will be driven by the hope that the tough teacher or editor will finally realize how much talent and determination you really have.

Even if the pleasure you seek is the confidence that you can make a living by doing something that appears easier than laying bricks or selling them (but is actually much more difficult), you still need to start with a sense that acting out on the stage of the page pleases you and that pleasing an audience pleases you.

Few accomplishments are as rewarding and meaningful as creating a literary work through which visions of the human experience are shared or, at a more modest level, through which people are entertained and diverted for a moment. When that sharing happens, the world is a better place—if only because it's a little less lonely. These are lofty and distant goals. On a day-to-day basis, writers learn to find pleasure in the pains of creation.

What can we do about stoking the fire? Not much. The passions, the needs, the ongoing or anticipated pleasures that provide the fuel are as individual as each writer. Without this passion, nothing can happen. But it is not enough. Having passion without technique is one sure way to dampen the fire.

ATTITUDES

The mere *desire* to be a writer is not sufficient. You need to train yourself in certain habits of mind and work and to develop the attitudes that can help carry you from the desire to the reality. This chapter focuses on one attitude in particular—*taking a professional stance* toward your work, your audience, and your editor.

While you can have many motives for writing, usually the reader has only one motive for reading: to experience writing that pleases both in its shape and subject. Of course, both experts and students in a field—let's say nuclear physics—might slug their way through poorly expressed prose to get information they need in order to understand the Big Bang—but most of us would not. To satisfy the readers' desire for writing that pleases, you have to be aware of their needs and then take pains to satisfy them. In fact, 90 percent of what is "creative" in creative writing grows from a professional attitude toward taking pains over what the amateur thinks of as mere details.

For most of us, the *mature* stance toward writing that we are talking about here does not simply happen.

Good creative writing is good writing. In all good writing, the conventions of English mechanics and usage (grammar, punctuation, spelling, word order) remain relevant. These conventions ought not be looked at as a block to creativity; in fact, they are the very things that allow others to share in your creativity. For example, conventional spelling allows you and the reader to share a way of recognizing a word. Mispell to meny wurds and sea how rapidly the goodwill of your reader disappears.

Of course, you may take license with these conventions for special purposes. For example, you may have a character who speaks in ungrammatical ways, or you may decide not to use capitals or punctuation for particular effects (as did e e cummings, the poet). These are purposeful decisions you make from your knowledge and control of the language system. However, flawed prose does not become good poetry. Carelessness, slovenliness, and ignorance do not become virtues just because you are doing "creative" writing.

A professional writer is not satisfied with mere self-expression. If you write only for yourself, you have severely limited your audience. In any case, your writing will become more effective when you are aware that you must please, involve, awaken, provoke, excite, move—other people. The sense of a potential audience should create in you both energy and a feeling of obligation. Unless you make something happen to a reader, you are not doing anything worthwhile *as a writer*. (There are therapeutic uses of writing, of course, but those are not concerns of this book.)

How can you determine your success? One way is by being in a course or workshop that will provide feedback from the instructor and the other participants. They are your sounding boards, to be replaced at some point by editors and by your own developed editorial capabilities. Learning to invite and make positive use of this feedback—even of harshly negative commentary—is essential to your growth as a writer.

Listen carefully, take notes, and keep an open mind. Of course, you can't write and revise merely to satisfy others. You are the boss. However, you shut your ears to such responses at your peril. The reactions of your teacher and your fellow writers help you develop a consciousness of audience, and your responses to their comments can sharpen your own editorial skill.

Being a writer means being a reader in a new way—being more conscious of how the game is played. Almost without exception, great athletes are fans of their sport, artists visit galleries and museums, musicians attend concerts. It is reasonable for writers to read, both for pleasure and for professional development. You don't have to reinvent everything about writing to be creative. Existing stories, plays, and poems are the essential context for new work in each genre. As a writer, you must have a knowledge of genre conventions, the scope of literature, and the contemporary literary environment. If you have aspirations to poetry, you should be constantly reading poetry. You need to read your contemporaries as well as the major voices of each literary period. Read, analyze, ponder, imitate, and record your impressions.

As you read, keep your eyes open for blunders you think the writer has made, and work out how you might have handled the problem differently. Look for techniques that you can borrow and apply to your own writing. Imagine your own variations on another writer's characters, images, themes, or premises. Writing is a response to other writing just as much as it is a response to life.

Don't expect miracles. Part of being professional is having patience. Successful writing comes through a mixture of talent, learned skills, and commitment over a period of time. About commitment we have little to say—except that it is indispensable.

A Digression for the Classroom User

All we have said until this point assumes that you are serious about becoming a published writer. However, there are many other reasons for reading a book about or taking a course in creative writing. Let us discuss some of the possibilities.

◆ You always wanted to try writing something, so you thought you would take this course. A good enough reason. Your desire to experiment, to try something new, should be given an outlet. Take maximum advantage of this pleasant fact: your school has made this opportunity available to you. Though you may never go further with your writing than this course, you will have satisfied your curiosity. Certainly, you will come away with some sense of the demands placed upon a creative writer, and your appreciation of literature should only be enhanced by your having faced the series of complex problems that a successful writer must solve.

◆ You always had trouble with writing in other courses, so you thought you would take a course that focuses on writing. A good motive, but maybe this is the wrong course. A creative writing course is neither a remedial course nor a review of grammar and mechanics; successful creative writing builds on a firm control over the basic conventions of the written language. On the other hand, if you write correctly but not *effectively*, a creative writing course can help you. The attention to writing strategies, diction, organization, figurative language, and other issues can benefit any writer. All writing becomes creative when it escapes being bland, meandering, and impersonal. So, yes, your efforts in imaginative literature will make a positive contribution to your general writing ability—though only if the fundamentals are well in hand.

◆ You needed to fulfill a distribution requirement and this was the only humanities course that fit your schedule. A practical reason, certainly, but not an impressive one. The key to what happens now is your attitude. Others are in the course for more urgent, personal reasons. As a matter of respect for them, you have to agree to be serious about this endeavor. Be positive. Get the most out of the situation. You will meet some interesting people, and you will have fun reading their work as well as the work of accomplished, published writers. Remember also that everyone can benefit from the kind of engagement with language and human issues that this course will afford.

ON BEING UNPROFESSIONAL

You will have a productive, professional attitude when you no longer offer defenses for unsatisfactory work. Here is a small sampling of unprofessional stances toward criticism of one's writing:

1. "That's how I felt" or "that's what I believe," when somebody points to a writing problem in a work. This "defense" confuses the issue. If the criticism is about fuzzy diction, for example, by defending the legitimacy of our feelings or belief, we are avoiding the issue of the *effectiveness* of our writing. What often happens is that the writer has only managed to state an emotion or idea and hasn't made it live for the reader. Moreover, the excuse assumes that the reader cares about the "I" or that a record of personal experience or belief, in and of itself, has merit. The writer's job is to create experience through language. Of course, we always know (or do we?) what *we're* talking about, so that as readers of our own work we are privileged in ways that make us poor critics of it. The reader doesn't care how the writer feels. The real question is: Has the writer made the *reader* feel?

2. "But it really happened like that." This excuse focuses on events rather than feelings. We mistake a certain kind of accuracy in rendering events that are our source experiences with the needs of the work at hand. The mere fact that something really happened does not justify placing it in a story, play, or narrative poem. The writer's job is to use experience, not be used by it. If it is important *to the story* that the gas tank was one-quarter full or that early Beatles tunes were being played on the radio or that the predicted thunderstorm did not come, then give the reader such information. Remember that the demands of the story are not *necessarily* what happened, especially if what happened is downright tedious. Your job is to convince the reader that the event *happened in the story*, not that you saw it happen in the streets. Of course, if something is important to the story and did not happen, put it in—except in creative nonfiction.

3. "Doesn't 'creative' mean I can do what I want?" This is almost a meaningless question. It's similar to saying, "doesn't 'freedom' mean I can do what I want?" Both questions reveal frivolous attitudes. The freedoms we have are a result of our agreements to limit ourselves; we have responsibilities to others. Similarly, there are limitations—conventions of language and genre—that you must master as part of your responsibility to readers. We know we've said this before. We'll no doubt say it again.

4. "What are the formulae?" While we do have to work with and through conventions of the language system and of the genre, creative writing is not the same as mathematics. Trial and error is just as often the means to success as is a clear, logical plan. A writer cannot be the slave of prescriptions or

categories. Formula writing produces some kinds of popular literature and some superficially pleasing work, but nothing significant gets done by plugging material into formulas. The answers are always inside the writer, never outside. Your job is to make thinking in the conventions second nature so that you draw on them spontaneously rather than reach for them like so many cookie cutters. There are no easy answers.

5. "Isn't it just a matter of taste?" Certainly, it is a matter of taste whether someone likes avant-garde writing; it is a matter of taste whether one likes mystery stories; it is a matter of taste whether one likes long, elaborate sentences. Many aspects of writing, however, are also matters of knowledge about usable traditions. Someone may know these traditions better than you and know better how to manipulate them. Someone else may have read more widely than you. Someone else's taste may have more weight than yours right now because that person has greater experience. You ignore such judgment at your peril. However, if you feel strongly about something, from a detail to an entire work, stick to your guns. Just be willing to pay the price your confidence may cost. That price ranges from turning off a reader to being rejected by an editor.

6. "In his recent bestseller, Clancy Steiningway did the same thing you criticized me for. If he can get away with it, why can't I?" Sometimes poor writing gets published and sells well; sometimes famous writers get by on their reputations; sometimes other elements in a work are so effectively handled or the subject matter is so engrossing that stretches of poor writing or violations of useful conventions are overlooked. That such writing gets published is not an excuse for shoddy practice, and your instructor cannot in good conscience encourage bad habits. If Steiningway has gotten away with chaotic plotting, inconsistent characters, or leaden dialogue, rest assured that his work wasn't published *because* of these traits. Also, when the novice writer claims a parallel or precedent in the work of an accomplished (or honored) professional, that similarity is often quite superficial. Did you *really* do the same thing? Or perhaps Steiningway has managed to pull off something quite risky while the beginner has failed miserably. The point, then, is not to misunderstand the instructor's criticism: usually such strategies, devices, or styles don't work. Until you have Steiningway's skills, perhaps you should avoid such practices.

WORKING HABITS

Discipline is part of the professional attitude. You have to commit time to writing. We know one writer who pretends she is going to a job. She dresses, has breakfast, packs a lunch, and then is off to her writing space for a set period of time. She will not take phone calls unless they are associated with her writing work (the answering machine is her monitor), and she sits at her desk for at least two hours even if she has no clue about what she wants to write next. If inspiration has flown, she writes in her journal. Extreme as that discipline may seem, she is establishing for herself (and others) that she takes her writing seriously.

Another friend, who has a full-time job in local government, rises at 5:00 A.M. in order to get in an hour of writing before leaving for work. Many writers establish reward systems to help them get through a scheduled writing period. Promise yourself that after an hour (or five pages, or a chapter draft) you can have a snack, or surf the Internet, or browse the newspaper.

For some people, such bribes or strenuous regimens are unnecessary. These lucky people either have discipline built into their souls or are so fulfilled by the writing process that little can pull them away from it. Most of us, however, need to impose a routine upon ourselves so that we will write even when we are not in the mood. Once this discipline is established—once writing is a part of your daily routine—then you will not feel comfortable without it. When "it's time to write," you will be ready. Just like when it's time to brush your teeth or crunch those abdominals.

However, the commitment to "writing time" needs reinforcement. Here are some hints for keeping yourself writing and growing as a writer:

1. Make your writing space as inviting and efficient as possible. A large working surface enables you to have all your materials at hand without stacking them on top of one another. Paper, card files, pens, and pencils should all be at hand, as should resources such as dictionaries, handbooks, and style manuals. If you compose on a computer, take advantage of software that serves the same ends as these desk references. Have your computer and software reference manuals nearby. Keep disks or CDs on hand for backing up your files. Stock extra ink or toner cartridges. Above all, arrange for adequate lighting, a well-designed chair, and an ergonomically sound placement of keyboard and monitor.

2. If you need to be away from your writing space during writing time, be ready to write anyway. Have your journal with you.

3. Even when you are running hot on a piece of writing, a moment will come when you feel that your inspiration or energy is about to run dry. Rather than continue writing until you have squeezed all the juices from that session, stop in the middle of a sentence, or scene, or line that you are fairly sure you know how to finish. In your next writing session you will have some work that you can complete easily—a running start.

4. Don't talk about your work too much to friends, family, or teachers. Telling your story over a brandy to a fascinated lover has one doubtful benefit attached to two certain drawbacks. Talking out your idea does get you immediate feedback. If the feedback pumps you up, however, it also removes

that inner urge to do the communication the hard way—in writing. And if the feedback is negative, you might abandon an idea that is in fact a good one but just doesn't "sound" good in a crowded bar. Your job is not to talk about but to write about.

5. Don't keep yourself from moving onward in a piece of writing by looking for an ideal beginning, ideal phrasing, or ideal structure. The answer to the question "Where should I begin?" is the same answer you give to the question "Where does a 500-pound gorilla sleep?" In fact, not only can you begin writing your poem or story or play anyplace you want to, but also you need not be concerned about the conventions, coherence, logic, or any other responsibility to the reader—just so long as you are drafting.

   This paradox is only apparent, not real. It makes no difference where you begin or by what fits and starts you proceed. What counts is *where you decide—finally—to have your reader begin and proceed*. In other words, what counts is the final draft. Don't try to be perfectly polished as you go along, thinking you can avoid rewriting. Remember the fate of Grande, a character in Camus's *The Plague*, who believed he would write the perfect novel if only he could find the ideal opening sentence. He never got beyond the first sentence. So don't be afraid of letting the material flow undisturbed. In later drafts your editor-self can take over from your writer-self and channel the flow in useful directions.

6. Part of your work as a writer is to involve yourself in your craft by reading, attending plays, and going to hear other writers read from their work. Stay engaged in the world of writing; by supporting other writers, you are supporting the craft that you hope will support you. Read to discover how accomplished writers have solved the problems that you will be facing.

7. Almost all good writing is the result of rewriting. Make the process of revision an essential part of your attitude toward writing. In a first draft, you will usually only set down the material you need to shape and perfect. Assume that several drafts are needed to bring any writing project to success. Think of that first draft as a rough-cut piece of wood that must be sanded with finer and finer grades of sandpaper. Of course, if the rough cut is out of proportion, it must be discarded and replaced.

8. Leave some time between drafts. We tend to know what we mean when we've just thought it and (supposedly) pinned it down in writing. Some distance allows us to discover inadequacies. Generally, give yourself at least a day away from a draft before revising it. After all, how can you "revision" if you haven't first stopped looking at something?

9. Take the risk (for the benefit) of requesting feedback. If you are writing for publication, you have to contend with readers' responses to your work. You have to be ready to accept criticism and to assess that criticism. Remember, however, that it's easier to please your parent or spouse than an editor of a journal or publishing house. Seek frank advice.

10. Find your own best working habits. Discover what works for you and stay with it. When your writing goes stale, try something new: shift the time, rearrange the space, accelerate or slow down the revision process, seek new reading experiences.

Most important of all, you must set high standards and be ready for disappointment. As coaches say about exercise, "No pain, no gain." We are not suggesting that writing is a form of self-punishment, but it is a constant struggle. Still, just as athletes can find great pleasure in preparing for the game, you can find as many pleasures in the process of writing as in the results. Think of the analogy to an athlete again. If only the results—the winning or losing—matter to you, you can find them in something as unimportant as tossing a coin.

Something else must be at the heart of the endeavor to invest so much love and caring in, let us say, hours of exercise for one minute on a balance beam. There must be satisfactions in the exercise itself—the doing. What we do as writers is practice, plan, and engage ourselves in the intricate pressures of choosing well, tearing apart, rediscovering, rebuilding—in short, recognizing that literary works *become*.

A WORD ABOUT INTENTIONS

Eudora Welty said: "It was not my intention—it never was—to invent a character who should speak for me, the author, the person. A character is in a story to fill a role there, and the character's life is defined by that surrounding—indeed is created by his own story" (from *One Writer's Beginnings*, Harvard University Press, 1984). The implication of Welty's statement is that her writing isn't a disguise for something she wishes to hide in her fiction, a kind of sugar coating for what she would like us to swallow about morality, politics, or the ultimate purposes and significance of almost anything. Although any character in a play or story, any speaker in a poem, is a partial revelation of the writer, the *intention* to reveal one's self or sell one's views is not a necessary or useful approach to the art.

The truth is that you can't help but reveal yourself when you write honestly. Your worldview is the lens through which you look at experience, choose plots, characters, images, and settings. The conscious pressure of trying to make a point—of sending a message—can block the flow and distort the final shape of any literary work. An artwork, when it goes well, has a life of its own, its own demands. Sometimes *it* has something to say, and you need to let the writing process make such discoveries.

To quote Welty again, "If somewhere in its course your work seems to you to have come into a life of its own, and you can stand back from it and leave it be, you are looking then at your own subject—I feel."

Aside from thematic or moralistic intentions, we often find ourselves highly motivated by aesthetic ones—we want to put the demonstration of craft before anything else. We act like the tennis player who falls down after every difficult shot to punctuate its difficulty. "Look how clever I am" or "look how hard I am trying," such an attitude appears to say. However, no one enjoys reading a collection of skill exhibitions—not even creative writing teachers. Writings that only call attention to their author's virtuosity are rarely successful. What you learn about the craft of writing should serve your own efforts; it should not be the subject—even the hidden agenda—of what you do.

Nor should you approach your work as if preparing a treasure hunt. Don't put yourself in the position of having to explain that you have purposely buried "hidden meanings" for the reader to dig out. Writing is not like a jigsaw puzzle that the reader puts together after searching out the missing pieces.

In the best writing, themes often emerge while the writer keeps struggling with language and following the characters around. Though it is convenient to begin with an idea, an image or a situation is a better starting point. Trust yourself, trust the reader, and trust the writing process. Don't ask, "How am I going to get across to my reader that our involvement in Afghanistan or Iraq was the result of economic forces?" Ask, "What would my character do next?" "How does he or she feel about these circumstances?" "What words will resonate with the words I have just put down?" Only in the late stages of revision, when a work has announced its purpose—*its* intention—can we allow ourselves some calculating decisions, and then only to be true to the work we have come to understand.

Does this trust in the process mean that writers proceed with blind ignorance about where they are going? Sometimes yes and sometimes no. That's not the issue. Even a writer with a plan needs to be open and flexible. A writer's intentions are not what finally matter, and holding on to intentions too fiercely or justifying a work in terms of intentions is a more serious blindness than writing without a clear direction.

In spite of what we have just said, we are not partisans of the idea that art is an end in itself. There is no reason for literature except to communicate something about what it means to be human. What Cynthia Ozick calls "a corona of moral purpose" (in "Innovation and Redemption: What Literature Means") surrounds every significant work of literary art.

This moral purpose is different, however, from saying that literature must be narrowly or explicitly didactic. We each have our own way of knowing that literature affirms our ability to choose. In writing, we are choosing—asserting our freedom, our capacity to grow and to change. When we do this for ourselves, we do this for others as well: we do it for everyone. This, as Ozick points out, is the essential, implicit moral of creative acts.

2

Keeping a Journal

WHY KEEP A JOURNAL?

As you've probably already noticed, we have decided to use sports metaphors and analogies in this book. This strategy is not merely stylistic, it is also thematic. We truly believe that writing (some might say all art) satisfies a basic human impulse—the need to play. Actually, people are never so serious or intent as when they are playing. Just look at the face of someone about to make a golf shot. Watch a diver prepare for a difficult dive. See how a defensive back in a football game has no other reality than the unfolding play.

This chapter is about one way that writers prepare for playing the game well. We say "one way" because a successful writer's practices cannot be reduced to a formula. On the other hand, it makes good sense to imitate the stance and gestures of those who have made it to the major leagues. What worked for them might just work for you.

Almost all writers keep a journal. Some keep several different journals or notebooks:

- ◆ *A working journal* in which they practice writing and work out parts or whole drafts of a poem or story or essay or play.
- ◆ *A journal of ideas* for future writing or a record of work in progress.

◆ *A commonplace book* in which they jot down quotations from their reading, along with their reactions, as models or for inspiration.

Most writers keep a single journal to serve all of these purposes.

What follows is an excerpt from a real journal that contains aspects of all three. The Greek poet George Seferis is reading to get himself started on his writing; he is reacting to his daily experience; he is free-associating; and, finally, he is starting to develop a poem.

Tuesday Morning, October 8, 1946

I have been working on Cavafy again since last Saturday afternoon. I am reading articles about the poet written in the past and more recently. They bore me. Too much "literature," too much padding in all of them; very few noteworthy observations. I don't yet know if I'm in Cavafy's ambience. A thought put aside for the moment: *I am trying to return to the habit of working.* [Italics added]

I'll read every morning—I started yesterday—about a hundred lines of the *Iliad*.

Yesterday and today were superb days, too much for me; they distract me; I feel terribly lost. As in a ruined house, I have to put many things in order. I don't know if I'll ever be able to reconstruct it.

After swimming: the light is such that it absorbs you as blotter does ink; it absorbs the personality.

Days are stones. Flintstones
that accidentally found each other and made two or three sparks,
stones on the threshing floor, struck by horseshoes,
    and crushing many people.
pebbles in the water with ephemeral rings,
wet and multicolored little stones at the seashore,
or lekythoi, gravestones that sometimes stop the passerby
or bas-reliefs with the rider who went far out to sea
or Marsyas or Priapus, groups of phallus-bearers.
Days are stones; they crumble one on top of the other.

from *A Poet's Journal*

Journal keeping can get even more elaborate than we have described. Some writers keep separate journals for all aspects of their work: drafts, exercises, dreams, ideas, quotations, newspaper clippings, and so on. We even know one writer who keeps a separate journal for submissions to publications and payments for manuscripts. Most of us are hardly so organized or need to be, and so we recommend much less elaborate journal keeping for you.

The point is to keep a journal. It makes writing a regular part of your life. Many would-be writers hope that an occasional stab at a short story or a poem when the mood strikes them will produce significant results. That attitude is something like expecting to play a par round of golf by playing only once a month. Writing takes practice and preparation.

Let us put the matter less kindly. You should take an armchair writer about as seriously as you take an armchair athlete. Writers write; posers talk about writing. The journal is one place for you to be a writer.

YOUR JOURNAL

Go out now and buy yourself a journal. We suggest that it be either a ruled composition book with a hard cover (approximately 81/2 by 11 inches) or, if you want something more portable, a hardcover "record book" (5 by 8 inches) with ruled lines. The essential idea is to keep your journal in a form that ensures permanence. Avoid loose-leaf notebooks or spiral notebooks from which you can inadvertently rip pages. Tiny flip notebooks don't give you enough room to jot down more than a few words. (Many writers, however, do carry around some kind of small notebook for ideas that come to them in the middle of a workday or a dance.) If you carry your journal around with you, be sure to write your name, address, and phone number at the beginning along with the statement that, in case of loss, you will reward the returner.

Now that portable computers and PDAs are affordable, the last practical obstacle to keeping an electronic journal has been removed. And, if your journal keeping tends to be a desk-bound activity anyway, why not perform this task with your word processor? The choice of recording technology is yours; see what works best for you and take advantage of it.

Once you have your journal, you need to make it part of your daily routine. At first you will probably need a conscious strategy for keeping it up. Pick a time of day that you promise *always* to write in it. The time you choose should be one that works for you, but it makes sense to choose one in which you are not likely to be interrupted by a phone call or the meter reader.

If you can't keep your writer's notebook every day, then set up an appointment with it for at least three times a week. If you're having discipline problems, find some way to reward yourself for keeping it or to punish yourself when you don't. You may have to modify your behavior to develop the journal-keeping habit, but once you have developed the habit, you will no more think of not writing in your journal than you would think of not brushing your teeth.

It won't do simply to greet the blank page with "Hello, dear journal, I've got nothing to write. Goodbye." That's like doing one push-up and feeling that you have exercised. You have to give the journal enough time so that you can work up a sweat—twenty to thirty minutes a session minimum, enough to get you beyond simply saying "hello" and into the rhythm of writing. Put it another way: you have to run more than a block to get into running.

Journal keeping has nothing to do with feeling inspired. You write in it because you are or want to be a writer. And even when INSPIRATION has deserted you, you write on to prepare yourself for her—or his—return.

WHAT TO WRITE IN THE JOURNAL

It's your journal. What you stuff it with depends on your way of looking at and reacting to what you see, learn, and remember. In brief, you write what you want to write. We will, however, offer you some basic principles that can make your journal more useful over the short and long run. Unless your classroom instructor asks to see your journal as part of your course work, the journal is the writing place in which you have no commitment to anyone but yourself.

In some writers' journals, you might find:

what they did that day
lists of books to read
drafts of letters
quotations
columns of words
bits of dialogue
dreams
ramblings about events and people
memories
anticipations
story possibilities
descriptions
lists of intriguing words and phrases

. . . in short, anything.

Some of this material simply keeps them working as a writer. Some of it is the record of their thoughts, a place to hold and look at their past self at some future time. Some of it will end up in writing meant for other eyes.

John Steinbeck kept a journal in which he blended observations about his daily life with reminders to himself about the ongoing challenges of his work-in-progress, *Grapes of Wrath*. Here is an excerpt:

> Early start this morning. Can't ever tell. Worked long and slowly yesterday. Don't know whether it was good, but it was a satisfactory way to work and I wish it would be that way every day. I've lost this rushed feeling finally and can get back to the easy method of day by day—which is as it should be. Got the iron gate for an autograph. That is a

bargain. Today I shall work slowly and try to get that good feeling again. It must be. Just a little bit every day. A little bit every day. And then it will be through. And the story is coming to me fast now. And it will be fast from now on. Movement fast but the detail slow as always. I seem to be delaying pretty badly today. Half an hour gone already and I don't care because the little details are coming, are getting clearer all the time. So the more I wait, the more of this book will get written. How about the jail. Today, the preacher and Tom and the raid on the tent and the killing of the preacher. Tom's escape. Kills. Goes back to the camp to hide. Tom—half bitterness, half humane. Escapes in the night. Hunted, hunted. Over the last pages Tom hangs like a spirit around the camp. And in the water brings stolen food. Must get to work now. The thing speeds up.

from *Working Days: The Journals of the Grapes of Wrath*

Though anything goes in the journal, you do have a responsibility to yourself as a writer. Imagine, for example, that you have written the following sample journal entries:

September 6. I met a strange man on a train and was he interesting. He told me about his life. He might make an interesting story.

1995. The mountains in the north of Italy are simply tremendous. So big and with such lovely names.

April. I really feel low today. It's the lowest I've felt in years. He disappointed me in the worst way.

Friday the 13th. A good idea for a story about a future world based on an incurable disease. I wonder what would happen?

Suppose today you decide to look back over your old journals because your mind is sluggish and you want some ideas for a story or some precise information about an event in the past that has come up in a poem or personal essay. These old journal entries would leave you few triggering images with which to recapture the past, let alone your past feelings. The entries lack alertness, an awareness of the senses, discrimination, contemplation, or imagination. They indicate that you had worked neither at seeing nor at reporting.

Before we make additional suggestions, it may be worthwhile to say something about the relationship between the journal and the growth of the writer's imagination. The very effort put into keeping a journal over a period of time starts to sharpen both memory and awareness, both within and without the journal. Because you know you are keeping a journal, you start to become more conscious of your surroundings, more sensitive to the flow of your experience, your thinking, and your reading. You are more aware precisely because you know you are going to write, and as you write, you become more conscious of what you need to be aware of next time. The cycle is continuous, a whirlpool that sucks you deeper into both the world and yourself—that is, your material as a writer.

The journal entries just cited have little value as a library of memories, feelings, ideas, or pictures. They have no value as writing because they are stylistically flaccid. You need to run a bit of a game on yourself. Since you will be a different person when you read it, write the journal for that different self. Think of each entry as a time capsule you have sent to you. The following entry should make the principles clear:

> September 6, 1967. Today sat next to a lawyer on the metroliner to N.Y.C. (Going to see my agent about the paperback rights to Forever Never) He was a large man, rather rumpled—his clothes, his face, his body. He saw I was reading Williams' book about famous negligence cases. Told me had worked for Williams and before that Nizer. Spent the whole trip telling me that he was the one who planned the jury trials. Then started to tell me about cases he had won but they all sounded like cases I had read about in books on famous legal events. Said he was going up to New York to assist on the Yukonsky case but, of course, he would be kept out of the limelight. While he was telling me all this garbage I realized that he believed it—or at least believed it while he was telling it. Good potential character. Perhaps a metaphor of the writer. We believe it when we tell it. I asked for his card. "Sorry, I'm having them printed up now," he said when we left the train and he was back into rumpled reality. My god, did I really write "rumpled reality"? And now I just made it worst. He was wearing a worsted wursted suit.

When you compare this entry with the earlier ones, some principles of journal keeping should be clear:

1. Date each entry fully and precisely.
2. Make your journal entry as specific as you can.
3. Start trying to find the hard nouns and verbs that capture the feel of the situation.
4. If you are being flabby, tell yourself to straighten up. Talk to yourself in your journal. And play with the material. Start thinking about it. Let yourself go.
5. Look for associations in your past or in literature—anything that will help you recapture the emotion and feel of the event at some future time.

All this work in your journal hones skills you will need when you sit down to begin constructing something for an audience.

GETTING STARTED

Open your journal.

An effective first entry might be a brief overview of your life. Hit the most memorable points, especially the turning points when, had events or choices been different, you think your life might have been different. Don't try to be complete at this point. Leave yourself material for the entries that will come as you work into the journal-keeping habit. In later sessions start adding:

1. Your likes and dislikes.
2. Detailed sketches of people who are important to you—parents, brothers and sisters, friends and relatives, enemies, and so on. (See Anaïs Nin's sketch of her dance teacher later in this chapter.)
3. Memory portraits of homes, rooms, toys.
4. The truth about your weaknesses (it's permissible to write about what you think are your strengths too), your fears and anxieties.

What you are engaged in is self-exploration, the writer's archaeological dig. Even a writer who is writing in a naturalistic tradition filters the world through his or her own mind, a mind shaped by memories and experiences.

Write spontaneously—a suggestion easier to recommend than to follow. Try the technique used in this passage:

June 5, 2004. One of my earliest memories.

I am five years old and I am sitting on my red tricycle on the slate side-walks in Scranton, Pa. Behind me is our house, an attached house. Did it have a front porch? I must ask Dad. I know I am not supposed to cross the street but I want to play with a friend who lives in the house opposite. For some reason, perhaps she is busy baking or with my baby sister, I cannot ask my mother. It is August and I hear a humming sound. I now know it is the cicadas but I think it is the sound of people talking over the telephone wires. I do not remember having talked on the phone but I had heard my father talking to Uncle Joe about business and my mother talking to Aunt Syl. It is so hot I can smell the asphalt. My friend's house is green. I want to cross that street. Why not? There are no cars and no people. Suddenly I am aware that I am I and that my parents are other people. I have this deep sense of me. It comes as such a surprise that thinking about this new thing I forget that I want to cross the street.

Notice that the sentences are in the present tense. The writer is trying to capture the names, feel, smell, sound, color . . . the moment. Because we invented this journal entry, we can also tell you another fact; because we couldn't remember everything, we put in elements that felt as if they should have been there. Where did we get those elements? From other past experiences. We lied about the precise experience to capture for ourselves the true feel of the experience. Put the earliest memories you have into your journal. Why are they important to you?

Spontaneity does not mean sloppiness, and by "sloppiness" we are not referring to handwriting (though an unreadable journal entry will be useless for future exploration and to your biographer). Even though you wish to keep the material flowing, try different ways of saying it, look for the precise word, and keep a running commentary to yourself on exact information you will need later to make the journal entry complete.

Your family, with its experiences and stories, is important material for your journal. It is the stuff out of which you can build completely imagined scenes, even in stories having nothing to do with your family. And it may be the stuff of the stories and poems and plays you wish to write. Who are the characters in your family tree, what happened to them, and what do they mean to you? Because celebrations, dislocations, operations, vacations, maturations, and more are the stuff of life, they are the stuff of literature. In your journal, start practicing your re-creation of them: having your first birthday party, moving to a new house, getting your driver's license, realizing that one of your parents had a specific fault.

Keeping Up

What we have suggested up to this point are ways to build the journal-keeping habit through the subjects you know best. In fact, you will probably return again and again to these same subjects as events in your life shake out more memories. However, your life will flow on, and in your journal you will paste more word snapshots of daily events, ideas, character sketches, and pieces of your reading.

From your reading, copy short passages that appeal to you and then analyze the reasons for this appeal. What strikes you in your reading tells you something about yourself as a writer-in-the-making. Be alert to other writers' techniques and comment on them, even imitate and parody them. For example, if J. D. Salinger is one of your favorites, copy a paragraph that you think is representative of his work and then model a paragraph of your own on his sequence of sentences, saving even the shape of the sentences: introduce new characters, nouns, verbs, and modifiers. Or follow Ben Franklyn's practice when he was young. He read articles in the *Tatler* and *Spectator*, put them away, and then tried to reproduce them as closely as possible. Such imitation is a way of involving yourself in the world of words and of making your journal a laboratory in which you experiment with your medium—language.

As a writer you will of course keep reading, and your reading is always a source for journal keeping, even on those days you feel wiped out, empty of anything to say. It is those days that test your mettle and mental as a writer. Keep going.

1. Write a letter in your journal—to your parents (the letter you always should have written), to someone you want to curse out, to an author you admire.
2. Open a dictionary at random and look at a page of words. Jot down a few that interest you because they are strange or suggestive. Play with them.
3. Try to recapture in detail the last moment you felt pleased with yourself.
4. Retell the plot of a book—even one from your childhood.
5. Turn on some music and free-associate: just write anything that captures your emotional response to the music.
6. Freewriting is often hampered by our paying too much attention to the accumulating product. Try freewriting on the computer *with the screen turned off,* allowing yourself to read what you have written only after the writing session is over. After practicing this technique for a while, evaluate the results.

Nothing much may come of all this except the habit of keeping to your discipline, but that is no small matter. And we know that it is easier to write "discipline" than it is to summon reserves for running that last mile when your legs are leaden. Sometimes you won't; sometimes you will. What separates the writers from the pretenders is that most times the writers keep going.

WHAT WILL YOU DO WITH IT ALL?

In most of your journal writing, you will practice your craft and discover yourself. In fact, some people can fall so in love with journal keeping itself that it becomes all their writing. Interesting books, such as the *Diary of John Evelyn,* have actually come from dedicated journal keepers:

> 29th June 1678. Returned with my Lord by Hounslow Heath, where we saw the new-raised army encamped, designed against France, in pretence, at least; but which gave umbrage to the Parliament. His Majesty and a world of company were in the field, and the whole army in battalia; a very glorious sight. Now were brought into service a new sort of soldiers called *Grenadiers,* who were dexterous in flinging hand grenados, every one having a pouch full; they had furred caps with coped crowns like Janizaries, which made them look very fierce, and some had long hoods hanging down behind, as we picture fools. Their clothing being likewise piebald, yellow and red.

We are grateful to Evelyn because he has left us a detailed picture of his time. You will notice that his journal entry, even though he did not intend to create a work for public consumption, has many of the virtues of journal writing that we have suggested, all of which can be summed up in one expression: "a sense of detail."

As fine and useful as a journal like Evelyn's is, we assume your motive is to produce writing that will be read during your lifetime—to do some public good, for fame and approbation, for money, for revenge . . . for any or all of the motives that drive writers. The danger in journal writing is that you get immediate satisfaction from your most approving audience, yourself, and so may stop at the starting line.

Your journal is a *resource* for the writing that you hope will be published. Most of the time, of course, nothing transfers exactly from the journal into your public writing. Read and compare the following entry from Hawthorne's journal with the passage that actually occurs in his *The Blithedale Romance.*

> In a bar-room, a large oval basin let into the counter, with a brass tube rising from the centre, out of which gushes continually a miniature fountain, and descends in a soft, gentle, never ceasing rain into the basin, where swim a company of gold fishes. Some of them gleam brightly in their golden armor; others have a dull white aspect, going through some process of transmutation. One would think that the atmosphere, continually filled with tobacco-smoke, might impregnate the water unpleasantly for the scaly people; but then it is continually flowing away, and being renewed. And what if some toper should be seized with the freak of emptying his glass of gin or brandy into the basin? Would the fishes die, or merely get jolly?
>
> Journal entry for May 16, 1850

> The prettiest object in the saloon was a tiny fountain, which threw up its feathery jet, through the counter, and sparkled down again into an oval basin, or lakelet, containing several gold-fishes. There was a bed of bright sand, at the bottom, strewn with coral and rock-work; and the fishes went gleaming about, now turning up the sheen of a golden side, and now vanishing into the shadows of the water, like the fanciful thoughts that coquet with a poet in his dream. Never before, I imagine, did a company of water-drinkers remain so entirely uncontaminated by the bad example around them; nor could I help wondering that it had not occurred to any freakish inebriate, to empty a glass of liquor into their lakelet. What a delightful idea! Who would not be a fish, if he could inhale jollity with the essential element of his existence.
>
> from *The Blithedale Romance*

Some material disappears, such as the tobacco-smoke, and some material is added, such as the detailed description of the sand. Most interesting of all is the shift from an abstract narrator in the journal to the first-person narrator of the novel. The material in the journal is the seedling that Hawthorne nurses into a full passage, pruning and adding as he needs to. Still, he had a seedling.

Study the following extended journal entry from *The Diary of Anaïs Nin, 1931–1934*:

October, 1933

The death of Antonio Francisco Miralles in a hotel room, alone, of asthma. Miralles, my Spanish dancing teacher.

Whenever I stepped off the bus at Montmartre, I could hear the music of the merry-go-rounds at the fair, and I would feel my mood, my walk, my whole body transformed by its gaiety. I walked to a side street, knocked on a dark doorway opened by a disheveled concierge, and ran down the stairway to a vast room below street level, a vast cellar room with its walls covered with mirrors. It was the place where the little girls from the Opéra Ballet rehearsed. When I came down the stairway I could hear the piano, feet stamping, and the ballet master's voice. When the piano stopped, there was always his voice scolding, and the whispering of smaller voices. As I entered, the class was dissolving and a flurry of little girls brushed by me in their moth ballet costumes, laughing and whispering, fluttering like moths on their dusty ballet slippers, flurries of snow in the darkness of the vast room, with drops of dew from exertion. I went down with them along the corridors to the dressing rooms. These looked like gardens, with so many ballet skirts, Spanish costumes hanging on pegs. It overflowed with the smell of cold cream, face powder, cheap cologne.

While they dressed for the street, I dressed for my Spanish dances. Miralles would already be rehearsing his own castanets. The piano, slightly out of tune, was beginning the dance of Granados. The floor was beginning to vibrate as other Spanish dancers tried out their heel work. Tap tap tap tap tap. Miralles was about forty, slender, erect, not handsome in face but graceful when dancing. His face was undefined, his features blurred.

I was the favorite.

He was like a gentle Svengali, and by his eyes, his voice, his hands, he had the power to make me dance as well as by his ordinary lessons. He ruled my body with a magnetic rule, master of my dancing.

One day he waited for me at the door, neat and trim. "Will you come and sit at the café with me?"

I followed him. Not far from there was the Place Clichy, always animated, but more so now, as the site of a permanent fair. The merry-go-rounds were turning swiftly. The gypsies were reading fortunes in little booths hung with Arabian rugs. Workmen were shooting clay pigeons and winning cut glass for their wives. The prostitutes were enjoying their loitering, and the men were watching them.

My dancing teacher was saying to me: "Anaïs, I am a simple man. My parents were shoemakers in a little village in the south of Spain. I was put to work in an iron factory where I handled heavy things and was on the way to becoming deformed by big muscles. But during my lunch hour, I danced. I wanted to be a dancer and I practiced every day, every night. At night I went to the gypsies' caverns, and learned from them. I began to dance in cabarets. And today, look!" He took out a cigarette case engraved with the names of all the famous Spanish dancers. "Today I have been the partner of all these women. If you would come with me, we could be happy. I am a simple man, but we could dance in all the cities of Europe. I am no longer young but I have a lot of dancing in me yet. We could be happy."

The merry-go-round turned and sang, and I imagined myself embarking on a dancing career with Miralles, dancing, which was so much like flying, from city to city, receiving bouquets, praise in newspapers, with joyous music at the center always, pleasure as colorful as the Spanish dresses, all red, orange, black and gold, gold and purple, and red and white.

Imagining . . . like amnesia. Forgetting who I was, and where I was, and why I could not do it. Not knowing how to answer so I would not hurt him, I said, "I am not strong enough."

"That's what I thought when I first saw you. I thought you couldn't take the discipline of a dancer's life. But it isn't so. You look fragile and all that, but you're healthy. I can tell healthy women by their skin. Yours is shining and clear. No, I don't think you have the strength of a horse, you're what we call a *petite nature*. But you have energy and guts. And we'll take it easy on the road."

Many afternoons, after hard work, we sat at this little café and imagined what a dancer's life might be.

from The Diary of Anaïs Nin, 1931–1934

We can observe that this entry is much more than a recording of the day's events and that it wasn't tossed off to meet a deadline. Nin's impulse is to fashion material as she recalls it, a sure sign of someone who is already practicing the art of storytelling. Not only does this memory portrait collect fine details of place and atmosphere, but it also pretends to record conversation. Since this entry was written five years after Nin gave up dancing, the dialogue she attributes to herself and to Miralles has to have been created. Nin is *telling a story* based on the force of her memories as they well up. Notice how she strategically employs the merry-go-round image: you are not yet likely to have developed such a sure sense of how an image can link memories and provide a structure for the entry. Nin is at this time working toward the stories and novellas that will reach an audience in a few years. Her diary, begun in childhood, has truly become a writer's workbook. In fact, many critics believe that Nin's published diary volumes, the entries reworked several times from their handwritten originals, are her most significant achievement.

The following entries are from the diaries that James Boswell kept. Though he probably did not realize it yet, he was gathering material for his *Life of Johnson*, one of the world's great biographies, and was learning to become a writer. The entries we have selected cover a three-week period (July 16 to August 3, 1763) just after Boswell met Johnson and began the journal. Though these selections represent less than 20 percent of the total journal writing Boswell did during this period, they illustrate, among other things, how through time a journal can reveal the patterns of one's own life. Boswell's entries, while not as consciously literary as Nin's, show him becoming the master of details that are the life of all effective writing. His way of moving from description to reporting to contemplation, his other- and self-directed observations—this very jumping from topic to topic—is the way most writers are likely to proceed. You may find that Boswell's model is the one you want to follow.

SATURDAY 16 JULY. . . . [Dr. Johnson] advised me to keep a journal of my life, fair and undisguised. He said it would be a very good exercise, and would yield me infinite satisfaction when the ideas were faded from my remembrance. I told him that I had done so ever since I left Scotland. He said he was very happy that I pursued so good a plan. And now, O my journal! art thou not highly dignified? Shalt thou not flourish tenfold? No former solicitations or censures could tempt me to lay thee aside; and now is there any argument which can outweigh the sanction of Mr. Samuel Johnson? He said indeed that I should keep it private, and that I might surely have a friend who would burn it in case of my death. For my own part, I have at present such an affection for this my journal that it shocks me to think of burning it. I rather encourage the idea of having it carefully laid up among the archives of Auchinleck. However, I cannot judge fairly of it now. Some years hence I may, I told Mr. Johnson that I put down all sorts of little incidents in it. "Sir," said he, "there is nothing too little for so little a creature as man. It is by studying little things that we attain the great knowledge of having as little misery and as much happiness as possible."

*

At present we have an old woman called Mrs. Legge for a laundress, who has breakfast set every morning, washes our linen, cleans the chambers, wipes our shoes, and, in short, does everything in the world that we can require of an old woman. She is perhaps as curious an animal as has appeared in human shape. She presents a strong idea of one of the frightful witches in *Macbeth*; and yet the beldame boasts that she was once as handsome a girl as you could clap your eyes upon, and withal exceedingly virtuous; in so much that she refused £500 from the late Lord Hervey. She was servant in many great families, and then she married for love a tall strapping fellow who died. She then owns that she married Mr. Legge for money. He is a little queer round creature; and claiming kindred with Baron Legge, he generally goes by the name of

The Baron, and fine fun we have with him. He serves as porter when we have any message to send at a distance.

To give a specimen of Mrs. Legge, who is a prodigious prater. She said to Bob this morning, "Ay, ay, Master Robert, you may talk. But we knows what you young men are. Just cock-sparrows. You can't stand it out. But the Baron! O Lord! the Baron is a staunch man. Ay, ay, did you never hear that GOD never made a little man but he made it up to him in something else? Yes, yes, the Baron is a good man, an able man. He laid a married woman upon the floor while he sent the maid out for a pint of porter. But he was discovered, and so I come to know of it."

MONDAY 18 JULY. At the head of St. James's Street I observed three Turks staring about in a strange manner. I spoke a little of English, French, and Latin to them, neither of which they understood a word of. They showed me a pass from a captain of a ship declaring that they were Algerines who had been taken by the Spaniards and made slaves. That they made their escape, got to Lisbon, and from thence were brought to England. I carried them with me to a French house, where I got a man who spoke a little Spanish to one of them, and learnt that they wanted to see the Ambassador from Tripoli, who though not from the same division of territory, is yet under the Grand Signior, as they are. I accordingly went with him to the Ambassador's house, where I found a Turk who could speak English and interpret what they said; and he told me that they had landed that morning and had already been with the Ambassador begging that he would get liberty for them from the Lords of the Admiralty; and that he had ordered them victuals. I gave them half a crown. They were very thankful, and my Turkish friend who spoke English said, "GOD reward you. The same God make the Turk that make the Christian. But the English have the tender heart. The Turk have not the tender heart."

⌒🐀

WEDNESDAY 20 JULY. Dempster argued on Rousseau's plan, that the goods of fortune and advantages of rank were nothing to a wise man, who ought only to value internal merit. Replied Johnson: "If man were a savage living in the woods by himself, this might be true. But in civilized society we all depend upon each other, and our happiness is very much owing to the good opinion of others. Now, Sir, in civilized society, external advantages make us more respected by individuals. A man who has a good coat upon his back meets with a better reception than he who has a bad one.

"Go to the street and give one man a lecture of morality and another a shilling, and see who will respect you most. Sir, I was once a great arguer for the advantages of poverty, but I was at the same time very discontented. Sir, the great deal of arguing which we hear to represent poverty as no evil shows it to be evidently a great one. You never knew people labouring to convince you that you might live very happily upon a plentiful fortune. In the same way, you hear people talking how miserable a king must be. And yet every one of them would wish to have his place."

⁂

THURSDAY 21 JULY. I remember nothing that happened worth relating this day. How many such days does mortal man pass!

FRIDAY 22 JULY. Mr. Johnson said that Mr. Hume and all other sceptical innovators were vain men; and finding mankind already in possession of truth, they could not gratify their vanity by supporting her; and so they have taken to error. "Sir," said he, "Truth is a cow which will yield such people no more milk, and so they are gone to milk the bull."

⁂

He maintained that a boy at school was the happiest being. I maintained that a man was more so. He said a boy's having his backside flogged was not so severe as a man's having the hiss of the world against him. He talked of the anxiety which men have for fame; and how the greater it is, the more afraid are they of losing it. I considered how wonderful it must be if even the great Mr. Johnson did not think himself secure.

TUESDAY 26 JULY. I called upon Mr. Johnson.

We talked of the education of children and what was best to teach them first. "Sir," said he, "there is no matter what you teach them first, any more than what leg you shall put into your breeches first. Sir, you may stand disputing which is best to put in first, but in the mean time your backside is bare. Sir, while you are considering which of two things you should teach your child first, another boy has learnt 'em both."

THURSDAY 28 JULY. I sat up all last night writing letters and bringing up my lagging journal, which, like a stone to be rolled up a hill, must be kept constantly going.

⁂

SATURDAY 30 JULY. Mr. Johnson and I took a boat and sailed down the silver Thames.

We landed at the Old Swan and walked to Billingsgate, where we took oars and moved smoothly along the river. We were entertained with the immense number and variety of ships that were lying at anchor. It was a pleasant day, and when we got clear out into the country, we were charmed with the beautiful fields on each side of the river.

We talked of preaching, and of the great success that the Methodists have. He said that was owing to their preaching in a plain, vulgar manner, which was the only way to do good to common people, and which men of learning and genius ought to do, as their duty; and for which they would be praised by men of sense.

When we got to Greenwich, I felt great pleasure in being at the place which Mr. Johnson celebrates in his *London: a Poem*. I had the poem in my pocket, and read the passage on the banks of the Thames, and literally "kissed the consecrated earth."

We supped at the Turk's Head. Mr. Johnson said, "I must see thee go; I will go down with you to Harwich." This prodigious mark of his affection filled me with gratitude and vanity. I gave him an account of the family of Auchinleck, and of the Place. He said, "I must be there, and we will live in the Old Castle; and if there is no room remaining, we will build one." This was the most pleasing idea that I could possibly have: to think of seeing this great man at the venerable seat of my ancestors. I had been up all last night yet was not sleepy.

SUNDAY 31 JULY. In the forenoon I was at a Quakers' meeting in Lombard Street, and in the afternoon at St. Paul's, where I was very devout and very happy. After service, I stood in the center and took leave of the church, bowing to every quarter. I cannot help having a reverence for it. Mr. Johnson says the same. Mr. Johnson said today that a woman's preaching was like a dog's walking on his hinder legs. It was not done well, but you were surprised to find it done at all.

Johnson said that he always felt an inclination to do nothing. I said it was strange to think that the most indolent man in Britain had written the most laborious work, *The English Dictionary*. He said he took ten years to do it; but that if he had applied properly, he might have done it in three. . . .

WEDNESDAY 3 AUGUST. I should have mentioned that on Monday night, coming up the Strand, I was tapped on the shoulder by a fine fresh lass. I went home with her. She was an officer's daughter, and born at Gibraltar. I could not resist indulging myself with the enjoyment of her. Surely, in such a situation, when the woman is already abandoned, the crime must be alleviated, though in strict morality, illicit love is always wrong.

from *The Heart of Boswell*

Here are some entries from the journal of novelist and short story master John Cheever. While in the first two entries Cheever addresses the business of writing, in the extended ones he sets down observations that could find their way into fictional works. Note Cheever's mix of precise detail and thematic pointing.

✒

The first page of a new journal, and I hope to report here soon that the middle section of the Wapshots has fallen into shape. I expect that I will continue to report here that I drink too much.

✒

The O'Hara book—he is a pro, a gifted man. There is the sense of life being translated, but I think also an extraordinary vein of morbid sexual anxiety. I would like "The Scandal" to be clear of this. I think the difference is between a fascinated horror of life and a vision of life. He is good and rough and not so lacy as me, but I hope to come to better terms.

⁀🐟

The firemen's bazaar. Seven o'clock. A July night. A rusted and battered backstop stands behind the circle of trucks and booths turned in against the gathering darkness like a circle of covered wagons. Parents and children hasten along the roads that lead to the bazaar as if it might all be over before they got there, although in fact they will get there before it has begun. The sumptuary revolution makes me feel old. Both the boys and the girls are wearing skintight pants, and there are many cases of ungainly and sometimes painful tightness. And in the crowd there are reminders of the fact that there are still some farms outside the village limits. I see a red-faced man, a little drunk, followed by an overworked woman who has cut her own hair as well as the hair of the four shabby children that follow. These are the poor; these are the ones who live upstairs over the shoe store, who live in the cottage down by the dump, who can be seen fanning themselves at their windows in the heat. When you leave at six to catch an early plane, these are the ones that you see at dawn, waiting by the bus stop with their sandwiches in a paper bag. But it is the children I enjoy most, watching them ride in mechanical pony carts and airplanes, suspended by chains from a pylon. Their brilliance, this raw material of human goodness. A very plain woman in the last months of pregnancy, who looks out at the scene calmly and with great pride in this proof of the fact that someone has taken her in his arms. Many of the girls have their hair in rollers half concealed by scarves. Like primitive headdresses and, in the darkness, like crowns.

⁀🐟

All Hallows' Eve. Some set piece about the community giving a primordial shudder, scattering the mercies of piety, charity, and mental health and exposing, briefly, the realities of evil and the hosts of the vengeful and unquiet dead. I see how frail the pumpkin lanterns are that we light on our doorsteps to protect our houses from the powers of darkness. I see the little boy, dressed as a devil, rattling a can and asking pennies for unicef. How thin the voice of reason sounds tonight! Does my mother fly through the air? My father, my fishing companions? Have mercy upon us; grant us thy peace! Although there seemed to be no connection, it was always at this season that, in the less well-heeled neighborhoods of the village, "For Sale" signs would appear, as abundant as chrysanthemums. Most of them seemed to have been printed by children, and they were stuck into car windshields, nailed to trees, and attached to the bows of cabin cruisers and other boats, resting on trailers in the side yard. Everything seemed to be for sale—pianos, vacant lots, Rototillers, and chain saws, as if the coming of winter provoked some psychic upheaval involving the fear of loss. But as the last of the leaves fell, glittering like money, the "For Sale" signs vanished with them. Had everyone got a raise, a mortgage, a loan, or an infusion of hopefulness? It happened every year.

from *The Journals of John Cheever*

THE JOURNAL, JOURNALING, AND JOURNALISM

While most journal writing is for the benefit of its author and does not anticipate a reader, the journal (or notebook) entries of the professional journalist—especially of the roving correspondent—make their way into print quickly. Indeed, often daily (*jour*-ly). A skilled observer's record of significant events, persons, and places travels from notebook to newspaper with only mimimal polishing and pointing. Often, editors invite dispatches that reflect the engagement of the writer, who is allowed to be part of the story.

In 1973, *The New York Times* assigned novelist James Jones to report on events in Vietnam following the Paris peace talks and during the initial stages of American withdrawal. Many of the pieces he wrote were published in the *Times*, several appeared in other publications, and all (previously published or not) were collected in a book. "Sandbags" has the feel at once of raw journal work and something shaped for an audience:

We had used them in my war. My personal experience with them had been mostly in Honolulu, right after Pearl Harbor, when we built or reinforced beach positions in and around Waikiki. But nowhere that I knew them did they ever reach the civilized, well-groomed aspect that they had in Vietnam.

Almost always they were green-colored. This made them match in color the interlocking, built-up metal members also in use for fragmentation and direct-fire protection. Thus adding a certain esthetic value. Sometimes the sandbags went up a full two stories. What was amazing about them was the way they kept their shape and their form at such heights. Later I got a closer look at them, and asked about them. A technique had been developed for spraying them with oil, and some composition. This hardened and made them as solid as any masonry, once they were placed. It accounted for their trim shipshape appearance, neat and military, squared off in their even lines and mounting pyramidal corners. They were everywhere in Vietnam. And only at the far-flung Border Ranger outposts I visited later, which were cut off and unreachable for resupply except by air, were there ever sandbags in disrepair, rotting and spilling and unshapely.

It was a consolation to know that, whatever else happened, we could always claim truthfully we had taught the South Viets how to take care of their sandbags.

This "personal journalism" done on the fly is not too far removed from the creative nonfiction treated in Chapter 11, though the latter has the benefit of a much more thoroughgoing process of revision, refinement, and rethinking.

From *Viet Journal*

The Journal as a Literary Form

In our discussion of Nin's *Diary*, we have already noted the critical and popular acceptance of the diary or journal as a literary form. Its appeal stems from the sense of intimacy and spontaneity it can convey. Some such works, like those of Nin and Samuel Pepys, probably are heightened and embellished with a potential reader in mind. Others, like Sherwood Anderson's *Paris Notebook, 1921*, are clearly private works whose interest is in what they tell us about the influence of this Paris trip on Anderson's subsquent career. It fascinates because it was not meant for publication—and because Anderson is always a good writer.

Roger Aplon's *Barcelona Diary* is a contemporary work that began simply as a writer's notebook or sketchbook but took on a life of its own. Aplon dignified it as "the work I would pursue until it no longer satisfied or had become stale in some way." A mixture of poems and prose poems, descriptions and meditations, Aplon's work evokes the interaction of place and an individual sensibility. Many of the entries underwent considerable revision, while others remained close to their first draft nakedness.

Here is entry number 56—"In Those Days":

There are women here, mature women, who ride the bus with dignity & a delicate fan to compliment their silks & striking prints & some sport a cane or hand-sewn umbrella or a clutch from Riera or Cartier to hold their private needs for a trip to Sonia's for dinner or Dr. Font's for that sore tooth or, Yes, an afternoon rendezvous in Guell Parc with a certain gentleman from her youth who is widowed & . . . & while I watch she nonchalantly opens her fan & begins, with her wrist cocked just so, to stir the air & with it a sly smile seems to come or is it a hint of perspiration caught in the corner of an eye which has made her turn this delicate rose or is it a memory or vision of herself with her first fan at a cotillion or summer fiesta when she was a girl in Tarragona & the young men would come to her mother & ask her to walk with them & it was the fan which kept her engaged & wise to the talk & time & whether the air had warmed or cooled & the name of the man had changed & she was on her own as she was mostly in those days and could do not wrong.

Aplon has created an imaginary portrait that is informed by his immersion in the spirit of Catalonia. Engaging in itself, it gains strength as it resonates with its companion pieces in Aplon's intricate mosaic.

SUGGESTIONS FOR JOURNAL WORK

1. Write a character sketch that incorporates an anecdote modeled on Boswell's treatment of Mrs. Legge. Now try one modeled on Nin's portrait of her dance instructor.

2. Report a conversation in your journal, capturing the personal style of one of the participants as accurately as Boswell has captured Dr. Johnson's.

3. After you have been keeping a journal for a while, reread it to see whether any patterns have begun to develop. Note, for example, Boswell's concern with controlled and uncontrolled sexual passion.

4. Holidays and special events provide opportunities for catching individual behavior within group behavior and custom. Prepare entries like Cheever's sketches of the firemen's bazaar and Halloween.

5. Take a journal piece that you have previously written for yourself and revise it with a reader in mind. How has it changed?

6. Attempt an "interior portrait," a meditation prompted by a passing stranger, on the model of the entry from Aplon's *Barcelona Diary.*

After a time—and we would not say what that time might be—your journal will become a resource not only for passages such as those found in this chapter but also for whole works. Often you will find that ideas or impulses appearing over a period of time in your journal start to form a pattern that sparks or confirms a story, essay, poem, or play. Our space being limited, we cannot give an example of such a development in operation. You will simply have to trust that, in time, the effort made on the practice field will pay off in the game.

Reread Boswell's entry of 28 July!

3

Point of View

WHAT IS IT?

We are fated—some might say "doomed"—to experience, observe, and understand everything from a *point of view*, a metaphor for having a mental attitude or opinion. We say: "That's how he sees it" or "That's your story." Of course, it is easier to detect another person's point of view than one's own. But on reflection you know you have one too, even when you are commenting on someone else's. It is no wonder, then, that writers share with readers the common definitions of the metaphor: one, we always look at something from one viewpoint (our scenic prospect, so to speak) and two, as a consequence, our reactions must be different from someone else's, if only by a millimeter.

Writers share the common fate, but they are highly aware of its power and can manipulate it for effects in their works. When Mark Twain had a naïve twelve-year-old narrate the events in Huckleberry Finn, he made a fateful decision. When Barbara Kingsolver chose to have four different daughters of a missionary and their mother tell of their African experiences in *The Poisonwood Bible*, she made a fateful decision. In these novels—one told by a naïve boy and the other told by girls of various ages and their mother—the writers can only tell aspects of the story and so the reader can only see aspects of the story. Indeed, the writers might choose to change the point of view, but then they would be limited by their new position. As for readers, they expect everything from a poem to a play to have one, for characters to have one, for narrators to have one, and for the writer to have one, even when it is difficult to discern. Because writers also expect that a reader will bring a point of view to the work, they make a host of decisions to anticipate reader expectations, Chapter 1. Think of the fatefulness of Allen Ginsberg's decision to tell *Howl* as if he were a latter day Walt Whitman.

In life and in art, one may move from one perspective to another. A house that looks good to us from a distance, we see, on close inspection, actually needs a new roof, glass in the windows, and paint. Our changed view may bring a change in our feelings or judgment about whether or not to buy it. The realtor, even if she sees the flaws, will probably "see" the house quite differently: "It's a steal," she says. In fact, it looks different to different people viewing it from what may seem to be the same perspective: a painting contractor, a ten-year-old who has lived there since birth, a neighbor who doesn't like the present owners. In sum, the way in which writers manipulate point of view shapes their writing and their audience's experience of the work.

WHO WILL DO THE TELLING?

We began this book with a point of view.

That point of view involves both decisions we made before we began writing and decisions we made, consciously or unconsciously, as we were writing and revising. Though the aims of this book are different from the aims of a story, poem, or play, the essential point-of-view question is the same: who is going to do the telling? As you will see, deciding who "who" will be is not merely a matter of deciding whether the speaker will be first, second, or third person and whether the "voice" will be an omniscient one, a limited one, the voice of someone who has been directly involved, or that of an onlooker (see "The Range of Perspectives" later in this chapter). Who the narrator will be concerns viewpoint to the world and the audience. Point of view is, then, partly about how to tell.

In planning and writing this book, for example, we had to decide whether to pretend we were authorities delivering the gospel from on high about formulas for writing success or, at the other end of the spectrum, whether to act as close friends at a table discussing writing processes and problems. We finally decided to take a position somewhere between authority and collegiality. Our decision about viewpoint derived from what we believed our audience already knew and what it needed to know about writing, as well as our premise that while ideally all matters are open to discussion, some guidelines and an introduction to standard techniques help when you are starting to play the game. In this sense, choosing a point of view is closely related to searching for a tone or style that communicates just where we stand about the writing process. Point of view, considered this way, is a process that is closely connected with *what* to tell, how much to tell, and how to tell it.

Our point of view was not a settled matter. It evolved as we tried to grapple with the subject, as we talked with and explained ideas to each other, and as we reviewed the notes we kept during our meetings (a version of the writer's notebook). It also developed from what we already knew about writing and editing, as well as from what we found out along the way.

In shaping what and how we tell, we knew that point of view would determine your response. What if we had written: "Point of view is implicated in every decision the writer makes, including diction. Structure your point of view to maximize effects." We suspect that one of your reactions would be to see such a statement as a sign that we were hidebound rule makers. Since we actually feel that successful writing involves continual decision making and because we do not care for the platform and the bureaucratic, we are more likely to say, "Point of view affects everything you do in your writing, including your choice of words." For example. we haven't decided just to speak in the first-person plural (we) and to address the second-person (you) reader. We have created a narrator with an attitude toward the material and toward the reader. Even writers of nonfiction prose concerned primarily with imparting information, such as the writers of this textbook, are doomed to think about point of view.

First-person compositions can have carefully defined narrators or spokespersons who are distanced from the author. In "A Modest Proposal," Jonathan Swift creates a speaker who describes a problem (starvation in eighteenth-century Ireland) and then argues in a cold, calculating way for a solution (raise Irish children as food for the English dinner table) that readers are not expected to accept. The sham point of view allows Swift to dramatize the oppression of the Irish in the guise of someone who wants to do good but who is, in fact, as callous as Swift's English audience. Many writers develop a **persona** through whom they engage their readers. Among today's newspaper writers, Miss Manners has developed a huge audience for her advice column. Her persona is not exactly the same person as her creator. The "Dave Barry" who is the subject of humor columns supposedly based on his experiences is probably not quite identical with the Dave Barry who creates those columns.

The "I" with which a writer of nonfiction prose chooses to address others has much to do with who these others are and what the occasion is. Because writers don't use the same style for all audiences, they don't project an identical self from one writing task to another. The opportunity to choose a persona, and thus a point of view, grows out of our multiple roles in everyday life. We speak to our old friends in one way and to our supervisors in another. For a given situation, one aspect of who we are takes over, and we automatically find the right voice. We can't help but choose the child's point of view in addressing our parents. However, as writers, we can deliberately choose such a point of view for specific ends; for example we can choose to provide a child's voice for an adult to produce an effect. Similarly, we can make a point one way by pretending to be bewildered, another way by pretending to be (or truly being) authoritative. Point of view is so powerful that it is the linchpin for every other aspect of writing.

Let us examine how point of view operates in Shelley's "Ozymandias." After you read the **sonnet,*** go back over it and try to isolate the various points of view it incorporates. Make a list outlining (1) whose mind is being reflected and (2) what attitude is revealed in each case. Then read the commentary that follows.

> I met a traveller from an antique land
> Who said: Two vast and trunkless legs of stone
> Stand in the desert . . . Near them, on the sand,
> Half sunk, a shattered visage lies, whose frown,
> And wrinkled lip, and sneer of cold command,
> Tell that its sculptor well those passions read
> Which yet survive, stamped on these lifeless things,
> The hand that mocked them, and the heart that fed;
> And on the pedestal these words appear:
> 'My name is Ozymandias, king of kings:
> Look on my works, ye Mighty, and despair!'
> Nothing beside remains. Round the decay
> Of that colossal wreck, boundless and bare
> The lone and level sands stretch far away.
>
>   1817

Immediately, we are told that the "narrator" or "speaker" heard a story. As readers, we recognize the first person point of view. But that's only the beginning of point-of-view complications. The remainder of the poem is the speaker's report of the traveler's experience. We can't be sure if Shelley's **persona** is quoting the traveler or merely paraphrasing what the traveler told him.

Let us construct a fiction of what happened in the writing process that may have led to his decision about point of view:

1. Shelley hated tyrants and believed that the poet's task was to challenge tyranny in preparation for the creation of more perfect societies. Let's not worry about how he came to this position.

---

*Boldface terms are defined in the glossary.

2. In a book, in a dream, from a friend—somehow—an image came to Shelley of a tyrant whose monument stands in a wasted land. He jots the image down in his journal, perhaps even first imagining that the statue is intact. Maybe he launches into the poem immediately. Maybe he writes a first draft in his journal and, coming across it years later, is moved to complete it. No matter.

3. At some point, Shelley had to decide who would tell the story. The most obvious person is himself, or, rather, the voice he creates to tell the story of Ozymandias's statue. Shelley could have cast the traveler as the persona and saved the extra step of narrating through someone who encountered the traveler. Perhaps Shelley feared that his message would be discounted by readers who would identify such a speaker with the poet, who was known to hate tyrants. Locating the story in another's experience can be a way of increasing the reader's readiness to accept it. At the same time, Shelley's surrogate (our secondhand narrator) hears the tale and passes it on to us, and if we know Shelley's attitude (point of view) toward tyrants, we can quickly catch his point. The poem is not, finally, addressing the haughtiness and transient stature of Ozymandias, but of all tyrants—especially those of Shelley's own day.

4. Looking further, we can see that the poem contains no less than four points of view: what Ozymandias thought of himself (the inscription still visible on the pedestal); what the sculptor thought of Ozymandias (through capturing his inner nature in stone); what the traveler records of his own experience; what the persona retells upon hearing the traveler's story. At some point, Shelley found that this layered perspective projected his feeling about tyranny most effectively. The character of Ozymandias—of tyranny—becomes a shared understanding of sculptor, traveler, conveyor-poet, and reader. Only the king himself is left out, his haughty words—actually blasphemous words—shown to be absurd.

Though some of our speculations are fictive, this exploration tells something about point of view. Point of view involves a series of finely adjusted decisions. Many of them you will have to make as you discover the needs of your story; nevertheless, you will save yourself a good deal of grief if you start working them out before you write. We know one writer who plunged into a novel told in the first person and on page 110 found out that the narrator had to die. The writer then had to figure out how a dead person could be talking and who was going to tell the rest of the novel. Could he rewrite all 110 pages with a deadline just two months off? Not to leave you wondering, the novelist invented a second narrator to find the dead narrator's tape recording. What do you think of this solution?

Now that you've had a chance to think about point of view for a while, do the following exercise in your journal:

OZYMANDIAS EXERCISE

1. What kind of person is the traveler in Shelley's poem? How do you know?

2. Do you think Shelley's narrator is paraphrasing or quoting the traveler? How do you support your position? What difference does your position make on how the poem works?

3. Compose a description that takes a different attitude toward this statue and its subject. Try the point of view of an archaeologist or a painter or a child.

4. Imagine that the traveler (or a traveler of your own invention) had stumbled across a crumbling, isolated monument that we are all familiar with—the Statue of Liberty, or the Lincoln Memorial, or something else that you choose. Write a description that makes your point through what the traveler has told you of his (or her) experience.

EXERCISE

We said earlier that the point of view you choose affects many other aspects of writing. Because point of view touches on attitude and personality, it can affect the words that you choose and even the sentence patterns with which you string them together. Examine the following passages and jot down what you think about each narrator. We've commented at the end.

> 1. In the fall the war was always there, but we did not go to it any more. It was cold in the fall in Milan and the dark came very early. Then the electric lights came on, and it was pleasant along the streets looking in the windows.
>
> from Ernest Hemingway, "In Another Country"

> 2. There was music from my neighbor's house through the summer nights. In his blue gardens men and girls came and went like moths among the whisperings and the champagne and the stars. At high tide in the afternoon I watched his guests diving from the tower of his raft, or taking the sun on the hot sand of his beach while his two motorboats slit the waters of the Sound, drawing aquaplanes over cataracts of foam.
>
> from F. Scott Fitzgerald, *The Great Gatsby*

3.   Joseph, who whilst he was speaking had continued in one attitude, with his head reclining on one side, and his eyes cast on the ground, no sooner perceived, on looking up, the position of Adams, who was stretched on his back, and snored louder than the usual braying of the animal with long ears, then he turned towards Fanny, and, taking her by the hand began a daliance, which, though consistent with the purest innocence and decency, neither he would have attempted nor she permitted before any witness.

from Henry Fielding, Joseph Andrews

4.   I went along up the bank with one eye out for pap and 'tother one out for what the rise might fetch along. Well, all at once, here comes a canoe; just a beauty, too, about thirteen or fourteen foot long, riding high like a duck. I shot head first off the bank, like a frog, clothes and all on, and struck out for the canoe. I just expected there'd be somebody laying down in it, because people often done that to fool folks, and when a chap had pulled a skiff out most to it they'd raise up and laughed at him. But it warn't so this time.

from Mark Twain, Huckleberry Finn

5.   This is just a kid with a local yearning but he is part of an assembling crowd, anonymous thousands off the buses and trains, people in narrow columns tramping over the swing bridge above the river, and even if they are not a migration or a revolution, some vast shaking of the soul, they bring with them the body heat of a great city and their own small reveries and desperations, the unseen something that haunts the day—men in fedoras and sailors on shore leave, the stray tumble of their thoughts, going to a game.

from Don Delillo, Underworld

Our reactions: (1) Understated, matter of fact, direct—as if told at a bar. A person whose emotions are masked. (2) A wistful fellow with a romantic imagination. Slightly adolescent, but polished too. (3) An entertainer, self-conscious effect-maker. He revels in his circumlocutions and false delicacies. An ironist. (4) An unlettered youngster; impetuous, observant, worldly wise. (5) Aware of detail and slightly superior to the scene he describes. He sounds a bit like a travelogue announcer.

THE DECISION AND ITS CONSEQUENCES

Granted, some of the preceding examples may indeed be close to the author's voice rather than a persona created especially for the work; however, from our point of view as readers, we can hear the story only through the narrator's voice, which shapes our response to that story. Consciously or unconsciously the writer has the following decisions to make. He or she must:

1. Choose a narrator, usually first or third person.
2. Decide what the narrator's attitude will be.
3. Decide how the reader should respond to the narrator and how to make the narrator create that response.

Let us further explore the decisions involved in number 2.

Imagine: a baseball game. Nine players are on the field. A batter is at the plate. Perhaps there are one or more base runners. Umpires are at their positions. So are coaches. Each manager is in a dugout along with his assistants and the other players—some of the players are also out in the bullpen. Ball and bat-boys or girls are doing their jobs. Fans are in the stands, along with vendors of snacks, drinks, and souvenirs. Security guards patrol the area. In the press box, sports journalists are hard at work. Mini-studios hold members of the radio and television broadcast crews.

Think of all the people who are involved in the scene, all the potential stories. But perhaps there is just one story to tell: the simple story of the game.

Who should tell it?

As soon as we attempt to answer this question, we see that there is an intimate connection between the telling and what is told. The shortstop's story can never be the same as the ball-girl's or the visiting manager's. Which story holds the truth? Which truth? The decision about who tells the story (even if the "story" is about someone's feelings as expressed in a poem) makes the story take on certain contours. No convincing narrator is totally objective, and the subjective perceptions and needs of the storyteller make the story come out the way it does.

Umpires are neutral, but the umpire's story is about calling the game, not playing in it. A journalist may not favor either team, yet his love for the game itself—or for his job, or his wife, or his lunch—can affect how he reports what he sees. And *his* story is, at bottom, about reporting.

Consider the rookie's wife. She sits in the stands behind home plate. She is seven months pregnant, worried about her husband's future in baseball and their future together. What does she see on the playing field? Does the umpire block her view of the pitch that her husband doesn't swing at? Does a memory of their first meeting distract her? Does the pitcher care about this? Does he even notice her? What is the pitcher's story—a fable of blisters and beer?

By this time the point about point of view should be clear. Decisions regarding point of view involve as many combinations and possibilities as a baseball game. Like many other concerns, it has endless reverberations.

Let's dig into point of view a bit more.

Imagine: a multilevel house built of flagstone and redwood with large expanses of glass. The house is sprawled out along the side of a mountain. To the right is a small vineyard, where a young woman sits on a weathered bench, reading. Near her an Irish setter sleeps in the shade. A narrow gravel road winds around the side of the mountain, and branching off from it a dirt driveway leads to the house. It is late afternoon, and, though the low sun shines brightly, there are signs that it has rained within the hour.

Now imagine two men. One is hiking through a valley below the mountain. He looks up at the house. What could he see? Given his position, how would he describe it? The other man is driving past it on the narrow mountain road. Does he see what the hiker sees?

One meaning of point of view has to do with the physical perspective a viewer can have on the subject. The hiker, far below the house, can see it in less detail. From his perspective and distance, he may not be able to make out the materials of the house; perhaps he won't see the woman or the dog. If so, both might as well not be there. What the man in the car will see depends upon how fast he is driving and how long he can risk taking his eyes off the road. If he comes to a stop, he will be able to take in far more detail than the hiker down below.

EXERCISE

Choose a place—perhaps your workplace or a building at your school—and describe it from different physical and psychological vantage points. (For example, how might a French chef see a McDonald's?)

Going back to our two men and the mountain house, let us do some more imagining. We need to give the men identities. Suppose the hiker, let's call him Chick, is a stranger who has come here to flee a complex life in Chicago. He is tired and thirsty, soaked from his exertion, the humidity, and the wet grasses he has tramped through. How does this circumstance affect what he sees when he looks up at the house? How will his situation color his perception? Now imagine that the hiker is the woman's husband. They have lived together in the house for three years, and he has worked on every inch of it. Each day he walks to the valley to pick up mail and food at the general store. He then climbs the mountain again and joins his wife for wine and cheese in the vineyard. He raised the setter from a pup. What does *this* hiker see when he looks up at the house?

If we imagine each of these hikers as the narrator of a story in which looking up at the house from the valley triggers an important scene, we can readily understand the importance of point of view. Each narrator will see the house at that moment through a unique lens because he relates to the house differently and has different expectations. Let's see what might happen with

Chick, whom, at this point in the story, a third-person narrator wishes us to know a bit better:

> Chick saw the tangled geometry of a rambling house halfway up the mountainside. To the right, a splash of color told him some-one was home—someone who might offer a bit of hospitality if he could just manage to push himself up the slope. The house swam in a flux of long shadows and little mirrored explosions of the sun, reminding Chick that he'd better start moving before it got dark. He doubted they got many strangers stopping in such an isolated spot, particularly strangers carrying $100,000 in their knapsacks. He'd have to be careful.

Now it's your turn. Imagine the driver. Is he a lover? A detective? As he slows to swing onto the access road, what does he see? What does he think? Perhaps the house is for sale and he has come to examine it. Put the situation in motion. Just when does the noise of the car wake the dog? When is the central conscious-ness—the driver—aware of the dog?

Now let's turn the game around. A young woman has been sitting on a bench in the arbor alongside her elaborate mountain home. She puts down her book (what is she reading?), stands, stretches, and faces the valley. She is pretty sure that she can make out someone just reaching the bottom of the mountain slope. Then she becomes aware of a car slowing to turn into her driveway. Freeze the frame: what does she see in this frozen moment? Now roll the camera: follow her consciousness of what's going on in the world around her.

One more, final, wrinkle. Make the character who waits in the arbor a man and make the other characters women.

As we have seen, the term *point of view* covers a wide range of results that come from a writer's decisions. Deciding to tell a story in the first or third person is merely the first decision. The usefulness of the information readers receive depends upon how the writer has filtered the material through a narrator's consciousness and what coloring that consciousness has given to the information. For example, we get the information about what has happened in Emily Brontë's *Wuthering Heights* from Lockwood as reported to him by Nelly Dean, and much of her information is secondhand. In Daniel Defoe's *Moll Flanders* we learn all that happens from Moll, but the whole experience happens to her directly. Though both novels are written in the first person, there are far more differences than similarities. In F. Scott Fitzgerald's *The Great Gatsby* a character who is not at the center of the action tells the story; in Camus's *The Plague* we receive, without knowing it until near the end, all of our information from a first-person narrator who hides his identity and presents the story clinically. Technically, all these works are first person, but, from the writer's point of view, both the possibilities and limitations are infinite.

THE RANGE OF PERSPECTIVES

Third Person

The third-person narrator speaks from outside of the story as an onlooker or reporter rather than as a participant. The degree to which the narrator is given access to external and internal information and the degree to which the narrator is allowed to express judgments about that information determine more precisely the narrative stance. Within the broad third-person category, the narrator has three options:

Full Omniscience. The fully omniscient narrator accesses the minds, feelings, and dreams of all the characters in the work. Thus the author, through the narrator, can shift focus along the way, giving the reader a variety of perspectives. In the opening chapter of Alice McDermott's *Charming Billy*, we receive a complex image of Billy through the thoughts of people attending his wake. The reader wonders which is the true view and the novel flows from this mystery. This kind of omniscient narrator also shifts back and forth between subjective and objective approaches, sometimes becoming engaged in explaining, interpreting, assessing, and moralizing on the events and characters. The narrator may at times comment extensively, a technique we call *editorializing*. The absence of any limitation on the narrator's information (and presence) can create havoc for an inexperienced writer. The tendency is to lose focus, to bully the reader, and to subjugate the story and characters to thematic concerns in unattractive ways.

Limited Omniscience. The limited omniscient narrator stands behind the shoulder of one character, usually the major character, and conveys to the reader only what that character experiences, knows, and feels. Other characters are treated objectively: what they say and do is recorded. However, what the central character thinks about them is an important ingredient. Sometimes, on top of this limited omniscience, the narrator is allowed a bit of knowledge or speculation beyond what the central character knows in order for the reader to gain perspective on that character, to get outside of the main character's head. Most successful stories and novels use some variation of the limited omniscient point of view.

Objective Limitation. The objective limitation point of view is most like that of the dramatist. Setting, action, and dialogue are the only tools the author allows the narrator-self. Readers are given no direct access to the minds of the characters and are left to form judgments on their own. This perspective is as difficult, in its own way, as unlimited omniscience.

First Person

In first-person point of view the narrator is one of the characters in the story or novel, either a witness to the events or a participant. The narrator's relationship to the events and to the other characters determines what can be convincingly revealed from the chosen perspective. The first-person narrator does not have access to the minds of others (unless the narrator is a psychiatrist revealing professionally gained knowledge—a cute trick). At every moment of the story's progress, the first-person narrator is being characterized by the way he or she thinks and speaks.

Central Character. When the narrator is the central character, the fiction is borrowing the appeal of autobiography. The author has to be careful to restrain this kind of narrator. It is easy to sacrifice the development of the story to the narrator's ego. Often first-person narration is an exploration of how memory works and how a person comes to understand, with the passage of time, the meaning of events that happened years earlier. Ralph Ellison's *Invisible Man* is a powerful example of this technique.

Minor Character/Witness. "I was there" can be almost as compelling as "It happened to me." This kind of narrator has to be a true personality, not merely a convenient reporter of events. The reader must be able to gauge the degree of emotional interest—bias—of this narrator as well as of the central character narrator. Why is it important *to the teller*, Nick Carroway, to relate the events in *The Great Gatsby*?

As you can see, there are places where these categories overlap. Certain kinds of third-person narration come very close to first-person witness, but more than pronoun choice should separate these perspectives. The thirdperson narrator, even if given a personality as in Henry Fielding's *Joseph Andrews*, is primarily there to tell the story. The first-person minor character is *involved* in some way, even if not in terms of the main action. Of course, in fictions like those by Arthur Conan Doyle, Dr. Watson works with Sherlock Holmes, he doesn't just know about him or see him from afar.

EXERCISES

1. Describe an object:
   a. as if you secretly desired it.
   b. as if you were trying to, but could not quite, conceal your contempt for it.
   c. as if you had never seen anything like it before (you are from Alpha Centaurus).

    d. as a child of ten might describe it.

    e. as your roommate, mother, father, sister, or brother might describe it.

    f. as someone who is blind might describe it.

2. Look at some full-page newspaper or magazine advertisements. What, besides the product itself, is being "sold" in each case? What is the point of view of the ad copy? What kind of "speaker" is presented in each case? Write some ad copy for an object you own, but first imagine a person (or type of person) to whom you are trying to sell the object.

3. Here is a passage from "The Dead," a story from James Joyce's *Dubliners* in which Gabriel Conroy is the major character. After studying the paragraph, rewrite it in the first person. Then, after comparing the two versions, read the commentary that follows the excerpt:

> Gabriel could not listen while Mary Jane was playing her Academy piece, full of runs and difficult passages, to the hushed drawing-room. He liked music but the piece she was playing had no melody for him and he doubted whether it had any melody for the other listeners, though they had begged Mary Jane to play something. Four young men, who had come from the refreshment-room to stand in the doorway at the sound of the piano, had gone away quietly in couples after a few minutes. The only persons who seemed to follow the music were Mary Jane herself, her hands racing along the keyboard or lifted from it at the pauses like those of a priestess in momentary imprecation, and Aunt Kate standing at her elbow to turn the page.

As Joyce has written it, Gabriel's consciousness is part of a larger scene, some of which he is probably not paying attention to. If he became specifically aware of the other people and their attentiveness to Mary Jane's performance, some of his self-centered insularity would be lost. Gabriel is part of a social situation that Joyce is looking at satirically. For *Gabriel* to say Mary Jane's playing is "like . . . a priestess's" would give him too much distance from what is going on. Changing "Gabriel" and third-person pronoun references to first person will bring about only a mechanical difference.

Rewrite the paragraph, this time from Mary Jane's point of view. Now try Aunt Kate's. Each time, pay attention to how many other elements of the story can change when you change perspective. In some of your refashionings, allow yourself to revise the order of the material, the language, the implications. Try writing a similar paragraph in which someone is preparing a meal while another character, perhaps your main character, reacts to what he or she sees in such a way that we learn about both characters.

4. Though point of view is usually—and properly—treated as a concern of prose (the identification of the narrator), it is also a legitimate concern of the poet. This is especially true when the speaker is clearly identified and characterized. Often we are asked to understand how the truth of what is being perceived depends upon who is doing the perceiving. This theme is one thread in

Myra Sklarew's "Leaving." After reading this two-part poem, respond to the questions and tasks that follow it.

His Song

I go out foraging against
the molten core rising
rising daily inside me

against the voice saying
What did you mean to be in your life?

against the slow thought
that would come
when I drove out
on a Sunday

Ways I could change my life

But this other
this danger is too compelling
I tell you I'd die for it
The threat
of that man
with his sack of evidence
with his knife out after me
in the dark
slashing my tires
to keep me
from running off
with his wife

It doesn't matter now
It's what I want

My whole life is back there
leaning against the porch rail
thinking itself down
along the narrow edge
of the years

But it's not strong enough
to keep back
what's broken through
that part of me I set onto another
never quite fitting

It's something I can't do without
that friction to raise up a feeling
against the questions
that won't leave me
against the answer
out there in front of me

Her Song

After he left
I posted innocence
at my door

When he spoke
of his reason for leaving
I knew my own part in it
but I never said a word

At first it was good
filling up the boxes
with his books of naked girls
putting them
by the front door

But then
there was the empty closet
a white pill
on the floor
in the corner
the familiar smell

At night
innocence
like the book beside me
brings no comfort at all

nor the thin legs
of self-righteousness
nor the stem and leaf
of selfhood

Why is it
in my dream
it seems perfectly natural
to be taking off my clothes
in front of two men
who are naked

Perfectly natural for one
of the men to enter me
until I become aware
of someone else
standing in the corner
of that room

from *The Science of Goodbyes*

In this poem, the author attends to both the husband's and wife's point of view about a broken relationship. "His Song" and "Her Song" step into the consciousness of two people who now share only the legacy of their failed marriage.

    a. How does each view the past and the present?

    b. Is each point of view handled convincingly?

    c. Rewrite the poem so that the man tries to express the woman's attitude and the woman tries to express the man's.

    d. Rewrite the poem from a third-person perspective. Do more than merely changing the "I" to "he" or "she."

    e. Imagine that the couple has a child who is now about fifteen-years-old. Rewrite the poem (in prose if you wish) from the child's perspective.

    f. Imagine another conflict between two people: father and son, jail guard and criminal, hostess and gate-crasher. Present the contrasting points of view in a two-part poem in which each mind is entered (as in Sklarew's) or in a piece of dialogue.

    g. Now, in prose, recast this conflict from an outside perspective: first try third-person omniscient, then objective.

5. Read William Goyen's "Rhody's Path" (pp. 46–52) and then consider the following questions.

    a. Can you tell the approximate age of the narrator at the time of the events? How? Is there a distance in time or maturity established between the events and the telling?

    b. Is the narrator male or female?

    c. Why does Goyen have the narrator refer to "we" rather than "I"? Can you think of other circumstances in which such use of the first-person plural would be appropriate?

    d. Does Goyen create an authentic "voice" for his narrator? What are its characteristics?

    e. How would you describe the personality of the narrator? Why does the narrator seem so self-effacing?

    f. In what ways would the story be different if Rhody told it? If Mama or Idalou told it? If a third-person narrator told it?

    g. Prepare an overall assessment of the relationship between Goyen's point-of-view decision and the theme of individual versus family identity.

Rhody's Path

WILLIAM GOYEN

Sometimes several sudden events will happen together so as to make you believe they have a single meaning if 'twould only come clear. Surely happenings are lowered down upon us after a pattern of the Lord above.

Twas in the summer of one year; the time the Second Coming was prophesied over the land and the Revivalist came to Bailey's pasture to prove it; and the year of two memorable events. First was the plague of grasshoppers (twas the driest year in many an old memory, in East Texas); second was the Revival in the pasture across from the house.

Just even to mention the pestilence of hoppers makes you want to scratch all over. They came from over toward Grapeland like a promise of Revelations—all counted to the last as even the hairs of our head are numbered, so says the Bible and so said the Revivalist—making the driest noise in the world, if you have ever heard them. There were so many that they were all clusted together, just one working mass of living insects, wild with appetite and cutting down so fast you could not believe your eyes a whole field of crops. They hid the sun like a curtain and twas half-daylight all that day, the trees were alive with them and shredded of their leaves. We humans were locked in our houses, but the earth was the grasshopper's, he took over the world. It did truly seem a punishment, like the end of the world was upon us, as was prophesied.

Who should choose to come home to us that end of summer but Rhody, to visit, after a long time gone. She had been in New Orleans as well as in Dallas and up in Shreveport too, first married to her third husband in New Orleans, then in Dallas to run away from him in spite, and lastly in Shreveport to write him to go to the Devil and never lay eye on her again. We all think he was real ready to follow the law of that note. Then she come on home to tell us all this, and to rest.

Rhody arrived in a fuss and a fit, the way she is eternally, a born fidget, on the heels of the plague of hoppers. They had not been gone a day when she swept in like the scourge of pestilence. She came into our wasteland, scarce a leaf on a tree and crops just stalks, dust in the air. So had the Revivalist—as if they had arranged it together in Louisiana and the preacher had gone so far as to prophesy the Second Coming in Texas for Rhody's sake. She could make a man do such.

Already in the pasture across the railroad tracks and in front of the house, the Revivalist was raising his tent. We were all sitting on the front porch to watch, when we saw what we couldn't believe our eyes were telling us at first, but knew soon after by her same old walk, Rhody crossing the pasture with her grip in her hand. We watched her stop and set on her suitcase to pass conversation with the Revivalist—she never met a stranger in her life—and his helpers, and we waited for her to come on home across the tracks and through the gate. Mama and Papa and Idalou and some of the children stood at the gate and waited for her; but the bird dog Sam sat on the porch and waited there, barking. He was too old—Idalou said he was eighteen—to waste breath running to the gate to meet Rhody.

The hooded flagpole sitter was a part of it all. He had come in advance as an agent for the Revival and sat on the Mercantile building as an advertisement for the Revival. He had been up there for three days when the grasshoppers come. Twas harder for him than for anyone, we all imagined. The old-timers said he had brought in the plague of hoppers as part of prophesy. They raised up to him a little tent and he sat under that; but it must have been terrible for him. Most thought he would volunteer to come on down, in the face of such adversity, but no sir, he stayed, and was admired for it. He couldn't sail down his leaflets that advertised the Revival, for the grasshoppers would have eaten those as fast as if they had been green leaves from a tree. But the town had already had leaflets enough that read, "The Day of Judgment Is at Hand, Repent of Your Sins for the Lord Cometh . . . "

The first night he was up twas a hot starry night. We all sat on the porch till late at night rocking and fanning and watching him. There he was over the town, a black statue that hardly seemed real.

When the Revivalist first appeared at the house to ask us for cool water, we invited him in on the back porch. He was a young man to be so stern a preacher, lean and nervous and full of his sermon. His bushy eyebrows met together—for jealousy, Idalou told us after he was gone, and uttered a warning against eyebrows that run together. He started right out to speak of our salvation as if it might earn him a drink of water, and of his own past sinful life in cities before he was redeemed. He wanted our redemption, the way he went on sermonizing, more than a cool drink of water; but water was easiest to provide him with and best at hand, as Aunt Idalou said after he had gone. He was a man ready to speak of his own frailties and Mama praised him for this. He wanted to make us all free and purged of man's wickedness, he said, and his black eyes burned under his joined eyebrows when he spoke of this. When he had left, one of the children—Son—helped him carry the pail of well water to the pasture, and then we all broke into sides about who would go to the Revival the next night and who would watch it from the front porch.

When Son came back he was trembling and told that the Revivalist had two diamond rattlesnakes in a cage, right in Bailey's pasture, and that he had shown him the snakes. Then he told us that the preacher was going to show how the Lord would cure him of snakebite as a demonstration of faith. He had converted and saved thousands through this example of the healing power of the Lord, saying his famous prayer as he was struck by this rattling spear, "Hand of God, reach down and help antidote the poison of the diamond rattler of Sin."

Rhody added that she had already found out all this when she came through the pasture and stopped to converse with Bro. Peters—she already knew his name where we hadn't. Then she added that the Revivalist and his company—a lady pianist and three men who were his stewards and helpers—were going to camp in Bailey's pasture during their three-day stay in town and that at the last meeting, the flagpole sitter himself was going to come down and give a testimonial. She further informed us that she had taken upon herself the courtesy to invite Bro. Peters and his lady pianist to eat supper with us that night. We were all both excited and scared. But Mama and Idalou began at once to plan the supper and went in to make the fire in the stove to cook it with.

Rhody was not much changed—a person like Rhody could never change, just add on—as she was burdened by something we could not name. We all noticed a limp in her right leg, and then she confessed she had arthritis in it, from the dampness of New Orleans, she said. Her face was the same beautiful one; she had always been the prettiest in the family, taking after Granny who had been, it was a legend that had photographic proof right on the wall, a very beautiful young woman. But Rhody's face was as if seen through a glass darkly, as the Bible says. More had happened to Rhody during the years away than she would ever tell us. "Some of the fandango is danced out in her," Aunt Idalou said, and now we would all see the change in Rhody that we all hoped and prayed for.

Rhody was thrilled by the sight of the flagpole sitter. She said she was just dying to meet him. She told us that this town had more excitement in it than any city she had been in—and that included several—and she was glad she had come on home. She unpacked her grip and took out some expensive things of pure silk her husbands had bought for her, and there were presents for us all. Then she put her grip in the pantry as though she was going to stay for a long time but no one asked her for how long. In the early days, Rhody had come and left so often that her feet had trod out her own little path through Bailey's pasture and we had named it Rhody's Path. It ran alongside the main path that cut straight through to town. We never used it, left it for her; but if she was gone a long time, Mama would say to one of us who was going to town, "Use Rhody's Path, the bitterweeds are taking it over, maybe that'll bring her home," the way mothers keep up their hopes for their children's return, though the weeds grow over and their beds are unused. Mama kept Rhody's room the way Rhody had it before she left for the first time, and the same counterpane was always on the bed, fresh and clean, the big painted chalk figure of a collie was on the dresser, the fringed pillow a beau had given her with "Sweetheart" on it, and the framed picture of Mary Pickford autographed by her, "America's Sweetheart." "She's got sweetheart on the brain," Mama used to say. She carried sweetheart too far.

Anyway, the Revivalist took Rhody's Path to come to supper on. Around suppertime here came Bro. Peters and the lady pianist across Bailey's pasture on Rhody's Path, he tall and fast-walking, the little pianist trotting behind him like a little spitz to keep up with him. They came through the gate and onto the front porch where we all greeted them, and Rhody was putting on a few airs of city ways that made Idalou look at her as if she could stomp her toe. We were introduced to the pianist whose name was Elsie Wade, a little spinster type with freckled hands and birdlike movements of head. Miss Wade asked the Lord to bless this house and said that good Christians always gathered easily as if they were blood kin, which they were, Bro. Peters added; and we all went in the house, through the hall and onto the back porch. It was a late summer evening and the vines strung across the screen of the porch were nothing but strings after the grasshoppers had devoured them, but through the latticework of string we could see the distant figure of the flagpole sitter that the setting sun set aglow. Rhody kept wanting to talk about him. She said she thought he looked keen up there. Bro. Peters told that the flagpole sitter had been a drinking man, wild and in trouble in every county of Texas and Louisiana, until he was saved by a chance Revival Meeting in Diboll where he was sitting on the County Seat flagpole as a stunt for something or other. The night he came down to give himself to the Lord at the meeting brought wagonloads of people from far and wide, across creeks and gulleys to hear and see him, and many were saved. From that time on he gave his services to the Lord by way of the difficult and lonely task of sitting on a flagpole for three days and nights as a herald of the coming Revival. The flagpole sitter and the diamond rattlers were the most powerful agents of the Gospel and redemption from sin and literally brought thousands of converts into the fold, Bro. Peters told. Rhody said she was dying to meet him and Bro. Peters assured her he would make the introduction personally on the last night of the Revival.

We sat down to a big supper for summertime: cold baking-powder biscuits, cold kidney beans, onions and beets in vinegar, sweet milk and buttermilk, fried chicken—there was nothing green in the garden left after the grasshoppers had taken their fill. Idalou told Bro. Peters and Miss Elsie Wade that she had fed the Devil with some good squash that she had rescued from the grasshoppers but burnt to a mash on the stove; and Bro. Peters said that the Devil liked good summer squash and if he couldn't acquire it through his agents of pestilence he would come by it on a too-hot stove—but that he was glad the Devil left the chicken; and all laughed, Rhody loudest of all.

Afterwards we went to the porch and while Idalou played the piano Son sang some solos, "Drink to Me Only," etc. But Rhody spoiled the singing by talking incessantly to the Revivalist. Then Elsie Wade applied her rolling Revival technique to the old piano that no one could talk over, not even Rhody, and made it sound like a different instrument, playing some rousing hymns which we all sang faintly because of our astonishment at the way such a slight little thing as she manhandled the piano as if it was a bull plow.

In the middle of one of the songs there was somebody at the front door, and when Idalou went she found it to be a man from Bro. Peters' outfit over in the pasture. He was anxious to speak to Bro. Peters. Idalou asked him in, but Bro. Peters, hearing the man's voice, was already in the hallway by the time the man entered. "Brother Peters!" he called. "One of the diamond rattlers is aloose from the cage." Bro. Peters ran out and Elsie Wade seemed very nervous, inventing a few furbelows on the treble keys as she looked back over her shoulder with a stiff pencil-like neck at the conversation at the front door. Her eyes were so small and glittering at that moment that she seemed like a fierce little bird that might peck a loose snake to death. Idalou invited her to wait in the house, though. "The diamond rattler is our most valuable property," Elsie Wade said, "next to the flagpole sitter."

All night long they were searching for the diamond rattler with their flashlights. We locked all the doors and stayed indoors and watched the lights from the windows. We started a bonfire in the front yard. There were fires in many places in the pasture. The bird dog Sam was astonished that we brought him in the house, but he would not stop barking; and Idalou said he would die of a heart attack before daylight if they didn't catch the valuable property of the viper, he was so old. It was a sinister night. At a certain hour we heard that the flagpole sitter had come down to help find the scourge of Sin. And then suddenly like a shot out of the blue Rhody jumped up and said she couldn't stand it any longer, that she was going out to help the poor Revivalist in his search for the diamond rattler. Everybody objected and Aunt Idalou said over her dead body, that Rhody's arthritis would hinder her if she had to run; but Rhody, being Rhody, went anyway. So there was that anxiousness added.

We all watched from the parlor window. In the light of the bonfire's flame we could see the eerie posse, darting here, kicking there, and we saw that the Revivalist carried a shotgun. The flagpole sitter had arrived in such a hurry and was so excited that he had not had time to take off his long black robe and hood that he wore on the flagpole, and his priestlike shape in the light of the fires was the most nightmarish of all. On went the search through the dark hours after midnight, and it seemed the Revivalist was looking for his Sin, like some penance, a dark hunter in the night searching for evil. And now Rhody was by his side to help him, as if it could be her sin, her evil, too. They seemed to search together.

We never knew, nor will, exactly what happened. When we heard the shot and saw flashlights centered on one spot, we knew they had found the snake; and when we saw them coming on Rhody's Path toward the house, the Revivalist carrying in his arms something like a drowned person, we knew it was Rhody. They came up on the porch, the Revivalist saying sternly, "Call the doctor, she was bitten on the hip by the diamond rattler and has fainted." He bit her bad leg.

They laid Rhody on the bed and Bro. Peters began saying his famous prayer asking the Lord to reach down and pluck the poison from his child. "The snake is killed—the flagpole sitter shot him," one of the men said.

It was Aunt Idalou who scarified the snakebite with a paring knife and saved the life of Rhody until the doctor got there. Though she did it without open prayer, she prayed to herself as she worked on Rhody and used solid practical ways of salvation—including leaves of Spanish dagger plant in the front yard which Son ran and got, and hog lard. When the doctor got there he marveled at the cure and said there was little more to do except for Rhody to rest and lie prone for a few days. Idalou said she could count Rhody's prone days on one hand and Rhody commented that at least the snake had the common sense to strike her bad leg.

When the commotion was over and danger was passed, someone asked where the Revivalist was. He was nowhere to be found. In the early morning light, just breaking, we saw the pasture empty. There was no sign of anybody or anything except the guttering black remains of the bonfires. The flagpole on the Mercantile Building had nothing sitting on it. The whole Revival company had vanished like a dream . . . and had it all been one, the kind Rhody could bring down upon a place?

We hoped that would teach Rhody a lesson, but Aunt Idalou doubted it seriously. Anyway, Rhody stayed on with us till the very end of summer. Then one day there was that familiar scrambling in the pantry and it was Rhody getting her grip out. There was a mouse's nest in it. She packed it, saying she was going to Austin, to get her a job or take a beauty course she had seen advertised. When she had finished it, she told us, she might come back to Charity and open her a beauty parlor. We all doubted that, knowing she couldn't stay put for long in any one place, beauty or none.

We all kissed her good-bye and Aunt Idalou cried and asked the plain air what had branded her youngest child with some sign of restless wandering and when would she settle down to make a household as woman should; and we watched Rhody go on off, on the path across the pasture with her grip in her hand, going off to what, we all wondered.

"Well," Mama said, "she'll pull a fandango wherever she goes. But through some miracle or just plain common sense of somebody always around to protect her, with hog lard, or just good plain prayer, she'll survive and outlast us all who'll worry ourselves into our graves that Rhody will come to put flowers on, alive as ever." Rhody went out and took the world's risks and chances, but simple remedies of home and homefolks rescued and cured her, time and time again. She always had to touch home, set her wild foot on the path across the pasture that led back to the doorstep of the house, bringing to it across the pasture, from the great confused and mysterious world on the farther side, some sign of what had lately happened to her to lay it on the doorstep of home.

But with the world changing so fast and all old-time word and way paying so quickly away, she will have to correct *herself* in the world she errs in and by its means; or, in some way, by her own, on her own path, in the midst of her traveling. Surely we knew she needed all of us and had to touch us there, living on endurable and permanent, she thought, in that indestructible house where everything was always the way it had forever been and would never change, she imagined; where all, for her, was redeemed and put aright. Then, when she got something straight—what it was no one but Rhody ever knew—she'd gather her things and go off again.

"The sad thing is," Idalou said, rocking on the front porch looking at the empty pasture and the sad-looking path that Rhody took, "that years pass and all grow old and pass away, and this house will be slowly emptied of its tenants." Had Rhody ever considered this? And what would she do when all had gone and none to come home to?

But surely all of us who were listening to Idalou were thinking together that the path would remain, grown over and hidden by time, but drawn on the earth, the pasture was engraved with it like an indelible line; and Rhody's feet would be on it, time immemorial, coming and going, coming and going, child of the path in the pasture between home and homelessness, redemption and error. That was the way she had to go.

❧

As you continue experimenting with point of view, you will become more and more aware of its ramifications. Selecting the appropriate narrator or persona for a story, poem, or even an essay has a lot to do with the shape of the work: what information, in what order, with what coloring, reaches the reader. Once you have made—or remade—this fundamental decision, you are destined to follow out its logical consequences.

4

Language Is Your Medium

THERE IS NO SUCH THING AS A SYNONYM

Although everything is important in writing, obviously words come first. They are the writer's nuts and bolts, nails, screws, and bricks. Just as cabinetmakers develop an acute sense of the limits and purposes of materials—the strengths, lengths, thicknesses, and the infinite other properties of bolts, glues, and woods—so do writers develop a heightened awareness of the infinite properties of words. A cabinetmaker knows that you don't use a tenpenny nail when you need a brad, or a hacksaw when you need a coping saw.

The writer must learn to make analogous judgments: when to use an adjective, when to use a Latinate word, a complex sentence, a nickname, a noun instead of a pronoun, a quiet word rather than a noisy one. Your first job as a writer is to master the medium of your trade—language itself. This is not a simple task.

You should already be using your journal to exercise your awareness of how words function in particular circumstances. However, it is not only when writers are writing that they are sensitive to words. Just as painters are aware of colors whenever they open their eyes, just as composers are alert to sounds even when they aren't writing music, so too are writers aware of words whenever words are near. Writers are always on a busman's holiday, listening to people use words and, in their reading, testing the choices of other writers.

Our purposes in this chapter are (1) to get you thinking about ways to hone your word sense, (2) to introduce the complex decision making that goes into finding the right words to nail your meaning to the reader's mind, and (3) to change some mistaken notions you may have about effective word choice (diction).

We offer one basic principle:

For a writer, there is no such thing as a synonym.

This principle may come as a surprise if you have spent years doing synonym exercises in English classes or if you have been repeatedly warned against repeating and advised to replace a word with a synonym. Teachers gave such exercises and warnings in the name vocabulary building. Or they had the notion that repetition was, somehow, almost a grammatical error. The writer's ideal, however, is to find the exact word or phrase for the job. We assume there is always a best choice. For a *best* choice, there is no substitute.

It is more important to know how words that appear to refer the same object or idea on the surface actually differ. For example, "diaphanous," "transparent," and "see-through" refer to the same quality of a material object. Given that you can use only one of the words in a particular circumstance, you must choose the one that not only will have the correct *denotation* but also will carry the *connotation* you desire. The criteria for choosing are easy to enumerate, less easy to apply. Your choice must be:

1. accurate
2. precise
3. concrete (unless an abstract term is clearly necessary)
4. appropriate
5. idiomatic

As you can see, these criteria for word choice are the same for "creative" writing as they are for "ordinary" writing. One of the bits of misinformation that hampers beginners is the idea that they must learn a special language. Actually, what they must do is learn the only language we have as well as they can. Creativity is not measured by the difficulty or sophistication of your words. Nor is it a sign of creativity to foil the reader's expectation at every turn by choosing words for their puzzle quotient. Finally, creativity does not license the misuse of language. Only a responsible, caring attitude toward language makes for good writing of any kind.

For the following passage, choose one of the alternatives—"diaphanous," "see-through," or "transparent"—to fill in the blank. Which criteria governed your choice?

> After she dismissed her ladies-in-waiting, the queen snuffed all but one of the candles. She slipped off the heavy flannel nightgown and put on a _____ gown before opening the secret door that led to the tower where Tristram waited.

Most writers would choose "diaphanous" because it feels right for a queen and for the world of secret doors and towers. The word is accurate in that it literally means what the writer intends it to mean. It is precise in that the *range* of meaning is properly limited. It is as concrete as something filmy can be—that is, it gives us an image. Most important here, the choice is appropriate in the context: "diaphanous" carries with it the sense of delicacy and romance that suits the queen's seductive intent. "See-through" sounds crass, and "transparent" sounds almost scientific ("having the property of transmitting rays of light through its substance"). Is "diaphanous" used idiomatically? Although it isn't the kind of word we use every day, it is consistent with a special style—the conventional *idiom* for historical romance writing.

What a word connotes, either alone or in a particular context, may differ slightly from person to person, depending upon one's experiences with life and language. There are no rules except be sensitive to chosing the most telling words for the context. Since connotations are in the ear of the listener; the point here is that when revising you must be aware of all the fine adjustments that may be necessary.

EXERCISES

1. A woman is preparing to meet a man. Write a brief passage in which "see-through" would be appropriate. Rewrite so that "transparent" would be the best choice.

2. Write a brief scene for each word in these triplets:

  a. eat/dine/consume
  b. flick/film/motion picture
  c. whiskey/liquor/booze
  d. lazy/languid/unenergetic
  e. sexpot/seductress/temptress
  f. teacher/mentor/professor
  g. frugal/cheap/economical
  h. clutched/gripped/held
  i. caviar/roe/fish eggs

3. Explain the difference between "know-how" and "skill"; a "fear" and a "dread"; a "job" and an "occupation"; a "helper" and an "assistant"; and "work" and "labor."

One way of sharpening your language skills is to practice and then evaluate word substitutions while you are reading already published works. In writing, however, we recommend a very sparing and qualified use of your paper or computer. A word chosen from a list simply because it is on the list is not likely to be an effective choice. The thesaurus can be a good memory jogger; it can provide you with a range of possibilities from which to make choices. However, once you abandon the belief in synonyms, the choosing becomes more complex, more exciting, and more professional. Thesaurus mentality assumes that any word on the list will do. The genuine writer knows that only one of them is best and that the best may not even be on the list.

That "for the writer there is no such thing as a synonym" requires one qualification. Pronouns point to other words and phrases and so, in a way, *they* are synonyms. Assuming that the reference is clear, pronouns can provide variety for the eye since "he" stands for "George" and "it" stands for balloon. (See excessive variation p. 67.)

CHOOSING WELL

Now let's take a closer look at the criteria listed earlier.

Accuracy

When a word choice is accurate, it is free from error. It is "correct" in the sense that its accepted meaning is the meaning the author intends. Unless a word choice is accurate, it has no chance of being effective. Here are some examples of inaccuracy in diction:

1. In his valedictory speech, Brad made *illusions* to Hollywood stars. [The writer has confused "illusion" and "allusion."]
2. Brad had won far *lesser* awards than his father who had twenty metals. [The writer has confused "fewer" and "lesser." Unintentionally, the writer has addressed the significance of the awards rather than the number of them.]
3. Another significant factor was her *leapfrogging* suspicion that graduate school was not, nor would it be, her *dispensation*. [Two words don't mean what the writer hopes they mean.]
4. Though conventional now, In the 20s, her grandmother was a flopper. [The word is "flapper" and "flopper" may create unintended suggestions and laughter. The reader has no way of knowing if the word comes from ignorance or mistyping.]
5. I tried to light the half-smoked Camel, but my fingers were shaking and I lit it twice. Finally, the *stogie* ignited. [A "stogie" refers to a cigar, not a cigarette.]

Among the unfortunate results of inaccurate diction is that the writer may (1) confuse the reader, (2) stop the reader who will mentally correct an obvious error but who will be annoyed and may lose respect for the writing, or (3) provoke unintended laughter when the writer wanted to cause a different reaction. One way to avoid the problems in the examples above is to avoid using any word that you haven't seen or heard often in context and to proofread carefully and often.

Precision

The meanings of words have greater and lesser ranges. It is just as accurate to call Mr. Rockwell the *spouse* of Mrs. Rockwell as it is to call him her *husband*. However, while "husband" is the more sharply defined term and thus the more precise, some occasions will dictate "spouse" as the better choice. Also we might say that "spouse" is precise in a legal context but not in other contexts. Here are some examples of damaging imprecision:

1. The small town *loomed* in the distance. [In the broad sense, "loomed" is accurate; however, its normal and expected usage has to do with figures, states, or images of impending doom or magnitude. A "small town" would be far less likely to loom than a mountain.]

2. The microwave time buzzed and the smoky aroma of cooking meat pene-trated her consciousness causing her stomach to lurch. [Many problems here. Did the *time* buzz, or the microwave or the timer? "Aroma" is accu-rate but not precise because we associate "aroma" with a pleasant smell, not one that turns your stomach. Is the ready-made phrase "penetrated her consciousness" accurate? Precise? Concrete? Appropriate? Idiomatic? Do we need to be told that the meat is "cooking"?]

3. The airline crash dominated the headlines: "Thirty dead, sixty-eight *wounded*." [We would expect "injured" in such a situation, even if the people have suffered wounds. As worded, the passage suggests a battle-field statistic rather than an accidental catastrophe.]

4. The club was *quite nice*. It *clearly* catered to an upper-class, upwardly mobile clientele. It was filled with twenty- and thirty-year-olds who had skipped lunch for the *healthy* pursuit of fitness. [In addition to using the weasel-word "quite" and the nonword "nice," this writer has shoved in the unnecessary word "clearly" and the self-evident word "healthy." When words are meaningless or useless, your diction is not precise. We see here a connection between being **pre**cise and being **con**cise.]

5. He clutched a long wooden staff with ornate carvings *inscribed* on it. [The probable redundancy and definite wordiness causes imprecision and fuzziness. How about ending after "carvings"? How about ". . . staff ornately carved" or "with ornate inscriptions"? At any rate, the carvings wouldn't be inscribed, the "designs" or "figures"—wreaths, snakes, legends—would be.]

The search for preciseness not simply a matter of choosing words. Context is a factor. The following description is, from one point of view, not precise:

> Harriet realized that Don had gone without saying goodbye. His empty coffee cup with the picture of black and white cows on it sat beside the business section of the *Times*.

Of course, "black and white cows" have a precise name—"Holsteins." Let's say, however, that the writer wants the reader to realize that to Harriet a cow is a cow is a cow. They all give milk. How can the writer communicate that it is Harriet who is being imprecise, not he:

> Harriet realized that Don had gone without saying goodbye. His empty coffee cup with the picture of black and white cows on it sat beside the business section of the *Times*. She could hear Don yelling: "How many times have I got to tell you that they are . . . ." What was the word? Holsters? Something like that.

Now the reader has a further picture of Harriet because the writer has let the reader know that her imprecision may be a bone of contention with her husband. The elegant solution dramatizes and characterizes.

Imprecise diction leaves the reader with an imprecise sense of the actions, things, or emotions that the writer wants to evoke.

Concreteness

Concrete diction is usually preferred over abstract or general diction. Concrete diction evokes images, bits of sensory experience. (See the "Imagery" section in Chapter 6, "The Elements of Poetry.") Compare the impact of these three statements:

> John exhibited emotional hostility.
> John was angry.
> John fumed.

The first is formal and abstract, though perhaps appropriate for a psychological case study. The second is abstract, but at least it is clear and direct. The third is concrete: it gives us, by way of metaphor, a vivid picture that conveys the meaning more forcefully, more economically, and more memorably than the other two. "Fumes" suggest the release of dangerous forces.

We are not saying that abstract language must be eliminated from all writing. Writers need words that point to concepts and categories as well as those that refer directly to sensory experience. However, it is always dangerous to depend too much on words that *tell* rather than *show*.

Writers need to choose language that creates a sensory world for the reader's imagination to inhabit. As they struggle with their craft, writers learn the fine balance between abstract and concrete formulations. However, as a rule of thumb we suggest that *when in doubt, make it concrete.* (**Figurative language**, discussed later in this chapter, often expresses the abstract in concrete terms.)

Concreteness—specificity of sensation—is a relative matter. Even terms that are not abstract can be made more concrete by being made more specific. In the sentences that follow, the italicized general terms are followed by more specific alternatives in parentheses:

1. The *girl* (child, toddler, daughter, princess, Alice) *cried* (wailed, sobbed, whimpered).
2. *He* (the student, Edgar) *got* (asked for, ordered, bought, demanded) *food* (Italian food, a pizza, a pepperoni pizza).
3. Edgar also ordered a *drink* (beer, Sprite, Guinness).

Though a good deal of the writer's search for the concrete occurs in revision, it is a good idea to acquire the habit of mind that recognizes abstract diction as the work unfolds.

EXERCISE

Revise the following for greater concreteness:

1. The man walked slowly down the street.
2. An emotional condition was manifest in her appearance.
3. The building seemed quite imposing.
4. Jane put on her clothes and ate some tasteless food.

The general principle for achieving concreteness is that you call things by the most specific name you can and you describe actions with the most specific verbs you can, leaving minimal work to be done by modifiers. Of course, to be concrete you have to be either observant or know enough to appear so. Most of us know that a forest is made of trees, but few of us are in the habit of thinking about what types of trees. The accomplished writer knows how to find and when to use the concrete word.

Appropriateness

When you choose your words, you have to please two masters. First, you need to consider how appropriate your diction may be for the audience you have chosen to address. Second, you have to consider how appropriate your diction may be for your genre, your character, and the set of circumstances, including the overall language context within which your decisions take place. Compare the diction in the following three sentences:

> The patient manifests the delusion that his *siblings* are poisoning his food. [psychiatric case history]
>
> Henry called in the private eye because he believed his *siblings* were putting curare in his pasta. [fiction narration]
>
> "I tell ya Doc, my *siblings* is out to get me." [speech of an uneducated person who wishes to impress]

Since you are part of an audience yourself, and since you will probably write for people like yourself, you already have a sense of what diction is inappropriate because it will offend. You don't use street language in a poem for a religious periodical. Similarly, common sense will lead you to consider the age, experience, and knowledge of the audience you wish to address. If you have any doubts regarding the diction appropriate for an audience, study the kinds of things your intended audience already reads.

Here is an example of choosing appropriate diction for audience and character. Let us say you are writing for eight- to twelve-year-olds:

> Tom arranged with Becky for a rendezvous at her house.

Your editorial self (or editor) tells you that your audience is not likely to know "rendezvous," and you know how looking up a word interrupts the flow of your own reading. So you agree to do the dictionary work for your young reader:

> Tom arranged with Becky for a rendezvous (a meeting) at her house.

You soon realize, or your editor does, that this solution won't do because the new version reads like an essay. You try some substitutions:

> Tom arranged with Becky for a meeting at her house.
>
> Tom made an agreement with Becky to present himself at her house.

The second try sounds like something corporate lawyers might say. The first is easily accessible, but the romantic overtones of "rendezvous" and your sense of Tom's show-off character (*he* might use such a word) are lost. And, while the thesaurus might tempt you with a word like "assignation," this temptation would have to be resisted on grounds already mentioned.

> Tom told Becky that he'd be at her house that evening.

Too bland. What about turning the problem with "rendezvous" into the solution? Suppose Tom does know the word—or almost knows it—but neither the reader nor Becky does.

"Let's rendezvous at your house," Tom said.

"I don't think my parents would like that and I'm not sure I would either," said Becky, tossing her head.

"We meet at your house all the time."

"Oh, is that all?"

You can see where one might go from here. In this case, a bit of inventiveness allowed you to teach a new word and to show Tom's character. The words that reach your audience must convey more than surface information; thus they must be appropriate to many purposes simultaneously. Consider the following passage:

> The death of a famous actress is the signal, as a rule, for a great deal of maudlin excitement. The world that knew her rushes up on that last stage where she lies with her eyes sincerely closed and joins, as it were, in her death scene, posturing and poetizing around her bier like a pack of amateur mummers. For a few days everyone who knew her is a road company Mark Antony burying her with bad oratory. The stage is a respectable and important institution, what with its enormous real estate holdings, but we still patronize an actress, particularly a dead one.
>
> from Ben Hecht, "Actor's Blood"

The narrator of this passage is not simply reporting the fact of someone's death. We can tell that the narrator is familiar with the world of acting ("scene," "mummers," "road company," "Mark Antony"). Moreover, the writer has chosen words to reveal a contemptuous or ironic attitude about Hollywood.

EXERCISE

1. In the preceding passage, locate and describe the word choices that reveal the narrator's attitude. Consider accuracy, precision, concreteness, and especially appropriateness.

2. Answer the questions that follow this passage, which is intended for a historical novel about fifteenth-century England:

> With sword or lance or any kind of sidearm Alex was a deadly practitioner. As a hand-to-hand blood spiller he was second to none. He knew a thousand songs, most of them dirty. He was a royster, a rogue, a ruffian, a fornicator, and a basterlycullion, but otherwise and in all other respects the best man in the world.

  a. Is the overall impact of this passage aided or hindered by words we might have difficulty understanding?
  b. Which words contribute to the historical flavoring?
  c. Given your understanding of the writer's purpose, do any of the word choices misfire? Why? What changes do you suggest?

3. Here is a passage from a story intended to be a *naturalistic* look at a contemporary problem. Can you find language in it that is more properly associated with escapist romance fiction? What is the consequence of this diction clash? (Regina is considering artificial insemination.)

> Regina nodded, mute, hugging the sheet around her neck. She wanted to ask him what her chances were, whether he thought it would work, how many babies were conceived this way. But part of her was tired of statistics and percentages, and the other part of her was just tired. So she pushed her fears down into a deep, secret place in her heart and forced a "brave girl" smile.

Appropriate diction, as we have seen, means many things. In a given context, any word or word combination can be appropriate. The writer's job requires an understanding of all the ways in which word choices can be appropriate or inappropriate.

Idiomatic Usage

An idiom is a word combination that has a unique grammatical construction or a meaning that cannot be logically derived from its combined parts. When we say "the kettle is boiling," we are speaking idiomatically (and probably putting words together in an untranslatable way). After all, the kettle is *not* boiling, the water is. Many of us, because we confuse idiomatic expressions with trite expressions, have been frightened away from using standard English idioms. While it is true that triteness is to be avoided, the rich idiomatic resources of our language should be employed whenever they are appropriate—and they almost always are appropriate.

The following sentences contain trite expressions:

1. He was *as handsome as a prince.*
2. She had a *devilish twinkle* in her eyes which, at times, would *flash with anger.*
3. Their marriage started out *all lovey-dovey.*
4. Whenever they went out for pizza, they would *travel down memory lane*, recalling the *long lost images of their youths.*

The following contain serviceable idioms:

1. Despite Elliot's good looks, Buffy could not *work up* any interest in him.
2. Elliot *ducked out* the back door rather than *face up* to Buffy's anger.
3. Elliot daydreamed about Buffy so much that he forgot to take classnotes.

Idioms tend to be metaphoric and therefore colorful. Most of all, they no longer appear metaphoric but rather as *natural*, and the natural is rarely misleading or ineffective. The advantage of such words and phrases as "work up" instead of "show" or "ducked out" instead of "left by" is that they create a sense of the character's action rather than the writer's telling. Trite expressions, on the other hand, signal their tiredness to an alert reader who will sense that the writer has *plugged in* the first available *off-the-rack* phrase to arrive quickly at the bottom line. These are constructions whose impact has been worn away through overuse. Of course, what might be trite in one circumstance can actually accomplish the writer's purpose:

> Priscilla had always thought Jeffrey as handsome as a prince—in fact,
> a character in the romances she read by the hour.

In this example, the author used the trite expression to characterize Priscilla's way of thinking as "trite."

Generally speaking, then, you want to avoid the trite, but *not at the expense of the natural*. Examine these alternative passages:

1. In spite of the statistical probability that the situation would eventuate negatively, and half-wondering if she wanted it to, she perpetrated a fraudulent optimism upon herself and aimed her countenance in the direction of the inevitable harsh resolution.
2. Hoping against hope, she faced the music.

Neither of these renderings is effective. However, the first is so clotted, tortured, and *unnatural* that, if we had to choose, we'd select the trite yet smooth and spontaneous movement of the second.

In brief, you will usually want to work at a natural, idiomatic diction that captures the quality of friendly rather than academic or professional talk. There are exceptions, of course. Writers of historical fiction might appropriately use a more formal or archaic diction in order to suggest the past.

EXERCISE

1. Match the phrase in the left column with the idiomatic form on the right:

withdraw his assertion	bank on
expect to receive	tune in
not the route usually taken	shortcut
adopt a different attitude	pay off
redeem a loan or note	back down
adjust for sharper reception	change one's tune

2. Write two short scenes, the first using any three items from column "A" and the next using the parallel items from column "B." Now examine the differences.

A	B
wait for a favorable opportunity	→ bide one's time
accept an offer	→ bite at
look for an implied meaning	→ read between the lines
extort all one's money	→ bleed white
disclaim further responsibility	→ wash one's hands of
spent money foolishly	→ blew
exclude	→ rule out
malfunction	→ break down
perform	→ carry out
suited to	→ cut out for
eat greedily	→ wolf down

Like any other language tool, idioms can be misused or inappropriately used. Still, we encourage you to use idioms rather than to go out of your way to avoid them and end up with stuffy or overwritten prose. Here are some guidelines:

1. Prefer a common idiom to eccentric diction: Buffy felt that he had *no call* to *jump down her throat* simply because she forgot the mustard.
2. Prefer nothing to trite diction: He was handsome (*not* "as handsome as a prince"). Buffy felt a mess (*not* "as if she had been through a meat grinder").
3. Prefer something you may think is trite to a forced expression: When they walked by without saying hello, Buffy felt that she had been given the cold shoulder (*not* "as chilled as a lobster in a freezer").

SOME DICTION PROBLEMS

Many novice writers have the mistaken notion that they should "write writing." That is, they believe effective writing consists of verbal prestidigitation and pyrotechnics. They believe that the words need not be chosen for specific tasks but rather that the words chosen need to sound important and weighty. Some beginners were actually taught to worship words for words' sake; some simply pile word upon words as a substitute for thinking. The end result of believing in this false god is twofold: (1) the writing becomes padded and/or inflated; (2) problems in effective word choice are actually disguised. But even before that happens, the false god leads the writer to put enormous efforts into the wrong type of work: the work of impressing rather than convincing the reader.

We might have discussed the various guises in which padded and inflated diction choices appear under one or another of our major headings: accuracy, precision, concreteness, appropriateness, and idiomatic naturalness. However, the following strivings after quick effects appear often enough to merit a separate section. They are not positive criteria for emulation, but negative habits to be avoided.

Overwriting

Many of the subclasses discussed elsewhere in this section could be placed into this category. You *overwrite* when you pad your language without adding meaning or impact, as in the following example from the beginning of a story:

> It's funny how certain things, the biggest moments and the smallest *passing thoughts alike, how they* can *both* become your sweetest memories later on. And, *years later*, when the places and the people who gave you these tender times are gone, their memories become *starbright* highlight colors for the tapestry of your life.

The problems in this passage cannot be solved only by removing the obvious overwriting (in italics). Taking out such overblown adjectives as "starbright" is only the first step. One still needs to deal with the padding sewn tightly to the rather obvious, even silly, thought that both the big and little occurrences can become sweet memories. This type of overwriting can disguise paucity of thought even from the writer. (Of course, the passage might work if it revealed a rather foolish character's habitual style.)

One type of overwriting grows from a virtue, the virtue of presenting precise detail for the reader. This virtue becomes a problem when the writer becomes too ambitious and gives us too many details to absorb. In the following passage, which describes someone the major character sees once and never again, the writer's purpose is to describe a representative character in a subway crowd.

> He was dressed in the standard Washington attorney uniform—conservative suit, solid color shirt, Ivy League tie, tan raincoat, Irish walking hat. Yet behind his Yuppiestyle glasses, his face had a devilish twinkle accented by a dimple you could dangle barefoot in and brown hair that strayed past the regulation length, curling at least an inch down his collar.

Since there is no reason in the story to give us all this detail, the elaboration becomes a distraction. In fact, when we look carefully at exactly what the narrator has told us, we wonder—as we did in the former case—if the words are attached to any authentic observations. Do faces "twinkle?"

Overmodification

This kind of overwriting comes from the admirable attempt to be concrete. However, the piling up of adjectives, adverbs, and prepositional phrases is a signal that something is wrong and that the writer has done the wrong kind of work. Often the muscle of sentence structure and meaning gets covered over by the modifying fat. Adverbs and adjective create concrete images when they specify a class for which no concrete word exists. For example, if you need to describe the walls in your character's room "red walls" you'd be hard put to find a single word that will do the job. Sometimes choosing a more specific noun or verb is the solution. In the following cases, the modification is unnecessary because its meaning so overlaps the meaning of the modified word.

> A faded *woven tapestry* hung from the *lintel of the door.* [Most tapestries are woven; "lintel" is the part of the door from which one would assume something as large as a tapestry would be hung.]

> Her lungs felt as if someone had stabbed her *with a knife.* [Here a trite simile is automatically continued to its predictable end. Without the unnecessary final phrase, the expression is sharper.]

What modifying words can be cut or phrases reduced from the following passage?

> "A sad saint is not a saint," she often said, one of her many expressions from a seemingly endless tape. These quotes poured out from her with force or tenderness as the situation demanded. In a less energetic person, remarks such as these would bore, but Bridget's desire to serve gave her ebullient Christian advice a distinctive palatable flavor.

A useful writing principle is to avoid adjectives and adverbs unless the modification is absolutely necessary to present an exact picture.

Another type of overmodification occurs when you use such intensifiers as "very," "definitely," or "certainly." The problem is that "very red walls" does not help the reader see "blood-red walls." And one person's "very" may be another person's "kind of." The weasel word "seemed" leads the reader to falsely expect another reality: "George *definitely seemed* ready to ask for her hand in marriage and got down on his knee to do just that." After a time, such word choices lead a reader to doubt whether the writer has a picture of the situation she is writing about.

Saying It Twice

Redundancy is a common problem and has many causes, some of which we have already addressed. In the example that follows, the writer refused to pay attention to what her words were saying, or were supposed to say:

Directly in front of me, a modern glass and steel tower, *illumination provided by lights* in its occupied rooms, sparkled like a monolithic crystal. [There is some nonsense in the closing simile; can you detect it?]

Excessive Variation

This problem used to go by the name of "elegant variation," but the issue has less to do with elegance than with a learned fear of repeating key words and phrases. With or without the "help" of the thesaurus, many writers act as if repetition were a deadly sin. While repetition *can* become deadly, often the means taken to avoid it create even worse problems. In the following passage, the student writer seems to be driven by a misguided but honest desire to avoid repeating his key noun.

> As Jim entered the turn, the *motorcycle* seemed to sink into the ground. He could feel the shocks being compressed as the force of the turn pushed him and his *machine* to a lower center of gravity. As he leaned into the turn, he stuck out his knee for balance. It was hard to remain in control, but Jim calmly, smoothly, lifted his head, twisted the *vehicle* upright, and pulled back with his right wrist. Instantly, the *bike* shot forward, its front wheel once again coming off the ground. Already entering the next turn, Jim shifted his weight forward and braked hard. Slowing to 100 miles per hour, he leaned the *Kawasaki* once more over to the left. Passing by the pits, he could see David and Georgetti keeping track of his time while Rhonda displayed it on the leader board for him to see. At the end of the first session, Jim pulled his *trusty mount* back into the pit.

The result is a scattered effect, as well as some uncertainty about whether or not the writer is always referring to the same thing.

Latinate Diction

Linking up a series of polysyllabic words from Latin roots makes your writing self-consciously learned and unpleasantly pretentious. It also slows the reader down, as the following sentence illustrates:

> Jane held to her assertion despite Bill's remonstrance to the contrary. [Can you put this into plain English?]

Archaic Diction

This habit usually springs from a misguided notion about how to sound "literary" or "poetic." We no longer believe that such words or expressions as "yore," "thee," "o'er," or "finny prey" (for "fish") confer a poetic or dignified quality to writing. In fact, the convention of our day is that effective writing demands the words and rhythms of everyday speech. "Alas" and "ill tidings" sound like attempts to impose emotions rather than create them.

Sonic Boom

Sometimes intentionally, sometimes not, a writer allows the sounds to drown out meaning by calling too much attention to themselves, as the following case demonstrates:

> The blustery day threatened to batter the delicate blossoms that had drawn *gaggles* of *gawking* tourists to the nation's capital. [One might argue that the alliteration on "b" has a positive effect, but certainly the italicized words make too much noise.]

If, as we have suggested, all successful writing comes from editing and rewriting, then every good writer must become a word detective, hunting down the criminal elements in early drafts and taking them out of circulation. Breaking bad habits is only part of the job, however. A writer must develop a positive working sense of what makes for effective diction—accuracy, precision, concreteness, appropriateness, and idiomatic usage. A writer must understand what it means to live without the comfort of synonyms.

EXERCISE

Locate and describe the diction problems in the following passages; then provide improvements.

1. I entered the office promptly at seven o'clock as usual, the nostalgic noises of the small-town daily reverberating against my ears, transmitting a sense of urgency. I liked my work; it gave me an opportunity to keep my thumb on the pulse of the mainstream of the city's affairs.

2. Rosa stormed from the room. I could hear her heels tiptip in harmony down the steps. The slamming door sent a thud throughout the whole empty club that I could feel even upstairs. I mentally surveyed the damage I'd just done.

3. A little past ten in the morning and I'd already brought two star-crossed kids together for who knows how much future happiness.

4. She had never mentioned the incident to anyone, not even Mark, and tried to avoid Cooper whenever possible. If only she'd come up with a clever, gentle put-down, she thought, she could have curtailed the problem without this awkwardness between them. As it was, she spoke to him from a cool distance. [The incident is an attempted rape.]

5. Just as they began to move out of the driveway, the police car drove in front suddenly and blocked their car. If Sybil hadn't dissuaded him from leaving earlier, they would have escaped.

6. As I spoke, I felt exhilarated as I watched the sea of eager eyes and scribbling hands intently following my words. Stimulating young minds athirst for knowledge and open to new ideas was spiritual in a way, certainly far more uplifting than listening to a priest.

7. The first thing that Jeff noticed when he was walking into the room was the smell of evergreen.

8. I couldn't lose this chance. Not when I was getting nearer to finding the murderer. Maybe this call would give me the clue that was keeping me from solving the case.

9. With a cold gleam in her eye, Katherine swung again and struck him hard in the ribs and across the stomach. An audible gasp of air escaped from the man's bloodied lips.

10. Well, things change as time passes, he told himself. He then dismissed these thoughts with the hope that perhaps if he just let things sort themselves out, they might just come to a suitable conclusion.

11. The chance that he might lose her caused him evident stress, and to help the situation, she lowered some of her defenses and began to open up.

12. My uncle looked sadly at me. Thoughtfully, he patted down the gray lateral hairs spread thinly across his tanned veined distinguished head.

13. "I told you not to go!" shouted the angered captain as the sound of his voice drifted out of focus.

FUN WITH WORDS

Word play is an important activity. It can help you build an active vocabulary, sharpen your diction, and freshen your word combinations. In his poem "Because I Never Learned the Names of Flowers," Rod Jellema shows us the sheer fun of word play and the power of expectation. Even though the tone and technique are playful, any reader can recognize the genuine emotion in this love poem.

> it is moonlight and white where
> I slink away from my cat-quiet blue rubber truck
> and motion myself to back it up to your ear.
> I peel back the doors of the van and begin
> to hushload into your sleep
> the whole damn botanical cargo of Spring.
>
> Sleeper, I whisk you
> Trivia and Illium, Sweet Peristalsis, Flowering Delirium.

Sprigs of purple persiflage and Lovers' Leap, slips
of Hysteria stick in my hair. I gather clumps of Timex,
handfuls of Buttertongues, Belly buttons, and Bluelets.

I come with Trailing Nebula, I come with Late-Blooming
Paradox, with Creeping Pyromania, Pink Apoplex,
and Climbing Solar Plexis,

whispering: Needlenose,
Juice Cup, Godstem, Nexus, Sex-us, Condominium.

from *The Eighth Day: New & Selected Poems*

Part of the fun of Jellema's poem is to discover the strange tension between what we expect (names of flowers) and the actual words and phrases that the poet has put in their places. To most novices, and perhaps even to some experts, there is something almost convincing about these new "names." Some of this impression has to do with the Latinate formulations that sound like those used in botany. This love poem, of course, is filled with physical passion and a grand madness. Still, one could almost draw a picture of each imaginary flower.

EXERCISE

1. Look up each word that you don't know in Jellema's poem. How is the meaning of each appropriate, ironic, or fanciful? Which words overlap in meaning? How does this overlapping influence the effect of the overall poem?

2. Rewrite or extend Jellema's poem with "flowers" of your own.

3. Make a specialized word list. Perhaps you know or can find out something about computers, astronomy, chess, film editing, or even flowers. Now work this list into a surprising yet revealing context—an apparent nonsense that makes a kind of sense.

4. Rename the components of a sport or game and see what happens when you describe the game with these new words. Example: (for baseball) bat = stem, base = pillow, ball = gourd, and so on.

5. Copy the recipes for some bar drinks (a Tom Collins, Martini, Pink Lady, or White Russian, for example). Now introduce abstract words (rage, loss, enthusiasm) in place of the original ingredients. Concoct a love potion, a youth potion, or a drink that will increase your intelligence.

Exercises like these help waken your sense of language. Remember, however, that liberties you can take in exercises sometimes exceed those you can take in works intended for publication. Word play helps you go beyond your concern for diction that is *literally* accurate, precise, concrete, appropriate, and idiomatic. It allows you to enter the world of *figurative language*, a world you must explore in order to make your writing lively.

FIGURES OF SPEECH

Writers achieve economy and vividness of expression through figures of speech, those complex ways of perceiving and phrasing comparisons and contrasts. At bottom, metaphors, similes, and other figures of speech are not literary devices; they are the ways in which our minds try to make sense of experience. Everyday language is filled with these constructions. When we speak of "the head of a pin," "the teeth of a gear," "the shoulder of a road," or "a dead-end street," we are speaking figuratively. To call someone "spineless" is not to make a literal statement, but a figurative one. Colloquial expressions like "get off my back" attest to the figurative habits of mind that generate new ways of communicating our ideas and feelings.

Some of the most successful figures eventually turn into clichés—dead metaphors that have lost their imaginative punch. Let's explore a few of these.

What genius first came up with the expression "he's (or she's) a brick" to make a point about a friend's dependability? Does the image of the brick come to mind when the expression is used? Do we any longer enjoy the particular areas of overlap between two relatively unlike things—a human personality and a construction material? Once we stop seeing the brick, the metaphor is dead and may have become a cliché, an expression to be avoided unless selected for special, limited purposes (to make fun of it, for instance) or an idiom.

In the following poem by William Matthews, the cliché "it's a tough nut to crack" becomes resuscitated by its context:

Hope

Beautiful floors and a lively
daughter were all he'd wanted, and then—
that the dear piñata of her head

not loose its bounty, the girl's
father scored the soles of her new shoes
with a pocketknife, that she not slide

nor skid nor turn finally upside-
down on the oak floors he'd sanded
and buffed slick long before she first

gurgled from her crib. Now he's dead
and she's eighty. That's how time
works: it's a tough nut to crack

and then a sapling, then a tree, and
then somebody else's floor long
after we ourselves are planted.

from *Selected Poems and Translations 1969–1991*

Matthews has given us back the reality of the nut, the literal truth from which the metaphorical use springs. The nut holds the seeds that become the sapling, the tree, and finally the floor. Also, "planted" appropriately suggests a renewal that follows burial.

Here is a passage that contains another dead metaphor: "After the leader worked his way over the log that bridged the chasm, the others *followed suit.*" Though we would no longer stop to enjoy the buried picture of cardplayers playing out the same suit that had been led, we know what the phrase means: it seems like a *literal* statement to us now and not a *figurative* one.

We don't have to avoid every expression that we recognize as a dead metaphor. In fact, we can't. As we insisted earlier, many of these formulations are simply available idiomatic expressions that work far better than outlandish alternatives that some writers invent to avoid sounding trite.

Figurative expressions are literal lies. In the equation of **metaphor**, two unlike things (events, traits, or objects) are asserted to be identical: A = B. "The moon is a ghostly galleon tossed up on silvery seas." Well, the moon is no such thing, but claiming that it is—discovering an area of overlap between the way this particular moon looked and the appearance of a certain ship under certain circumstances—allows the writer to tell us much about the way things felt, not just the way they looked.

Examine the metaphor closely. What phase of the moon is suggested? Is the sky clear or cloudy? Is the work from which this passage is taken one of hard-boiled cynicism or romantic adventure? How do you know?

Direct statements of identity, "X is Y," are not the only constructions that release metaphor. The ways in which parts of speech unexpectedly relate can release subdued metaphors. The passage "Each footstep puffed a plume of dust" contains two metaphors. In the second, we are asked to see a relationship between the particular shape the dust took and a plume or feather. Of course, dust and feathers often go together, but not in this way. To give a footstep breath with which to puff likens that action to animal or even human behavior. This special kind of metaphorical expression is called **personification**.

Examine the poem by Robert Bly that follows. The first stanza contains two personifications, the second contains a metaphor, the third a **simile**—a figurative linking in which A is explicitly likened to B.

Three Kinds of Pleasures

I

Sometimes, riding in a car, in Wisconsin
Or Illinois, you notice those dark telephone poles
One by one lift themselves out of the fence line
And slowly leap on the gray sky—
And past them the snowy fields.

II
The darkness drifts down like snow on the picked cornfields
In Wisconsin, and on these black trees
Scattered, one by one,
Through the winter fields—
We see stiff weeds and brownish stubble,
And white snow left now only in the wheeltracks of the combine.

III
It is a pleasure, also, to be driving
Toward Chicago, near dark,
And see the lights in the barns.
The bare trees more dignified than ever,
Like a fierce man on his deathbed,
And the ditches along the road half full of a private snow.

from *Silence in the Snowy Fields*

Telephone poles can't actually "lift themselves" or "leap." Saying so attributes human characteristics to them. "Darkness" does not literally "drift" into anything because it has no substance. The poet's imagination has suggested that darkness is acting like something else—dust, perhaps. The comparative formulation that closes the poem—"The bare trees more dignified than ever, / Like a fierce man on his deathbed"—tells us about the trees in a striking way. Bly's simile makes these trees unforgettably dignified. He has taken two unlike things, found a linking aspect, and exploited it to the hilt. Whoops!

In the examples just given, a literal lie made something not only vivid, not only fresh in expression, but clear as well. Though it seems paradoxical, effective figures of speech do just that—lie to make things clear. Without this heightened clarity, figurative language is no better than muddy language of any kind. The writer of the following passage probably felt proud of the way in which he made an abstraction concrete—one of the goals of much figurative expression. We wonder, however, if the meaning is clear: "Time is like a trail cut through the woods that we crawl down with our noses in the dirt."

What can anyone learn about time or about human nature here? Nothing. What has gone wrong? For one thing, the writer has lost sight of his original intention. The simile, which begins with an attempt to characterize *time* through images of distance and motion, abruptly shifts to concerns that have no clear relevance to time. However, if the time under discussion was the time spent humbling ourselves before authority, the extended simile just might work.

The following poem is an exercise constructed almost entirely out of similes. What is the effect of each one? Of the entire catalog?

Anatomy of Melancholy

The blue tears stain my cheeks
  Like a leaky fountain pen
Spurting its juice on white paper,
  Like a ripe blueberry
Bursting upon a milk-white tablecloth.

A droopy head hangs low
  Like the daisies knocked down by
Blowing gusts of wind,
  Like the signpost ran into
By the drunk kid in the red Corvette.

The thin lips pressed to viseful grip,
  Like a sad clown's inverted grin

Stamped on white facepaint,
  Like the crescent moon hanging
Upside down in the darkening sky.

A saggy flesh drapes the frame
  Like the Auschwitz inhabitants doomed
To the fuming chloride showers,
  Like the jowls of the bulldog
Standing guard at the house next door.

As with any other tool at our disposal, similes and other figures of speech can be overused or go haywire. In the preceding case, while many of the expressions are successful, the parts are not subordinated to the whole. After a while, the reader ceases to be in touch with what the poem is about; the piling up of similes becomes an end in itself rather than the means to an end.

One more point about similes. They are not simply comparisons using *like* or *as*. The sentence "Jane looks like her sister" is a literal comparison (it is actually true) rather than a figurative one. Remember, it is the discovery of an area of likeness or overlap between two essentially different terms that is the basis for a figurative expression.

FIGURATIVE LANGUAGE EXERCISE

1. Expand three of the following statements: first with a literal comparison, next with a metaphor or simile, last with an **analogy**—the resemblance in a number of particulars of two things otherwise unlike. In doing this exercise, don't worry about saving all the words from the statement. The goal is vivid communication that is both clear and suggestive.

Example: My Model T takes off rapidly.

> **Literal comparison**: My Geo accelerates just like your Miata.
> **Figure of speech**: My Geo takes off like a bullet.
> **Analogy**: My Geo reminds me of a well-preserved old athlete. Like him, it isn't as young as it once was, but it too has been kept in top condition through proper care and exercise. Just as that athlete can still hold his own among the youngsters, so my old car continues to show up well in competition with the newer cars.

   a. A Boy Scout knife is a handy tool.
   b. My dog is very affectionate.
   c. The exam was extremely difficult.
   d. Lisa has a lovely complexion.
   e. When I came home, my parents were up waiting for me.
   f. News of violent crime dominates the front page.
   g. The giant crane lifts the building materials.

2. Complete the following sentences, using or creating vivid figurative expressions:

   a. When he smiled, . . .
   b. The sun . . . through the trees and . . . whatever it touched.
   c. When I heard the tailpipe clatter on the road, . . .
   d. They shook hands carefully, like . . .
   e. She drew deeply on her cigarette, . . .

Though we have been giving examples from poetry, figurative language is part of all kinds of writing. Indeed, it appears to be a natural way of talking and thinking. When a teenager says "I'll meet you if I can get a *set of wheels*," he is using the part for the whole, a figure of speech call **synecdoche**. When the reporter describes the debate on *the hill*, she is referring to Congress by the place in Washington associated with it. This figure of speech is called **metonymy**. (See Chapter 6, p. 142, for an example from Dylan Thomas.) Though such figures of speech are part of the writer's toolbox, problems emerge when the figures go berserk. Metaphors and similes can be so farfetched, so forced, that readers will either tune out or be so dazzled by the writer's ingenuity that they will miss the point. More often, the problem is that elements in the metaphor are in conflict with one another. We call such a construction a **mixed metaphor**. The writer who puts down "My spirit, like my blood, slowly drips from my body, white feathers now turned crimson" has lost hold of effective figurative logic. It would seem that the spirit is being likened to white feathers, but it is also likened to blood. Once it is blood, it can't drip on itself, turning itself crimson; it must have been crimson to begin with. Such a mishmash gives a reader a headache. Mixed metaphors often come from overwriting, allowing needless complexity and elaboration to ruin a workable insight.

When we use images suggestively, they turn out to be more than descriptive. They may involve the sort of figurative comparisons discussed earlier in which one term is equated or related to another in a special way. Sometimes images generate associations in which the second term is not named, but still understood. When an image represents something other than or beyond itself, it is being used as a **symbol**.

Many symbols are conventional: their meanings are shared by a community or culture. Our flag is one such symbol; the cross is another. Traditionally, the color white is a symbol of purity, red of passion, purple of royalty. No one can refer to a snake or serpent without suggesting the meanings developed in the story of Adam and Eve. We use symbols of this sort all the time, often without even thinking about them.

In our own writing, we can also generate meanings in a particular work through local symbols. For example, in the following poem by A. E. Housman, "London" is used to suggest all that is opposed to gentleness, innocence, and inexperience. It becomes a symbol for a worldly toughness and a worldly style.

> From the wash the laundress sends
> My collars home with ravelled ends;
> I must fit, now these are frayed,
> My neck with new ones, London-made.
>
> Homespun collars, homespun hearts,
> Wear to rags in foreign parts.
> Mine at least's as good as done,
> And I must get a London one.

Often there is little distance between symbolism and synecdoche or metonymy. You could say here that "collars" symbolizes all of the person's clothing, style, and way of life. If you think the reference is only on the concrete level, you might say that "collars" is the part that stands for all of the speaker's garments (synecdoche). Housman's reference to "hearts" is the conventional one in which the vital organ represents the center of emotion.

EXERCISE

Evaluate the diction in the following passage from James Agee's *The Morning Watch*. How does Agee make his diction accurate? Precise? Concrete? Appropriate? Idiomatic? Where does he use figurative language? How much does he depend on modifiers? Is this dependence justified?

> At the far end of the break in the woods along the far side of the track they saw the weathered oak tower and soon, walking more briskly along the ties, the relics of machinery and the dead cones, puttycolored sand and the wrinkled sandstone and, at length, the sullen water itself, untouched in all

these cold months. There were black slits along the sides of the tower where planks had fallen during the winter. The water was motionless and almost black. The whole place, familiar as it was, was deadly still, and seemed not at all to welcome them. As they left the track to round the near end of the Sand Cut there was a scuttling among the reddened brambles but although they went as fast as they could on their soft feet and threw rocks where the brambles twitched with noise they got no glimpse of whatever it was, and soon the scuttling stopped.

STYLE

Consider what judgments you might make about the writer of each of the following four passages, all of which use the same information:

I. Also passed by Congress was legislation which prohibits the expenditure of appropriated funds to influence the awarding of federal grants, contracts, and loans, and requires that an applicant for a federal grant, contract, or loan disclose any payments made with nonappropriated funds that would have been prohibited if made with appropriated funds.

II. The new law that Congress passed states that you can't use money from one government grant, contract, or loan to get another one. Also, the law requires you to disclose any money you spend to get government money.

III. What's the world coming to? Now Congress has passed a law that stops self-respecting lobbyists and gun-makers from using money from one government dole to wheedle another government dole. And, get this, even if you use your own money to lobby for some government largess, you have to tell about it. There go the general's free tickets for Redskin games.

IV. The work was going slowly and badly. Bill had assigned me the Herculean chore of turning dark bureaucratic prose into instructions for the contract men (and sometimes, but not too often, women), delivery date yesterday but five o'clock today would do. My screen was filled with so many drafts that I thought I might blow out the computer's brain. My instinct was simply to say: "Don't do bad things with government money." Then I added: "Like using it to get the next contract." That wasn't going to fly. The Congressional bill wasn't quite that simple. I took two aspirin to comfort my headache, due only partly to the argument with JoAnn the night before. Perhaps the easiest approach was to make a list of all the possible ways our contract people could violate the law and put "thou shalt not" at the beginning.

You would have little difficulty in describing these styles—cool legalese, abstract reportorial, sarcastic editorial, tough guy narration—and understanding them as versions of formal, informal and colloquial style. These large categories are part of our reading glasses, the lenses through which we see the work. When we know the style, we already know something about what we are going to read, and that makes us more comfortable. Usually we recognize the style in the first few sentences or paragraphs.

Decisions about diction are primary ingredients in the creation of style. Earlier in this chapter, we reviewed the fundamental considerations that lead to effective word choice. A writer's work is made even more effective through the consistent use of a vocabulary stylized to achieve specific ends. The style of a literary work is part of the reader's experience—the dress of its content. And the dress must be tailored to fit. Not only must it fit the body of content, it must also be appropriate to the occasion. No sweat suits at a black tie affair.

The range of styles is infinite. Here is a list of broad, contrasting alternatives that have to do with diction:

- ◆ The diction may be modifier-heavy—or eliminate modifiers altogether.
- ◆ It may tend to be polysyllabic—or monosyllabic.
- ◆ It may be formal—or slangy.
- ◆ It may be connotatively rich—or spare.
- ◆ The figurative language may be lavish—or sparse.

Important as it is, diction is only one element of style. Other elements include sentence shapes and lengths; clause relationships; attention to the sounds and rhythms of language; and the projection of wit or humor (through puns or surprising juxtapositions). The style of a work is the sum-total of its linguistic gestures. Many writers and critics relate style to *voice*, the latter meaning the verbal characteristics by which an author's or narrator's personality is expressed. Most readers of fiction could immediately recognize the following selection as written in the Hemingway style.

The taxi went up the hill, passed the lighted square, then on into the dark, still climbing, then leveled out onto a dark street behind St. Etienne du Mont, went smoothly down the asphalt, passed the trees and the standing bus at the Place de la Contrescarpe, then turned onto the cobbles of the Rue Mouffetard. There were lighted bars and late open shops on each side of the street. We were sitting apart and we jolted close together going down the old street. Brett's hat was off. Her head was back. I saw her face in the lights from the open shops, then it was dark, then I saw her face clearly as we came out on the Avenue des Gobelins. The street was torn up and men were working on the cartracks by the light of acetylene flares. Brett's face was white and the long line of her neck showed in the bright light of the flares. The street was dark again and I kissed her. Our lips were tight together and then she turned away and pressed against the corner of the seat, as far away as she could get. Her head was down.

"Don't touch me," she said. "Please don't touch me."
"What's the matter?"

from The Sun Also Rises

Typically in a Hemingway story the reporting of the character's emotion is kept well in check, though we are aware that deep feelings are present. Hemingway creates some of the affectless reporting through terse sentences. Even the long opening sentence appears clipped because of the repetition of "then." The sentences are like a frame in a film, each beat (see Chapter 13) coalescing into a scene. Strangely, the segments of the sentences coordinated with "and" (some say that Hemingway even overuses this construction) do not appear joined. Things are just run together, without a logical connection. Drop the "ands" and the picture is the same even though we lose the rhythm. Providing coherent links would radically change our impression and eliminate the detached tone as in the following rewriting: "Her head was back and I could see her face in the lights from the open shops. When we passed the shops, it was dark again. Then I could see it again when we came to the lighted Avenue des Gobelins." Another typical element in Hemingway's style is the chariness of his adjectives and adverbs. He doesn't say "kissed her passionately." Their lips were "tight together," communicates something tamer and constricted. What's up? Once you realize that Jake Barnes and Brett cannot make physical love, the mechanical nature of "pressed" is clear. You will also notice that the verbs tend to be monosyllabic—"went," "were," "saw," "turned," and "pressed." All these elements add up to a style in which the effects appear flattened. It suits the sense of valuelessness and purposelessness that pervades this novel about the Lost Generation.

If the subjects and emotions they tackle call for such a style, writers may choose a more lavish style than Hemingway's. In the following passage from Stanley Elkin's *The MacGuffin* the third person narrator presents the way the hero thinks in sentences like this one:

> And Druff, who at his time of life—it was at *least* past late middle age in his head and even later than that in the cut of his cloth, his chest caving behind his shirts, emptying out, and his torso sinking, lowering into trousers rising like a tide and lapping about him like waves—hard by, as he was, the thin headwaters of the elderly—and was the first to admit the outrageousness of his surmise and discount the chinks in his argument, discounted his vulnerabilities anyway and suddenly knew the man, his driver, the chauffeur Dick, was some kind of spy.

The complex sentence—with its zigs and zags before it comes to a precise piece of information—exactly fits the way that Druff's mind is working as well as the inclination of Stanley Elkin to see the world in complex ways. It may not be everyone's cup of style but it serves both his purpose and the readings habits of his audience.

A unique style readily identifiable as yours is hard to come by. Hemingway, Ginsberg, Tom Wolfe, Emily Dickenson and a host of other writers with striking style had models that they knew and imitated. We wouldn't recommend trying to search for a totally unique style just for the sake of being unique. Rather, search for and imitate the style or styles that fit you and the work at hand.

EXERCISES

1. Benjamin Franklin practiced writing clear prose by imitating the articles he read in the *Spectator*. Imitation is an effective way to think about and develop your own style. Franklin would read an article, put it aside, and later try to recreate the original as closely as possible. Then he would compare his version with the original. Choose a passage from a writer you admire or something you have read in this book. Study it. Put the passage aside and do what Franklin did.

2. Consider something you intend to write (or have already written), then choose a passage from another writer, study the style, and then apply the techniques you have observed to writing your piece.

EVOKING STYLES

In the service of their works, writers often evoke styles from other contexts. The intent is to bring to mind the outward appearance of a form normally found in another framework. For example, in *Harry Potter and the Sorcerer's Stone*, J. K. Rowling uses several devices that allow the reader to swallow (with a smile) this absurd biographical entry that gives Harry Potter information he needs to know:

Albus Dumbledore

CURRENTLY HEADMASTER OF HOGWARTS

Considered by many the greatest wizard of modern times, Dumbledore is particularly famous for his defeat of the dark wizard Gindelwald in 1945, for the discovery of the twelve uses of dragon's blood and his work on alchemy with his partner, Nicolas Flamel. Professor Dumbledore enjoys chamber music and tenpin bowling.

Early in the novel, Rowling establishes that each packet of a children's candy called Chocolate Frogs contains a card of a famous figure from the history of wizardry. Three elements attach the strange fictive world to our mundane world: candy, chocolate, and collectable cards of some admired figure (a baseball player, for example). The brief biography on Dumbledore's card imitates the style of such entries: not only do figures have their public significance but they also have their private hobbies and lives. Typically the biographies are sketchy, mention what the person is famous for, and conclude with a personal element. In this way, Rowling communicates information that Harry Potter and so the reader need to know but also she creates a sense of verisimilitude by alluding to a "real" world form and style to her imaginary world. She relies on the style to tell us about the content. (See verisimilitude on pp. 226–230.)

In the following passage, the writer attaches a fairy tale style to a story meant to take place in the modern world:

> Once upon a time there was a poor unmarried mother who lived in a shelter with her three-year-old daughter. The little girl had beautiful curly auburn hair and big green eyes. People used to tell her mother that she certainly was a pretty child. The mother was pleased to hear it. One day when the mother was out with her little girl seeking a job she met a man.

The style the writer has chosen is signaled by the word choice and the rhythm of the first sentence as well as by brief sentences suitable for a child (even if, as is this case, the writer intends the story for adults). The writer intends to draw our attention to the fairy tale quality because her story will allude to elements in a well-known fairy tale placed in a contemporary setting, "a shelter."

In the sense that we have been discussing it here, "style" is closely related to "form." In every genre, writers use natural style-forms for a myriad of purposes. A poet might use the style of a letter or list to help shape an idea or emotion (see Chapter 7 for examples). A dramatist might characterize someone by making him sound like a manual on how to win friends and influence people as Arthur Miller does with Willy Loman in parts of *Death of a Salesman.*

Writers may, of course, wrong headedly evoke a style that they think advances their purposes but that, in fact, works against them, as in the following example:

> Harken O Life to profound elocution
> Blazoned in Starlight for thee to behold.
> Grand vision of Spirit before evolution
> Proclaiming thy destiny yet to unfold.
>
> From out of the nothing transposed to potential
> My unspoken purpose delayed revelation
> Awaiting the pattern of matter's essential
> Vitality wakened to free animation.

This style is intended to evoke the dignity of the Bible or of such poets as Milton and Robert Blake. However, for a variety of reasons, it does not create in the reader a sense of reverence, as the author undoubtedly intended. One is hard put to think of god as speaking in rhymed couplets with a beat we associate with light-hearted poems such as "The Night before Christmas." Choosing "elocution" for the divine word is hardly appropriate because it conjures up an image of someone who is speaking at a debate tournament. Indeed, much of the diction appears old-fashioned, and self-conscious. There is no way to modify this verse without finding a contemporary style more appropriate to the view of the universe as formed by the natural forces of evolution. (Also, see "sonic boom" in Chapter 7, p. 68.)

Except as a *tour d' force* it is wisest to avoid the diction, sentence structure, and narrative pace of a George Eliot for a short-short story that involves the hero writing a love rap. The principle is: you can't avoid having readers see another style in your writing but, if you don't want to lose them, you had better select a style that is useful for expressing your content and narrative.

INCOMPATIBLE STYLES

Writers who have been working in other forms frequently are unaware that they are bringing to their poetry, fiction, and drama a style that is not suitable. When they have successfully written papers, reports, or other documents for school or work, they may find it difficult to switch gears and so, in a genre requiring another style, the reader hears echoes of the academic, legal, or bureaucratic voice. It is easier to illustrate this problem than to describe it abstractly.

The following passage is from a story intended as an exploration of how the character deals with the death of her husband.

> Rita reported her unhappiness about the death of her husband. Years as a military wife imbued her with an acceptance of change. She had moved constantly and found herself quick to adjust. Now, however, she has an intrinsic need to work as well as a financial need. She feels the "intrinsic" fails to fulfill the psychological need. She feels her job is unrewarding in either aspect.

The word choices and sentence structure here remind one of a social worker's report about a client. The writer is cool, distant. The writer has sent the wrong signals. A simple revision can change the style so that readers will immediately feel that they are entering a story.

> Rita felt depressed even though she was used to change. A woman married to a soldier had to learn how to survive the constant moving about from base to base, from north to south. That constant uprooting she accepted. But when Ed was killed in Iraq, she found that she would

have to work. Work both for the money and to busy her mind. Her job as a manager at Ben and Jerry's failed miserably to give her much of the first or any of the second.

The revision allows the reader to know what Rita's "intrinsic need" was and why she had it. Rita's "feels" rather than a narrator "reports" and the style is active. Of course, the writer might have placed the original version into the mouth of a social worker to characterize her as cold and professional.

In the following passage we do feel that the writer is telling us a story but the style feels lugubrious, flat, and mechanical.

> When she saw the figure she braked, skidding around a little bit, out of instinct or compassion. At first she felt good that she could be helping out someone on a night like this, but then thoughts started flashing across her mind and horror broke out.

Even though we take this passage as part of a story and not a newspaper report, it sounds like a synopsis or summary reporting. Too many actions are piled into the sentences and too much of the action and thought is hidden in subordinate clauses or vaguely expressed. Rather than readers entering the moment, they are distanced by the summaries and imprecise diction.

A forward-moving revision might go as follows:

> She saw the figure by the side of the road. She braked so hard the car fishtailed. Finally it stopped half way onto the shoulder. Had she stopped because she felt sorry for the man standing in the downpour? Why did she always want to help out? But when the car had come to a standstill, she realized that picking up a stranger at night was dangerous and she felt dismay replace her pity. How she could have been so unthinking, so stupid?

Notice that the revision brings the point of view closer to the character's by having her act and feel rather than have the narrator report her action and feeling. The action is told in brief, punchy sentences that lengthen when we enter her thoughts, and the diction is simpler. The reader feels in the presence of a story rather than a report.

Sometimes beginning writers will use a style appropriate to other forms, like the travel article or advertising. Sometimes they will use a style appropriate to another sub-genre—a romance style in a tough-guy detective story. Unfortunately, readers are more likely to forgive you for a distasteful idea or a mixed metaphor than they to forgive you for sounding like something they didn't expect when they picked up the magazine or book and started reading.

EXERCISE

1. Edit any of the following passages to fit the audience proposed.

   A. This is the beginning of a detective story written for a general audience. [Consider that the style evokes a real estate sales pitch.]

   > I spoke into the box, explaining that I was the investigator from the agency Mr. Delamour had called. The box spoke back in a soft but clear velvet tone. "Good morning. Please pull around to the front door, Mr. Hardner."
   >
   > Through the Italian brick and iron gate winding around groomed shrubbery was a modestly sized mansion of the same Italian flavor and extravagance. Green lawns bordered with mulched flowerbeds which bordered with the extremely black driveway. The pieces of shrubbery scattered across the lawn had all been clipped into garish sculptures of nude women in surrealistic frolic.
   >
   > There was also a fountain next to the side walk of a nude female spilling water out of a jar. This was not as accosting as a large black dog galloping up to me who was undoubtedly named Duke or King. Being a P.I., I had these problems frequently, so when he came up to sniff my crotch or bite me I grabbed the back of his neck and undramatically kneed him in the throat. He didn't bother me again.
   >
   > I rang the doorbell and stared into the black windows on the black door. After the three-tone bong the door opened and the velvet voice in a satin blue outfit greeted me.

   B. This is a portion of a short story intended for a sophisticated audience that reads literary magazines and *The New Yorker*. [Consider both the romance tone and the real estate pitch.]

   > This woman was beautiful—I could not deny myself the pleasurable task of mentally noting this creamy face from a magazine resting on a loosely wrapped body of perfect proportions. I pulled out my notepad.
   >
   > "You can call me Lana . . . Ah, would you care for any thing to drink."
   >
   > "No thank you, ah well actually I'm a bit thirsty; a glass of ice water would be great."
   >
   > She left the front hall and I proceeded to take note of every thing in this first room. Cream walls, stairway up, brown and beige tile floor, generous mirrors, and a dark stained desk stand with erotically twisting carved legs. The real legs came back into the foyer.
   >
   > "Here you go."

2. Look back at the passage by Agee. What are the effects of the long opening and closing sentences? How do these serve to set off the shorter sentences in the middle of the paragraph, especially the shortest, central one? Compare this strategy of sentence relationships with that used in William Matthews's poem (p. 71).

3. Reread William Goyen's "Rhody's Path" (Chapter 3) and see if you can find stylistic features that evoke regional culture.

4. As we've noted, style is, in part, a function of personality. What elements of style reveal the narrative voices in passages presented on pages 36–37? Contrast the literalness of Hemingway's diction with the figurative richness of Fitzgerald's. Why does Fielding's narrator say "the animal with long ears" instead of "ass"? Is a genuine decorum at work here? Or just an allusion to decorum? What does this decision have to do with the fact that Fielding considers his work mock-epic? Many of James's structures involve interruptions of subject from verb, verb from object. What are the consequences of this stylistic manner?

5. Compare and contrast the styles employed in two of the essays found in Chapters 11 and 12.

༖

A STYLE CHECK LIST

The following check list is partly an abstract of other sections in this chapter. We invite you to copy it. Put it under your keyboard and review it often.

1. If you find yourself struggling for an image or a phrase, stop writing. Close your eyes and look at the subject again. What did you see? Show *that* to your reader.

2. Flee the category, the summary. Return to what you specifically saw—even in your mind's eye—specifically. "She felt good" doesn't create a picture.

3. Name the things and actions with hard nouns and verbs.

4. If you are pleased by your own cleverness in word or image choice, probably you should delete the phrase. When in doubt, take it out.

5. When you finish your first draft, pretend you are an editor and have to suggest that 20 percent of what the writer has submitted must be deleted. Find the 20 percent in your piece and cut it.

6. Keep your sentences active and friendly. Passive voice hardly ever; operators never. An operator occurs when your verb is not the real action. "He made a decision" instead of "he decided." Both slow the reader and create a negative impression.

7. Learn the style conventions and expectation of your audience—no matter how foolish. Even if you have to use it, be conscious that you are using it. Consciousness is the antidote to style rot. We're thinking here, for example, about the particular style that romances once demanded, a style filled with adjectives and adverbs to create breathlessness.

8. Don't *try* to impress your reader with stylistic fireworks. Pyrotechnics draw attention away from content.

9. Pay no attention to rules that lead to unclear writing or writing not suitable for your purposes. "After he left the room, Eleanor was the first person to whom he spoke." That passage is grammatically correct but not suitable for narration. "Eleanor was the first person he spoke to."

SUMMARY

If personal "style" is the result of a host of conscious and unconscious choices in everything from dress to speech, we might conclude that a writer (or artist) doesn't have to worry about "style" since, no matter what you do, your writing will have style. And that is, as a matter of fact, a correct conclusion. But having a style and having a useful style for your purposes and audience are not necessarily the same thing.

Beyond discovering and honing your general-purpose style, you will need to develop an ability to invent styles for specific projects and purposes. If you use Latinate diction combined with long, highly subordinated sentences, your style might sound like that of a professional or bureaucrat who is trying to communicate laws, ideas, abstractions, or summations. Use simpler words and shorter sentences for a style that appears to be a simple reporting of actions and thoughts. Use many adjectives and adverbs, and you give the impression of being ornate (lavish, gushy, generous). Avoid adjectives, and your style becomes plain (curt, Spartan, stingy). Similes and metaphors, like decorative rocks in the lawnmower's path, can slow the pace of your prose. Short sentences speed it up.

None of these generalizations are always true. Some philosophers express quite complex ideas in relatively simple, jargon-free sentences. Some prose that is filled with adjectives moves rapidly.

Experiment with a variety of styles and consciously imitate writers you admire as part of your writing apprenticeship. And read diligently, with an eye to discovering the relationships between stylistic causes and their effects.

Consistency in style (within a work) is almost always a virtue.

5

Invention and Research

*Origin*ally, the word *original* meant the source, the starting point, the cause of a series of effects. The spring is the origin of the river; the poet of the poem. In this sense, the term only describes; it does not evaluate. In time, it came to mean the primary instance of something after which only copies or imitations were possible. Because we tend to value a copy less than its original, we can be led to an irritable striving after originality in everything—as if the only valuable creation is one in which the creator has done everything in a totally new way. But even the Mona Lisa would fail this test. Insisting that imitation is always bad and that originality, meaning uniqueness, is always good can be a trap for the beginning writer.

Don't fall into it.

In the first sense of the word, you can't help but be original—you are *originating*—causing something to come into being that wouldn't occur without your effort. To accept the modern all-or-nothing sense of the word dooms you to failure because you have set an impossible goal: to invent materials and shapes that have no precedents.

The search for this type of total originality can develop into mere eccentricity—one of the archaic meanings of *original*. The reader can easily grow weary of the following three kinds of works:

1. Those that strive after unique effects without any justification.
2. Those that result from believing that "creative" means anything goes—poor logic, faulty mechanics, and factual inaccuracy.
3. Those that have no relationship to any shared world, natural or artistic. These works, almost by definition, will have no audience.

The false notion that the "original" is somehow independent of anything else can grow into the equally false notion that creativity is the result of brilliant flashes of the never-before-seen rather than the result of the more mundane but realistic ability-to-take-pains.

As you will see, the ability to think and act independently as a writer involves the ability to develop a mature work ethic.

ORIGINALITY AND THE EVERYDAY

Although originality in writing, as in other arts, is sometimes connected with the freaky, most often truly original writing is steeped in the usual—the everyday. Even contemporary horror stories, for example, create their effects by focusing on the lives of ordinary people into which the unusual enters. The chilling effect of such tales grows, in part, from the very fact that the werewolf is the local barber who loves apple pie and Saturday night bowling. You should not put yourself under *unreasonable* pressure to come up with startling ideas, exotic settings, tic-filled characters, and constantly surprising twists of plot.

Successful writing keeps a grip on probability and on universal human nature. If the writer can't present the ordinary in a vital way, the reader will never believe in what may be extraordinary in the work. Harry Potter goes to a strange school, but he has to study, sleep, and eat just as we do. And if the reader doesn't recognize the human truth of the writer's fabrications, then the work will be quickly set aside in favor of something else.

This is not to say that there is no room for invention. Indeed, there is always a great demand for it. However, invention is a means to an end, not an end in itself. Readers have expectations based on their experiences with other literary and dramatic writing, and those expectations are based on a familiarity with the conventions of language and genre. There is no baseball game until everyone is ready to play by the rules, and there is no positive effect on a reader who is confused, frustrated, or insulted. While it is possible to invent a game—or a world—in which the runners go clockwise, you need a good reason to do so.

Originality has more to do with the way in which familiar materials are combined than with a new way to say something that no one else has ever said before.

Your fresh vision in a poem, story, personal essay, or play will come from the unique combination that is you, but only so long as you have studied, thought deeply about, and responded honestly to your material. The masters of literature—Jane Austen, William Faulkner, William Butler Yeats, Eugene O'Neill, and Toni Morrison, for example—are intriguing first of all because they are believable. Granted, often they get us to believe something during our experience that we would not believe in another context. Perhaps we should say that they hold their visions with such conviction and record them so powerfully that the reader can't help but believe. And, even though these writers stay in touch with the world they know—which shares a great deal with the world we know—each is strikingly original. You are unlikely ever to confuse their visions with anyone else's.

To create a world of values, assumptions, social styles, issues, speech styles, and material setting that is unmistakable and therefore original is the writer's task. Though such worlds are based on what authors see around them, *they exist only in the pages of their books.* The London of Dickens, the Georgia of Flannery O'Connor, the Chicago of Saul Bellow, the Renaissance England of Karen Harper's popular "Elizabeth I" mystery series, the Pequod of Herman Melville, and the New Iberia, Louisiana region of James Lee Burke's Dave Robicheaux novels are truthful inventions imagined, ordered, and recorded for the very first time to serve important purposes in the work of each writer.

We should realize, too, that the fantasy worlds of Jonathan Swift's *Gulliver's Travels*, George Orwell's *1984*, J. R. R. Tolkien's *Lord of the Rings*, and J. K. Rowling's "Harry Potter" series are not greater acts of invention than the eastern towns set down by John Updike, the Vietnam of several Tim O'Brien novels, or the semi-imaginary Wessex in which many of Thomas Hardy's novels are placed. The land of tiny people Gulliver visits are real to him, and he is real to us, and that is what finally matters. Making your hometown real to a reader, or making the reader believe in the place you see only in your imagination or in a travel guide, calls for the same faculties of invention and originality.

EXERCISE

Read "First Day" in Chapter 12. What elements in the child's experience are part of a world you already understand and what parts are not?

THE RELATIONSHIP BETWEEN INVENTION AND RESEARCH

The root meaning of *invent* is "to come upon" or "to find." In this sense it is related to *discover*. The origin of the word tells us that what we are after already exists, though perhaps only somewhere inside the writer. The meaning also suggests a seemingly paradoxical relationship between invention and

research. Many of the masterpieces of our literary culture, the "great originals" of our most individualistic writers, are the result of voluminous
research. Melville's *Moby Dick* is such a work. Critics have discovered the
many sources on whales and whaling that Melville used to help him create
this vast, imagined world. His reliance on research, however, does not dimin-
ish Melville's achievement. In fact, in some ways the marvel of what he
accomplished is only enhanced by the discovery of his methods, including his
dependence on facts.

The coastal Newfoundland of Annie Proulx's *The Shipping News* is
another marvelous blend of research and invention. Proulx has remarked
on the attraction of the region, the ways in which she came to know it as
an engaged writer-researcher (italics ours), and the issues that her field
work raised:

> Rarely have I been so strongly moved by geography as I was during
> that first journey up the Great Northern Peninsula. The harsh climate,
> the grim history, the hard lives and the generous, warm characters of the
> outport fisherman and their families interested me deeply. Yet I could
> also see contemporary civilization rushing in on the island after its cen-
> turies of isolation and the idea for *The Shipping News* began to form.
> *Over the next few years I made nine trips to Newfoundland, watching,
> observing, taking notes, listening.* I am keenly interested in situations of
> change, both personal and social, and in this book I wanted to show
> characters teetering along the highwires of their lives yet managing to
> keep their balance, lives placed against a background of incomprehensi-
> ble and massive social change.

In the introduction to her novel *Passenger to Frankfurt*, Agatha Christie
has some advice for writers that is worth repeating. She raises the novice's question, "How shall you get full information [for people, places, and events to give
your work verisimilitude] apart from the evidence of your own eyes and ears?"
"The answer," Christie maintains, "is frighteningly simple."

> It is what the press brings to you every day, served up in your morn-
> ing paper under the general heading of News. Collect it from the
> front page. What is going on in the world today? What is everyone
> saying, thinking, doing? Hold up a mirror to 1970 [when Christie's
> book was published] in England [or the United States, or your
> county seat].

> Look at that front page every day for a month, make notes, consider
> and classify.
> Every day there is a killing.
> A girl is strangled.
> Elderly woman attacked and robbed of her meager savings.

Young men or boys—attacking or attacked.
Buildings and telephone kiosks smashed and gutted.
Drug smuggling.
Robbery and assault.
Children missing and children's murdered bodies found not far from their homes.

Can this be England? Is England *really* like this? One feels—no—not yet, *but it could be.*

And yet one knows—of one's own knowledge—how much goodness there is in this world of ours—the kindnesses done, the goodness of the heart, the acts of compassion, the kindness of neighbor to neighbor, the helpful actions of girls and boys. Then why this fantastic atmosphere of daily news—of things that happen—that are actual *facts*? To write a story in this year . . . you must come to terms with your background. If the background is fantastic, then the story must accept its background.

Christie's point is that we must do all we can to feel the pulse of the world around us, to be engaged, to look outward as well as inward, and to make our personal sense out of the cascade of facts that rushes past, selecting what we need for our work.

Agatha Christie's imagination and inventiveness were remarkable, but her writing comes alive because she created a world that her readers and characters can live in together. Like most successful writers, she knew the value of research—of finding the facts that she needed to stimulate her imagination and to weave into the fabric of her work.

Take her advice and make one of your journal practices the kind of newspaper reading (or research) that she suggests: *Scan the front page every day for a month, make notes, consider, and classify.* You'll find that imagination and facts are inseparable, that invention and research are parts of the same process.

Newspaper headlines bring us in touch, quickly and succinctly, not only with what's going on in the world but also with stuff for the imagination. Can you imagine any crime writer who would ignore the following headline?

9 Bodies Found in Fort Myers Storage Unit
Funeral Director Who Rented Unit Lost License 6 Weeks Ago

Perhaps you are tempted to outline your own story as your imagination explores the suggestions in the headline. In the news article that follows, which facts do you find most provocative? What kind of opportunities for exercising your own originality are lurking in this information? Where could you do further research on this topic? What else do you want to know? What else *don't* you want to know?

FORT MYERS—Nine badly decomposed bodies were found in a rental storage unit Monday east of Fort Myers after the manager of the storage business noticed a pungent odor coming from the unit rented by a former funeral director.

Authorities say more bodies may be found.

The storage unit at AAA Storage on High Cotton Road off Ortiz Avenue east of Fort Myers was being rented by Finley Carter, 44. Carter owned and ran a funeral parlor on Dr. Martin Luther King Jr. Boulevard until six weeks ago when his license as a funeral director was revoked by the state Department of Business and Professional Regulation, said Lee County sheriff's spokesman Tim Hetz.

He said a family from Collier County had taken a loved one to the funeral home. But none of the bodies have been identified.

Only one body had a toe tag.

All were in various stages of decomposition, the oldest having been there for months. They were transported to the Lee County Medical Examiner's Office where the task of identifying them is under way. Hetz said the hands on some of the bodies had decomposed down to the bone. Others had leathery faces.

"There were big, huge bugs crawling around," Hetz said.

Some of the bodies of the five men and four women were in caskets, but others were in cardboard boxes and some were "out in the open," said Sam Johnson, an investigator with the Lee County Medical Examiner's Office.

Numerous complaints about practices at the funeral home had been filed with Dr. Judith Hartner, director of the Lee County Public Health Unit, which prompted the investigation by the state agency, Hetz said.

"(Hartner) had a list of people who complained about this funeral home, and so when (Carter) was closed down, there were some bodies not accounted for" Hetz said. "But not these."

Two bodies, one from Collier and one from Brevard, had been taken for burial, Hetz said. "We don't know anything further . . . The question is, who are these nine?"

The discovery of the bodies is being investigated by the sheriff's department and the Medical Examiner's Office, but no charges have been filed against Carter.

The problem is that authorities don't know what charges can be brought against Carter, Hetz said. Improper disposal of a body is a second-degree misdemeanor, he said.

"But in his situation he is only required to keep (bodies) at 40 degrees or embalmed," Hetz said, referring to Carter being a licensed funeral director until a few weeks ago. And there is no penalty for not following those procedures, he said.

To compound matters, the law doesn't address how long a funeral director can keep a body, Hetz said.

Carter was located Monday about 4 p.m. in the Hampton Inn hotel on Daniels Parkway in south Lee County, Hetz said. When confronted by deputies, Carter told them he wanted to talk to an attorney. Johnson said he hopes Carter cooperates and provides identification of the bodies.

"Identification," Johnson said. "That will be difficult. That is our primary concern."

Johnson couldn't estimate how long it will take the Medical Examiner's Office to identify the bodies if Carter doesn't provide information.

"I think Mr. Carter will cooperate," he said.

Carter had owned and operated his funeral home for 12 to 15 years, Johnson said, and he's personally known him for many years. He said he was aware that Carter had fallen on bad times.

"(Carter) has always been very professional and unfortunately in the last year he has come upon some trouble," he said.

As Agatha Christie insisted, such reports from the newspapers are among the great sources for the ongoing research that a writer needs to be doing even without a specific project in mind. Of course, when you do have a project under way, relevant items will leap out at you once you're in the habit of being on the alert for anything you can use.

SEARCHING AND IMAGINING

New information is often liberating and stimulating, especially for the writer whose imagination can take a few fresh facts and combine them in a way that gives them new meaning. On a more sophisticated level, many writers have created their most important work out of intense, prolonged periods of learning. Gary Snyder has combined his formal Zen training and his explorations of American Indian culture into highly personal yet universally acclaimed poems. Writers who do a great deal of translation, like Robert Bly, are in fact "researching" into language itself and into the sensibilities of writers whose poems grow out of another culture.

Fiction writers, no less than writers of nonfiction, need to establish through research an authentic sense of place and time in a story or novel. How did people dress in 1944? What were hairstyles like? What songs were popular? What were new parents in a certain part of the country naming their children? What is a likely Parisian neighborhood for an American cultural attaché to live in today? How can one effectively suggest this place? How would this person get to work? To the theater? What do the Japanese call a wrench? How does a film maker organize a shoot on location? How much annual rainfall is there in the Iraqi desert?

Writers need to know how to answer questions like these and how to involve their imaginations in the new information that their narratives require. Of course, staying close to home and to one's personal experience minimizes this kind of research, but it doesn't eliminate it. A twenty-five-year-old writer trying to recapture what her hometown was like when she was twelve may have a great deal of work to do. The answers to these questions about people and places can be found in unexpected sources, such as high school and college yearbooks. Almost everyone you know has saved such treasures, and schools and colleges usually keep complete sets of these annual publications. Any writer attempting to create the illusion of a time and place in twentieth-century America will find the yearbook a fascinating research tool. (For the twenty-first century American, the electronic yearbook is becoming popular.) One's own yearbooks are great memory joggers, and yearbooks outline, both in words and in pictures, the values of a culture as recorded by and for students. In their pages, one can see a whole range of individuals, from the most popular to the most obscure. One can discover the common interests (clubs, sports teams, school events) that formed the bases for relationships. In most yearbooks the faculty and administration are portrayed, and the final pages often carry advertisements from local merchants. It is not difficult to build on the "facts" found in this source, a source readily available and waiting to be mined.

The 1955 issue of *Corral*, the yearbook of Calvin Coolidge High School in Washington, D.C., reveals many features of 1950s culture. For example, running a bank within a school was fairly common. The bank managed savings accounts, collected dues and fees, ordered government savings bonds, cashed checks, and sold tickets to student events. Business students received practical training in banking operations, while all students were encouraged to take an interest in their personal finances. Such high school activities are rare today. A person looking through the *Corral* will find that Calvin Coolidge had a large Latin Club, a Junior Red Cross, and a new chapter of the Future Homemakers of America. The school population, to judge by the pictures and names, was almost exclusively white and heavily Jewish. Today Calvin Coolidge High School is in the heart of what, for a generation, has been a middle-class black neighborhood. A researcher comparing *Corral* yearbooks at five-year intervals would see changes in educational philosophy and cultural values as well as demographic changes in the school's neighborhood.

EXERCISE

Research, through yearbooks, the character and environment of high school life in your hometown or your present location at five-year intervals over a twenty-five-year period. Make a list of significant changes. Look for ideas, images, characters, and situations that you could use in a creative work. For example, consider two high school friends who haven't seen each other for many years meeting again at the funeral of one of their classmates.

CLASSROOM EXERCISES WITH YEARBOOKS

1. Single out two or three individuals in a group portrait, and record the thoughts each has about the others. How does each feel about sitting for this photograph?

2. Turn to a page of names in the middle of the alphabet. Describe, as carefully as you can, what each person looks like. Imagine each five years later, ten years later. What are these people doing now? How do you know? How have the additional years altered appearances?

3. Which teachers or administrators receive special recognition? Can you tell why? Do their appearances fit their jobs or specialties? Explain.

4. Create an extra page in the yearbook for each of the following:

    a. a special interest club that didn't exist
    b. a sport that you've just made up
    c. a school event that would have been unlikely then
    d. a group portrait for those who were absent when yearbook pictures were taken

5. Outline plans for a high school yearbook (or equivalent) for a society of the future, one with different values.

Other tools for this kind of research include picture magazines, *Look* and *Life* in particular for older material, as well as newsmagazines like *Time* and *Newsweek*. Convenient summaries of contemporary events and issues are useful sources for plot ideas, background, or just occasional realistic detail that will make a work authoritative and lively. Local publications— regional travel magazines, newspapers, almanacs, Chamber of Commerce brochures, metropolitan entertainment guides, and "shoppers"—are obvious places for a writer to discover information with which to be original in the best sense.

When you need compact sources for developing settings that will depend almost entirely on research, travel guides are indispensable, and so are detailed maps. Don't make the mistake, however, of using a current travel guide to help you develop a sense of Los Angeles in 1933. The American Guide Series published under the Federal Writers' project during the late 1930s is a major resource. In addition, many small towns and counties have historical associations and archives.

Special exhibition catalogs from galleries and museums can help you get the feeling for a period. *Making Mischief: Dada Invades New York*, published by the Whitney Museum of American Art, is one such volume. Responsible yet accessible histories, like David Halberstam's *The Fifties*, are good starting points for exploring the cultural texture of the past. More specialized studies, such as Philip D. Beidler's *Scriptures for a Generation: What Were We Reading in the '60*, can be used to help shade characterization by reinforcing the currents of ideas and the likely allusions sweeping through the cultural environment.

The interaction between research and invention is twofold: (1) you search because you need facts to fill your imagined world; and (2) facts themselves, whether sought or randomly discovered, stimulate your imagin tion. Moreover, factual accuracy contributes to **verisimilitude** (see pp. 226–230).

Beginning with Facts

One problem of the beginning writer, as well as the experienced one, is confronting the blank page. Finding the thing (issue, experience, memory, feeling, person, wish) to write about is an endless problem, and, paradoxically, not a very important one *if* we admit that much of what we do as writers is practice or warming up. The journal is always available as a safe place for false starts or as a source of inspiration. What's important for a writer who is blocked is simply to get started, not to find the germ of an idea that will surely lead to a masterpiece. Hard facts are good places to begin. You can research your way into a creative effort that will give you satisfaction and confidence in your ability to break through the block next time. Perhaps research is too heavy a word; *search* is the main issue here.

The following poem by Charles Ghigna was inspired by an article that appeared in a 1976 issue of *The Birmingham News* about a boy who was struck and killed by lightning as he attempted to drive his father's tractor out of the rain and back to the barn.

An Alabama August

The deep steel of our field machine
opens red earth wounds
under a darkening sky
where James rides.

The ground gathers clouds to her breast
as a thunderbolt breaks the hidden drums

of sparrow ears
and turns my brother black.

In the morning
I find the burned machine,
the sunken footprints of my father.

from The Southern Poetry Review

The news article sent the poet's imagination soaring. The facts that he appropriated are colored and transformed by a search into his own emotions. The
"I" who tells the story is an invention of the poet, a way, perhaps, of getting
close to the tragedy.

Many of the poems and plays of Robert Peters begin with research on the
subject characters, into whom he breathes new life: his own. Research and
invention have resulted in such original works as *Hawker*, based on the writings of a nineteenth-century Cornish clergyman; *Picnic in the Snow*, about
Ludwig II of Bavaria; and *Kane*, about the great Arctic explorer. Here is "Capturing Ducks" from *Kane*:

A bolsa is a swift device
for dropping ducks to the ice:
tie ivory weights to braided sinew
and as the ducks come winging past you
let your multiple gadget fly
flipping upwards towards the sky.
With luck the weights will snag a duck
and choke its neck and break its back.

The human voice is fine in fog
for dropping eiders on the bog:
their feathers are so stiff and soaked
their clumsy bodies sailing low
can't veer and swing and bank for danger.
Hide yourself in their line of flight
and shout aloud with all your might.

Slogged with wet, they try to turn
but freezing, frenzied,
drop and churn amidst the snow,
frantic to elude your blow.
You wring their necks with a practiced flip
then quickly grab and whirl your bolsa
as more sodden ducks wing towards you.

Various sources must have nourished the poems of Adrien Stoutenburg, a
writer whose works are filled with information about nature and history. Here is
a brief excerpt from her sequence poem *A Short History of the Fur Trade*.

> In summer, even chiefs went bare,
> though seldom without the pointed jewels
> of claws strung into necklaces,
> of clacking halos of dead teeth
> strung through their black and dancing hair.
>
> Beaten hides of bison kept out the cold,
> and their swift horns, headgear for warriors,
> blazed like new moons turned into bone,
> or served as flagons for an antelope's blood,
> while the cosmetic bear, crowded with fat,
> supplied his oozing brilliantine
> to blaze on scalps and in a stone lamp's
> rancid flame.
>
> from *Land of Superior Mirages*

Of course, Stoutenburg's poem is no mere listing of facts. She has transformed her material into a highly personal, emotional statement. Her originality is in her selection of material, the freshness of her imagery, the connotative charge of her language. Nevertheless, a passage like the one just quoted is rooted in facts that the author had to master about the fur trade and American Indian culture.

Stephen Bluestone's poem on Moses Miamonides is the first part of a three-part poem entitled "Three Figures in the Landscape." In each, Bluestone imaginatively enters the spiritual world of a Jewish philosopher. This poem, and much of Bluestone's work, illustrates the interplay of research and imagination. Bluestone writes:

The Maimonides section from "Three Figures in the Landscape" was part of an attempt to answer the question: What did the world look like to the human eye at different times in history? Each section of the poem required a considerable amount of research. I also choose three figures whose views of the natural landscape would involve some spiritual question or crisis: Moses Maimonides, Baruch Spinoza, and Martin Buber. In the case of Maimonides I had to look for images of nature from the 12th century, long before landscape painting as we know it. I found these images in the decorative margins of the hand-written books of the time and in medieval Arabic carpet figurations. My purpose in this poem was to reconstruct Maimonides' vision of the seamless unity of the world. During a violent storm at sea on his transit from Cordoba to Acco, Maimonides experiences "the high/sensual seas" and "the almost-touch/of the sky." As a result of this experience, Maimonides clears his mind not only of chaos but of reason. He eventually sees that each of the attributes of God, no matter how expressed, is mercy. In the mind of this great intellectual genius "the world/winged like a bird whose body is thought/took flight." In my own mind, this poem (all three parts of it) was an exercise in point of view. What I learned from doing it was that no one should ever attempt point of view without engaging in a great deal of research—much of it seemingly unrelated—into the life and times of the character involved. Only then does the inner spiritual life of that character stand a chance of becoming the subject of a poem.

Here is the poem:

> While the prophets dreamed of chariots
> and angles (always dreaming, he said,
> the true landscape), his mind grew
> like the shoots and tendrils of a vine;
>
> others saw visions or plainly knew
> what trailed from the fringes of garments,
> fell down from heaven like stars;
> some spoke with messengers, unafraid;
>
> but he kept his start eye on words
> that were neither red, green, nor blue,
> among meanings that shifted like clouds
> across the figureless carpet of sight.
>
> Once, escaping Cordoba, sailing to Acco,
> fleeing from Spain and its madness,
> a storm nearly wrecked him, the high
> sensual seas almost took him down;
>
> he never forgot that almost-touch
> of the sky, those mountains of waves
> that rose and roared like a woman,
> jumped like chaff in the sifter.
>
> Still, he cleared his mind of the chaos,
> its systole of reason, its reflex
> and diastole of fear. He saw that each
> of the attributes, thirteen in all,
>
> of God is mercy. This occurred
> as he wrote, exhausted by lamplight,
> straining the husks, And the world,
> winged like a bird whose body is thought,
>
> took flight. In the dry harbor
> of Fostat, a three-hour ride from Cairo,
> after medical service to caliph and harem,
> he salvaged the sleepless nights—
>
> It was then that the single
> and seamless body of the prophets
> (whose inflamed flesh was dreams) lay open,
> tossing the soul and its laws.

from *The Laughing Monkeys of Gravity*

BEAUFORT SCALE

BEAUFORT NUMBER	NAME	MILES PER HOUR	DESCRIPTION
0	calm	less than 1	calm; smoke rises vertically
1	light air	1–3	direction of wind shown by smoke but not by wind vanes
2	light breeze	4–7	wind felt on face; leaves rustle; ordinary vane moved by wind
3	gentle breeze	8–12	leaves and small twigs in constant motion; wind extends light flag
4	moderate breeze	13–18	raises dust and loose paper; small branches are moved
5	fresh breeze	19–24	small trees in leaf begin to sway; crested wavelets form on inland water
6	strong breeze	25–31	large branches in motion; telegraph wires whistle; umbrellas used with difficulty
7	moderate gale (*or* near gale)	32–38	whole trees in motion; inconvenience in walking against wind
8	fresh gale (*or* gale)	39–46	breaks twigs off trees; generally impedes progress
9	strong gale	47–54	slight structural damage occurs; chimney pots and slates removed
10	whole gale (*or* storm)	55–63	trees uprooted; considerable structural damage occurs
11	storm (*or* violent storm)	64–72	very rarely experienced; accompanied by widespread damage
12	hurricane*	73–136	devastation occurs

*The U.S. uses 74 statute mph as the speed criterion for hurricane

Imagine that something you are working on requires meteorological information. You need to describe the approach of a hurricane, or you want to use increasing wind velocities metaphorically to address an emotion—a rage—building in one of your characters. The scale that Sir Francis Beaufort devised—a "found poem" in itself—is just what you need. Reproductions of this scale are found in most dictionaries.

Now go ahead and build a descriptive paragraph or a short poem out of this "research" material.

The material you have researched for one purpose can jostle your imagination in other ways. For example, you might try to make your own version of such a scale. How about a scale that rates men's clothing styles by the effect they have on women? How about a scale that deals with the effects of different kinds of speakers (or jokes) on the listeners? Be true to the terse, efficient nature of the *Beaufort Scale*. Keep your language similarly flat—objective in tone.

EXERCISES

1. From a travel guide (book, magazine, etc.), research material for a description of a place you've never been. Develop a sketch that could be used as a setting or scene for a short story.

2. Gather a few provocative human interest stories from the newspaper. Building on the facts, develop a story sketch or a draft for a poem.

3. See if it's possible to generate material from a combination of details from two or more of the news clippings.

4. Use your imagination to build a story sketch from an ad in the classified section of the newspaper. Here are some ads that we found:

- CHAIRS 4 cane bottom chairs. $75 total. Need Work. One-caret diamond ring. Make offer.
- *Itek Quadritek 1201* 2 disc drive, RS232, good cond.
- Bushwacker, Sears, $70. BMX boy's bike, $40. Rocker, contemporary ladder back, $30.

5. Place a character you know within a well-known painting or photograph. Describe the character's situation from a first-person perspective and then in the third person. Try Da Vinci's "The Last Supper" or Renoir's "The Boating Party."

6. Research some historical material, such as a battle, a "first" in sports, a mechanical invention, a geographical discovery. Now build on your source imaginatively.

7. Have others (classmates) help you gather a library of high school and college yearbooks. Use them to develop character sketches, relationships, community portraits, and whatever else comes to mind.

8. Plan a few pages of a guidebook for a fictional town in a fictional country. It is the year 2030 A.D.

9. Draw or build a model for the "scene of the crime" of a detective story or a play set. Use sources like *Metropolitan Home* magazine or *Better Homes and Gardens* to give you some ideas. Now write a detailed description of the scene. *Note*: Does this place suggest wealth? Region? Taste? Age of owners or inhabitants? Keep the details reasonably consistent.

10. Furnish an "interior" room—the room inside you (or inside another person). Let a reader know about the intangible qualities of your character from the way in which you describe this metaphorical space (soul, heart, complex of emotions). Again, use decorating magazines as a source.

11. Do some research on the tools necessary to perform certain specialized tasks: to shoe a horse, build a model plane, tune a car, hook a rug, cut a diamond. Now develop a story sketch, an essay, or a poem that enlivens the old expression "a poor workman always blames his tools."

12. Scan the *Yellow Pages*. Study the entries under "Restaurants" or some other equally large category. Base a description of the town on your research, or sketch a series of characters in terms of their dining-out preferences.

13. In a microfilm reading room or other library source, find a newspaper for the date of your birth. Write a short narrative placing the fact of your birth in the context of local, national, and international events.

MIND EXPANDERS

1. Examine the palm of your hand. Use your observations to develop a map of a place that has never before existed. Give your reader a guided tour.

2. Closely observe a cloud formation, a cluster of tree roots, or some other suggestive natural phenomenon. Do fifteen minutes of freewriting in which you allow the images to generate a train of associations. (Research the names of clouds and use this vocabulary as the core of a few quick character sketches.)

3. How are building nails sized? Use this information imaginatively.

4. Investigate the holdings of a desk drawer, a wallet, or a pocketbook. Build a character sketch from this inventory.

5. Take the dictionary definition for a word and expand what you find into a story, poem, or personal essay. Try *rust* or *palm*.

6. Ask a classmate to tell you a personal or family story in no more than ten minutes. Take notes on the story; then, in twenty minutes, work up a version of the story incorporating characters drawn from your own experience.

FIELD WORK

The following prose sketches by Sharon Spencer, taken from her book *Ellis Island: Then and Now* (and originally published in the 1984–1985 issue of *Paintbrush*), are responses to a visit she made to Ellis Island accompanied by Dennis Toner, a photographer. Her visit to this set of abandoned buildings was research. Her interest in finding the voices of those who had come through this gateway to the United States required an act of imagination, an act stimulated by the visit itself, by Toner's photographs, and by Spencer's knowledge of the immigrant experience.

After studying Spencer's work, make a visit to an abandoned or out-of-use or radically altered location. Respond to the present situation and find out about how this place used to be. Let your imagination create a dialogue between voices of the past and the present, or allow the ghosts of the past to revisit their old territory. If you can, bring along a friend who enjoys photography and share your perceptions of place. Try working with the photographs as well as with your own impressions.

ELLIS ISLAND: THEN AND NOW

SHARON SPENCER

During the first quarter of the century immigrants entering the United States from Europe were examined in an enormous room in a massive red brick building on a small island situated between New York and New Jersey. It is called Ellis Island. Half of us Americans of European ancestry are descendants of at least one person who was examined in this room by immigration inspectors. The newcomers had to prove that they were in good physical and mental health, that they were capable of earning a living and that they were neither prostitutes nor anarchists. Many people, it is unclear just how many, were unable to prove these things. Refused entry, they were forced to endure the return voyage by steamship. This meant a second period of eight weeks in steerage, the dirty, badly ventilated and often dangerous part of the ship below the water line. Many immigrants died on the journey to America. Who can know how many more perished on the return trip? There was another group, too, the people who were afflicted with serious diseases: they were quarantined on Ellis island.

Today Ellis Island has been abandoned. It is "surplus government property." The only inhabitants are birds, primarily seagulls, and about two hundred thousand rats . . . .

Looking In, Looking Out

So this is America? A big empty room. It must have been beautiful once. A palace in ruins. Where are the people now?

Oooooh, it's so damp! I shouldn't have wandered away from the group. Ivan thought I'd enjoy this so much. His treat. But I feel feverish, chilled. It's so damp!

Where am I now? Here, looking in. Yes, but where are the others? I shouldn't have gone off by myself. Ivan will worry.

Oh look! There's Mamma. A big fireplace. Mamma, I can see you. "By the Fireplace." "*U Kamina*." Remember that lovely song? It's so cold out here in the garden. No, not cold. Damp. It's autumn. Wet, misty, clouded over. But you, Mamma, are inside by the warm fire. "*U Kamina*," Mamma:

> Alone, you sit by the fireplace
> And watch the fire go out.
> At times the flames flare up
> But then die down again.

You put her head between your hands, rock back and forth in your chair and silently curse the letter carrier. He has brought you nothing, not even one card from your daughter, who's run away to America, leaving you to sit alone by the fireplace.

> Love is like the fireplace
> Where dreams turn to ashes
> And your heart is chilled.

Mamma, I feel like a ghost. There is nothing here in America. Just this one big empty room that was once grand, loved and cared for, just as I once loved and looked after you, Mamma.

Oooooh, the wind feels cold! Weeds are growing inside the house. Mamma, speak to me. Say something. Just a word or two. Something. Mamma, I feel so sick, so cold. So confused. I don't know if I can find my way back to you.

❧

"Darling Katya,

"I sit here by the fireplace writing to you. Through the window I watch the rain fall on the apple trees and, Darling, though I am inside by the fireplace, I can smell the apples, and I can see your father as he was before the war. Imagine! We were married only eight months before he was killed. And you, Katya, eight months inside my belly, waiting to become the love, the only love that life brought me after I grew up.

"Forget the man who has left you, dear Katya. You still think of him, I know, and you will always think of him. It is inevitable, now that you have decided to let his baby stay alive inside of you. That man was ashamed of you, and he would be ashamed of your child too. So, Katya dear, it is better that you find for your child another father over there in America.

"Choose well, my darling.

"When I was your age, I didn't even suspect that life would be so long. For an old woman it is enough to sit by the fire in a small sod house and know that the garden will always grow enough for me to eat, enough to find my only happiness in the smell of ripe apples and a song remembered from the time long ago when I was loved by a man."

❧

Mamma, I hear your voice. You're calling me: "Come inside, Katya dear. Come in and sit here with me beside the fireplace. We will warm ourselves while we listen to the sound of the rain falling on the apple trees." Oh, Mamma, I can hear your voice! "Come inside," you call, "Katya, come to me and we will sing '*U Kamina*' together."

I want to come in. Oh so badly! But how can I get inside? Oh, there's a long stick. It looks strong. The windows are broken. Maybe I can knock out some more panes of glass. I can climb inside where it's warm and safe. I'll just knock out one or two more. There! Now I can climb inside and sit by the fire. I will drink hot tea. I will rest against Mamma's knee. I will go to sleep, finally, sleep . . .

"Hey, Mother! What're you doing with that stick?"

It's Ivan. He looks upset. "Oh, nothing. I just thought I'd . . . "

"Mother, that's called 'breaking and entering.' You can't do that."

"Oh! I'm sorry. I didn't mean to hurt anything . . . anyone. I just wanted to climb inside where it's warm."

"That's all right, Mother. It's my fault. I shouldn't have let you wander off. Let's go back to the ferry slip. The group's going back to Manhattan now. Shall we have some coffee? Maybe you'd rather have tea."

"Oh, Ivan. You're such a good boy. I'm so glad you're here. Tea. That sounds very nice now. Yes, I'd like to have some tea."

"You don't need that stick any more."

"Oh no. Of course I don't. For heaven's sakes, what was I doing with it in the first place?"

Fatima

There is a crash. The sound of glass shattering. A woman's voice, at first low, then a flow of words, high and sharp. The words stop. There is the sound of short regular screams, evenly paced, mechanical. A shrill calliope of terror. Two immigration inspectors are standing in a wide corridor filled with light.

"What's going on in there?" one asks, jerking his head toward the door marked WOMEN.

"Locked herself in. On the way over she went crazy. No one can control her. Not even her husband."

"Is that him?"

A man is walking up and down in the bay area in front of the large bright windows. He is young, dark, bearded. He is wearing a black suit. On his head is a white turban, around his throat a red and gold scarf. Head lowered, he walks up and down, clasping and unclasping his hands. He does not seem to notice the immigration inspectors.

A calliope of terror. The short sharp screams continue to pierce the morning. Then there is a heavy thud. A flow of words, high and sharp. A scream, prolonged.

The pacing man lifts his head, covers his face with his hands, groans.

"Who's handling this?" asks one of the inspectors. "Allen. She's Allen's case."

"So it's back to Damascus for this one, right?" The screams continue. Then a sustained flow of sharp words. The pacing man stops, crouches, his elbows on his knees, face in cupped hands. He murmurs swift urgent-sounding words into his hands.

"What's he doing? Praying?"

"Beats me!"

Four men wearing white uniforms come hurrying down the corridor. One holds a ring of keys, another, a hypodermic needle.

The crouching husband throws them a swift glance. "Say, did you see that woman before she locked herself in the restroom?"

"No."

"She was some sight! Tall and wild looking. Wearing those white robes they like. Black and red scarves. Lots of jewelry. Tense as she was, she still looked like a queen!"

"What'll he do if they send her back?" "Who knows? He can go back with her. He can stay here. Or he can send home for another wife. Maybe he already has another wife. They do that, you know."

EXERCISE

Visit a local museum or gallery. Bring your notebook or a small notepad.

1. Survey the various kinds of exhibits. Pay attention to the ways in which stories are told and messages are expressed by the displays. Consider the overall purpose of the museum as well as of the specific exhibits.

2. After twenty minutes, choose three exhibits for more intense observation, reaction, and note-taking. Describe each of the exhibits, including just what about it caught your attention and made it seem important or intriguing. Take notes for about fifteen minutes, then find a good place to sit down and write.

3. Now, choose *one* of the three exhibits that you singled out and elaborate your notes by freewriting and by making up questions about the exhibit. Also, jot down notes on how to transform this material into a piece of fiction. Spend about fifteen minutes on this activity.

4. Choose a direction and spend five to ten minutes on what you hope is the beginning of your rough draft. You are aiming for a short, short story or at least a story episode.

5. Develop the full rough draft to share with a classmate or friend. Of course, you can return to the museum or gallery for further "research" and stimulation.

The idea is to let the exhibit fire your imagination.

After you have received some feedback on the piece, revise it for emphasis, color, and flow. Make the language interesting, but not outlandish. The initial descriptions are a springboard, not the finished product. Need a plot? Well, pretend you are the curator of a museum and you discover, one day, that an item is not where it's supposed to be . . .

RESEARCH AND ELECTRONIC MEDIA

Over the last two decades, writers have been able to take advantage of the amazing surge in technology that has put not only information, but also images and sounds into readily accessible electronic formats. Standard print media (books, magazines, newspapers, and so forth) have been rivaled and supplemented by the compact and easily searchable CD and DVD technologies. Representations of specialized collections that fill buildings are now available on a handful of slim disks. For example, the United States Army Center of Military History has published a 3-disk CD-ROM set entitled The United States Army and the Korean War. This resource contains a library of information. In fact, it includes "the complete collection of the Center of Military History books, monographs, posters, and brochures on the Korean War." A writer needing ready access to such material—perhaps as background to a novel set in Korea during the war—can easily move back and forth between note-taking, drafting, and information retrieval without leaving his computer station—a station that is likely to be as portable as the box of disks.

Moreover, investigators can select from various electronic sources to create their own collections of written information, illustrations, and music. With a scanner, one can digitize, store, and rearrange material selected from print media. These possibilities are a quantum leap from the last major time-saving technology—photocopying.

Writers with access to the Internet can benefit from this electronic research bonanza. Worldwide resources in almost every subject of interest can be retrieved with a few simple taps on the computer keyboard or mouse. Telephone directories, maps, medical information, scholarly articles and bibliographies, encyclopedias, newspaper files, library holdings, and even information about where to market your creative efforts can be found on the Internet. Whether you need a recipe or an illustrated list of military insignia, information about the average temperature in Santa Fe, or population growth figures, the information is floating out there in cyberspace.

Special interest groups maintain forums on the Internet through which member-subscribers exchange information and ideas, seek expertise, and make themselves available to solve research problems. Messages posted for circulation carry the individual e-mail addresses of participants as well as an address that can direct a question to the entire membership list. Queries to the right lists can bring a writer in contact with many congenial experts willing to share their knowledge.

Almost all internet material is now presented through the World Wide Web, a graphic electronic medium that can handle illustrations (including moving pictures) and sound as well as text. Once you have established a connection to the Web via an internet server (through your school, business, or a commercial service provider such as America Online), you can choose from among various "search engines." These require only that you enter key terms for the kind of information you seek. Some trial and error is necessary, but most researchers can find what they need (and more of it) more quickly through this computer-assisted network than by any other means. Usually, the material you want to have at hand can be printed or saved to your own computer's disk. Sometimes, information providers charge a fee to download files or to send textual material by fax or mail.

EXERCISE

Look for more Ellis Island information on the Internet. You are likely to find the following:

1. Ellis Island photos by Philip Buehler with Buehler's commentary. Use Buehler's photographs to spark your imagination in the same way that Sharon Spencer used those of Dennis Toner. A few clicks will reveal Buehler's interest in the 1964–1965 New York World's Fair, material that can lead to fruitful comparisons with the 1939 event.

2. At "http://www.ellisisland.org" you will find the Ellis Island Home Page, which leads to further information on the Immigration Museum and the American Family Immigration History Center. Though many of the searches that can be conducted online require registration and fees, researchers can benefit from near-instant responses and an enormous savings in travel expenses.

One of the great advantages of the World Wide Web is that providers of information are able to update their sites without the delays of other communication means. The Web often has the freshest information. But it also, perhaps as a consequence, conveys the most misinformation as well. Beware! As with any other collection of resources, reliability is not guaranteed. You will need to question the authority and reputation of electronically distributed information. The accuracy and utility of the information found on the Internet is no better than the goodwill, care, and skills of those who make it available.

THE TIME CAPSULE GAME

On special occasions, societies have attempted to communicate with the future by sending a time capsule, a sealed container holding artifacts, statements, aspirations, images of the present. The time capsule buried at the New York World's Fair of 1939–1940 is a well-known example. The makers of time capsules might be thought of as inverted archaeologists, scientifically burying a culture instead of digging it up. Into the Fair's time capsule went copies of popular magazines, mail-order catalogs, card-game rules, airline timetables, newsreels, comic strips, coins, watches (one with a Mickey Mouse face), a compact, and other items.

1. List items for your hometown's time capsule to be opened in 200 years.
2. List items for your school's time capsule.
3. Research a community of 100 or more years ago and list items for its time capsule to be opened now.
4. List time capsule items for a society that you invent. Now exchange lists with a classmate and describe the society suggested by your classmate's list.
5. Characterize someone by what he or she would put in a personal time capsule.
6. Draft a time capsule poem.
7. Write a glossary of contemporary slang to put in a time capsule.
8. Imagine a situation in which unexpected changes create unintended impressions on those who open a time capsule.
9. Is the time capsule an act of vanity or humility? Write a sketch or film scene about someone who buries a personal time capsule.

As you have now discovered, invention and research go hand in hand in writing just as they do in other creative processes. No scientist ever made a major breakthrough without gathering information and exploring various approaches to the problem at hand. The original thinker in any field is a person who keeps at least one foot on the ground. Though we have said nothing in this chapter directly about writing, we are convinced that the discovery and amplification of raw material for creative works are creative acts in themselves.

6

The Elements of Poetry

THE NATURE OF POETRY

Of all the literary forms, poetry focuses most intensely on language itself. Like other writers, poets tell stories, create characters, and formulate ideas, but these activities do not give poetry its special distinction. A display of language, an exploration of language, is always a special part of what poetry offers. Of course, no writer is unconscious of the impact of words in themselves; still, poets give the most concentrated attention to their medium: language.

Poetry distinguishes itself in other ways as well. First of all, it looks different on the page from other kinds of writing. We recognize a poem by its ragged right-hand margin and its relatively narrow blocks or columns of type. The right margin is uneven because where and how lines end is a defining element in poetry. While all writers compose in sentences and paragraphs, poets have this other unit—the line. The line itself can be defined in many ways, as we shall see. According to William Matthews, "the line in prose is like a fishing line, cast out as far as it will go, straightforward. And the line in verse goes out from the margin, turns back, goes out again, etc. Thus poetry is often linked to dance. The serpentine line of verse goes more down the page than across it." [From "A Note on Prose, Verse, and the Line" in *A Field Guide to Contemporary Poetry and Poetics*, edited by Stuart Friebert and David Young. New York: Longman, 1980.] In almost every significant work, the line is not only poetry's visual signal, its garment, but also its basic unit of expression.

Poets are alert to and exploit the *physical* aspects of language far more than writers in the other genres. The fact that language is made out of sounds and rhythms has always been a special truth for poets. Indeed, poetry's origins are oral. The transmission of story, chronicle, and experience from one generation to another was the driving motive of the earliest poetry. Voice to ear. Patterns of sound and rhythm were, at first, memory aids. In a way, they have never lost that function, though over the generations other functions have become even more important, including emphasis and organization.

Poetry has other distinguishing characteristics. It is the form that most intensely conveys emotion. In fact, poetry is often called the language of emotion. Poets put a high premium on language loaded with sensory materials (images) in order to recreate emotions in us as we read. Poetry stirs us through its mysterious economy that communicates more than the words would seem to allow.

Because of these special considerations, writing poetry can be fun and yet frustrating. We want to say so much and to say it so well that our goals seem unattainable. Our tools are so various and interdependent that it is difficult to make everything work in harmony. Nevertheless, as in any other endeavor, practice coupled with knowledge and determination will carry any writer a long way toward success. It's important not to expect to get there all at once.

In this chapter we invite you to explore the many possibilities, demands, and satisfactions of writing poetry. We begin with a basic introduction to poetry's conventions. Since these conventions are fairly specialized and jargon-filled, some of you will find our review demanding. Stay with us. You wouldn't want to whittle without some wood and a knife. In Chapter 7, we provide a series of exercises that will keep you busy creating poems. Chapter 8 reviews the beginners' problems and illustrates the revision process.

THE LINE

The line and the various strategies of line break are fundamental concerns of poetic craft. At the very outset, the shape on the printed page announces the work as a poem. Consider these lines from "Fog Township," a free-verse poem by Brendan Galvin:

> It's that delicate time
> when things could spill
> any way, when fog
> rides into the hollows,
> making bays, and Cathedral
> and Round Hills are
> high islands. Brooks
> have already churned back
> into their beds to trickle

their own placid names
again, and cloud shadows
have drawn across
the landscape's lightest
movements. Now I begin
to hear something trying
to come through, a message
tapped on twigs out there:

Galvin has chosen relatively short lines to project both his descriptions of a place and his reactions to that place. The flow of images, the fog itself, and the short but regularly **run-on** lines (lines ending without punctuation) keep us moving from one unit to the next. No set number of syllables or accents are repeated—just a limited *range* that the reader's eye and ear get used to.

Consider these variations of Galvin's first sentence:

1. It's that delicate time when things could spill
   any way,
   when fog rides into the hollows, making bays,
   and Cathedral and Round Hills are high islands.

2. It's that delicate time when things
   could spill any way, when fog rides
   into the hollows, making bays,
   and Cathedral and Round Hills
   are high islands.

3. It's that delicate
   time when things
   could spill any
   way, when fog rides
   into the hollows,
   making bays,
   and Cathedral and Round Hills are high islands.

Although the language of the poem does not change, our experience does. One reason for this change is that the differing line constructions send different pieces of the developing message; that is, the rate at which we absorb the material and the ways in which the materials relate differ in each case. These differences occur because the white space around each line acts as a temporary frame, and as we read, we add frame to frame, often overriding or suspending the logic of **syntax**. Decisions about lines and line break become decisions about the poem as an *experience* or a sequence of experiences.

As you can see, line length and line break are devices that control emphasis. For example, isolating "making bays" in variation 3 gives that phenomenon more emphasis than it has in the other variations. Moreover, the contrast between that line and the considerably longer line that follows heightens our awareness of just how short the earlier line is. It also forces us to consider why the last line is so extended. What difference does it make? This is the question we must ask over and over again as alert readers and adventuring writers.

Notice, for example, that the last lines of variation 1 and variation 3 are identical but their impact is quite different because the preceding line is of equal length in one case and much shorter in the other. Obviously, the effect—the expressiveness—of a given line length is a function of its context, the environment of other lines that surrounds it.

But that's not all.

The position of a word on a line influences the emphasis it receives. Generally speaking, what's at the end of a line receives the greatest emphasis, what's at the beginning of a line receives secondary emphasis, and the material in the middle gets the least emphasis. At the beginning of Galvin's poem, "time," "spill," "fog," and "hollows" receive the greatest emphasis. Their placement gives the first full syntactical unit (sentence) a different flavor than is projected by the three variations. Galvin's decision to split a line between the words "fog" and "rides" gives each word relatively equal emphasis and impact. Compare the effect in the original with that in the variations.

QUESTIONS

1. What is the effect of keeping the words "high" and "islands" together, with "high" at the beginning of a line?

2. To what extent do Galvin's line breaks capitalize on or spring similarities in sound ("fog"/"hollows," "Cathedral"/"are," "Brooks"/"back," and so forth)?

3. What is the effect of the pauses marked by punctuation *within* lines?

4. Continue to explore the differences among the three revisions of Galvin's lines.

5. What is the fewest number of syllables per line? The most? The norm (most frequently found or average)?

Here is the rest of "Fog Township":

> the spring genius of this
> foggy township knitting up
> cable and chain to bind
> the acres, among moss stitches
> laying down her simple
> seed and fern stitch,
> complicating the landscape
> a pattern a day: daisy

stitches and wild oats,
berry knots interspersed
with traveling vine
and dogwood. Her needles
cut from oak tips,
click like sparks fired
across a gap, and I
imagine her crouched on
a stump, hair wet, pulling
April back together.
But for the lethargy that's
floating in this fog
in nets so fine they can't
be seen, I might walk around
out there until I meet her,
or scare off the jay
who's chipping for sustenance
along a pine's gray limb.

from *Seals in the Inner Harbor*

EXERCISE

1. Recast this poem in lines ranging from eight to ten syllables. How do the effects of the two versions differ?

2. Recast the poem in widely varying line lengths. What has happened to the experience?

3. Recast the poem as prose. How does the prose version differ from the original? Now, without looking at the original, can you reconstruct the line breaks?

4. Write your own poem about fog and how it makes you feel. Pay special attention to how fog alters things. Employ as many different senses as you can. Experiment extensively with line lengths and line break.

5. Experiment with line length and line break to communicate the different effects of fog, rain, snow, and bright sunshine.

◆ *Question*: Is line length a function of seeing or of hearing?

By now, we hope one thing is clear: your lines and line breaks should not be the result of accident or whimsy. The line is a unit of composition and revision, not an afterthought practiced upon a stretch of prose. As a fundamental principle of composition, the line must become *a way of thinking*.

THE LINE AND METER

Poets don't invent the sounds and accents of the language while in the process of writing poems. These features are inherent in the language itself as it is spoken and heard by everyone. **Rhythm**, loosely defined as the recurrence of stressed (accented) syllables, is not a device but a given. Poets pay special attention to this natural dimension of language: heightening it, systematizing it, and using it expressively.

One convention of the poetic line is to identify it with the repetition that is rhythm. Knowing how this convention operates is a means to expressive power. Though this knowledge is not essential—you can certainly begin writing a poem without any consideration of these matters—it is most useful for you to examine the means by which you can create desired effects.

The special terms we use to discuss these physical features of language sound curious and remote, but they are our only available means of sharing observations about how poems work.

Traditionally, line length in English poetry is defined by a system of measurement called **meter**. There are three basic conventions of measurement in English poetry: the counting of stressed syllables, the counting of total syllables, and the counting of units comprised of some combination of stressed and unstressed syllables. *Note*: when we say a syllable has *stress*, we mean this relatively; it has more stress (takes more emphasis in natural pronunciation) than those that surround it.

The earliest English poetry—called Old English or Anglo-Saxon verse—was based on a line in which only stressed (or accented) syllables were counted without regard to the total number of syllables. It was as if the poets and their audiences heard verbal music only in terms of the stresses and somehow filtered out the unstressed syllables. This poetry was dominated by the convention of a four-stress line, the accented syllables emphasized by repeated initial sounds (**alliteration**). The lines typically had a strong internal pause (**caesura**) between the second and third stressed syllable:

> They *came* to the *court*yard | | *fac*es a-*flame*

This is a tradition that has never vanished, and a good deal of contemporary verse that seems unmeasured is really a version of the long-lived accentual line. Poetry whose lines are defined in this way is called **accentual verse**.

Read aloud the following lines from Dave Smith's "Night Fishing for Blues" and you will hear the strong-stress accentual rhythms.

> At Fortress Monroe, Virginia,
> the big-jawed Bluefish, ravenous, sleek muscle slamming
> at *rock*, at *pier* legs, *drives* into *Che*sapeake
> *sha*llows, *con*voys *rank* after *rank*,
>   *wheel*ing through *flume* and *flute* of *blood*,   5
>   *some*thing like *hunger*'s *throb* *hook*ing

un*til* you *hear* it and *know* them *there,*

                                   the family.
           Tonight, not far from where Jefferson Davis

hunched in a harrowing cell, gray eyes quick   10
as crabs' nubs, I come back over plants
deep drummed under boots years ago, tufts of hair

*floa*ting at my *eyes, think*ing it *right* now
           to *pitch* through *tideturn* and *mud*slur
           for *fish* with *teeth* like *snapped sa*bers.   15

                              from *Cumberland Station*

There is no fixed line length here; rather, an insistent beat emerges from the piling up of stressed syllables in lines that roughly approximate the traditional four-stress measure. Many lines (3–7, 13–15) reinforce the four-stress pattern—the norm—though the variation from it is pronounced. Lines 5 and 6 illustrate the interplay of sound and stress, not only by alliteration, but through repetition of internal vowel sounds (**assonance**) as well. Note the long "u" sound in "flume" and "flute" and the more subtle short "u" linking "blood," "something," and "hunger."

EXERCISES

1. Write a short poem using a four-stress line. In writing accentual verse, pay no attention to the *total* number of syllables in a line—only the stressed syllables.

2. Develop an accentual stanza using a preset variation. For example, let lines 1 and 4 have three stresses per line, let line 2 have four stresses, and let line 3 have five stresses:

  (1)   /   /   /
  (2)   /   /   /   /
  (3)   /   /   /   /   /
  (4)   /   /   /

Repeat your pattern for three stanzas.

In contrast to accentual verse, lines in **syllabic verse** are defined by the total number of syllables without regard to accent. This system is not highly expressive in English poetry or in the poetry of other languages in which the contrast between stressed and unstressed syllables is well defined. Syllabic measures do dominate the poetry of some languages, such as Japanese and French. Syllabic verse *has* had its English language partisans. Many feel that the arbitrary discipline forces decisions that bring surprising results. Marianne Moore's work represents syllabic poetry at its most inventive. Her elaborate stanzaic poems may be analyzed as intricate syllabic patterns. Here are the last three stanzas of "The Fish":

> All
> external
>   marks of abuse are present on this
>   defiant edifice—
>   all the physical features of
>
> ac-
> cident—lack
>   of cornice, dynamite grooves, burns, and
>   hatchet strokes, these things stand
>   out on it; the chasm is
>
> dead.
> Repeated
>   evidence has proved that it can live
>   on what can not revive
>   its youth. The sea grows old in it.

> from *Collected Poems*

Another example of syllabic verse is the following poem by Peter Meinke:

Goalfish

> are nomadic slipping
> sideways through shallows in tight
> schools along shoreline breaks
> to some warm shady weedbed
> of our lake
>
> They're serious these goal-
> fish mouths frowning like bankers
> heads shaking eyes round as
> nickels   *This is serious*
> *Serious*
>
> When young the sweet darters
> make easy prey greengold scales
> glinting like Spanish coins
> translucent tails signaling
> Swallow me
>
> to the big fish cruising
> and cashing in near deep holes
> In winter even their
> parents eat them as they flick
> back and forth

under rock and dock   If
they survive growing bars from
belly to fin they'll do
the same to their own fry sons
and daughters

until time to move on
and they weave across borders
among hooks angling like
untranslated questions to
the slack at the end of the line . . .

from *Scars*

EXERCISE

1. Reline Moore's stanzas. Can you discover any changes in expressiveness?

2. Experiment with a set syllabic line of seven or more syllables. Then try a shorter line. Finally, try a stanza of alternate syllabic line lengths (like Moore's).

3. Notice how the short fifth line in each of Meinke's first five stanzas seems to pack special power and suggest closure. What, then, justifies the longer line that ends the poem?

4. Meinke's "Scars" works without punctuation until the final line which trails off with an ellipsis. What is the effect of this sudden introduction of a form of punctuation? What does it signify?

5. What other typographical device has replaced punctuation in Meinke's poem? Is this device expressive? How does this work to reveal the poem's thematic concerns?

When most people think of meter, they think of the system that measures units of stressed and unstressed syllables each of which is called a **foot**. This system came into English poetry after the Norman Conquest (1066), perhaps from the mixing of the accentual Anglo-Saxon tradition with the syllabic tradition of the Norman French. We call the poetic system that counts these packages of stressed and unstressed syllables **accentual-syllabic verse**.

Four distinctive units (or feet) are the building blocks for poetry in the accentual-syllabic tradition. Each unit is named by a term borrowed from ancient Greek **prosody**. The dominant unit is the **iamb**, a package that consists of an unstressed syllable followed by a stressed one ($\breve{}/$), as in the word "up*on*." The great majority of poems in accentual-syllabic verse have their lines defined by the iamb. The inverse of the iamb is the **trochee**, in which a stressed syllable is followed by an unstressed syllable ($/\breve{}$), as in the word "*but*ton." The **anapest** is a sort of stretched iamb; it contains two unstressed syllables followed by a stressed syllable ($\breve{}\breve{}/$), as in the phrase "in the *phrase*." Its inverse ($/\breve{}\breve{}$) is the **dactyl**, an elongated trochee, as in the word "*bat*tery."

Lines dominated by one or another of these feet are named by adjective–noun combinations in which the first term announces the type of foot and the second the number of feet in the line. Thus, we may have iambic, trochaic, anapestic, or dactylic *monometer, dimeter, trimeter, tetrameter, pentameter, hexameter, heptameter,* and so forth. For example, an "anapestic trimeter" is a line of three anapests. Though these terms are sometimes annoying, they are analogous to more familiar constructions from other systems: "dual exhausts," "triple play," "quadraphonic sound," and "quintuple bypass," for example. The point is that they form the available language for talking about what we observe.

To discover and indicate the metrical nature of a poem, we employ the process called **scansion**, in which we mark the stressed and unstressed syllables and divide the line, when appropriate, into feet. This technique makes visible what our ears tell us. By carefully scanning—reading, listening, and marking—we can discover that Andrew Marvell's "Thoughts in a Garden" is cast in iambic tetrameter:

How vainly men themselves amaze
To win the palm, the oak, or bays,
And their incessant labours see
Crown'd from some single herb or tree,   4
Whose short and narrow-verged shade
Does prudently their toils upbraid;
While all the flowers and trees do close
To weave the garlands of repose!   8

Though Marvell's use of his measure seems quite regular by the standards of modern practice, we can see that he was not a slavish metermongerer. The life of metrical poetry is not in the endless reproduction of a pattern, but in the lively interplay of a background beat—the norm—with expressive variation. Marvell's first three lines march briskly along, establishing the pattern. However, the fourth line begins with a variation (or substitution) before settling down once again into the iambic groove. The fifth and seventh lines are again regular, while the sixth and eighth stray playfully from the norm.

You can create variations for emphasis: notice how the word "crown'd" gains extra force as a consequence of the unexpected change in meter: a trochaic for an iambic foot at the beginning of the line. Another effect of substitution is to change pace. In line 6, the valley (made visible by scansion) of unstressed syllables after the initial iamb quickens that line in relation to those around it.

The unit of two unstressed syllables that we discover in lines 6 and 8 is called the **pyrrhic foot**. This unit is often found in poetry dominated by iambs or another of the four major poetic feet, but it can never in itself be the basis for a line. If you try to write a pyrrhic line, you'll soon discover how the nature of the English language defies you. Another foot used only for variation is the **spondee**, a unit of two stressed syllables. The effect of the spondee, or of any piling up of stressed syllables, is to create illusions of deliberateness, weight, slowness, or power—quite the opposite of the effects made possible by pyrrhic substitution. The pyrrhic–spondee combination in the second line of the following passage (also from Marvell's "Garden") illustrates the sharp contrast, pushing against the iambic norm, that lifts the poet's adjective–noun combinations off the page:

˘ /|˘/| ˘ /| ˘ /
Annihilating all that's made
˘ ˘| / / | ˘ ˘| / /
to a green thought in a green shade.

Here is the opening stanza of Wyatt Prunty's "What Doesn't Go Away." After scanning it for yourself, compare Prunty's contemporary handling of iambic tetrameter with Marvell's:

His heart was like a butterfly
dropped through a vacuum tube,
no air to lift it up again;
each time the fluttering began,
he opened his eyes, first seeing
his family staggered around the bed,
then seeing that he didn't see.
While he died, the nurses wouldn't budge,
blood pressure gone too low, they said.

from *What Women Know, What Men Believe*

Notice how Prunty fashions a compromise between the artifice of iambic tetrameter and the colloquial flow of contemporary speech patterns. Observe also, in the stanzas by both Marvell and Prunty, the role that internal pauses play in breaking up what might otherwise become too mechanical and repetitious. You can vary meter and caesura placement to create energy and pace.

EXERCISE

Here are some workshop exercises done by Lisa Schenkel, a student in one of our classes. She was asked to write a short passage in strict iambic lines, then to introduce a preponderance of stressed syllables, and then to work it through once again with the metrical balance leaning toward unstressed syllables. Study the results and give yourself the same assignment.

Sunday Evening Matisse

1. In strict iambic:

> Unlike the other nudes, she stands at ease
> and watches. Paint in hand, he strokes a breast
> with quickness. Black, the lines relax the splash
> of pink—her feathered hat. Undaunted
> and ready, Barbra breaks her silent stance
> and laughs until he puts his paints away.

2. With piled stresses:

> Unlike other nudes, she stands, slouches, smiles
> from the door, winks and watches. Black strokes
> curve to breasts, pink splashes feather a hat.
> Playful, he paints her unposed. Teasing, she flings
> pink her hat, spills blue paint slick on tile floors,
> slips into the room laughing, and leaves footprints.

3. With unstressed:

> So at ease, she's a bit unlike the other nudes.
> She stands with her hands on her hips, as if
> impatient for him to finish. Her lips tilt in a
> smile as he hurries to capture her. With a dab
> of paint he attacks the canvas with a clutter of pink
> hat, and black brushstrokes below match her stance.

LINES AND RHYMES

You will want to control how sharply lines are defined and how regularly that definition is reinforced. It is easy for readers to respond to a line that ends with a pause marked by punctuation. Such a line is called an **end-stopped** line. One that concludes with no such syntactical pause is called **run-on** or **enjambed**. You can sense the difference by comparing the following passages from Alexander Pope's "Eloisa to Abelard" and Robert Browning's "My Last Duchess." Read each passage aloud and jot down your reactions to how each poet handles the line.

> Those smiling eyes, attempering every ray,
> Shone sweetly lambent with celestial day.
> Guiltless I gazed; heaven listened while you sung;
> And truths divine came mended from that tongue.
> From lips like those what precept failed to move?

Too soon they taught me was no sin to love:
Back thro' the paths of pleasing sense I ran,
Nor wished an angel whom I loved a man.

༄

Sir, 'twas not
Her husband's presence only, called that spot
Of joy into the Duchess' cheek; perhaps
Fra Pandolf chanced to say, "Her mantle laps
Over my lady's wrist too much," or, "Paint
Must never hope to reproduce the faint
Half-flush that dies along her throat." Such stuff
Was courtesy, she thought, and cause enough
For calling up that spot of joy. . . .

Even though both poets are writing in the same verse form, rhymed iambic pentameter couplets, each uses the line in a rather extreme and distinctive way. Pope, by ending each line with a pause, reinforces his rhyme words and creates the feeling of sharply isolated lines and couplets being added one to another. Browning, on the other hand, weakens the impact of the rhyme words, and so we feel that the lines and couplets flow into one another. Each writer's technique is appropriate for his ends.

Browning's model is the basis for much formal work by contemporary poets, and even for poets writing in free verse. It allows for a dynamic tension between the mechanical ideal of metrical regularity and the spontaneous utterance of human speech. In the following poem by Annie Finch, a poem in **terza rima** the varied enjambment is a tremendous source of energy: The surprising enjambment is one unpredictable element in a predictable pattern of rhyming. Another surprise is the slight variation in line lengths:

Thanksgiving

for Julian

Earth is getting ready to harden and dim
in an unmoving winter. A dry yellow curl
bends the grasses the long year has tufted and brimmed.

The tops start to flatten hushed by the hurl
the wind sends through the trees, and soon the will bow.
layered on grain, quick-shadowed like pearl,

sky-think gray clouds anchor down to plow
the black plunging earth. As the furrows grow strange
and dark with their shadows, the morning grows. How

Can a harvest this cold wrinkle open and change?
Laced into earth by their last anxious stalks,
the fields wait. Nothing's there, in the sky's empty range,

but the emptying wind that listens and talks,
or else barely stutters, stumbling by
on its way to bring snow. The day-darkened hawks

slow their long wheeling, up the thin sky,
and then push back downward with shuddering grace
to catch the dry answer this time makes. The high

piled grain, the bleached houses and barns, lean. You place
fourteen dense kernels of looming seed-corn
with care in my left hand. Their saffron-hard trace

of the sun is alive, a long memory torn
from a stalk. So smooth, they call quiet, as loud
as your opened eyes spoke the first day you were born.

from *Eve*

The preceding examples reveal one more fact about the poetic line. **End rhyme** is its most powerful signal. Indeed, end rhyme communicates line length to the ear, and this device can have as much force as the visual signal of the wide white space that follows a line break in print. However, because end rhyme is such a powerful attention getter and one so strongly identified with poetry, beginning writers often overuse it. The result can be noise that obscures meaning.

Contemporary poetry is characterized by less emphatic rhyming as well as less predictable line lengths. In Maxine Kumin's poem, there are instances of true rhyme on stressed syllables as well as the more subdued echoes of rhymes on unstressed syllables (blister/after) and of matched final consonants (line/on):

Stopped Time in Blue and Yellow

Today the violets turn up blue
in the long grass as ever
a heaven can, the sea-calm color
of promises ballooning into view.
Stems long enough to lace
around your oval wrist,
small petal face
the wash of Waterman's ink,
vigilant cat's eye at the center
yellow as the sluice box where cows drink.

Today under the blue line
that covers your pulse I feel
the small purling sounds
your body makes, going on.
Time squats in the blue-spurred grass
like a yellow blister
and love in the long foreplay of spring
follows skyblue after.

from *Our Ground Time Here Will Be Brief*

QUESTIONS

1. Why do you think Kumin uses less prominent repetitions of sounds in the second stanza than in the first?

2. What principle governs Kumin's line breaks?

3. How do the shortest and longest lines in this poem work expressively?

EXERCISE

Write a poem in which you experiment with various line lengths. Make your shortest line a single word.

THE LINE AND FREE VERSE

Most poets today write in **free verse**, a term describing a wide variety of practices in which the traditional, quantitatively defined line is replaced by lines defined far more loosely and subjectively. The poems by Galvin and Kumin that we have already examined are, relatively speaking, "free"—especially if we set them alongside the excerpts from Pope or Browning or even Prunty. If you read Kumin's poem aloud, you will hear a slight pause at many of the line breaks, even when no punctuation occurs. Kumin separates sentence parts in a fairly predictable manner, trusting her ear for colloquial speech patterns. *One convention of free verse is to break lines at natural, syntactical pauses, whether they are punctuated or not.*

In the following excerpt from Margaret Gibson's "Affirmations," line break works similarly. However, Gibson sometimes departs from line breaks governed by syntax. Such variations depend more for their effects on what the eye sees than on what the ear hears. *This visual focusing is one major device for emphasis in free verse.*

> An Eskimo shaman
> will take stone, and with a pebble sit quietly
> for days tracing on stone a circle,
> until snow and mind are one.
>
> Gazing into the whirl of a knothole   5
> I sit out winter. Someone mutters inside.
> Just one tremor before the walls give me
> another white word for snow
> this wood desk shimmers, as if wind

had reached wood's spellbound   10
galaxies and seen
the pole star
turning.

from *Long Walks in the Afternoon*

Gibson allows line break to replace punctuation on occasion, as in lines 5 and 8. Her practice suggests that for the free verse poet, *line break serves as a kind of punctuation*. As such, it is a way of visually scoring a feature of the *spoken* poem.

Another device illustrated by this passage, a device explored in our examination of Galvin's poem, is the power of position. The placing of "spellbound" at the end of one line and "galaxies" at the beginning of the next gives the word "spellbound" more emphasis. Moreover, the hesitation at the line break creates a moment of suspense: we know that the line has ended with an adjective that demands a noun, and when the fulfillment of our expectation comes at the beginning of the next line, it comes with extra force. *Many free verse poets use line break as a strategy for surprise and suspense—or even for multiple meanings.*

Consider the various ways of reading the following lines:

When she cried
Wolf
Tears down her face
Ran

Is "Wolf" the object of the verb, as in the half-dead metaphor of "crying wolf," or is it the subject of the main clause that follows an introductory "when . . . " clause? Is the first word on the third line a reference to crying or a synonym for "rips"? This kind of controlled ambiguity is a device used by many contemporary poets.

When all is going well, every decision a poet makes about the length of lines and the placement of end words and opening words helps the poem communicate. In "Figure Eights" by Siv Cedering, even the white spaces between stanzas are functional. One could almost say that these spaces "mean" something in this brilliant reproduction of the experience of skating:

My back toward the circle, I skate,
shift my weight, turn toward the center.

The skill is in the balance, the ability
to choose an edge, and let it cut

its smooth line. The moon is trapped
in the ice. My body flows

across it. The evening's cold. The space
limited. There is not much room

for hesitation. But I have learned a lot
about grace, in my thirty-third year.

> I lean into the cutting edge: two circles
> interlock, number eight drawn
>
> by a child, a mathematician's
> infinity.

> from *Letters from the Floating*
> *World: Selected and New Poems*

The stanza breaks at "cut / its smooth line," "flows / across it," and "room/ for hesitation" seem to enact what the words describe.

Cedering's decision to shape this poem in unrhymed couplets has other consequences. The most obvious of these is that the appearance of the poem becomes a visual imaging of its content: the paired lines help us "see" the idea of pairing represented in the poem by the skates. Such visual communication is another element in much free verse poetry—and even in traditional poetry. *Poems on the printed page have a visual (typographical) level of communication; they have shapes that may or may not correspond to the poem as an experience for the ear.*

The argument for free verse is at once simple and profound: experience does not come to us in measured doses, and an art in the service of creating or re-creating experience must be free of such restrictions (which is not the same as being free of *all* restrictions). The kind of free verse that uses the loose measures of phrase and clause employs, then, a conservative principle. After all, unlike the flow of experience itself, coordination and subordination are logical relationships. Still, it can be argued that these units of sentence-building are units of thought *as it works itself out*, not subjugated to the tyranny of metrical prosody and packaging. Line break reveals, even heightens, what the justified right-hand margin of prose typesetting hides. Cedering's decisions reveal even more as they allow her to register the acts of attention and muscular discipline of the skater.

In much free verse (Gibson's and Cedering's work included), poets break lines between syntactical units and between words that would otherwise seem glued together. These subtle interruptions, as Denise Levertov explains in "Technique and Tune-up," duplicate how "The mind as it feels its way through a thought or an impression often stops with one foot in the air, its antennae waving and its nose waffling" (from *New & Selected Essays*, 1992).

In his essay "Intricate Song's Lost Measure" (*Sewanee Review*, Spring 1979), Alan Helms observes that the free verse poet's prosody is initially private, "arising from the occasion of the poem rather than adopted for it, whereupon his line becomes more important in establishing the terms of his rhythmical contract" (257). Helms argues (as have John Hollander and Paul Fussell) that before the free verse poem can be shared, the *method* of the poem must be shared. The reader must feel some kind of security about what is going on, that the poet's decisions (especially decisions about the line) make sense even as the easily quantifiable metrical dimension is abandoned.

If the experience behind the poem involves how life is fragmented and how one's feelings can undergo abrupt and extreme changes, then a free verse technique in which lines are scattered, syntax is fractured, and margins jump around is, in fact, a prosody that does rise from the poem's occasion. Helms chooses the opening of A. R. Ammons's "Muse" to illustrate this point, noting how the shift from rising to falling rhythms helps to produce the feeling of struggle that accompanies the task (our task) of bringing the fragments together into sense:

> From the dark
> fragmentations
> build me up
> into a changed brilliant shape
>
> realized order,
> mind singing again
> new song, moving into the slow beat and
>
> disappearing beat
> of perfect resonance:
>
> how many
> times must I be broken and reassembled!
> anguish of becoming,
> pain of moulting,
> descent! before the unending moment of vision:
>
> from *Collected Poems, 1951–1971*

With this rhythmic contract, Ammons moves closer than a metrical poet can to representing the process of perception. Or, to return to Levertov's observations, such practices "notate the tiny nonsyntactic pauses that take place during the thinking/feeling process."

It is a mistake to think that meter altogether vanishes in free verse composition, though it is true that metrical expectations and predictability are no longer at work. Consciously or unconsciously, metrical passages emerge. *The impact of a sudden metrical stretch in a free verse poem is akin to the impact of metrical variation in traditional prosody.* In the latter, a pattern is temporarily broken. In the former, what we will for convenience call a "non-pattern" is broken by the emergence of a metrical stretch. In the broadest sense, the signal sent to the reader is the same: the variation calls attention to itself and places special attention on the local language. Often, the variation signals change.

Sometimes, as Annie Finch suggests (in *The Ghost of Meter*, 1993), the emergence of meter has symbolic cultural weight; it may signal an attitude toward authority in that meter itself represents authority (the old, established way). In her chapter on "Contemporary Free Verse," Finch argues, for example, that the iambic pentameter line closing the following passage in Audre Lorde's "A Litany for Survival" amplifies Lorde's sense of betrayal by authorities. Observe the metrical "lightness" of the second line (mostly unstressed syllables) that precedes the ponderous iambic stomping that follows.

for by this weapon
this illusion of some safety to be found
the *heavy-foot*ed *hoped* to *silence us.*

from The Black Unicorn

Though free verse abandons preset metrical repetition, it does not abandon all types of repetition. The incantatory cadences of Walt Whitman depend
on repetition of grammatical structures, often introduced by word repetition, as
in this passage from "Respondez":

Let insanity still have charge of sanity!
Let books take the places of trees, animals, rivers, clouds!
Let the daub'd portraits of heroes supersede heroes!
Let the manhood of man never take steps after itself!

This device, which provides cohesion and continuity, is often combined with
lists or catalogs, as in Whitman's classic "To a Locomotive in Winter" and
Allen Ginsberg's "Howl," two poems in which the ghost of meter asserts itself.
For more on lists and initial word repetition (called "anaphora"), see Section 8
of Chapter 7.

Free verse, when it is effective, is not the result of spontaneous composition or a disregard for the relationships between means and ends. Like all good
writing, effective free verse comes from a mastery of the medium, and especially
from considered decisions about how the line, even without a predetermined
meter or length, can communicate. We agree with George McWhirter's assertion found in the Winter 1980 issue of *Epoch*: "A line is a controller, concentra-
tor of a poem's voice and focus. The line delays, directs the attention, lets it fall
on the right thing, the right inflection, phrase or word at the right moment. It
is the major domo of the poem."

EXERCISE

1. Compose a free verse poem in which line breaks are determined by
punctuation.

2. Following Gibson's example, write a poem in which decreasing line length is
used expressively. Now try another in which line lengths expand.

3. Experiment with line breaks and stanza breaks that separate parts of speech
(subject from verb, verb from object, preposition from object, adjective from
noun, adverb from verb).

4. Use line break and line placement (see the discussion of the Ammons poem)
to register one or more of the following experiences: alienation, interrupted

sleep, attending to one person or task while remembering another, a scene of confusion (police raid on a demonstration, for example).

5. Compose a free verse poem in which you occasionally *and strategically* break out into meter.

LINES IN COMBINATION

Broadly speaking, you can choose one of two major traditions for combining lines into poems: the **stichic** and the **stanzaic** (or **strophic**). The stichic tradition is to write a continuous poem whose overriding unity and cohesiveness are promised by the unbroken column of type. An example of this tradition is Galvin's "Fog Township." The stanzaic tradition is to write a segmented poem in which white spaces (blank lines) divide the total work into smaller, quasiindependent units, as in the Wordsworth poem that follows.

The contrasting visual experiences send the reader different signals, creating different kinds of expectations. While we recognize the general look of poetry— the fairly uniform left-hand margin, the ragged (unjustified) right margin, the narrower-than-prose column shape—we further recognize and are "preset" to respond to a range of more particular typographical designs. The following two-stanza poem by William Wordsworth promises something even before we begin reading it:

A Slumber Did My Spirit Seal

A slumber did my spirit seal;
  I had no human fears:
She seemed a thing that could not feel
  The touch of earthly years.

No motion has she now, no force;
  She neither hears nor sees;
Rolls round in earth's diurnal course,
  With rocks, and stones, and trees.

The visual message of this poem immediately suggests twofoldedness and symmetry: we expect that the shape of thought or emotion will somehow correspond to the halved whole—and it does. The shift from past tense to present tense is the key to the "before and after" structure. In turn, that structure justifies the decision to cast the material in two *equal* stanzas. The line indentations suggest a further division of each stanza, a division echoed by the end rhyme (*ab/ab*).

Stanzaic poems and poems in **fixed forms** are most effective when some kind of correspondence exists between outer and inner divisions or form. Each of the following two Italian sonnets by Jay Rogoff pivots between the eighth and ninth line; when the rhyme scheme changes, the poet takes us from the scene of the crime to the interrogation room:

Murder Mystery 1

Inkstains upon the oriental rug.
Blood mingles with them. Blood today is king.
The lyre lies on the bed strung with one string.
Protruding from her wounds are points stuck snug
as bees' abandoned stingers, which cops unplug.
Only the radio is left to sing.
The floor littered with crow quill pens. "Bring
'em here," says the sergeant with a shrug.

The poet, crammed into his seat with bright
lights blinding, when interrogated, said,
"I don't know what you mean." A lie. The light
was brightened, handcuffs clamped. He stood and read
a poem. Finished, he sobbed, "We used to fight.
I'd never *kill* her. But I'm glad she's dead."

Murder Mystery 2

Inkstains upon the oriental rug.
The poet at a queer angle. Like a spring
wound round his neck, a strangling catgut string
has popped his eyes. His hands clutch poems and hug
them to his heart. The cops' most violent tug
won't pry them. A pen lies like a torn wing.
From the hall a woman's voice begins to sing.
"Book'er," the sergeant says. "Prints and a mug."

She sat handcuffed. Her robe trailed on the floor.
"What do you know?" "Nothing." "A man is dead."
"A poet," she corrected. "I know no more."
The light was thrown upon her laureled head.
"He did it to himself," she added. "You're
a liar." "No, this is my lyre," she said.

Some poets might emphasize the overall unity of the sonnet; others, like Rogoff, develop material that coincides with the divisions signaled by the rhyme scheme. To put it simply, a mitten tells us one thing about a hand, a glove tells us something else.

Whether writing poems in traditional or in free verse structures, the poet chooses or invents groupings to achieve expressive ends. Just as the unequal sections of the Italian sonnet promise a change of scene or direction, just as the narrowing line in Gibson's "Affirmation" affects the reader's response by isolating less and less, so does the diminishing stanza in Theodore Roethke's "The Moment" direct the poem's emotion and meaning:

We passed the ice of pain,
And came to a dark ravine,

And there we sang with the sea:
The wide, the bleak abyss
Shifted with our slow kiss.

Space struggled with time;
The gong of midnight struck
The naked absolute.
Sound, silence sang as one.

All flowed: Without, within;
Body met body, we
Created what's to be.

What else to say?
We end in joy.

from *The Collected Poems*
of Theodore Roethke

The poem's structure—each stanza a line shorter than the one before it—guides our understanding of what's at stake: two people coming together, stripping away both time and space in the process. In their connection or uniting, they are what's left of the world, but they contain it as well.

If you think about it, the business of defining lines and line combinations leads to a prior consideration of whether your poem exists primarily in *time*, as a sequence of words, sounds, and rhythms to be heard, or in *space*, as a sequence of signs printed on the page. The work of most contemporary poets hovers somewhere in between, so that reading—finding the essential poem—becomes an act of mediation between what we hear, however silently, and what we see. In addition, you must consider how much the full communicative strength of your work depends on your reader's knowledge of traditions either employed, alluded to, or intentionally defied. You must be aware of your assumptions and the demands they place on your readers: you need to gauge the risks you are taking by depending on or ignoring conventions—even the conventions of free verse.

The two poems that follow illustrate contrasting assumptions about the essential nature of poetry and about the audience. Karen Swenson's "Time and the Perfume River" is in a fixed form, the **villanelle**, and it gets much of its strength from manipulating the conventions of that form. Consequently, while the poem can reach any reader, it has greater resonance for the reader who is aware of the dynamics of the form and who is familiar with other villanelles. "The Waves," by Mary Oliver, follows only the rules that the poet has discovered for this individual poem. Moreover, Oliver has given special emphasis to the typographical level of the poem, allowing that experience to sit in sharp contrast to sounds, rhythms, and even syntax. Swenson's poem also has a strong typographical impact; the visual shape underscores—or outlines—a musical shape that communicates to the ear. These patterned repetitions of sounds delineate the poem in time.

Time and the Perfume River

Small Buddhas smile above their blooms
on gilded family altars, glide
along the curves of the Perfume,

that river named before the dooms
of war ripped Hue's old gilded hide
and Buddhas' smiles above the blooms.

The river waves are slapping tunes.
Greens sputtering in a wok provide,
slong the curves of the Perfume,

the smoke of incense. Children's spumes
of laughter rock small boats whose guide
is Buddha's smile above his blooms.

Those years death rode the river's flume
his rotting incense justified
along the curves of the Perfume

by leaders' greed for power's boom.
War's drowned now in the river's tide
where Buddhas smile above their blooms
along the curves of the Perfume.

from *The Landlady in Bangkok*

The Waves

The sea
    isn't a place
        but a fact, and
            a mystery

under its green and black
    cobbled coat that never
        stops moving.
            When death

happens on land, on some
    hairpin piece of road,
        we crawl past,
            imagining

over and over that moment
    of disaster. After the storm
        the other boats didn't
            hesitate—they spun out

from the rickety pier, the men
    bent to the nets or turning
        the weedy winches.
            Surely the sea

is the most beautiful fact
  in our universe, but
    you won't find a fisherman
      who will say so;

what they say is,
  See you later.
    Gulls white as angels scream
      as they float in the sun

just off the sterns;
  everything is here
    that you could ever imagine.
      and the bones

of the drowned fisherman
  are returned, half a year later,
    in the glittering,
      laden nets.

from *Dream Work*

QUESTIONS AND EXERCISES

1. From Swenson's example, describe the villanelle form. What is repeated? How many times?

2. What is the effect of the difference between the first five sections and the longer final section with its concluding couplet?

3. Can you determine if Swenson is taking any liberties with an even more restrictive tradition?

4. Swenson begins her lines with lowercase letters (unless uppercase is otherwise demanded). Why does she use this contemporary practice in a long-lived fixed form?

5. Find and study five or six other English villanelles, including Dylan Thomas's "Do Not Go Gentle Into That Good Night." After exploring the possibilities, try a villanelle of your own.

6. Compare and contrast the conventions and effects of the villanelle (pp. 133–134) with those of the English (Shakespearean) sonnet and the Italian sonnet (see Rogoff's "Murder Mystery" sequence, p. 132).

7. Invent a form that borrows some of its features from the villanelle and some from the sonnet.

8. What is the relationship between (visual) form and content in "The Waves"?

9. Does the fact that the stanzas are not self-contained seem accidental or purposeful?

10. Is there any inner logic that insists on or justifies the stanzaic appearance of this poem?

11. Can this poem be read aloud so its stanzaic nature is communicated?

12. Does a free verse poem cast in visual stanzas work with or against our expectations in order to gain its effects?

IMAGERY

For many poets, a poem begins with an **image**—a piece of language that relates sensory experience. Though all writers employ **imagery** and the many figures of speech that are built from images, poets *depend* on this type of language. (See the discussions of **concreteness** and **figurative language** in Chapter 4, "Language Is Your Medium.") Because poetry aims at intensity and economy of expression, imagery and figures of speech have special value to the poet. Sensory experience is primary experience: we see, feel, taste, smell, and hear before we think, analyze, choose, and argue. By staying close to imagery, the language of the senses, you can bring your readers close to a fundamental animal awareness of the world we inhabit. At the same time, by choosing carefully and by letting associated images coalesce, you can evoke complex states of awareness.

The image in the title of this Roland Flint poem controls the poem by giving it a center and a circumference. If we let ourselves respond fully to what the earthworm image generates, we find a poem that is about processes, transformations—perhaps about poetry itself.

Earthworm

I think of a girl who hated to walk in the rain,
Loathing to step on them. I hope she got over that.
We liked to keep one on the sidewalk
And line it up with another
For an excruciating race,
Or put it back in the grass
And watch its progress. Burrowing.

We said, when he's underground,
And worming, the earth goes right through him.

I still think of him that way, lank, blind,
Both ends open, refining whatever comes,
Dirt among rose roots, yeasty bodies.

He doesn't look for trouble. He just follows warmth,
At the earth's curve, coming up only for rain
And the feet of girls.

from *Resuming Green*

Flint's poem works through a series of sensory triggers to reach out for emotions and ideas. By building upon his central, generative image, the poet keeps his writing concrete, cohesive, and immediate. The earthworm changes what passes through it. The language of the poem invites us to ask *what else works in this way* without ever leaving the heat-seeking earthworm behind. The poem also asks *what, like the earthworm, is undervalued because it seems unattractive or doesn't call much attention to itself.*

Observations that discover likenesses are the geneses of many successful poems. Even such rarefied emotional experiences as the sudden sense of absence can be captured by the patient poet who asks, "What is it like?" over and over again. "Gloves," by Jean Nordhaus, is alive with focused images that finally take us to a place beyond and within.

> When all the birds roost
> suddenly
> the bare tree
> bursts into leaf.
>
> plumb, tapered, brown, true
> a flock of
> weathervanes
> nosing into
>
> the wind, they hang
> to the branches
> like gloves, then
> leave suddenly
>
> leaving the branches,
> the branches
> full of in-
> visible hands.

from *A Language of Hands*

EXERCISE

1. Trace the connections between the images and figures of speech in these two poems.

2. How does each poet use the line to isolate or connect images?

3. Examine each poem in this chapter to see whether line, imagery, or something else functions as the primary structural element.

4. Write your own poem by enlarging upon a central image or building a series of associated images.

The interplay between lines and images creates much of the dramatic tension in contemporary poetry. Investigating the possibilities of various line–image units will lead you to an understanding of one more expressive convention.

EXERCISE

Analyze the following poem by William Heyen in terms of line construction, line break, lines in combination, stanza breaks, and imagery. Pay special attention to the images of light. What are the key organizational devices of this poem? How can you use what you have learned from reading like a writer?

The Return

I will touch things and things and no more thoughts.
—Robinson Jeffers

My boat slowed on the still water,
stopped in a thatch of lilies.
The moon leaned over the white lilies.

I waited for a sign, and stared
at the hooded water. On the far shore
brush broke, a deer broke cover.

I waited for a sign, and waited.
The moon lit the lilies to candles.
Their light reached down the water

to a dark flame, a fish. It hovered
under the pads, the pond held it
in its dim depths as in amber.

Green, still, balanced in its own life,
breathing small breaths of light, this
was the world's oldest wonder, the arrow

of thought, the branch that all words
break against, the deep fire, the pure poise
of an object, the pond's presence, the pike.

from *Long Island Light:*
Poems and a Memoir

1. What happens between stanzas 3 and 4, 5 and 6?

2. What sound dominates the close of the poem? What is its effect? (You might want to review this question after reading the next section.)

3. What figure of speech is "small breaths of light"? How does it work?

4. What does the poem have to say about the concrete versus the abstract?

5. Write your own poem in which you use one or two enjambed stanzas that force the reader to move over the white space in a way that underscores meaning.

SOUND PATTERNS

In our discussion of the line, we referred to the basic sonic devices: rhyme, alliteration, and assonance. Now it is time to look more closely into the expressiveness of sounds and sound patterns. In speech and in most prose, the various sounds in our language system occur at random. However, the poet can pattern the occurrence of sounds by repeating them in close proximity or at regular intervals. As with meter, some feature of language that occurs in a haphazard way when we speak or when we write prose is now given a conscious patterning for purposes of emphasis, cohesiveness, or organization.

When Poe, in "The Raven," writes of "this *g*rim, un*g*ainly, *g*hastly, *g*aunt, and ominous bird of yore," he is employing alliteration (repetition of initial consonant) on four stressed syllables in order to underscore his adjectives by linking them sonically. When Shelley, in "Mont Blanc," writes of pines that "in the m*a*ngled soil/Br*a*nchless and sh*a*ttered st*a*nd," a similar—though somewhat quieter—effect is achieved through assonance (repetition of vowel sound). In both cases, the reader's attention is drawn to words linked by sounds, and the words themselves are linked together. *Note*: we are not referring to the *spelling* of words, since identical sounds are often spelled differently: "stuff"/"enough."

Rhyme is simply a more complex echoing: usually a repeated vowel–consonant combination, as in the pair "streams"/"dreams." Often, as in the pair "free"/"see," the matching of the final vowel constitutes the rhyme. Because rhyme (or "true rhyme") is more emphatic than the other devices, it is customarily used, as we have seen, to signal the ends of lines and to define stanzas. Rhyme sharpens meanings by asking readers to consider the semantic relationships between the words whose sounds mirror one another.

The following lines resulted from an assignment to develop a six-line stanza using true rhyme:

> Early one morning, an Amtrak train
> Rumbles north through the ivory expanse
> Of Maryland landscape. The muffled terrain

> Is sliced by the tracks. Slung like a lance,
> The careless freight, by folly and chance,
> Splatters the snowbank with that human stain.

This first draft exploits the power of rhyme effectively by emphasizing words important enough to carry the extra attention they receive. After leading us to anticipate alternating rhyme (*abab* through line 4), the poet makes a couplet (lines 4 and 5) that interrupts the pattern. This interruption unsettles the reader, who waits for some new resolution of pattern. The waiting produces suspense, and then surprise, as the culminating image is delivered with the return of the *a* rhyme.

While repetition of any sound has the broad effect of calling attention, more specialized effects can be achieved through a sensitivity—in both writer and reader—to the nuances of the various sounds. When Poe repeats the harsh gutteral *g*, the effect is quite different from that of Keats's lines from "To August": "Thy hair soft-lifted by the winnowing wing; / Or on a half-reaped furrow sound asleep." In Keats's lines, harsh sounds are almost altogether absent and never prominent.

Although we hesitate to say that sounds *mean* anything, we do feel that they *suggest*. Let's consider consonants first. The following chart shows the range of consonant sounds. The family groupings have to do with how the sounds are pronounced as well as how they strike the ear.

CONSONANT SOUNDS

liquids; *r*, *l*	"semivowels" along with *w* and *y*, considered the most musical consonants
nasals: *m*, *n*, *ng*	firmer, but still "soft"
fricatives: *h, f, v, th, dh, s, z, sh, zh*	produced by vibration or friction, abrasive
plosives: *p, b, k, g, t, d*	produced by blasting open a closed space . . . can't be prolonged . . . called "hard" consonants

Here is a student experiment in using sounds. The assignment was to write two short passages of poetry, the first with language that is dominated by softer consonants, and the second emphasizing the plosives.

> 1. Summer came on slow as a lizard's blink,
>   on a flotilla of white wicker chairs and lawn games,
>   and all we knew of time was a lurid glow
>   in the West-Northwest that we watched from the headland,
>   watched it sink seamless into Thursday.

> 2. Kirk burned for a while on alternate doses
>   of hard bop and crack. He smoked Kents tit for tat

with the most brutal of the night beasts and
    once hocked his axe
for a Palo Alto whore. Even now, dead by the hand
of an outraged husband, he looms over my shoulder
slipping me jacks to cinch a high straight.

EXERCISE

1. In the preceding experiment, which lines or passages seem most successful at linking sound and sense? Where would you make improvements? Revise these passages; then go on to do your own experiments with the consonant groups. Recite your work out loud. Listen for the similarities among sounds from the same family. Notice how they can almost be mistaken for one another. For example, the word "fish" and the first syllable of "visual" create a near rhyme—in fact, a near identity.

2. Listen and respond to the sounds in the following word pairs. How do the contrasting sounds make you feel?
  a. pillow / cushion
  b. coast / shore
  c. beast / animal
  d. referee / umpire
  e. whiskey / booze

Now pronounce each word in the following vowel chart slowly and deliberately. Feel the work your mouth has to do to make the sounds.

VOWEL SOUNDS

bee	high-frequency	vitality, speed,
bay	(alto) vowels	excitement, stridency,
buy		exhilaration, light
bit	middle-frequency	
bet	(tenor) vowels	
bat		
bird		
bud		
bar	low-frequency	sobriety, awe, gloom,
bough	(bass) vowels	doom, largeness,
boy		darkness
bought		
book		
bone		
boot		

This vowel scale groups families by frequency characteristics that can be graphed on an oscilloscope. An interval of high-frequency sounds shows a busy, jagged pattern with many peaks and valleys. Low-frequency vowels, on the other hand, show fewer oscillations over the same interval. Like the consonant families, the vowel families are related by how they are produced. The high-frequency vowels are made toward the front of the mouth in a relatively closed space. You can feel a tension in the facial muscles as you pronounce them. The low-frequency vowels begin far back in the mouth, which is open and rounded as these sounds are manufactured.

As with the consonants, repetition of vowels from one or another category can help give emotional coloring to the passages bonded together by these related sounds. For example, the last stanza of Dylan Thomas's "The Hand That Signed the Paper" gains much of its solemnity from the way in which low-frequency vowel sounds dominate the passage, especially toward the end of lines.

> The five kings count the dead but do not soften
> The crusted wound nor stroke the brow;
> A hand rules pity as a hand rules heaven;
> Hands have no tears to flow.

Conversely, in his elegiac "Do Not Go Gentle Into That Good Night," Thomas urges not self-pity or gloom, but active resistance to death; here the strident high-frequency vowels take over:

> Grave men, near death, who see with blinding sight
> Blind eyes could blaze like meteors and be gay,
> Rage, rage against the dying of the light.

Turn back to the six-line stanza that begins on page 139. Notice how the strident *a* sound promotes the feeling that the speaker's otherwise flat voice can veil but not hide his recognition of anguish.

EXERCISE

As you have already done with the consonant sounds, explore the effects of piling up vowel sounds from one and then the other side of the spectrum.

1. Write an "aw" poem in which the vowel in words like "call" and "appall" and "thought" is dominant. Notice, again, that spelling is not the key to pronunciation.

2. Write an "ee" poem.

3. Experiment with the ways in which various classes of consonants and vowels work in combination. For example, mix high-frequency vowels and fricative consonants.

OFF-RHYME

Contemporary practice tends to favor subdued sound patterns. **Off-rhyme** (also called **slant rhyme**, *near rhyme*, and *half rhyme*) is used more frequently than true rhyme, and the aspiring poet should experiment with the varying intensities of rhyme in order to discover what kinds of effects are possible. One form of off-rhyme is **consonance**. This is a matching of consonant clusters around changing vowel sounds: "blood / blade," "cut / cat / cot / caught," "dance / dunce." The following lines from John Ciardi's "At My Father's Grave" indicate the power of this slight discord.

> A leaf is not too little. A world may rest
> in no more shade than spiders weave. Defend
> the nit on every underside. I roost
> on less than it, and I must yet be found
> by the same bird that found St. Francis dead.

Two lines later, "dead" is echoed by "deed." There is something slightly grating in this kind of rhyming, and it is appropriate to the emotion that Ciardi expresses.

EXERCISE

Experiment by alternating full rhymes with consonance.

1. Try these end words in your poem: "blend, blonde, blind, bland."

2. Now use these: "cuff, cough, calf; meat, mat, might, moat."

Consonance has an eerie richness about it; other types of echoing in use today are far more subdued. Often the repetition of final consonant sounds, or the pairing of related consonant sounds, serves for rhyme. Listen to the end sounds in the first stanza of Philip Levine's "For Fran."

> She packs the flower beds with leaves,
> Rags, dampened paper, ties with twine
> The lemon tree, but winter carves
> Its features on the uprooted stem.

The quiet alternate rhyming of the fricative "vs" pattern and the nasals sets just the degree of containment Levine needs for his gentle homage to his wife.

Another kind of off-rhyme uses assonance in the end words: "ice / prize," "crisp / din," "loud / growl."

EXERCISE

1. Write six lines of alternating rhyme in which the odd-numbered lines end with dental consonants (*d*, *t*) and the even-numbered ones end with fricatives (see chart on p. 140).

2. Write a five-line passage in which the final consonants of the end words are nasals but the other sounds are in contrast.

There is no point in arguing, as some conservatives are apt to do, that this isn't rhyme or that poets just can't rhyme anymore. The subdued echoes illustrated by Levine's quatrain are the convention of our time for those who choose to rhyme at all. These modulated echoes can move a sensitive reader (listener). A skilled poet will have mastered their effects.

The sounds of the language are among your most important tools. While it is possible to write without regard to sound or meter, these physical phenomena do their work anyway. In a sense, they just *will not* be ignored. Any dimension of language that we choose to ignore is ignored at the risk of our sending unintended, ineffective messages to the reader, even the reader who has no conscious concern with these matters. The subterranean effects of sounds and rhythms are part of the "magic" of poetry. As with all magic, one needs knowledge and skill.

Our review of the fundamentals is now over. Of course, we have only skimmed the surface of these issues. Each poet chooses the devices and strategies that solve the problems of each developing poem—but there can be little in the way of informed choice without information. Each poet, as well, must discover, through trial and error as much as by any other means, his or her poetic balance between spontaneous utterance and traditional measures and forms. Each must do what Eavan Boland describes herself doing (in her introductory essay to *The Making of a Poem: A Norton Anthology of Poetic Forms*): ". . . pushing the music of dailyness against the customary shapes of the centuries."

The conventions of poetry are, finally, the features by which poems are recognized and do their work.

7

Practicing Poetry

1. UNSCRAMBLING

We have scrambled the fifteen lines of Susan Astor's poem, "The Poem Queen." The original has five 3-line stanzas rhyming *aab*. Reconstruct Astor's poem. *Hint*: the first and last lines are in the right place.

The Poem Queen writes a poem a day,
To please her when she is alone
She has more power than they know,
It will be read.

Some say hers is a magic throne
Has found a way to burn the snow;
Her pen is her divining rod;
Turns gold to lead.

She uses it to handle God,
In her spare time pauses to pray
She has a soldier and a drone
And blossom bread.

That she eats custard made of bone
Or in her bed.
And tame the dead.

Now exchange your reconstruction with those done by others in the class. Discuss the pros and cons of each version, as well as the original—which most people will be able to discover after a little trial and error. Astor's poem appears at the end of this chapter. Answer these questions about it:

a. By what logic are the stanzas ordered?
b. What is the effect of the repeated rhyme sound in the half-size third line of each stanza?
c. What about the short line in itself? What effect does it create?

2. IMITATION

Model a "character poem" of your own on Susan Astor's. Use her stanza form five times. Titles might be "The Prom Queen," "The Car King," "The Duke of Disco," "The Computer King," "The Punk Queen." Exchange and discuss the results with your classmates.

3. RECASTING

Recast the poem you have just written into the following forms.

Ballad Stanza. This form rhymes *abxb* or *abab* and alternates iambic tetrameter with iambic trimeter, as in the following example:

> About the dead hour o' the night
> She heard the bridles ring;
> And Janet was as glad at that
> As any earthly thing.

Write four stanzas (you'll need sixteen lines instead of the fifteen in your original version).

Terza Rima. This is a three-line stanza that rhymes *aba bcb cdc* and so forth, the enclosed sound of each stanza becoming the enveloping sound of the next. (See Annie Finch's "Thanksgiving" on pp. 124–125.) Write five stanzas, and stretch the lines out to iambic pentameter. Compare these two variations with each other and with your original.

Shakespearean Sonnet. This is an English form rhyming *abab cdcd efef gg*. Take notes on the different effects the different forms create, as well as the problems each form creates for you.

Blank Verse. Write twelve lines of unrhymed iambic pentameter. This time the poem should be **stichic** (continuous) rather than divided into sections. How difficult is it to get rid of the rhymes?

4. More Unscrambling

Here is a scrambled free verse poem by Roland Flint. See if you can recover the original. To make things difficult, we have changed some of the punctuation and capitalization. When you have taken your best shot at this, compare your version with those of your classmates before looking at the original (found at the end of this chapter).

Too young to be dying this way,
he checks his meters, checks his flaps,
and I am drifting back to North Dakota
and airplanes.

With the white silk scarf of his sleeve
he pulls back the stick,
steers a laborious, self-propelled combine,
where butterflies are all gone brown with wheat dust.
It is hot today, dry enough for cutting grain.
and hurtles into the sun.

Engines roaring,
red-faced, sweating, chafed,
he shines and shines his goggles,
dreaming of cities, and blizzards—
And where some boy
screams contact at his dreamless father.

Hint: The original has four sections, the last consisting of a single line.

As well as developing skills and techniques through analysis and imitation of other poetry, to engage the reader, the poet exploits the power of what might be called natural forms—the letter, the notice, the memoir, the list, the recipe, the ritual, the description, and the entire toolbox of familiar shapes.

5. Memory Poem

Try a free verse "memory poem" of your own. Begin with some feeling, image, or event in the present that triggers a flashback to an earlier version of yourself. Perhaps you can fashion the poem around an action like swimming, running, dancing, or driving a car. Here is a memory poem by Hilary Tham. Compare this treatment of the speaker's father with the portrait in "Chinese Medicine" (Chapter 12).

Father

1

It was better than carnival day to see
you, the heroine in the opera, slender
in a gown of sequined silk, diamond
pins in your elaborate wig, your hands
arcing in grace-lineated gestures
as your voice stroked and stretched,
fish glistening upstream
against the roaring of cymbals.

Older, your waist thickened,
you played the hero, strode high
over invisible doorsills, rode unseen horses,
made invisible cities fall
with serpentine ripplings of flags while drums
pounded through my ears and my blood.
Later, you played the saxophone in the band.
I knew you could do anything.

2

My first memory is you, playing
with me and Sister who died.
You sloped a plywood board,
conjured Monte Carlo's Grand Prix
for our little lead cars.
You were commentator and sound effects
and we were squeals and admiration.

3

Those were rain days in our growing season,
and rare. You sowed and followed
the freedom of butterflies, abandoned us
for flights with beautiful women.
Returning for the harvest, you are surprised
there are blackbirds in your ricefield.

from *Paper Boats*

6. FORMULA POEMS

One kind of structure is the familiar formula, in which a cataloging or listing of directions and ingredients gives the material a focus, a limit, and—if some degree of parallel grammatical structure is used—a basic rhythm. Here is an old recipe for a cocktail called "Golf Links."

1/2 wineglass rye

1/2 wineglass sweet catawba

2 dashes lemon juice

1 teaspoon syrup

2 dashes orange bitters

1 dash angostura bitters

1 dash rum

rinse cocktail glass with Abricotine, strain into same, dash with Appolinaris and dress with fruit.

Allowing our imaginations to take over, we can alter the proportions, ingredients, and procedures in order to provide, let's say, recipes for hate, ambition, or love. How are you feeling right now? Can you devise a recipe for a drink that will reproduce that feeling? It might include a jigger of stars, a dumpster full of dandelions, a twist of madness, a pinch of turpentine, a teaspoon of powdered California. Get the idea?

Here is a student "recipe poem" that relates two kinds of pleasure:

Jazz Sundae

I love that sultry flavored trumpet
topped with rich, creamy, soothing sax.
Add a dash of drums, and a sprinkle of keyboard.
Then cool to taste.

And here are some other formula ideas: menus (how about one for a restaurant called Nuclear Café?); 15,000-mile service (on your heart, perhaps); a weather report; a state of the union address; a promissory note; being read your rights (*Mirandized*); a pledge of allegiance; prayer; an ad in the personals column; the box score of a baseball game.

A major kind of formula, related to the recipe, gives directions (to go somewhere, to fix something, to assess something). Of course, one kind of process can always be imaginatively transformed into another, gaining strength from the contrast between the familiar formula and the new material it holds. Working with an imaginary map, give directions (in a poem) for getting to forgiveness, ecstasy, indifference, the fountain of youth, inner space, hysteria, or the end of a poem.

Examine a process that you know very well: how a bill becomes a law, how to knit a sweater, how to pitch a curve ball, how to parallel park, how to build a kite, how to drive on ice. Now give someone else directions—allowing, of course, an imaginative transformation to take place. For example, turn building a kite into a love poem.

Another kind of formula poem involves playing with plot patterns or similar literary conventions. "French Movie," by Pat Shelley, is a response to this assignment: *set the scene; put a person or persons in it; bring in another person or element and make something happen.* Here's the poem:

Apricots are falling in the rain;
The new young prunes are growing whiskers;
Two old grandfathers, lost in ruminant thoughts,
Sit among the pails of geraniums
Eating the morning's squash blossoms.

When the old nurse comes out
And leans to pour them a cup of soup
One old grandfather pinches her tit.

from *Bogg* #56, 1986

Try a formula poem of your own based on the directions given in italics preceding the Shelley poem.

7. RITUAL POEMS

Ritual poems are closely related to formula poems but have more to do with behavior patterns outside those of language and literature. The job of a ritual poem is to discover or assess the feeling and meaning latent in such behavior. Because ritual implies order, structure, and a sense of inevitability, poems that deal with ritual have a ready-made attraction for the formalist poet. Here is a poem by Baron Wormser that says something about the impact of soap opera patterns on the patterns of our lives, and vice versa.

Soap Opera

If each witless age creates an image of itself,
Ours is of a woman crying for help
Amid a crowd of well-groomed friends.
She is hysterical, tormented, saddened, upset.
In a few minutes she will be better

And stay that way until she cries again.
It was nothing that made her cry.
Ralph had told Joan that Bill might die.
She looks at us through harsh light
That jumps off the linoleum and glass.

She is crying again and has locked the door.
She is not ugly or stupid or poor.
That's why she cries like this.
No one has told her what to do,
And she is forced to always look for clues,

To check the way adolescents dress and swear,
To listen to commentators
And remember the news.
She has opened the door.
Tom looks at her and smiles.

They kiss. It might be reconciliation
Or tenderness or thoughtless urge.
Adroit music surges over the throw rugs
And well-waxed tiles. We are convinced.
Happiness is the best of styles.

from *Good Trembling*

Write a ritual poem about a sporting event, a wedding, a holiday meal, a shopping trip. How do you get ready for work, for a test, for a date? What were Sunday mornings like when you were a child? Friday nights? Are there rituals at the restaurants or bars you go to? Employ some kind of formal repetition of sound, rhythm, phrase, or line that enhances the feeling of ritual, of routine, that you are describing.

Having trouble getting started? Here is a suggestion that we've adapted from Ross Talarico's book, *Creative Writing Exercises*. Divide a sheet of paper into two columns. Head one column "hunter" or "fisherman" or "soldier" and the other column "priest." Now, under each column make a list of five items connected with the person (occupation) named. Now add to the list three action verbs associated with each heading. These word lists are the raw materials for your poem. Try to interweave the words from each list ("stalking the Bible," "chalice of bait," "plaid flannel cassock") rather than allowing the poem to fall into two separate sections. The name of the poem? *Ritual.*

8. List Poems

Inventories and lists are useful ways to brainstorm for a poem and good journal exercises. More than that, however, many successful poems are little more than well-selected lists ordered and phrased for maximum effect. Lists are forms of analysis and classification; as such, they can help us come to terms with large subjects or issues without resorting to abstract language or generality. In Shakespeare's *The Tempest*, Prospero threatens to punish Caliban with this list of traumas:

For this, be sure, to-night thou shalt have cramps,
Side-stitches that shall pen thy breath up; urchins
Shall, for that vast of night that they may work,
All exercise on thee; thou shalt be pinched
As thick as honeycomb, each pinch more stinging
Than bees that made 'em.

Lists can be narrowly restricted: things in the pantry, in a bureau drawer, on a desk, in a supermarket, in a wallet or pocketbook. Many lists lead to poems that gain their strength not only from the selection but also from careful decisions about which arrangement of items is most telling. Often, successful poems are constructed out of lists that contain items at once literal and figurative, or that mix the two together. Examine Sue Standing's "A Woman Disappears Inside Her Own Life":

> There comes a time when she has to say goodbye
> to the cat, and stop watering the plants.
>
> She wants to be more than a curator
> of dissolving objects.
>
> The song her tongue keeps
> reaching for stays out of tune.
>
> The nautilus adds one chamber each moon,
> while she fills a room with rue.
>
> She leaves a clue
> inside the telephone book:
>
> underlines the names of friends
> who have already left town.
>
> She puts on all her necklaces—
> the clay beads from Peru,
>
> the feathers from New Mexico,
> the ostrich eggshells from Africa.
>
> She wears her lapis lazuli earrings
> and her aquamarine ring,
>
> the lightning bracelet
> and the tortoise shell combs.
>
> She tries to fix one emotion
> like a photograph of the room.
>
> Someone has stolen her maps,
> except one drawn in mauve
>
> on thin parchment.
> She will go there.

from *Deception Pass*

Walt Whitman, Allen Ginsberg, and Gerald Stern have created many fine poems using the list or inventory. Apply some of their techniques to a few list poems of your own. Don't always let logic rule in stringing items together; see where your imagination takes you. Put at least one of your poems in unrhymed, uneven couplets. Consider some of the following ideas: a basket full of gifts (wishes) for someone, an auction catalog for a hypochondriac's estate, items in a patrolman's memo pad, a time capsule for yourself to be opened twenty years from now, what Thomas Jefferson might bring back home if he visited a major city of today, a vegetable for each month of the year.

Anaphora is a device connected with formulas, rituals, and lists. It is the repetition of a word or words at the beginning of lines. Cornelius Eady takes it a bit further than usual, repeating whole lines and phrases. The effect is incantatory.

The Dance

When the world ends,
I will be in a red dress.
When the world ends,
I will be in a smoky bar
   on Friday night.
When the world ends,
I will be a thought-cloud.
When the world ends,
I will be steam in a tea kettle.
When the world ends,
I will be a sunbeam through
   a lead window,
And I will shake like the
   semis on the interstate,
And I will shake like the tree
   kissed by lightning,
And I will move; the earth will move
   too,
And I will move; the cities will move
   too,
And I will move; with the remains of
   my last paycheck in my pocket.
It will be Friday night
And I will be in a red dress,
My feet relieved of duty,
My body in free-fall,
Loose as a ballerina
   in zero gravity,
Equal at last with feathers
   and dust,
As the world faints and tumbles
   down the stairs,
The jukebox is overtaken at last,
And the cicadas, under the eaves,
   warm up their legs.

from *Victims of the Latest Dance Craze*

9. DRAMATIC POEMS/CHARACTER POEMS

In "The Dance," Eady is not the woman in the red dress. He has invented a character and spoken in her voice. This kind of poem, called a dramatic poem, comes in two major types. One is the **soliloquy**, in which a character speaks (or thinks out loud) to no one in particular. The other type, the **dramatic monologue**, imagines a full dramatic scene in which the occasion for the utterance is clear. In such poems, we can usually sense that a particular listener is intended, as in a play.

You are probably already familiar with works like Tennyson's "Ulysses" and Browning's "My Last Duchess." Eliot's "The Love Song of J. Alfred Prufrock" is a variation of that mode, an interior monologue in which Prufrock's character is revealed while the dramatic situation is subdued. Pretending to be someone else and speaking through that other person requires imaginative leaps and new considerations of language: just how would that character see the world, meditate, speak. Paul Zimmer has peopled book-length collections with a variety of fascinating characters. Here Eli speaks of Wanda, the central character of Zimmer's most engaging volume:

Eli and the Coal Strippers

At last I could not bear
The heavy memories of Wanda
And the farm. I sold out
To the bulldozers, let them
Slaughter woods, knock down
The old barn, topple great
Stones of the ancient people
And rip the top soil back
Till they had taken what
They wanted. They covered
It again as a dog would
With its turds.

        Now I taste
The blood of the farm in
My water. When wind blows
Hard I smell the agony
Of the land rising like
My memory of Wanda at
The windows of this house,
Looking at fields in early
August, foretelling the end
Of all we had begun.

from *With Wanda:*
Town and Country Poems

Through how he presents his vision of experience, Eli tells us about himself. That is, Zimmer invents Eli and knows him well enough to let Eli do the talking. Perhaps it is easiest to begin working in this mode by transporting yourself into the mind of someone you know or into that of an historical character. Can you imagine Marilyn Monroe's last phone call? Suppose George Bush had a chance to talk to George Washington; what would Bush say?

Employ the figure of speech called **personification** to give life—personalities and voices—to nonhuman entities. There is an old cliché about the tales that walls could tell if they had ears. Why not *become* that wall? Find speech for an overturned motorcycle, a perfume bottle, a hairpin. (Leave out the identifying label, and you will have a riddle.) In the following poem, Karl Shapiro gives voice to a cut flower.

A Cut Flower

I stand on slenderness all fresh and fair,
I feel root-firmness in the earth far down,
I catch in the wind and loose my scent for bees
That sack my throat for kisses and suck love.
What is the wind that brings thy body over?
Wind, I am beautiful and sick. I long
For rain that strikes and bites like cold and hurts.
Be angry, rain, for dew is kind to me
When I am cool from sleep and take my bath.

Who softens the sweet earth about my feet,
Touches my face so often and brings water?
Where does she go, taller than any sunflower
Over the grass like birds? Has she a root?
These are great animals that kneel to us,
Sent by the sun perhaps to help us grow.
I have seen death. The colors went away,
The petals grasped at nothing and curled tight.
Then the whole head fell off and left the sky.

She tended me and held me by my stalk.
Yesterday I was well, and then the gleam,
The thing sharper than frost cut me in half.
I fainted and was lifted high. I feel
Waist-deep in rain. My face is dry and drawn.
My beauty leaks into the glass like rain.
When first I opened to the sun I thought
My colors would be parched. Where are my bees?
Must I die now? Is this a part of life?

From *Collected Poems*

Effective dramatic monologues are dramatic because they are little scenes, usually with a specific listener. Set your persona in a situation that will force revelations. What will the pot have to say to the kettle? What will a woman who has changed her mind say to the man she was about to marry? What will an election loser have to say to his or her loyal supporters?

10. EPISTOLARY POEMS

Epistolary poems, that is, poems written in the form of letters, can be voiced through invented characters or, as in the opening passage from the following poem by Richard Hugo, they can be modes of expression for very personal material.

> My dearest Kathy: When I heard your tears and those of your
> mother over the phone from Moore, from the farm
> I've never seen and see again and again under the most
> uncaring of skies, I thought of this town I'm writing from,
> where we came lovers years ago to fish. How odd
> we seemed to them here, a lovely young girl and a fat
> middle 40's man they mistook for father and daughter
> before the sucker lights in their eyes flashed on. That was
> when we kissed their petty scorn to dust. Now, I eat alone
> in the cafe we ate in then, thinking of your demons, the sad
> days you've seen, the hospitals, doctors, the agonizing
> breakdowns that left you ashamed. . . .
>
> from *Selected Poems*

Now, how about trying an epistolary poem that

- reviews your qualifications for an imaginary job.
- describes the highlights of a trip you are taking.
- asks forgiveness from someone you've betrayed, insulted, or somehow brought suffering to.
- admits that you might have been wrong about something.
- admits your fondness for chocolate, Mickey Mouse, old clothes, sentimental greeting cards, liver, gossip columns.

11. TIME WARP POEMS

Have you ever wondered what would happen if a legendary or historical character was relocated to our own times? What if Benjamin Franklin found himself in Silicon Valley? What if Ulysses led his mariners to a modern American port, like Baltimore? What if the biblical Miriam found herself at a women's rights rally? While it may be tempting to see such an exercise as leading to humorous results, it can also lead to the sensitive probing of important, universal issues. Before reading Stephen Bluestone's "Isaac on the Altiplano," consider Bluestone's comments:

"Isaac on the Altiplano" is but one of countless retellings and elabo-rations of Genesis 22, the chapter that deals with the sacrifice of Isaac, also known as the "Aqedah" (or binding) in Hebrew. My version is a parallel one that sets father and son in the Andes and makes them Aymara Indians. This Isaac is even more zealous than his father; in this retelling Isaac knows he is to be sacrificed, is impatient for it to happen, and leads the old man to the high place "where air is as thin/as a knife blade and breath is locked in stone." Isaac hates the life down below, the life of oppression and poverty, in which his people live in villages with "bent backs/against the stiff sides of impossible peaks." This Isaac (whose name means "he who laughs" in Hebrew) can only find happi-ness in leaving the intolerable life of his people behind to seek a death blessed by the gods. And so, the Isaac in this poem loves the gods more than he loves his father, more than he loves the brief moments of joy celebrated by the holiday dancers and musicians, the women clapping hands, the villagers drinking chicha far below. Is this Isaac an idealist? A realist? Does he understand more than his father does about the future of his people? Are the Aymara gods necessarily gods of mercy? Was the sacrifice in this instance Isaac's own idea of what the gods demand? Obviously this character is wholly invented, but his origin is in Genesis 22, which is a blueprint for one of the most profound explorations in all of religious literature of the relation between God and man and father and son.

Here is the poem:

Isaac on the Altiplano

Say there are high *cordilleras* sharp as glass
against a black sky, a country of lost cities
with the ghosts of children playing on the slopes
of the shining day, places where air is as thin
as a knife blade and breath is locked in stone.

Down below, it is holiday time, with dancers
in flower hats and shawls, women clapping hands,
and men playing flutes; there is *chicha*, too,
the smack of it, along with the graceful prows
of bundle-reed boats on the waters of the Great Lake.

Isaac waits, having come ahead of his father,
impatient to hear the sound of the wind.
Isaac hates the damp cellar of the Andes,
the cobbled keep of the mines; like his father,
he hates the *Aymara* villages, with their bent backs
against the stiff sided of impossible peaks . . .

And now the sky is near enough to touch;
he turns to watch the old man struggle up behind him

much too slowly, a bird entering darkness
too heavy for wings or the lift of song.

"Here I am," he says to his stiff-legged father,
a pale and brittle figure gasping for breath.

> *Isaac kneels to be blessed; he laughs*
> *while the gods, like butterflies, converge on the spot,*
> *their yellow wings beating like slow hearts,*
> *their empty veins drinking his love.*

from The Laughing Monkeys of Gravity

12. SYNESTHETIC POEMS

Synesthesia is the mixing of senses, or the describing of one sense in terms of
another. It is a natural phenomenon of thought and language to experience one
sense in terms of another. For example, a friend's tie can be called *loud*, a musical performance can be *hot*, a smile can be *sweet*. May Swenson uses this technique in "The Blindman."

The blindman placed
a tulip on his tongue for purple's taste.
Cheek to grass, his green

was rough excitement's sheen
of little whips.
In water to his lips

he named the sea blue and white,
the basin of his tears and fallen beads of sight.
He said: This scarf is red;

I feel the vectors to its thread
that dance down from the sun. I know
the seven fragrances of the rainbow.

I have caressed
the orange hair of flames. Pressed
to my ear,

a pomegranate lets me hear
crimson's flute.
Trumpets tell me yellow. Only ebony is mute.

from New & Selected.: Things Taking Place

Swenson uses synesthesia to paint with hearing, taste, touch, smell. Write a
poem in which you describe the tastes of music, the feel of colors, the sound of
fragrances, or the smell of touch (or some combination of these blendings).
Refer to "Jazz Sundae" on page 149. Which senses are being mixed there?

13. PICTURE POEMS

Use a painting, sculpture, or photograph that you admire as the inspiration for a poem. Try to capture in language the energy, technique, and vision of life that the artwork has to offer. Here is a famous poem of this type by William Carlos Williams. What relationships can you discover between the way poetry works and the way the visual arts work? How about poetry and music?

The Dance

In Breughel's great picture, The Kermess,
the dancers go round, they go round and
around, the squeal and the blare and the
tweedle of bagpipes, a bugle and fiddles
tipping their bellies (round as the thick-
sided glasses whose wash they impound)
their hips and their bellies off balance
to turn them. Kicking and rolling about
the Fair Grounds, swinging their butts, those
shanks must be sound to bear up under such
rollicking measures, prance as they dance
in Breughel's great picture, The Kermess.

from *Collected Later Poems*

14. MUSIC POEMS

Choose a piece of instrumental music that has affected you deeply. Play it over a number of times, paying special attention to its rhythms and emotional colorings. Now try to render those same rhythms and emotions in a poem. Don't write *about* the piece of music, "translate" it into poetry.

15. FOUND POEMS

When nothing else works, pushing someone else's language around can be fun. It can be revealing too. Here are some things to do:

1. Look for ready-made poetry in your everyday reading (such as the *Beaufort Scale* reproduced in Chapter 5). Bulletin boards are good places to look. After you have selected a few of these found poems and copied them into your journal, take some notes on what qualities of expression make them seem poetic. Some possibilities: advertising copy, operating manuals for various products, weekly school lunch menus in local newspapers, announcements for auctions, correction notices (apologies) for

errors in the daily paper. Pay special attention to material that is highly patterned. The language of bridge and astrology columns is, in some ways, remarkably poetic. Share your discoveries in class.

2. Cut and paste! Take a column from a newspaper or magazine and cut it in half or in thirds lengthwise. Now rearrange the strips of type and look for vivid passages. Slide the strips up and down until effective word combinations appear. Now use them. Line up half-columns from different articles or news stories and see what happens.

3. Sculpt! Photocopy a solid page of print from a book, newspaper, or magazine. Now, working with masking tape or correction fluid (white-out), cover over (discard) the least interesting stretches of language, letting the more evocative words and phrases reveal themselves. Can you get a poem to emerge by chiseling away the unnecessary words?

4. X-ray! If sculpting is too messy for you, use a yellow highlighting marker to display the words and phrases you find most striking. Now try linking together what you have found into a poem.

These exercises, along with the ones presented in Chapter 6, should give you some feeling for the wide range of techniques, tools, and approaches to writing poetry. However, unless you have been especially fortunate, you are not yet likely to have produced anything of major consequence. Beginners have to begin. It is now time to write from your own need, your own imagination, and your own sense of what will be significant for yourself and for your readers.

Warning: Don't let the shape of the illustrative poems we have provided or the expected shape of finished drafts inhibit the process by which you explore. Poems can grow in many ways, not necessarily from beginning to end. If you work with a word processor, try the following.

EXERCISE

1. Enter a tentative concluding line for a poem so that it appears at the top of the screen. Now compose a line that will precede the line already written, entering it above the line written first so that that line is pushed down. Add lines in this fashion until the first line you wrote has reached the bottom of the screen.

2. Write a line to get started and then compose by alternating additions both above and below the original line.

In the next chapter we will review some of the problems you are likely to encounter on your way to mastering this demanding genre.

The Poem Queen

SUSAN ASTOR

The Poem Queen writes a poem a day,
In her spare time pauses to pray
It will be read.

She has a soldier and a drone
To please her when she is alone
Or in her bed.

Some say hers is a magic throne
That she eats custard made of bone
And blossom bread.

She has more power than they know,
Has found a way to burn the snow;
Turns gold to lead.

Her pen is her divining rod;
She uses it to handle God,
And tame the dead.

from *Dame*

August from My Desk

ROLAND FLINT

It is hot today, dry enough for cutting grain,
And I am drifting back to North Dakota
Where butterflies are all gone brown with wheat dust.

And where some boy,
Red-faced, sweating, chafed,
Too young to be dying this way,
Steers a laborious, self-propelled combine,
Dreaming of cities, and blizzards—
And airplanes.

With the white silk scarf of his sleeve
He shines and shines his goggles,
He checks his meters, checks his flaps,
Screams contact at his dreamless father,
He pulls back the stick,
Engines roaring,

And hurtles into the sun.

from *Resuming Green*

8

❧

Poetry Problems

As we have said before and will say again, all good writing is finally the result of editing and revising. Rarely do we put down in first draft what will be a finished work. This is certainly true in poetry. Even poems that we want to believe are ready to go soon after we have drafted them usually benefit from second thoughts. We need to look at the poem again, honestly, and with a rigorous editorial eye. Often, having solved the technical problems in a poem, we are ready to congratulate ourselves prematurely. Here are some common problems in the poems of beginning writers (and some experienced ones, too).

ARCHAIC DICTION

Some of the more obvious archaic words and phrases in the following poem have been set in italics. The problem with language that is so remote from common usage is that it sounds insincere. Paradoxically, the writer probably chose it because it sounded "poetic"; nonetheless, it is hard to take these formulations seriously. Though this student's technical skill is apparent, that skill is being undermined by bad habits of diction.

The Thief

The warm, the fevered pillows pushed aside,
I lay *amidst* the ever-present Night
While his sweet handmaid, his euphoric bride
Beamed through glazed panels with a *pallid* light.
Mid hoary trees her shadows could be seen
In contrast to that phosphorescent sheen.
I sighed, unshackled from my *torpid shrouds,*
And sleep's last fetters from the covers fell
Away. As I peered out, a sable cloud
Swirled *round* the *orb*—as if its soul to quell.
Who else but Luna would steal *o'er* my sill
While I, bedazzled, could no more lay still?

Diction like this is often accompanied by the old-fashioned poetic contractions—
"o'er," in this case—and by a tendency to disguise experience rather than reveal
it. "Glazed panels" are only windows: why not say so? Writing like this tends
to become formulaic; it expresses kinds of actions or emotions rather than
particular ones.

Can you find other diction problems in this poem? What revisions (substitutions) do you suggest? Can any of the poem be salvaged, or should the poet
begin again? Do you spot any problems in word order? Can you solve them?

THE ANONYMOUS VOICE

Characteristic of much greeting card verse—and of much unsuccessful poetry—is
the anonymous voice. The following poem by James J. Dorbin is an example of the
kind of writing that sounds as if it could be by almost anyone and is therefore
unconvincing. Along with problems in mastering the stanza form, this poem suffers
from the hackneyed figures of speech, the absence of particulars, the yearning after
vastness, and the overt **sentimentality** that add up to a typical beginner's effort.

Dreams

In a world of fantasy
dreams, like nets, were thrown
from a vessel hopelessly
adrift and all alone.

To cast a net and catch a dream
is no simple task.
Of any man it might seem
impossible to ask.

My dreams have come up empty,
Worthless, tangled, torn.

> —A rend too harsh for charity
> —A wound that must be borne.
>
> How long have I been dreaming?
> The ship sails out of sight.
> Sand's slipped through the opening.
> I've dreamed away the night.

A poem like this cannot be improved merely by local substitutions—nor should it be thrown away. The poet needs to begin again with honest materials. What, really, constitutes the kind of dream vaguely alluded to here? What is a convincing comparison? A fresh, evocative approach is required, one in which the poet leaves behind the world of decoration and soft disguises. In too many poems, the attention to form is not only a superficial attention but also one that limits the novice poet's focus. Overwhelmed by making the container, the poet has no energy left for other concerns.

The following poem is true greeting card verse. It is completely anonymous and offers a generalized sentiment without one concrete image. Unless you are writing for the card market, avoid using language in this way.

> *Giving*
>
> I give to you a part of me
> I give to you my heart
> I'll try to ask for nothing more
> Than friends that never part
> I'll give to you all my life
> I give because I care
> I give because a friend like you
> Is found so very rare.

Because this verse can be sent by anyone to anyone, whoever receives it will not feel special.

APPALLING ABSTRACTION

"Appalling abstraction" is in some ways like greeting card verse, but usually more urgent. However, the urgency is never convincing because the language makes no impact, no connection with felt experience. Intellectually clear, the formulations that follow do not begin to take on the concern for language that is poetry's province.

> If nurtured,
> The fantasy thrives.
> If neglected,
> The untested dream dies,

The imagination atrophies,
The soul perishes.

It's the same with us.
Barren years
Interlaced with frenzied passion,
Have sterilized our union,
Distorted our dreams,
Crushed our raison d'etre . . .

The writer here is working from an inner pain, but none of it comes through.

UNINTENTIONAL HUMOR

Novice poets are sometimes not aware of the ways in which diction can misfire, especially cliché-ridden words and phrases. In an attempt to give concrete force to an emotion, the writer of the following poem uses diction that is found—and belongs—in horror films and comic books.

Inside Out

I feel violence within,
churning.
A knife sits sharp and ready,
burning.
Deep red, warm gushing and
gurgling.
The brook of life silently
running,
Over sharp rocks, soft moss
glowing
To the cold ocean of death,
ending.

Because we associate a phrase like "gushing and gurgling" with literary modes that we don't take seriously, we are kept from taking this poem seriously. Miscalculations like these come in part from inexperience, in part from laziness—letting ready-made expressions find their way into poems. Ready-made language rarely convinces us that it expresses genuine experience.

JARRING DICTION

The result of not paying enough attention to connotation and to words in context can be diction that is jarring. The next poem, cast in free verse, mixes diction in unattractive ways.

Land Lord Dharma

I kneel
head erect
shoulders straight
hands on thighs
the warrior's posture

he enters
in long white silk robes
he looks so elegant—
from the warrior's shrine
he hands me implements
for my new quarters

first a flashing sword
with a slightly curved tip
to cut neurosis
and allow gentleness

then comes the black pen
with a rolled white scroll
tied with a ribbon . . .

The words "implements" and "neurosis" are in conflict with the poem's general diction. Additionally, "quarters" may be a questionable choice. The gains are obvious when we substitute "blessings" for "implements" and "masks" for "neurosis." Now "cut" seems off, if it wasn't clearly so before. What would be a better verb here? What substitute can you find for "quarters"?

FOR THE SAKE OF RHYME

Solving the puzzle of an intricate rhyme scheme is so exhilarating that you can become lost in a single dimension of a poem. The poet who wrote "Departure" conjured up the "braided ballad" form that rhymes *abcb/cede/dfgf* and so forth.

Departure

The smell of guava blossoms
appears to fill the air
and in the wind are waving
the palm leaves . . . and your hair.

I sit on the porch, craving   5
those kisses that you give
and think that these are times
in which it's good to live.

But in the end our crimes   10
seem to catch up with us,

and I must take a trip
with a distant terminus.

I board the hated ship
as you wave from the sand
and dream I cup your bosom   15
and feel it on my hand.

Among the problems lurking in this draft are the following:

1. Line 2 lacks poetic density; that is, the only function of most of the language is to get in enough syllables ahead of the rhyme word.
2. Unnatural (unidiomatic) word order undermines lines 7 and 8. More natural alternatives would be "and think that these are good times to live in" or "and think that it's good to live in these times." The poet has solved the problem of rhyme, but created a new one.
3. Inappropriate diction. The use of "terminus" in line 12 creates a clever rhyme but ruptures the poem's simple diction and earnest tone. It seems far-fetched, and it is.

There are a few other instances of these and related problems in the poem. Can you find them? What kinds of revision would you suggest? Should the poet stay with this demanding form, or should he abandon it?

Rose MacMurray's poem that follows is a more successful handling of the same form. Compare the two efforts (trimeter quatrains) before attempting your own.

Teen Mall-Rats Die in Suicide Pact

After the Mall closed down
they came and built a nest.
Monoxide was a high
and they could charge the rest.

No sweat to say goodbye,
monoxide was a gas.
The mall rats, curled in death,
have solved their maze at last.

We lay a discount wreath.
May their eternity
be one long shopping mall,
one Gold Card spending spree

and may their parents all
sign up for every course
in "Interfacing Grief"
and "Creative Remorse."

The Clash of Poetic Elements

This is a broad category, covering scores of discordant permutations of image, mood, sense, rhythm, sound, and other poetic ingredients. In the following example, the picture being painted and the meter used to reveal it are at odds with one another:

> They glide like spirits by the water
> Open to the tepid twilight
> Bearing alabaster candles:
> Rush-like figures clad in white.
> Thin and spectral, like the Shee-folk
> With their dripping, glowing wands . . .

This poet, who has such marvelous control over sound, meter, and language, does not coordinate the elements especially well. Whatever can "glide like spirits" will not move in this insistent, choppy rhythm. The pushy trochaic beat conflicts with anyone's notion of ethereality. A simple lengthening of the lines would help, but getting rid of those initial stressed syllables is mandatory. Things can't glide and march at the same time.

Writing Past the Poem

Sometimes poets are unable to throw away what they have put down on paper. They are more willing to revise than to delete. In Karen Malloy's "Bagged Air," the poet's inventiveness goes beyond the poem's need:

> The signs say no balloons.
>
> You are just another visitor,
> Hunted, fearful of the telltale coughs,
> the dripping of mysterious liquids suspended
> in bags,
> and harried eyes
> of people in white.
>
> Frailty, mortality, futility,
> the cheap pictures on the wall say it,
> so do the eyes from the beds,
> watching you pass.
> You walk on, holding roses for a shield
> against these exposed truths.
> Brown has begun to claim the healthy pink domain
> of a petal.
>
> Among carefree balloons, even the best
> leak gaseous blood,
> and submit

to the most basic laws of nature,
pulling them earthward.
That admonishing sign is humane—
stopping those who would give a doomed
bag of air
as a gift of cheer
here.

How can the last stanza be pruned? What is essential to conclude the poem?
Most of the poem *shows*, whereas the last stanza is dominated by *telling*. Can the
"message" of the conclusion be derived from a minor revision of the main part
of the poem, eliminating the need for the last stanza?

TREASURE BURYING

Burying treasure in an otherwise unsuccessful poem is the unfortunate practice
of overwriters. In the following piece, Alice S. James employs predictable
rhymes and overuses repetition. Moreover, she breaks the logic of her own
figurative expressions. Still, one extremely vivid and evocative stanza sings out.
We have set it in italics.

Desert Rain Poem

I am the desert
Dry and desolate
Shimmering in the sun
You were rain
And I watched the rain
Coming down
Against my sun-drenched pain

I am the African steppe
Dying into desert
The wind tosses over me
A blanket of sand

Shrouding once verdant trees,
Big dry holes—once lakes
Maybe small seas
Into oblivion

Some fountain of sorrow
Fountain of life
An ancient aching love
Brings on the spring rain
Just to pass my way again

Only searing sun-drenched
Pain, reigns
Raining down on me

I am the desert at night
Cold dark sand
Blows against my stark
Countenance
When I love, I rain
My rains to come
As long as the love
Keeps coming
So will the rains

Our suggestion to this writer is to start over again, rebuilding the poem from the third stanza, which could be an effective beginning. Three additional four-line stanzas, if they are equally compact and focused, should do to complete the idea of the earlier draft.

SAYING TOO MUCH

Even sophisticated writers can overwrite by saying too much. The following draft is slightly heavy-handed, though it is clearly the work of a careful and skillful writer.

January Thunder

As the heavy presence nears
bare branches falter and twist.
At the first crash of the axe
pines flail and lash,
stoop to the snow.

At the iron boom of the hammer
gusts of summer flare at the window,
ice pellets surge up.
Snow flooded by lightning,
blazes white beyond white.

In a workshop session the author agreed that the poem would be strengthened by the elimination of "heavy" and "blazes." Why do you think that the poet agreed? Do you see other possibilities for paring back so that less does more?

THE FALSE START

It should be obvious to a practiced writer that we often find our subject and warm up our language engines only after we have been writing for a while. In composition classes, students are warned about introductions that no longer work when the act of writing has taken the writer in unexpected directions. This type of false start happens in poems too.

Here is an early draft of a poem by Elizabeth Bennett.

A Small Explosion

Is it a coincidence
This forty years later
soft knock at the door?
the young girl, Makiko
with her father, Yasuo
their car broken down.
I pronounce her name wrong.
Her father explains
it means little jewel.

She looks at me
little jewel, eyes clear
as a freshwater pool
where fish still swim, hair
paint brush straight.
In the kitchen
she takes off her coat
Her T shirt says
Washington A Capitol City.

While her father phones
she plays with my infant son's
Steiff bear, fondles
its stiff fur.
When the baby cries
she makes a face
She pulls her long arms
inside her shirt.
See, I have no arms
she says to make him laugh.

This was not a first draft, nor is it the final one. In the published version, a number of changes have been made. Notice how the poem gets off to a quicker start by beginning with what had been the third line. Locate and discuss the other changes.

Small Explosion August 6th, 1985

A knock at the door,
the young girl, Makiko
with her father, Yasuo
their car broken down.
I pronounce her name wrong.
Her father explains
it means little jewel.

She looks at me,

        little jewel,

eyes clear as a freshwater pool
where fish still swim,
hair paint brush straight.
Her T shirt says,
                          Washington A Capitol City

While her father phones
she plays with my infant son's Steiff bear,
fondles its stiff fur.
When he cries she makes a face,
pulls her arms inside her shirt,
See I have no arms, she says
to make him laugh.

It is forty years later.

                              from *Poet Lore*, Fall 1986

PUNCH-LINE ENDINGS

Although they can be successful, too often punch-line endings reach for too much or too little. Poets can be tempted to rescue weak or trivial poems by clever resolutions. The next poem leans too heavily on its pressured close, a close that isn't strong enough to take the weight.

Lifeguards

Gopher holes blemished our back-
yard like acne
when the swimming hole
was dry
and it was too hot for kickball
Henry and I
took the hose
and filled them up
to the brim
We waited for gophers
to surface gasping
Patient hours
we sat on our shadows
but never saw
one

Back then
we didn't know
of escape tunnels.

The idea of bringing in a new perspective that answers a question is a good one, but the execution falls flat. The shift seems too self-conscious, and, once again, the decision to "tell" rather than "show" is part of the problem.

INEFFECTIVE LINE BREAK

It is often hard to detect an unsatisfactory line break without the frequent testing of alternatives. It is easy to cure such diseases as ending on function words (articles, prepositions, conjunctions) for no good reason, calling too much attention to words whose only job is to link more important words together. Most often, line-break problems result in obscuring key images and relationships between images and ideas. Examine the following passage:

> I hold a desperate starfish before I toss him back
> matched with my hand, our common five-shape
> a reminder of where we begin.

Here the writer wants us to observe the relationship between the human hand and the starfish, but both words are lost in the middle of lines. One solution would be to reconstruct these lines:

> Before I toss him back, I hold a desperate starfish,
> our common five-shape, matched with my hand—
> a reminder of where we begin.

There is some strategic improvement in placing the "before" clause in front of the rest. However, "our common five-shape" now has less emphasis, and its proper place in the movement from specific to general has been lost. Stronger yet is this shaping:

> Before I toss him back,
> I hold a desperate starfish,
> matched with my hand—
> this, our common five-shape,
> reminder of where we begin.

The language still needs some smoothing, but at least the key words/images— "starfish," "hand," and "five-shape"—are properly emphasized and clearly related to one another. Line break has controlled the emerging picture and idea.

OUT OF ORDER

Lines or sections that are not in the proper order can cause a poem to lack cohesiveness and focus. Linda Replogle's untitled poem is fairly effective as it stands, but it could be argued that the transposition of stanzas 2 and 3 would make an even stronger poem.

> The old man sits
> at the white kitchen table,
> his eyes big
> behind thick glasses.

Behind him, his wife
in a large apron
fries fish
at the kitchen stove.

He looks out, away,
into the garden.
Rain separates him
from the green hydrangea.

He puts the magnifying glass
down on the newspaper
and lifts the cup
hot from tea
with his fragile hands.

What are the losses and gains in the suggested rearrangement? What other arrangements are possible?

DERIVATIVE DRIVEL

Many beginning poets get lost in the worst habits of a poet whom they consciously or unconsciously imitate. Usually they capture only the most obvious surface features of a style or technique. The resulting poems are simply clumsy posturings: piles of mannerisms. Of course, the worse the model, the worse the imitation is likely to be. Here is an example of a poet striving for poetic density. The cop-out is at the end.

Red rock in the brain
and the proud darkness settles like a sifted house
deep in the synapse of ultimate mind.
Do you know what I mean?

And here is imitation beat generation sprawl:

I wandered in the big, empty, people-filled city
an ant in Miami Beach where I saw
dopers, fat landladies, displaced californians, cops
in Porsches right out of tv . . . and scrawled walls of
sneering, scarred, fearing, raging . . .
pimps and smarmy politicians, supermarket grandmas,
and I wanted to kick and smash and trash them all!

These are only a sampling of the many problems that both beginners and experienced poets encounter. We could fill a book with additional instances such as predictable rhyme, lack of unity caused by two poems being pressed into one, and stumbling rhythms. While writing poetry requires more than technical skill, without that skill no amount of vision or largeness of soul will be turned into a living poem.

We began this unit on poetry by talking about the line—the most obvious signal that we may be in the presence of a poem. It should be clear by now, however, that the mere ragged right-hand margin does not a poem make. To borrow the prestige of poetry by presenting pedantry, political argument, exhortation, or preaching in "poetic" lines—without *attending to craft* in the ways we have explored—is more likely to fool you than your reader.

> We have to shed ourselves of these snake
> politicians who crawl around each year
> and cover up all graft they take . . .
> Impeach those who dip into and make
> our pockets empty and dishonor this greatest land of all
> where men and women should stand tall!

The less said about this stuff, the better.

REVISION: A BRIEF CASE STUDY

By examining the material presented here, you will be able to follow the development of a short poem from its initial draft to its final form. Because this poem was short, and because the poet had worked with related material for a long time, the journey from inception to completion was relatively brief. Here is the first draft, actually eight lines of notes toward a poem that had the good luck of getting off on the right foot.

> (1)　His hands are fish that dart
> 　　　Htoward the center of ripples
> 　　　at the surface of his name,
> 　　　his neck a knotted trunk
> 　　　that shoots from a mulch of collar.
> 　　　Pull on the tie
> 　　　and his eyes will dance
> 　　　like paired skaters

To the right of the typescript, the poet later wrote some additional material:

> His heart is pumping coffee,
> he is counting out bus fare
> in ~~the dark~~ his pocket's dark.
> He hears the garbage truck's approach

> He is late with everything
> He is going to work

The next draft works at consolidating all this material:

> (2) His hands are fish that dart
> to the center of ripples
> at the surface of his name,
> his heart is pumping coffee,   /arteries surge with
> his neck/a knotted trunk   /is
> that shoots from a mulch of collar.
> He hears the garbage truck's approach,
> he counts out busfare in his pocket's dark,
> he pulls on his tie
> and his eyes dance like paired skaters
> gliding through red creases of ~~light~~ dawn.
> Today, he is going to be on time.

While the consolidation was in process, additional changes were introduced, the most important being the alternative phrasing for line 4. This and the earlier revision of "in the dark" to "in his pocket's dark" are the most significant so far. The next run through produced this:

> (3) His hands are fish that dart
> to the center of ripples
> at the surface of his name;
> his neck is a knotted trunk
> that shoots from a mulch of collar;
> his arteries surge with coffee.
> He hears the garbage truck's ~~approach~~ moan.
> and counts out busfare in his pocket's dark.
> He pulls on his tie
> and his eyes dance like paired skaters
> gliding through red creases of dawn.
> Today, he is going to be on time.

Notice that the revised fourth line of draft 2 has been moved down, anchoring a series of clauses that now move more logically through this segment of the morning. Moreover, by making each clause a line shorter than the one before it, the writer has echoed the focusing of awareness that is conveyed in the series of images: the disoriented initial coming awake, the body stiffness as he finished getting dressed, the boost of the caffeine. All along the way, the poem's rhythms have been improved.

In the next draft, the poem receives its title:

Meeting the Day

(4)　His hands are fish that dart
　　　to the center of ripples
　　　at the surface of his name;
　　　his neck is a knotted trunk
　　　that shoots from a mulch of collar;
　　　his arteries surge with coffee.
　　　He moves to the garbage truck's moan
　　　and counts out busfare in his pocket's dark.
　　　Today, he is going to be on time.
　　　He pulls on his tie
　　　and his eyes veer like paired skaters
　　　~~gliding through~~ that dance through
　　　the red creases of dawn.

　　Notable here is the decision to shift what had been the concluding line in previous versions, letting that intention—to be on time—serve as a bridge between the man's preliminary struggles and his final action of adjusting his tie—a sign of determination—and the visionary resolving image.

　　Looking back to the poet's initial jottings, we can see that his first idea was to present the man as a kind of marionette whose eyes would move if someone pulled on his tie. This possibility has not entirely disappeared from the succeeding versions, though it is no longer the main thrust of the image. The poet is still struggling with the complex "eyes . . . skaters . . . creases" business. In the final (published) version, the conclusion is less cluttered: the simile formula is dropped and one action verb controls the passage. Additionally, the close is visually reinforced by the lengthening lines.

Meeting the Day

His hands are fish that dart
to the center of ripples
at the surface of his name;
his neck is a knotted trunk
that shoots from a mulch of collar;
his arteries surge with coffee.
He moves to the garbage truck's moan
and counts out busfare in his pocket's dark.
Today, he is going to be on time.
He pulls on his tie
and his eyes become paired skaters
that veer through the red creases of dawn.

from Philip K. Jason's *Near the Fire*

9

❧

The Elements of Fiction

While this and the next chapter are constructed primarily to engage the writer of prose fiction, many of the principles we present here regarding structure, narration, character, and other storytelling elements apply to poetry and nonfiction as well. We do not revisit this ground in Chapter 11, *Creative Nonfiction*.

THE NATURE OF FICTION

Like all narrative, prose fiction contains the *history* of one or more characters or something that acts like a character (a talking dog, yellow Rolls-Royce, or computer). The writer shapes that *history* with the same tools one would use in literal *history*—except that "people" become *characters*, "talk" becomes dialogue, "reporting" becomes *narration*, and "places" become *settings*. The stories contain descriptions of where and how the characters live, what they do, and what they say, believe, or think:

> There was once upon a time a Fisherman who lived with his wife in a miserable hovel close by the sea, and every day he went out fishing. And once as he was sitting with his rod, looking at the clear water, his line suddenly went down, far down below and when he drew it up again, he brought out a large Flounder. Then the Flounder said to him, "Hark,

you Fisherman, I pray you, let me live, I am no Flounder really, but an enchanted prince. What good will it do you to kill me? I should not be good to eat, put me in the water again, and let me go."

"Come," said the Fisherman, "there is no need for so many words about it—a fish that can talk I should certainly let go, anyhow." With that he put him back again into the clear water. . . . Then the Fisherman got up and went to his wife in the hovel.

"Husband," said the woman, "have you caught nothing today?"

"No," said the man, "I did catch a Flounder, who said he was an enchanted prince, so I let him go again."

"Did you not wish for anything first?" said the woman.

"No," said the man, "what should I wish for?"

"Ah," said the woman, "it is surely hard to have to live always in this dirty hovel; you might have wished for a small cottage for us. Go back and call him. Tell him we want to have a small cottage, he will certainly give us that."

from Jakob and Wilhelm Grimm, "The Fisherman and His Wife"

Notice that the Grimms' story has the following elements:

- *time*—a "once upon a time" that is vague but efficient
- *setting*—a hovel by the sea (a place related to the action) in a fairyland with real poverty
- *characters*—the fisherman, wife, and Flounder-prince
- *reported actions*—catching Flounder and throwing prince back
- *dialogue*—revealing the Fisherman's easily satisfied nature and the wife's materialism

Even Charles Dickens's *Great Expectations,* Virginia Woolf's *To the Lighthouse,* J. D. Salinger's *Catcher in the Rye* and Rowling's Harry Potter series are made up of these elements. Whether you wish to write traditionally or experimentally, there is no way around gaining a mastery of them.

Of course, the story of your character in fiction will be different from a literal biography. One of the major differences is that in fiction it is legitimate to choose the events and make them come out as you like. In your story, fish can be turned into princes who make wishes come true. To put the matter another way, in fiction you can travel anywhere you want so long as you can convince your reader to take the trip with you.

Your story may grow from actual or imagined experience(s), character(s), image(s), or concept(s). No matter what generates your story line, you will have to create a **plot line** to carry it. As you can guess, we are not using "story" and "plot" interchangeably as we do in everyday speech. Here "story" is the name we give to imagined lives presented chronologically—an imitation of how we present events in a chronicle, biography, or history. Story, in that sense, is A to Z.

"Plot," on the other hand, is the name for the shape we give to the story materials by selection, arrangement, and emphasis. **Plot** involves (1) *what* of the story is told and shown, and (2) *when* each unit of showing and telling is presented to the reader.

In this chapter we present an overview of the elements of fiction, stopping for short examples and a number of exercises along the way. Some of the discussion refers to the stories in Chapter 12. You might want to read them before going on and then again as they are brought into discussion. Between the overview and the stories is a chapter on student problems in fiction.

PLOT AND WHAT IT DOES

Though the writing process itself can begin anywhere, we are beginning the discussion of fiction with plot because plot is the vehicle that carries all the other elements. Like a sentence and love, you should know a plot when you see one—though you may be deceived.

Here are several dictionary definitions for "plot":

1. a secret plan or scheme
2. the plan, scheme, or main story of a play, novel, poem, or short story
3. in *artillery*, a point or points located on a map or chart
4. in *navigation*, to mark on a plan, map, or chart, as the course of a ship or aircraft

Beginning writers often take the first definition as the significant one and so think their task as writers is to hide what is going on from the reader until they spring their surprise. The second definition, while accurate, is about as useful as saying that your plot should have a beginning, middle, and end. A rope needs the same thing. (The real problem for a writer is *how* to make particular beginnings, middles, and ends.)

Strangely enough, the third definition is a bit more to the point; in a way, the plot is the direction in which you have aimed the reader. The fourth definition is the most appropriate of all for writers. Sailors plot a course to get from here to there as safely and efficiently as possible considering their purposes and what is in the way. What the plot does is to organize the voyage.

For your reader, the plot may appear to be the equivalent of the story, the sum of all the events that "happen." Even a writer might try to report the chronological story line if asked "what is it all about?"

"It's the story of this man and woman who are caught in a cave-in. She doesn't like him and, at first, they fight all the time. Then, when they think they are going to die, they fall in love. Then they feel this breeze and then start to—"

The potential reader breaks in:

"Wait a minute. How did they get into the cave in the first place? Why doesn't she like him? How come they didn't feel the breeze right off?"

And when the answers to these questions cause more questions, the writer most likely will say, "Look. You'd better read it." The reason the writer can't satisfactorily tell you the plot by giving the chronological events is the same reason a chocolate chip cookie can't be experienced by having you taste butter, chips, flour, sugar, and vanilla. Because the story is mixed and baked in the plot, it is an error to think that a mere sequence of events is what the work is about.

This common error is understandable, however, because the actions the characters perform are usually the most visible element in the plot. Indeed, through these actions the reader sees what the writer has prepared: (1) a conflict or conflicts with complications, (2) a crisis or crises, and (3) a resolution—all contained within a series of actions the characters perform because of their needs and wants. For some readers, the plot is the writer's plan for keeping the characters in danger in order to keep the reader interested. And, for some readers, the only worthwhile plot is the type that keeps them at the edge of their seats or up past midnight waiting *for what comes next.*

These types of plots are not easy to make, and those who, like Stephen King or Ross Thomas, can hold our attention with their plots and satisfy our need to be on tenterhooks deserve our gratitude. They haven't written *Sons and Lovers* or *The Color Purple*, but they have entertained us. On the other end of the spectrum, some plots may be made up of subtler actions, not so "dramatic" in nature. Such plots satisfy us less by presenting a series of slambang actions that bring the characters to success or failure and more by expanding our understanding of human circumstances (see Joyce's "The Boarding House").

Both types of plots share with all plots the same purpose: to put the characters in motion so the reader can follow them to a satisfactory—that is, convincing—end that grows from what we have come to understand about the characters' needs, wants, abilities, weaknesses, situation, and so on. Plots provide a line to follow, they explain how and why what is happening is happening, and they involve us with the fate of the characters because the elements that make up the plot connect the character to our world (or wished for world) in a logical way. By "a logical way" we mean "*a process* to which our minds may give assent without believing." *This process need not be revealed chronologically.*

Experienced as well as inexperienced writers may confuse a situation (a premise, image, idea) with a plot, though the experienced writer will soon realize that something is wrong. The following list, for example, contains the root situations for six specific American works. These obviously could be the root situations for a million other works.

1. A young boy runs away from his cruel father.
2. A woman commits adultery in a rigidly puritanical society.
3. A family driven from its land seeks work and dignity in a foreign place.
4. In order to help his family, an old man commits suicide.
5. A young man loses the woman he loves.
6. A young black man comes North.

At this point, the preceding situations share one feature—each is a frozen statement of the characters' circumstances. In a plot, however, the situation is in motion.

The situations just listed may be thought of as images or pictures about which the story has yet to be told. Indeed, writers often begin with even less in mind:

1. The seventeen-year locusts come out.
2. Going to Wicoma Lake.
3. What if a man always told the truth?
4. An intelligent computer that wants to be fed graphics of food.
5. The last living veteran from World War I.
6. The last living veteran from World War IV.
7. The bag lady who has a Ph.D. in nutrition.
8. Aunt Susan who disappeared and no one talks about her.

These notebook jottings, the kind of pictures or ideas always popping into our minds, are the stuff from which we might build anything—poems, fiction, essays, or plays.

Here we should point out that writers work out plots in many ways. Some find out what will happen by writing along until the direction reveals itself, almost magically. Then they go back and make it all match up. Some construct elaborate outlines of each scene and transition and will not begin writing until they know every part of their story. Some start with characters and invent situations and plots for them to act in. Some start with plots and invent characters. Some start with abstract ideas and invent everything else to express those ideas. The starting places, if not infinite, are various, and you will find a way to work that is most congenial and productive for you. It is a sign of inexperience to ask a writer or a workshop leader: What is *the* way to go about developing a plot?

Wherever you start, you have to construct incidents—opportunities for your characters to be in psychological and physical conflict or motion. Keep in mind, however, that though a plot is made up of incidents, a mere series of incidents do not a plot make. Here is an example of a plot that a student outlined:

A. Kane never liked school much and one day had a major fight with Mr. Sonwil, his English teacher.

B. Another time, Kane and Leon, his brother, are wrestling, when Kane kills Leon.

C. Kane moves to NYC where he gets a job washing windows on the Empire State Building.

D. He meets a young woman who is free with her favors.

E. Kane decides to go to night school.

F. The woman goes to Africa with a wealthy man, and there she kills a tiger.

G. Kane goes back to the family farm.

H. One day, while plowing, he unearths a treasure.

I. The next day a bee stings him and he dies.

Each of these is certainly an incident. One can even imagine building from this outline a series of scenes in which actions occur (think of the opportunities for action in event C). However, we would be hard put to find any *connections* that make event A flow into event B and B into C, with event C also connecting to event A . . . and so on until they are all woven together. You might argue, of course, that if one eliminates item F, the events are connected because they happen to one character. Or, they are connected because they happen to the same character in chronological order. Or, that if all the events happen in New York to one character, and one event follows the other, everything will be connected. Such connections in time, place, and character can be virtues, but they do not create a sense that the events have a necessary and logical relationship, a syntax, that allows us to understand the events individually and as a whole.

EXERCISE

1. Take the incidents previously listed and try to find a syntactical relationship between them—some reason that Kane goes to New York and takes such a dangerous job, a reason to go home, a reason to find a treasure, a reason to die. Feel free to drop items out, change them around, and bring items in. Don't expect to end up with anything useful. It is the process of finding the connections and adjusting the events that is important for developing a plot from Kane's biography. Is there anything you can do with the name Kane? Is it necessary to begin telling the story with Kane's school days?

2. Once you have selected the key events, determined their relative importance (show or tell), and their connections, rethink the strategy of your plot line. Will simple chronology suffice? *When does the reader need to know* that Kane killed his brother? This is a different question from "when did it happen?" Reconstruct your plot as a sequence of revelations to the reader.

3. Create a list of incidents that might surround the following poem:

Written in Pencil
in the Sealed
Railway Car

Here in this carload
I am eve
with abel my son
if you see my other son
cane son of man
tell him i

from Dan Pagis, *Variable Directions*

In a sense, writers have to construct plots as they might sentences. All the nouns, verbs, adjectives, adverbs, articles, and conjunctions must be in their proper grammatical form and place to produce the effect of a sentence. You don't have a plot until all the parts produce an understanding of what each part is doing in the work. Just as a vase is not the space it contains, so a plot is not the simple addition of events; the plot *contains* events.

SETTING

We generally use the word "setting" in two senses. One sense has to do with the particular "somewhere" in which the characters function for a single scene—the kitchen, the palace, the street. That kind of "where" has to do with **scene**, and we discuss it later. In its second sense, **setting** refers to more than a specific space. It refers to the total environment for your story, with all of its cultural shadings as well as its physical landmarks and characteristics—medieval Burgundy, turn-of-the-century Sacramento, a boarding house inhabited by men at the edge of society in Dublin, contemporary cubistic Houston. These settings are not and should not be flat backdrops in front of which the action happens. From the character's point of view, that is where they live.

An effective setting is intimately related to the plot because what happens to the characters could happen *in the way it happens* only in that particular setting. Goyen's "Rhody's Path" cannot be divorced from its setting in rural Texas—the food, the way people talk, the pasture and porch, the values—and still have the same kind of impact and make the same kind of sense. The characters know that they are somewhere; therefore, the reader is more inclined to believe in and respond to their lives.

The physical place that the writer directly invokes in a particular scene is surrounded by a larger environment that the writer may directly or indirectly suggest. In stories such as Joyce's "The Boarding House" and Edward Jones' "First Day," the particular settings include more than streets and churches. Early twentieth-century Dublin and late twentieth-century Washington D.C. are societies and all that societies mean. Such environments are involved in our understanding of what happens as any individual character.

Chapter 5, "Invention and Research," provides many suggestions for working toward a control over setting. The following excerpts show how various writers communicate a sense of place.

> It was a tiny town, worse than a village, inhabited chiefly by old people who so seldom died that it was really vexatious. Very few coffins were needed for the hospital and the jail; in a word, business was bad. If Yakov Ivanov had been a maker of coffins in the county town, he would probably have owned a house of his own by now, and would have been called Mr. Ivanov, but here in this little place he was simply called Yakov, and for some reason his nickname was Bronze. He lived as poorly as any common peasant in a little old hut of one room, in which he and Martha, and the stove, and a double bed, and the coffins and his joiner's bench, and all the necessities of housekeeping were stowed away.
>
> from Anton Chekhov, "Rothschild's Fiddle"

> It was a bad time. Billy Boy Watkins was dead, and so was Frenchie Tucker. Billy Boy had died of fright, scared to death on the field of battle, and Frenchie Tucker had been shot through the nose. Bernie Lynn and Lieutenant Sidney Martin had died in tunnels. Pederson was dead and Rudy Chassler was dead. Buff was dead. Ready Mix was dead. They were all among the dead. The rain fed fungus that grew in the men's boots and socks, and their socks rotted, and their feet turned white and soft so that the skin could be scraped off with a fingernail, and Stink Harris woke up screaming one night with a leech on his tongue. When it was not raining, a low mist moved across the paddies, blending the elements into a single gray element, and the war was cold and pasty and rotten. . . . The ammunition corroded and the foxholes filled with mud and water during the nights, and in the mornings there was always the next village and the war was always the same.
>
> from Tim O'Brien, *Going After Cacciato*

> The school was on a large lake in the breast-pocket of the continent, pouched and crouched in inwardness. It was as though it had a horror of coasts and margins; of edges and extremes of any sort. The school was of the middle and in the middle. Its three buildings were middling-high, flat-roofed, moderately modern. Behind them, the lake cast out glimmers of things primeval, cryptic, obscure. These waters had a history of turbulence: they had knocked freighters to pieces in tidal storms. Now and then the lake took a human life.
>
> from Cynthia Ozick, *The Cannibal Galaxy*

We don't mean to suggest, with these examples, that the first thing you do in your story is to lay out the setting in full detail. More often, the impact of setting on the reader is cumulative, as it is in James Dickey's novel *Deliverance* or in any of the novels that Saul Bellow has placed in Chicago. When the writer has fully imagined the place (even if the place is only imaginary), that necessary sense of "being somewhere" will permeate the writing in hundreds of seemingly incidental details. The two worlds in Ursula K. Le Guin's *The Dispossessed* are her own inventions, but the characters who live there know them with the same sense of their own belonging or alienation as we know the settings of our own lives—or so it seems while we're reading. To put it another way, the reader believes in a setting—natural or imaginary—precisely because the writer has made one in which the characters believe.

If you look back over the examples, you will see that each passage not only conveys a material reality but also projects attitudes and emotion. Places are associated with feelings, often because of the events that happen there. The setting in "Rothschild's Fiddle," for example, is not simply a tiny town. Chekhov establishes that it is boring—a funeral would be more exciting. Economic conditions are poor. Existence is dingy. People have a sense of somehow being better than their circumstances—he's Yakov here and would be Mr. Ivanov in a bigger town. By implication, status is important to them. When handled effectively, then, setting—like everything else—is not only literal, but suggestive. How the character feels about and relates to the setting is often the "background music" of the work. Setting isn't established and forgotten. A setting is where the characters live. (For more about settings, see pp. 308–310 in the drama section.)

EXERCISE

Review the preceding examples and answer the following questions.

1. Describe as fully as possible the worlds that the characters live in: material, social, and spiritual.

2. What devices of language—diction and imagery—are used suggestively?

3. Do any of the passages contain **foreshadowing**, that is, suggestions of events to come?

4. Invent two or three additional sentences for each passage that maintain consistency of setting in both tangible and intangible terms.

5. Draft four descriptions of the same place, such as a shopping mall, a mountain vacation spot, a college or university, or an urban business office. Let each description register a different emotion or tone: nostalgia, torment, mystery, or farcical humor.

POINT OF ATTACK

Think of your narrative as being composed of two movements. One movement is *forward*, an unfolding of events in scenes that the characters have yet to experience. From their point of view, the future is as unknown as it is to the reader. Indeed, in some cases the audience knows what will happen even when the characters don't as in *Oedipus* or an episode of Columbo. As the characters move forward in time, the writer communicates to the reader (or viewer or listener) *past* events that are necessary for understanding the characters' present situation. This other movement, sometimes called backgrounding or **exposition**, evolves in the process of shaping a plot from a story line. Sooner or later you have to decide where you are going to have your reader begin reading.

The *first* forward-moving scene that you choose to show the reader is your **point of attack**.

You may do a lot of writing during your drafts before you find the point in the time line of the story at which the plot—*not the story*—begins. Where you begin writing anything makes no difference because the readers will only know where they began. Ultimately point of attach is one of your major decisions. Many other decisions follow from it. This is the rule of thumb: *have the reader start reading as far along the time line as is consistent with the effects you are trying to achieve.* The principle of beginning somewhere along the way—*in medias res*—has been distilled from the practice that worked even before Aristotle and still works for us. Even in fiction writing where you have a bit more lattitude in presenting background than in playwriting, start as late in the chronology of the story as you can.

The following Aesop fable, "Belling the Cat," gets to its one scene quickly, and that scene is within moments of the story's end.

> One day the mice held a general council to consider what they might do to protect themselves against their common enemy, the Cat. Some said one thing and some said another, but at last a Young Mouse stood up and announced that he had a plan which he thought would solve the problem.
>
> "You will all agree," said he, "that our chief danger lies in the unexpected and sly manner in which our enemy comes upon us. Now if we could receive some warning of her approach, we could easily hide from her. I propose, therefore, that a small bell be obtained and attached by a ribbon to the neck of the Cat. In this way we could always know when she was coming and be able to make our escape."
>
> This proposal was met with great applause, until an Old Mouse arose and said, "This is all very fine, but who among us is so brave? Who will bell the Cat?" The mice looked at one another in silence and nobody volunteered.
>
> from *Aesop's Fables*

The story dramatizes that it is easier to suggest a plan than to carry it out. Aesop relies on conventional characters (a foolish youth and a wise old mouse) and a conventional situation—we expect that mice will want protection from cats. The exposition is rapid: time = one day, place = a meeting, situation = an enemy to be frustrated. For the point Aesop wishes to make, we don't have to experience in detail the Cat's deprecations among the legions of mice, the process by which the meeting was called, or even the description of where it is being held (between walls, one is sure). Not only is the point of attack at the first and, one presumes, last meeting, but also that meeting is the only scene. Notice where we really enter the action: close to the end of the meeting when the Young Mouse stands to deliver his plan.

This basic principle cannot be repeated too often: *have your reader enter the story at a point that allows all irrelevant effects to be excluded*. We return to this point shortly.

EXERCISE

List all the information that happened before the point of attack in the following story excerpts.

1.   A Fox was eagerly watching a Crow as she settled in the branch of a tree because in her beak he spied a large piece of cheese. "That's for me, as sure as I'm a Fox," he said to himself as he walked up to the tree.

"Good morning, Mistress Crow," he began, "how lovely you look today. How black and glossy are your feathers, how bright your eyes. I am sure that your voice, like your beauty, surpasses all the other birds. Just let me hear you sing a little song, so that I may know that you are really the Queen of Birds."

The Crow was so pleased with all these compliments that she lifted up her head and began to caw. Naturally the moment she opened her mouth the piece of cheese dropped to the ground and was snapped up by the Fox. "That will do," said he. "This is all I wanted."

from Aesop's Fables

2.   Alice was beginning to get very tired of sitting by her sister on the bank and of having nothing to do: once or twice she had peeped into the book her sister was reading, but it had no pictures or conversations in it, "and what is the use of a book," thought Alice, "without pictures or conversations?"

So she was considering, in her own mind (as well as she could, for the hot day made her feel very sleepy and stupid), whether the pleasure of making a daisy-chain would be worth the trouble of getting up and picking the daisies, when suddenly a White Rabbit with pink eyes ran close by her.

from Lewis Carroll, Alice's Adventures in Wonderland

3.   Do the same thing for the first two paragraphs of Karen Sagstetter's "The Thing with Willie" (pp. 253–261)

Essentially, there are three reasons for choosing as late a point of attack as possible:

1. You have less to account for and avoid a lot of undramatic transitions.
2. You get the reader into the story faster.
3. You increase the tension because the reader waits for the unfolding of both the past and the present.

In Aesop's story, had we met Crow before she got the cheese, we probably would want to see how she got it. And now we'd have a story with different effects than we intended. The classic though deliberately amusing case of beginning too early and getting caught in too many explanations is Laurence Sterne's *Tristram Shandy*. Tristram decides to tell his life story from the beginning, his birth. Since he is an inexperienced storyteller, he feels he has to explain how he was conceived, and that decision leads him back and back into the past. As a result, he never gets born in the novel. Remember, the later the entrance, the fewer the explanations.

Getting the reader into the story quickly is not simply a matter of exploding into action as in the following opener:

> John grabbed the gun from the wall and shot the two men Swenson had sent to kill him. Then he flung himself out the window, crashing through the convertible top of the Maserati waiting below. Sheila gunned the 460cc engine and squealed away from the curb. The Bolix XG-5 on the other side of the street took off after them.
>
> How did John and Sheila get themselves into this bind? Well, six months before, Karl Ambler had called them and. . . .

Sure, this story begins quickly, but then it comes to a dead halt to orient us. And it starts on such a high level of action that the writer will have a hard time building up to it again. In fact, this point of attack feels like the final moment of the final scene.

A late point of attack works on your readers' natural curiosity about the purpose of or reason for something they are experiencing. The reader will trust you to fill in the background if there is something happening in the foreground. Only in rare circumstances will the reader tolerate investing hours of energy in a story before it really gets started. Of course, decisions about point of attack are connected to the nature of the fiction: a novel may begin earlier than a short story. In short stories or plays or poems, the point of attack is usually near the concluding event.

EXERCISE

List all the information (and scenes) you might have to prepare if you started *Alice in Wonderland* with Alice getting up in the morning and dressing. How might an earlier point of attack change our reaction to the story.

Though you never begin at the beginning—can one ever?—you still need to find an effective point of attack. The most practical point of attack is a natural one, one that is natural to life itself. Start with actual beginnings (weddings, new jobs, births, graduations, vacations); waitings (for friends, dinner, trains, mail, the long lost cousins, news); movings or relocations (into the forest, into a vehicle, out of town). Moments like these involve the kinds of tensions we are all familiar with, allowing readers to enter willingly the "let's pretend" of fiction.

Also these are moments connected to change in the lives of our characters. Readers are inclined to suspect that something is up with a character who going someplace to buy a pumpkin or who is starting her first day in school. Such natural beginnings focus your readers' attention. They raise questions about the future *and* the past that will pull the reader into your material.

EXERCISE

What is the effect of each of the following opening scenes?

1.   She was a large woman with a large purse that had everything in it but a hammer and nails. It had a long strap, and she carried it slung across her shoulder. It was about eleven o'clock at night, dark, and she was walking alone, when a boy ran up behind her and tried to snatch her purse. The strap broke with the sudden single tug the boy gave it from behind. But the boy's weight and the weight of the purse combined caused him to lose his balance. Instead of taking off full blast as he had hoped, the boy fell on his back on the sidewalk and his legs flew up. The large woman simply turned around and kicked him right square in his bluejeaned sitter. Then she reached down, picked the boy up by his shirt front and shook him until his teeth rattled.

from Langston Hughes, "Thank You, M'am"

2.   The king sits in Dumferling town
                Drinking the blood-red wine:
            "O where will I get a good sailor,
                To sail this ship of mine?"

            Up and spake an elder knight
                Sat on the king's right knee:
            "Sir Patrick Spence is the best sailor,
                That sails upon the sea."

from the anonymous ballad "Sir Patrick Spence"

3.   All of Olga Ivanovna's friends and acquaintances went to her wedding. "Look at him—there *is* something about him, isn't there?" she said to her friends, nodding towards her husband—apparently anxious to explain how it was that she had agreed to marry a commonplace, in no way remarkable man.

from Anton Chekhov, "The Grasshopper"

4.   It is five o'clock in the morning, Daylight Saving Time. I have been sitting on the balcony of the down-river room on the second floor of the Howard Johnson's motel on Canona Boulevard almost all night. In other cities motels may be escape routes to anonymity, but not for me, not in Canona, and not this morning.

from Mary Lee Settle, *The Killing Ground*

CHARACTER AND CHARACTERIZATION

We started this chapter with plot because without one your characters drift aimlessly. However, many critics would argue that we should have begun with character because it is the most important element of the story. Actually they are equally important and have to join in a satisfactory manner. The story from which your plot grows through exposition (largely *telling*) and scenes (*showing*) is about the life or a portion of the life of characters. Remember, you are writing fictional biography or autobiography or history that the reader will take as "real" during the time of reading. For example, *The Great Gatsby* is Nick Carraway's memoir about a fateful summer and *The Grapes of Wrath* is the chronicle of a dispossessed family. Even in pure allegories or the most action-oriented plot, we expect that what happens to the characters and what they do will grow from their natures, *or will appear to.* The pigs in *Animal Farm* who make up the communist oligarchy do wallow in comfort. So, whether you create characters to fulfill a situation or a situation to fulfill characters, the reader expects situation and characters to match. By "match" we mean:

1. What the characters do always reflects who they are or what happens to them as the story unfolds.
2. Their natures are understandable both in terms of the conventions of fiction or of what *has* happened to them. (Remember, the environment or **setting** is always happening to them.)

For the characters, there is no plot (usually). They do not think of themselves as characters (usually). From their point of view, they have lived and are living through events. They may plan or try to "plot" their lives in order to reach goals. They may "plot" against some other characters or vice versa. Like people, within the flow of events that *you* are charting for them, your characters wish to achieve their desires.

There are three possible types of characters in your stories or novels: primary characters, whose story you are telling; secondary characters, who are necessary for understanding the primary characters or carrying out the plot; and "uniformed" characters—doormen, waitresses, crowds—who are in the story to open doors, serve meals, and jostle the other characters; that is, to provide a credibly populated fictional world. In a way, this last type of character is a part of the setting. How much time you spend on characterization depends upon how much of the story the character carries. (See the later section, "Functionaries and Stock Characters.")

The word *character* comes from the Greek word meaning "an instrument for marking or engraving." By the fourteenth century the word in English had come to mean "distinctive mark," and by the fifteenth, "graphic symbol." Not until the seventeenth century was it used in anything like our modern sense—the sum of mental and moral qualities—and not until the eighteenth do we find it used in place of "personage" and "personality." The history of the word suggests that character is something imprinted, impressed upon, or scratched into universal human material to distinguish it from other material. It is the individual in the universal. A character in a literary or dramatic work is a *fictional personage* whom the reader recognizes by the distinctive traits the author has stamped upon or etched into the raw material. That character is "branded" so as not to be mistaken for anyone else.

A major error of beginning writers is to equate "character" with "actor"—to think that simply because one has given different names to the personages carrying out the plot, the task of characterizing has been done. What the writer should strive for is to convince the reader that (1) what happens, (2) where it happens, and (3) to whom it happens are intimately related. In fact, when you inspire in your reader a belief in the character, you usually can get your reader to believe any other aspect of the story. This "belief" we are speaking of refers to recognizing the character's reality *in the story* rather than its reality as part of the natural world. When we identify and individualize the characters, the reader can believe even in talking flounders.

The writer gives the reader four basic ways of identifying each character. For every Roderick Usher, Ahab, Elizabeth Bennett, Holden Caulfield, Invisible Man, Harry Potter, the writer constructs

- ◆ an identifiable way of behaving
- ◆ an identifiable way of speaking
- ◆ an identifiable appearance
- ◆ an identifiable way of thinking

The writer sets up and develops the identification either (1) by *telling* us information through straight exposition or (2) by *showing* us how the character acts. This showing includes, of course, how the character looks, speaks, and thinks and how other characters respond. All these elements are ultimately connected to the plot because without them what happens would not happen in the way it happens. And so once again, character is plot and plot is character.

In practice, the writer shapes our sense of the character's identity by mixing the basic techniques, as in the following passage:

> Much to his surprise, Grant felt relaxed, yet serious.
> "We may as well admit it's over, really over this time," he said.
> Alice wasn't convinced that this time was any different from the others. Her hand smoothed her shoulder length hair in a gesture that was part of her little arsenal of weapons in such situations. The gesture was always the first step in a delicate series of maneuvers that had kept them together. But Grant had prepared himself. "That's not going to work, you know." He had had enough. He was through.

Even in this brief passage, the writer uses all the tools of characterization. The first sentence presents the narrator's assessment of the situation. He (or she) tells us something about Grant. Then Grant, in his own words, reveals where he stands—and thus something about himself. Alice's actions characterize her and, in passing, give us some sense of how she looks while helping us understand the history of their relationship. But it also says something about Grant. We know that up to this point he has been indecisive about ending the relationship and that he had a weakness for Alice's physical charms that she could exploit. Grant's own words finish the job of establishing a changed situation, and the very way he speaks tells us something about his quiet but firm approach to this difficult moment. The closing sentences appear to be the narrator's report of what Grant is thinking, almost as if Grant had said it aloud. The reader understands by this point not only that the situation has changed but also a little bit about the nature of both characters. Such moments, repeated dozens of times in any particular narrative, give the reader a sense that a character has a specific psychological and moral organization, an identifiable way of looking at and responding to situations.

One thing to notice about the preceding sample is that it doesn't sit there screaming *characterization*. The ongoing business of characterization gets done while everything else is getting done. Only when a character is first introduced or at special moments in an extended narrative is a long, static section of characterization ever appropriate. Even then, most writers would have the character doing something—going or coming, at a meeting, already involved in some way with an event that established an element of the plot. Characters are more effectively presented to readers by actions and words than by analytical descriptions.

The problem with long, analytical descriptions is that the audience is given the end product—the summary case history—rather than being allowed to experience the character in action. The writer creates a greater sense of intimacy and engagement when a reader deduces the nature of characters from what they do, think, or say. These are the ways we get to know an individual's nature in life itself. Indeed, one of the reasons a reader comes to believe in a character is that the writer provides the same kinds of information by which we come to know real people; we don't come to know *them* through lengthy analyses. Remember, the characters created in a work of fiction are not "real" because they pass the test of measurement against real models. They are fictional personages in whom we agree to believe because of accepted, conventional means the writer has employed.

To create these believable characters, you must know more about them than can ever be told or shown to the reader. This in-depth knowledge is particularly true for major characters. The writer sets the game in motion by knowing the fictional personages so well that every move they make, every word they speak, every thought they have grows from a kind of intimate biography that allows the writer to answer the following questions:

1. When and where was the character born? Why does the character have that name? What is the character's background—economically, spiritually, educationally? Does the character have brothers and sisters? What are the family dynamics?

2. What does the character look like? How does the character speak? Move? Relate to others? What are the behavioral tics (like rubbing the side of his nose or hiccuping when nervous)?

3. What does the character do for a living? For fun? For a hobby? To kill time?

4. What is the character's psychological makeup? What are the character's memories—conscious and unconscious (as revealed in dreams and actions)? How self-aware is the character?

5. What significant events shaped the character's views and reactions?

6. *What does the character want and why?*

While all of these questions are important, the last is crucial. (For more on these elements of characterization, see Chapter 13.)

Knowing what your characters want and need can help you find situations that will put them in conflict with other characters or with the environment. It is the question that can connect character and plot, not in the sense that the pursuit of a goal is all that makes for a story line, but in the sense that knowing what the character wants and needs (even if the character doesn't) is the key to knowing how that figure will react to various circumstances. In Bel Kaufman's "Sunday in the Park" (pp. 267–270) what the woman, "she," really wants is paradoxical—a sensitive man who can beat the daylights out of the bully. As in life, the clash between the wants and needs of a character and the blocking forces of nature, social conditions, or the wishes of other characters is what creates tension. Without tension, stories and life are ho-hum—which is acceptable in life but not in stories.

Once you know your character, you will be able to present that character as a unique identity rather than just as a type (see "Functionaries and Stock Characters"). And once you know your character that well, you cannot avoid keeping to what may be the only unbreakable rule in fiction: *the character must behave according to his or her nature as the writer has established that nature.* Tom Sawyer may leave off being a romantic and become a cynic, but we'll have to see how that happened. Indeed, **how** that happened may be the story or part of it. Merely for the convenience of the writer in a particular scene, a character who studied atomic physics cannot ask another physicist: "By the way, who was Einstein?"

Writers, particularly novelists, often develop elaborate journal sketches of their characters' lives so that they can give those characters the degree of complexity, the multiple edges required for the type of fiction they are writing. Often they discover potential scenes or plot directions. In sum: individuality, consistency, and complexity result in successful characterization. They give the reader the opportunity to believe in the character.

You should, however, avoid the temptation to push everything you used in a character sketch into your story. The sketch is there only as a reference, a resource. The materials in the sketch must be used selectively and suggestively. You will need to choose or invent *representative* items that economically stand for many omitted possibilities. Essentially, doing the sketch will give you the knowledge and the insight necessary to set the character in motion. You can draw on that insight as you follow the character through a series of actions and reactions. (For more on characters see Chapter 13, "The Elements of Drama," pp. 296–302.)

EXERCISES

1. Write three elaborate character sketches. Make one of the characters approximately your own age, one five years younger, and one five years older. Two of them should be the same sex as yourself, the other of the opposite sex. Answer all of the questions listed on page 194 as well as others that you think of. Write the sketches out in full sentences and paragraphs. If you are assigned to do this in a short period of time, do the best you can and go back to amplify your sketches later.

2. Test out your character sketches with someone else. Find out what the sketch has not covered or made clear about your characters.

3. Make a list of situations for each character. In making the list, consider the kind of problem or set of circumstances that will best reveal what the character is made of. Take situation suggestions from others who have read your character sketches.

4. Imagine one of your characters as ten years older. Take some additional notes on the character at that age.

5. Have one of your characters look in the mirror and record what he or she sees (some first-person introspection). *Note*: This ploy has become a cliché—useful in practice sessions, dangerous in serious work.

6. Write about one character through the eyes of another.

Action

What characters do defines them, and these same actions are part of the materials that constitute plot. In a story or novel or play, every action must be convincing in this double way: (1) it must be consistent with what we know or will come to know about the character's inner state; (2) it must be necessary to the advancement of the plot and the revelation of theme.

Actions are related to motivations and reveal character. In James Joyce's "The Boarding House," when Mr. Doran passes Jack Mooney, the brother of the girl he has compromised, he notes his powerful arms and remembers how violent Jack could be. We realize that Mr. Doran is a physical coward as well as a moral one and that he will marry Polly. In Tony Earley's "Just Married," the serenity of the old couple in their wrecked car reveals their acceptance of life's various accidents. Their story of love and faithfulness over fifty years of being married to others, evokes the doubt and foreboding in the husband and wife who have helped the old couple. Will they be so faithful? Do they hold in their hearts a deep love for someone else? In this story, the action of the old couple affects the thoughts of the younger couple.

Actions are directly related to motivations. In Edward Jones's "First Day" (pp. 270–273), the mother takes the child to kindergarten at the wrong school not only because she does not understand the concept of school zones but also because she wants her daughter to go to the school close to her church. We learn about her desire to provide a better life for her daughter by the care the mother takes in dressing and in buying the school supplies. Certainly love motivates her, but just as telling is the fact that she can neither read nor write. She does not want her daughter to be a victim of ignorance as she is. We understand the pain the lack of these skills brings her because of her embarrassment when she asks for help in filling out the school forms. Overcoming the embarrassment becomes a sign of her pride and strong character.

EXERCISE

From one of the character sketches you have drawn up, develop a scene in which a character trait—impatience, for example—is revealed in action or actions. See if, at the same time, you can show how that trait developed.

Appearance

In life, appearances are significant, even if they are deceiving. When we meet people, they strike us first as images, and it is this first impression that we remember. How people respond to *our* images and how we believe we look are important to us (consciously or unconsciously), as is made quite clear when we consider the time we devote to our weight, our hairstyles, our clothing, and even our gestures. In fiction, even a single detail (Huck Finn's ragged pants) gives the reader some tangible image to hang on to. Such details usually hint at other aspects of the character or situation. In the collection of physical features that meets the eye is something of the buried individual.

The amount and kind of detail about your character that you give needs to be carefully measured and selected. Beginning writers tend to go to extremes, either (1) giving their characters too much of a physical embodiment or (2) neglecting to visualize their characters altogether, often insisting that they want to leave it to the reader's imagination. The writers who go overboard elaborate the appearance of the character far beyond what the reader needs or wants. In fact, when a writer lays out pages of excruciating detail about the character's appearance, the reader is likely to lose the *essential* picture. There is simply too much for the reader's imagination to carry. On the other hand, a character who is totally faceless (except for age and sex) has so many possibilities that the reader is left without anything to hold on to. Readers are also confused when too many different characters are described one right after another. Think of what happens when you are introduced at a party to an entirely new group of people.

EXERCISE

The following physical descriptions suggest the nature of the character. Examine the extent of such description in each passage and the techniques for presenting the description. See our comments following the first example.

1. Zadok Hoyle presented a fine figure on the box of carriage or hearse, for he was a large, muscular man of upright bearing, black-haired and dark-skinned, possessed of a moustache that swept from under his nose in two fine ebony curls. On closer inspection it could be seen that he was cock-eyed, that his nose was of a rich red, and that his snowy collar and stock were washed less often than they were touched up with chalk. The seams of the frock coat he wore when driving the hearse would have been white if he had not painted them with ink. His top hat was glossy, but its nap was kept smooth with vaseline. His voice was deep and caressing. The story was that he was an old soldier, a veteran of the Boer War, and that he had learned about horses in the army.

    from Robertson Davies, *What's Bred in the Bone*

Nothing is directly said about Hoyle's personality here, though the narrator has begun to show the character in a way that allows us to draw inferences we will test later in the novel. What Hoyle does to maintain his clothes suggests his pride in his appearance, as does his posture. The "fine figure" is an image that he has worked hard to create. Nonetheless, we receive the impression of a man who is competent within a limited sphere and who can be endearing (note the qualities of his voice).

Make a list of expectations about Zadok Hoyle from the materials presented in the paragraph. After each, answer the question, "What makes you think so?" Notice that Davies comes right out and *tells* us what Hoyle's appearance is rather than trying to find more "subtle" ways (i.e., having Hoyle look in a mirror or seeing Hoyle's appearance through another character's eyes).

Ask the same questions about the following passages. Note, for each, how much is *told*, how much *shown*. What role does *appearance* play in each passage?

2.   My grandfather, when I first remember him, lived over in the next county from us, forty miles west of Nashville. But he was always and forever driving over for those visits of his—visits of three or four days, or longer—transporting himself back and forth from Hunt County to Nashville in his big tan touring car, with the canvas top put back in almost all weather, and usually wearing a broad-brimmed hat—a straw in summer, a felt in winter—and an ankle-length gabardine topcoat no matter what the season was.

He was my maternal grandfather and was known to everyone as Major Basil Manley. Seeing Major Manley like that at the wheel of his tan touring car, swinging into our driveway, it wasn't hard to imagine how he had once looked riding horseback or muleback through the wilds of West Tennessee when he was a young boy in Forrest's cavalry, or how he had looked, for that matter, in 1912, nearly half a century after he had ridden with General Forrest, at the time when he escaped from a band of hooded nightriders who had kidnapped him then—him and his law partner (and who had murdered his law partner before his eyes, on the banks of Bayou du Chien, near Reelfoot Lake). He would plant one of the canvas yard chairs on the very spot where I had been building a little airfield or a horse farm in the grass. Then he would undo his collar button and remove his starched collar—he seldom wore a tie in those days—and next he would pull his straw hat down over his face and begin his inevitable dialogue with me without our having exchanged so much as a glance or how-do-you-do.

from Peter Taylor, "In the Miro District"

3.   On this particular evening, a Tuesday, most of the regular people . . . were down at the Rachel River V.F.W. Lounge. Drinks, for once, were at half price, in honor of Mr. and Mrs. Kevin Ohlaugs's son, Curt [who was back from the service] . . . The local radio-news lady, a thirty-three-year-old divorcee named Mary Graving, sat in the best corner booth of the V.F.W. Lounge. She was celebrating something secretly. From the beginning, she had intended to spend the whole evening there, so she had had the foresight to prop herself up in the right angle between the back of the booth

and the wall. By her elbow, someone had scratched on the wall a suggestion to the I.R.S. about what it could do with itself. Mary had arranged a smile on her face quite a while ago; now it was safely fixed there, and she herself was safely fixed, and although she was immensely drunk, she was not so drunk as the others, which meant she counted as dead sober.

When Mary Graving was sober, her face was too decided and twitchy to look good with the large plain earrings she always wore. She thought she was generally too grim-looking, and her earrings looked too cheerful at the edges of her face. Now that she was drunk, though, and wearing a red dress, her face felt hot and rosy. Her smile stayed stuck on, and she knew that the earrings—a new pair, especially cheap, not from Bagley's in Duluth but a product of the Ben Franklin Store in Rachel River—looked fine. She was not beautiful but she was all right.

from Carol Bly, "The Last of the Gold Star Mothers"

Thought

A reader knows the action of a character's mind two basic ways: (1) the narrator *reports* what a character thought, dreamed, or felt; and (2) the narrator directly *presents* the flow of the character's thoughts. Sometimes the narrator may present the flow as an **interior monologue**—an apparently realistic, because apparently uncut, recording of the complex flow of diverse thoughts, feelings, and images welling up within the character. **Stream of consciousness** is the extended form of interior monologue often going on for whole chapters, as in the works of James Joyce, Virginia Woolf, and William Faulkner.

An omniscient narrator can enter the mind of any character, but in most fiction the narrator chooses one character as a point of psychological reference, limiting our access to the thoughts (feelings, dreams) of that individual. Jumping back and forth among the minds of many characters is undesirable because it is difficult for the reader to follow. It *seems* unrealistic. Given the brevity of "The Boarding House," Joyce's decision to take us into the minds of three characters is especially unusual. He chooses to do this because his story is largely *about* their different perspectives and their understandings of one another. In recording his characters' thoughts, Joyce rarely tags the passages with phrases like "he thought" or "she pondered." The narrator slips into the character's mind and, with a minimum of fuss, tells us what's going on. Here are Mrs. Mooney's thoughts as she prepares to maneuver Mr. Doran into a proposal to Polly Mooney:

> There must be reparation made in such a case. It is all very well for the man: he can go his ways as if nothing happened, having had his moment of pleasure, but the girl has to bear the brunt. Some mothers would be content to patch up such an affair for a sum of money; she had known cases of it. But she would not do so. For her only one reparation could make up for the loss of her daughter's honour: marriage.

Here, Joyce's report of her thought comes very close to authorial comment, another means of characterization that we will discuss later. Joyce's intention, however, is to bring us close to Mrs. Mooney's thoughts, not to access them directly. The pronoun "she" signals that these are her thoughts. Of course, in first person narration, the narrators have no difficulty expressing what is in their own brains.

A more typical handling of a character's thoughts is this passage from Bel Kaufman's "Sunday in the Park":

> Her first feeling was one of relief that a fight had been avoided, that no one was hurt. Yet beneath it there was a layer of something else, something heavy and inescapable. She sensed that it was more than just an unpleasant incident, more than defeat of reason by force. She felt dimly it had something do with her and Morton, something acutely person, familiar, and important.

In this story, we are slightly more distant from the character's mind than in "The Boarding House" because we are aware that the narrator is reporting the thoughts rather than presenting them as a form of **indirect discourse**. (For indirect discourse, see pp. 203–204.) The more the character concentrates on his or her own thoughts, the closer the author makes the language of thought approximate the language of speech, and the more the reader feels like a direct observer of the character's inner life.

EXERCISE

1. Report the thoughts of two characters you have sketched. Work the thoughts into the flow of a scene.

2. Write interior monologues for two of the characters you have sketched, one of each sex.

Dialogue

What characters say to one another is a key way of dramatizing them, putting their needs and wants into action. While action, appearance, and thought reveal the character in ways that heighten his or her individuality, dialogue also insists that we see the character in immediate relationship to others. We might say that speech is the way in which *thought* becomes *action*. Dialogue used merely as a way of presenting exposition (facts necessary for the reader to understand the plot) will be stilted and boring.

The writer who uses dialogue well, understands that it performs multiple tasks. Let us say two characters are talking about whether or not to go to Boston. Ideally, the way they talk about going to Boston should carry the plot forward, reveal character, focus relationships, carry thematic implications, and—if convenient—provide some exposition. If a stretch of dialogue isn't working on many levels, then dialogue is not likely to be the best tool to use at that point.

Here's a passage from the short story "Corn" developed through conversation between Tobey, his wife René, and an old farmer. Notice how René's hesitance and Tobey's attempt to appear down to earth and the farmer's desire to make money fit together without spelling these desires out. The situation is that Tobey and René have been arguing about the best way to cook corn.

> "We'd like to set up our stove, go pick some corn, and cook it right here. We'll pay you, of course. It's kind of a scientific experiment." The Lab let Tobey scratch his ears.
>
> The old man considered the proposition. René just shook her head back and forth. The dog left Tobey and sniffed at her legs.
>
> "Could be danger of fire," the farmer said.
>
> "He's perfectly right, Tobey. You're perfectly right, sir," René said. "We're sorry to have bothered you."
>
> "But if'n I brought over the hose, we can set your getup right next 't the field and I could dowse any fire quicker 'in you can say . . . corn."
>
> "How much?" Tobey said.
>
> "Ten be too much?"
>
> "Throw in a dozen ears of corn?"
>
> "You pick 'em."
>
> "Done."
>
> Tobey backed the station wagon next to the field, set up the Coleman stove, attached the propane canister, filled their largest camping pot with water from the farmer's hose, and set it to boil.

Though it is clear from the context that Tobey is some distance from being a farmer, the quick fencing about price and amount shows him trying to act as he imagines a farmer would act. René's desire to flee the scene is signaled by her rapid acceptance of the farmer's apparent rejection. The farmer's willingness to accommodate them, despite the danger of fire, is a signal that he either wants the money or has another motive that will reveal itself later in the story.

The passage also illustrates some conventions of dialogue. Notice how *a paragraph indentation signals a shift in speaker*. Though in some cases writers will run the speeches of different characters in the same paragraph or bury a character's speech in a narrative passage, normally each speech has its own paragraph. This convention is a way of helping the reader keep the characters straight. We are so used to it that is has become an unconscious expectation when we read. As writers, we need to be helpful in these most ordinary ways.

Notice also how the **designators**—the words that tell us who is speaking—are simple and sparse. A single instance of "said" is all the exchange between Tobey and farmer needed, in part because there are only two speakers and in part because the dialogue is quick and sharp, like a duel. Beginning writers tend to become heavy-handed with these tags, no doubt out of a false worry about repetition. They try to juice up their prose by being inventive when they should be almost silent. "He snarled" and "she groused" and the like should be used sparingly, if ever. Not only are elaborate designators more comic than helpful, but they also signal the writer's insecurity about whether the reader will respond properly to what the characters have said. When the writer has shown the state of mind or the tone of voice in the dialogue, it is not necessary to do so in the designator. If the writer hasn't shown it in the dialogue, then the dialogue needs revision.

The designator in the following speech is both redundant and silly:

> "For God's sake, please don't go, Lettie," he implored in a piteous voice.

"He said" is sufficient. When the designator remains almost invisible, the reader is in closer contact with the dialogue and therefore with the characters. In fact, the writer can increase direct contact by judiciously dropping the designator altogether, as we have seen in the preceding passage.

You will want to read the extended discussion of how to create expressive dialogue in Chapter 14.

QUESTIONS

1. What would be the effect if the writer had added the tag "Tobey agreed" to Tobey's last speech in the preceding passage?

2. What are the surface and subsurface meanings (**text** and **subtext**) in the following the dialogue from Earley's "Just Married"?

> On the old woman's knee was a large drop of blood shaped like an apostrophe.
> "Well," said the old man.
> "Well," said the old woman.
> "I guess I wrecked your."
> "But it was just a car," she said. She patted his hand.
> "We just got married," he said.
> "Tonight," she said. "Six hours ago. In Huntsville. We stayed too long at the reception."
> "Everyone was there."

"All the grandkids. His and mine. We didn't want to leave."
The old man almost smiled. "Well," he said. "We did and we didn't."

EXERCISE

Write two pages of dialogue for any two characters. Create a simple conflict (should they go someplace or not; should they buy something or not). Do not use designators for any of the characters' speeches. *Remember*: The characters know what they are doing and what their situation is, so they are not likely to talk about it directly. Show your dialogue to someone else to see if they can understand the situation and keep track of each character. Better yet, read the dialogue with someone else as you might a play.

Indirect Discourse

The technique a writer can use to avoid unnecessary dialogue is to report or have a character report (as in a play) what characters said to one another. The technique is called **indirect discourse**. Let us suppose that you have developed a scene in which one character (A) has to tell another character (B) about what (C) said from an earlier scene. The reader already has heard the information and it doesn't need to have tediously elaborated:

> Addie entered the room where Franklyn was setting the table.
> "Hi, Frank."
> "Hi, Addie."
> "How you feeling?"
> "O.K., I guess. And you?"
> "O.K."
> "How did it go with Scotty?"
> "I went over there and we started to talk."
> "What did she tell you?"
> "It's not what she told me. It's what happened."
> "What happened?"
> "[Now Addie launches into a long retelling of a squabble that turned into a shoving match while Frank either fiddles his thumbs, the reader forgets he is there, or Frank interrupts with 'and then what happened.']"

With indirect discourse you can quickly get over such repetitious or dramatically weak material:

> Addie entered the room where Franklyn was setting the table. And after they exchanged greetings she told him what had happened with Scotty—including the business about the fight.

Sometimes, as in "Rhody's Path," dialogue is kept to an absolute minimum while the illusion of conversation is created through extensive use of indirect discourse:

> And then suddenly like a shot out of the blue Rhody jumped up and said she couldn't stand it any longer, that she was going out to help the poor Revivalist in his search for the diamond rattler.

Indirect discourse is also a way of avoiding the presentation of *any* dialogue that would be downright tedious or purely informational (not characterizing). In some instances, this technique serves when characterization is called for but the use of dialogue would force you to invent speeches for *other* characters. Notice, in the following example, how dialogue and indirect discourse are combined for maximum flavor and efficiency. A son has come home late:

> "I'm only an hour after I promised, Ma. What do you want from—"
> "It wasn't you who was doing the waiting."
> "But, Ma, I'm eighteen."
> He might be eighteen, she told him, but he wasn't a very grown-up eighteen. Because if he was he would understand exactly how she felt. What with no husband and Marcy and Joe gone heaven knows where, he should plan his time a little better. In any case, he was home now and she wanted him to get down to his homework right away. At least one of them would amount to something. . . .

The narrator can go on for quite a while like this, giving information as well as a sense of character without having to worry about the mother's exact words or the son's responses.

The consideration of indirect discourse is a reminder that it is easy to overuse or misuse dialogue. As a general rule, save dialogue for what only dialogue can accomplish. Indirect discourse is often the more effective choice.

EXERCISE

Finish what the mother in the example tells the son. Then break into a brief dialogue in which she demands an explanation as to why he was late. Then use indirect discourse to report his story.

Other Means

So far we have reviewed the direct means of characterization: what a character looks like and what that character does, thinks, and says. Often the delineation of a character is aided by what other characters say and think about him or her. In "The Boarding House" Joyce presents Mr. Doran's character, in part, by providing Mrs. Mooney's estimate of it. In "Rhody's Path" the narrator quotes Aunt Idalou to help the reader evaluate Rhody.

Another technique requires delicacy: *authorial comment.* It has the advantage of great economy, but the disadvantage of seeming coercive—as if the author doesn't trust our understanding. James Joyce allows himself this method in a well-known line from "The Boarding House": "She [Mrs. Mooney] dealt with moral problems as a cleaver deals with meat." Of course, Joyce's simile comparing her character to a cleaver has its own dramatic brilliance.

Functionaries and Stock Characters

In selecting characters and building them, you can exploit what the reader already is likely to know. Indeed, to have your narrator demonstrate that an aging mercenary soldier is cynical about the glory of war is to ignore that we know this characteristic by convention, just as we know that dissolute younger brothers of murdered noblemen might be the logical suspect. Because your work is not the first your readers have read, you can rely on such types for less important characters, giving the readers' imagination and experience some room. Foxes are clever and hungry: *always.*

Most of the figures who populate your work are merely functionaries: the drunk show girls at Gatsby's parties, for example. At one level, functionaries may be part of the scenery; on another level, they may have a line or two. The writer is best off relying on the reader's knowledge of the function or the type so that the figure can be sketched in quickly:

> The *waitress* brought our drinks and we got down to business. It was difficult to talk in whispers because a *well-dressed and well-lubricated stockbroker was telling all the world why the market had crashed.* Leroy wanted to go to another bar but I thought it would be a waste of time. He was annoyed and at every other word he'd ask me to repeat what I just said. He didn't touch his martini so I took it.

Had the writer said anything more than this about the waitress and stockbroker, we would feel our attention diverted from the central issue of the scene. Unless the functionaries have a significant role in the plot, they need not be characterized.

Using **stock characters**, on the other hand, requires more complex decisions. Stock characters are derived either from commonly held generalizations about racial or social types or from conventions of literature. Sometimes it is difficult to separate the generalization from the convention, as in the following list: the disrespectful, clever servant; the braggart, cowardly soldier; the tough prostitute with a heart of gold; the silent cowboy; the snobby Harvard grad; the farmer's daughter; the cynic; the incorruptible but sarcastic private eye; the shylock; the step'n fetch-it; the redneck; the effeminate cross-dresser; the geek; and so on. On the one hand, stock characters can easily become mere reflections of popular prejudices. On the other hand, stock figures can behave so according to type that they never become characters with their own wants. Plots driven by stock characters tend to be allegorical or popular but such stories often become predictable and boring or like comic books.

A social type (the dull professor or the airhead yuppie), of course, will not offend the reader as may the racial, religious, or sexual stock character. Offensive or not, such stock figures can play major roles in satire or comedy. The dirty old man lusting after a young bride has supplied the central focus for many plots. When you want only a "stock response," use a stock character, but be careful to weigh the risks involved.

The stock character can also provide the seed from which the writer builds a more complex character. Just as our understanding of real people may begin with placing them in general categories by which we first know them (gender, age, occupation, class), so may we begin developing our fictional people by first seeing them as types and then learning about them as individuals. For an extended discussion of this process, see the section on stock characters in Chapter 13.

EXERCISES

1. List the functionaries and stock characters in "The Boarding House." How does Joyce signal their identity?

2. Examine the major characters from "The Thing with Willie" and "Rhody's Path." In what ways can you see them as stock characters? What characterizing techniques did the authors use to develop them into complex characters?

3. There is a fine line distinguishing **stock characters**, an artistic convenience, and **stereotypes**, a potentially hazardous playing on prejudices. How would you categorize each of the following?

a. a redheaded, gum-chewing waitress

b. a dumb jock

c. a "yes, dear" husband

d. an "old salt"

e. a Jewish-American princess

f. a wicked stepmother

g. a Puerto Rican thief

h. a couple in polyester leisure wear

i. a nerd

j. a television evangelist

k. an aging spinster

l. an unmarried career woman

m. a punk rocker

n. a male nurse

Naming Characters

Finding appropriate names is not a trivial task, since your reader is often attracted or distracted by the name itself and by its seeming "rightness" for that particular character. A name must have credibility without being a cliché, and sometimes the name may have significance or suggestiveness. In choosing names, the writer must consider:

1. cultural stereotypes (if only to avoid them)
2. historical authenticity (is the name right for the times?)
3. regional probability (is a small-town Texan named Melvin?)
4. socioeconomic signals (is Poindexter the trucker?)
5. symbolic overtones (is Joshua leader or wimp?)
6. auditory features (what's an Ebenezer Scrooge?)

The following list includes names of characters from drama, fiction, and poetry. For the characters you know, check the "ring" of each name against the traits of the character. For the others, make a list of traits you would expect and then find out how close your portrait comes to the original.

1. George F. Babbitt
2. J. Alfred Prufrock
3. Becky Thatcher
4. Willy Loman
5. Franny Glass
6. Quentin Compson
7. Stephen Dedalus
8. Emma Bovary
9. Nick Adams
10. Joseph Andrews
11. Lemuel Gulliver
12. Moll Flanders
13. Isabel Archer
14. Oliver Twist
15. Holden Caulfield
16. Daisy Buchanan

Beware of names that are overly allegorical—Lancelot Hero—as well as names that do nothing to distinguish your character—Bill Smith, Sam Smyth, Joan Jones, Joy Jakes. In the latter case, the reader may become lost in the forest of one-syllable names.

An excellent way to get names for your characters is by "researching" in telephone directories, local newspapers, and—of course—high school and college yearbooks. Mix first names and last names. Try out your characters' names on your friends or an instructor.

The Relationship of Character, Plot, and Setting

Since fictional characters are "represented" persons, their lives are limited to the fictional work or works that shape them. A character has verisimilitude in terms of the *imagined* environment, not necessarily in terms of the world we know intimately or the larger world that we know something about. The reality of Rhody in "Rhody's Path" is bound up with the environment in which Goyen places her: the impact she has on *that* world and that it has on her. It is easy to grasp this point when we consider fairly exotic settings (like East Texas or the boarding house in Joyce's Dublin) and characters. However, the same truth holds in the more familiar world created by Bel Kaufman. The reality of the character is *inside* the story, not *outside* it. This means, in part, that the things the reader needs to know about a character are limited to the larger unity of the story. Not every character is given the same attention, the same degree of rounding.

The situation (or conflict) that shapes the plot also limits or controls what the reader needs to know about the character. We, as readers, need to know those things that bear on the circumstances at hand. For example, in "The Boarding House," Mr. Doran's inexperience with women is important, and, by suggestion, so is Mrs. Mooney's upbringing as a butcher's daughter. In another set of circumstances, we might need to discover other things about these same characters. As writers, we will know much more about these characters than the story allows us to share with the reader. Our concern for overall unity and focus will help us select just what must be known about each character. When the first words the old woman in "Just Married" speaks is "well" and the old man answers "well," Tony Earley gives us all we need to know about their imperturbability.

The art of characterization is at the heart of all successful fiction. For many writers, imagining their characters is where the process of storytelling begins. A sense of relationship to the characters is what keeps readers reading.

EXERCISES

1. From two or three of the character sketches you have done, draft an introductory section like the ones by Davies, Taylor, and Bly in the section on "Appearance."

2. Choose two or three of the "situations" collected for exercise 3, page 195. Group whatever materials from your character sketch you will be most likely to use in developing each situation.

3. Reread "Eli and the Coal Strippers" (p. 154) and develop a scene from Zimmer's hints about the relationship between Eli and Wanda. You might want to write about Wanda's leaving the farm.

4. In his afterword to "Just Married," Tony Earley tells us that the next day he had breakfast with the couple who sparked the story. Develop a scene with more of a focus on the narrator.

A NOTE ON THE NOVEL

Writing a novel involves all the basic techniques of writing shorter fiction—character and scene development, narration, dialogue—plus the demands brought on by the sheer magnitude of your promise to tell a long story. From a purely commercial point of view, when you undertake a novel, you commit yourself to writing a minimum of 40,000 to 60,000 words or 150 to 200 double-spaced typescript pages. And for some of the subgenres of the novel, like the historical romance, you may need to write 100,000 or more words because the reader expects a substantial beach book. Even with word processing, the task is daunting—both the original drafting and the revising.

However, the more serious difficulties are not those of filling up pages or preparing a manuscript. While a short story generally focuses on a single event involving only one or two major characters, a novel enters far more fully into the imitation of an unfolding life (or series of lives) while it places that unfolding in an elaborated setting that traditionally includes social background. The novelist must exercise intense concentration over a long period of time to manage the intricacies of characters' lives in an expansive plot. Authors of long fictions, even more than writers of short stories, must truly live with their characters.

Generally speaking you will need to do much more prewriting than might be necessary for a short story. Since novels tend to imitate either biographies, autobiographies, or histories, you will need to determine how your imagination will substitute for the nonfiction writer's research. Of course, you will need to do much of the same kind of research (see Chapter 5) to create a sense of authenticity. And you will have to be flexible: because you will be working on the manuscript for months, even years, your reading will expand your writing tools, and your experience of the natural world and the world of your novel will deepen. You will have many opportunities, *while you are writing*, to make discoveries about your characters and the moral, physical, and intellectual world(s) they inhabit. Rigid adherence to a plan over the months and years of the writing process that novels require is likely to be a foolish faithfulness.

Though you will want to jot down notes as ideas come to you for all writing projects, writing a novel calls for even more note taking. Much more is happening, more characters are moving across your stage, more time has passed since you set up the action. Think of yourself as the person who takes care of the props in a play or the continuity in a film. Like such managers, you need to know what your character was wearing and had in her purse in the last scene. Or, since four years have gone by since Jay Gatsby left for the war, how does he find out where Daisy is living? The sheer volume of events, props, and characters, and the time that elapses between writing Chapter 1 and Chapter 10, qualitatively change the task before you. Some authors dedicate a journal to keeping track of their ideas and plans for a novel, and then for keeping track of their progress (see Steinbeck excerpt, pp. 14–15).

If you have read this far, you already know that you have to study the genre and subgenre in which you plan to write. Particular subgenres—mystery, adventure, science fiction, romance, historical—are subdivided into even more types, and you should master the conventions and expectations of the audience (even if you intend to upset those expectations). You should have read in the genre for a long time before you try, let us say, an adventure story. If you try to write in a subgenre just because it is popular, you will probably fail.

A good part of your preplanning should involve especially careful thinking about who is going to tell the story (see Chapter 3). For example, if you are going to have to do a great deal of exposition (as, for example, in an historical novel), a first-person point of view may cause difficulties. How are you going to get a piece of information to your narrator? On the other hand, a story about growing up or a hard-boiled detective story may flow easily in the first person. If your point of view in a short story is not working, you have relatively little revising to do. Going back after writing a hundred pages of a novel can be a burden so daunting that you throw the manuscript in a drawer.

Always tell your novel in the past tense. Though you might have a prologue in the present tense to set the atmosphere, telling a whole novel in the present tense usually puts off a reader and poses exposition problems for the writer. It's been done, of course, but seldom successfully. Page after page of "she meets John and they go to the zoo where they look at the monkeys" creates unnecessary demands on the reader's attention. The novel has no emotional resting place. Everything appears to be so important and significant. Everything is happening now. The present tense may work in some short stories but, ultimately, it tends to create an evenness in the prose, an immediacy that allows for no hills and valleys.

All the decisions regarding plot, point of attack, character and characterization, and setting that we have already discussed become increasingly complicated when you tackle a novel. Perhaps the most important decision is to determine what to show and what to tell—and to be sure you know why. Because the novelist has to create a more sustained illusion of time passing, decisions about scene and summary are far more complex than they are for short stories. And, of course, such decisions must be made over and over again.

As a practical matter, what you show will be in scenes that combine description, narration, and dialogue (or interior monologue). Each scene will exist to reveal character and present action. If information is conveyed, it will be conveyed as a side effect of the scene. The scene must never appear to exist for the purpose of giving the information. When Hawthorne, in *The Scarlet Letter*, creates the scene in which Chillingworth doctors Hester and attempts to pull from her the identity of Pearl's father, we also learn about Chillingworth and Hester's marriage.

Most novels have twenty to forty major scenes of two to ten or more pages. Often one scene, with attendant description and exposition, makes up a chapter. If you find your scenes are a page or less and/or you have dozens in a chapter, you probably are writing scenes that exist only to give information (either to the reader or the other characters) or to provide a transition to another scene. In either case, the brief scenes are probably only for exposition and should be eliminated in favor of having your narrator simply tell the reader the key information.

Some novelists develop a complete life for each character: birthdate, parents, schooling, allergies, and so on. Many of your characters will exist only to help your major characters in their conflicts or to serve the plot. Ask yourself if it is really necessary to give a complete physical description of the doorman who appears only in a single scene. If you do need supporting characters, try to make those characters serve several functions. For example, Jordan Baker in *The Great Gatsby* not only serves as a foil to Daisy Buchanan, not only delivers necessary expository material, and not only becomes Nick Carraway's date for the summer (a parallel "love" story), she is also one of the characters who illustrates the decadence of contemporary society (she cheats at golf). A less sophisticated novelist might have employed several characters to fulfill these various roles.

Warnings: Do not revise while the novel is developing. When you discover in Chapter 4 that you need to revise one or more earlier chapters—anything from the name of a character to adding a scene—just put down a note to yourself to make the revision. Continue writing as if you had already made the change. Why? Because when you get to Chapter 5 and 6 and so on, you will find other revisions necessary for the earlier chapters. If you keep revising you will never finish the novel. (Word processing has the advantage of letting you return to the earlier chapters and drop in notes to yourself about the changes that will be needed and then jumping back to where you were.)

The challenge of the novel, then, brings a mixture of pleasure and pain. Most fiction writers (but certainly not all) learn to control the essential elements of their craft by working first in the short story, then going on to the longer form. The rewards of creating a peopled edifice in words are enormous, but the writer who accepts the challenge must camp out for a long season in those construction sites of the imagination, through bad weather and occasional strikes, while the structure takes shape.

EXERCISES

1. Prepare a chapter outline for a novel based on Hemingway's "A Very Short Story." Include comments on new characters, new scenes, and point of view.

2. Prepare dust jacket copy for your novel. This task should force you to focus on the essentials.

3. Develop a plot of four to five pages using the news article on pp. 92–93 as the foundation.

10

Narration and Its Problems

Your story, the interaction of situation (focused in the point of attack), setting, and characters, is **plotted** through alternating units of telling and showing, exposition, flashback, scene, and summary.

EXPOSITION

A writer needs ways to communicate information that will round out the readers' understanding of the unfolding story, which is **narrated** primarily through scenes and linking summaries. Most often this information has to do with events that precede the point of attack. The writing that supplies this information is called **exposition** (called "the back story" in drama). In Joyce's "The Boarding House," five introductory paragraphs supply family background necessary to our full comprehension of the dramatized events. We are told about Mrs. Mooney's unfortunate marriage, the reputation of the boarding house, and Polly's character and situation. The events that follow make sense—a particular kind of sense—because of what has been exposed. The first paragraphs in "The Thing With Willie" give the reader the context for the story's final paragraphs and an explanation of how Anna's interests and gentle character were formed.

The bridges between scenes also function as exposition when they prepare us for the point of attack of the coming scene. The term, however, usually applies to everything that we do not see happen in the forward movement of the story. In any case, exposition is almost always handled by *telling*, whereas scenes are conveyed by *showing*. Some of your most difficult decisions will involve discovering (1) how much of what happened before the point of attack is necessary to tell, (2) when to tell it, and (3) how to tell it most effectively and least obtrusively.

There are two kinds of information that the reader needs. First is information *about the world we all live in* that bears upon the characters in the story. If you are writing a story about, let's say, mountain climbing, how much does the reader need to know about Nepal, crampons, rappelling, hypothermia, atmospheric conditions? How much can you expect the reader to know already? How much can be gleaned from context? You need to gauge the reader's knowledge about the most relevant information and proceed accordingly, avoiding set explanatory passages that stop the action. When in doubt, the best principle is to expect the best of the reader. If you assume that you have to explain where New York City is, you will never make your way through the writing of a story.

Some fiction depends on introducing the reader to relatively unknown settings, the unfamiliar details engaging the reader's imagination. For example, novelist Dick Francis has made a career of letting his readers experience the world of horse racing. In works like these, the absorbing of new information is a central pleasure. A classic case is Defoe's *Robinson Crusoe*, which gains much of its power from having us learn the same things that Crusoe must learn to survive.

Most short fiction, however, needs to tell us only that, for example, the main characters are a couple with one child who live across from Central Park and read *the New York Times* every Sunday ("Sunday in the Park"). Your reader can intuit a lot from this little bit. In longer stories with more complex plots (as in a novel), the writer might spend time on even more exposition. In a subtle and amusing way, Hemingway's "A Very Short Story" is almost all exposition because it is a condensed novel and he has to tell us a good deal for us to understand the situation (man and woman fall in love, man goes off to war, woman doesn't wait, each suffers the consequences).

The second type of information the reader needs is information about the lives and circumstances of the characters *in the story*:

> Once upon a time, in a distant kingdom, there lived a princess who was an only child. Her name was Esmeralda and in every way save one she was the most fortunate of young persons.
>
> from Phyllis McGinley, *The Plain Princess*

Who, *where*, and *when* need to be established in almost every piece of fiction (including narrative poetry and drama), and little is ever gained by hiding this material from the reader. Making puzzles out of basic information, a novice's idea of creating mystery, more often loses the reader altogether. Look at the first paragraph of Bel Kaufman's "Sunday in the Park" (p. 267) to see how sure-handedly the basic expository work can be done and smoothed into the point of attack. In fact, effective exposition all by itself can please readers and appear to be dramatic.

However much you tell the reader about the background, you will know ten times more than you can expose. Your job is to anticipate the reader's needs as the story unfolds and to offer the right information—and no more—in the right place.

Again, most expository information is *told* by summary overviews of conditions, backgrounds, and settings. Directness is a virtue; don't worry over cute ways to make a simple point:

> NO: He walked up to the door. When the tall woman answered it, he handed her his card. She read on it: "Will E. Seridy, 7803 Wilson Lane, Exterminator."

> NO: Will looked into the handsome reflection that showed him a six-foot man of thirty-two with an intriguing cowlick of reddish hair.

These passages call more attention to the means of communicating the facts than to the facts themselves. The next attempt is simple, yet far more effective:

> Will Seridy walked up to the front door. A handsome man of thirty-two, the lanky exterminator had reddish hair that fell in a cowlick.

Save your creative effort for more important things.

Providing exposition is like giving your readers a map orientation before you show them where they are going: "You are right here. Now from this point. . . ." In the following example, notice how Saxe establishes his authority by just laying down the facts.

> It was six men of Indostan
>   To learning much inclined
> Who went to see the Elephant
>   (though all of them were blind),
> That each by observation
>   Might satisfy his mind.

> from John W. Saxe,
> "The Blind Man and the Elephant"

In this poem for children, Saxe orients us quickly to the situation so he can get to the material he wishes to show: what, after touching a different part, each of the six blind men will say an elephant is.

Exposition is frequently not placed at the beginning of a work, as our examples so far might indicate. Though chronologically it can convey information that precedes the point of attack, structurally exposition comes at the point the author feels is strategically effective. In "The Thing With Willie" Sagstetter holds back some of the key exposition until we are well into the story. The first scene is a flashback at the end of which we first hear the phrase "the thing with Willie."

The next scene begins with a conversation between Anna, the owner of the catering business, and Willie, the man who prepares the sea food. Part of that conversation is about their children:

> How's your wife? Okay?
> Yes, ma'am
> Your children? Gettin' big, I'll bet.
> My little boy Raymond isn't too good.
> Oh, sorry to hear that. What's wrong?
> He don't walk yet. Doctor don't know what to do.
> How old is he?
> He's four, ma'am
> That must be a worry. Sometimes they take their time. How about the others?

The key piece of exposition is dropped into the dialogue so quietly that we will only understand it later in the story when Willie brings the child to Anna's to ask her to bake a cake for his birthday. The child is not just slow: "A bag of limbs. Bones bundled together, but not holding him up. His head rolled around on his neck, and he was drooling." When we learn that Willie has just found out his wife is pregnant again, the information also appears random. However, it becomes the key piece of information that makes Willie's murder of his son and then of himself understandable and imparts additional poignancy to the story.

FLASHBACKS

Except for relatively rare cases in which a character flashes back to an event that the reader has directly witnessed, **flashbacks** dramatize events that happened before the point of attack. While exposition may or may not be presumed to occur in the mind of the character, a flashback is always presumed to be a remembrance. A memory moment like "As she reached for the peanut butter, Josie saw again the knife-scarred kitchen counter on which rested the fixings of all those homemade snacks her mother used to give her" is not yet a flashback but rather a piece of generalized exposition. It contains no events. Flashbacks are remembered **scenes** that interrupt the ongoing action. They serve expository purposes, but they dramatize rather than tell about something in the past.

> It was on her thirteenth birthday that the ceremony had come to an abrupt halt, her mother handing over the tools of the trade and the responsibility.
> "No more waiting on you hand and foot," she said.
> Josie was stunned. The words and the kindly, loving look in her mother's eyes seemed in conflict. She walked over to the counter and picked up an apron. "Which do you put on first, the peanut butter or the jelly?"

Today, she still imitated her mother's kitchen habits, though in everything else she had gone her own way.

Because flashbacks occur in the character's mind under the pressure of present circumstances, the reader assumes that whatever is revealed in the interrupting scene has some importance to the emotional development of the character. That is, a flashback should contain emotional facts, not simply material information. The placement of the flashback—or other exposition of past events—should be justified as a step in the experience you are creating for the reader.

The techniques of moving in and out of flashback scenes deserve special attention. You should get in and out of a flashback as quickly and directly as possible. Many times you can simply cut to the flashback, particularly if you use a typographical means (such as *italics*) to hold the flashback material. Here is an example of this technique. Miriam, at Phyllis's wedding, remembers a past event. Note the decision to put this flashback in the present tense for additional emphasis.

> Miriam heard the minister say, "Do you, Phyllis"—*She is standing at the punch bowl wondering why she came. She wants to be at the lab or back in her room listening to Bach. She sees the frenetic dancing and Robin talking animatedly at the other end of the room. Someone touches her on the shoulder and she turns to see Frank and he is saying,* "Do you . . . "
> And then she heard Phyllis saying "yes" and wondered how things would be now if she had said "yes" to Frank.

Normally you will cast flashbacks (and everything else) in the past tense. This is what readers are used to and what is easiest for them to follow. However, we note a growing tendency in contemporary fiction to use the present tense in narration and flashbacks.

Readers are also used to the simple conventions of phrasing that introduce interrupting scenes: "He remembered the time when . . . ," "She wished she could get back to when she was everybody's favorite, like on the day . . . ," "The smell was just like . . . ," and so forth. Here is a movement backward from Joyce's "The Boarding House."

> It was not altogether his fault that it had happened. He remembered well, with the curious patient memory of the celibate, the first casual caresses her dress, her breath, her fingers had given him. Then late one night as he was undressing for bed she had tapped at his door, timidly. She wanted to relight her candle at his for hers had been blown out by a gust. It was her bath night. She wore a loose open combing-jacket of printed flannel. Her white instep shone in the opening of her furry slippers and the blood glowed warmly behind her perfumed skin. From her hands and wrists too as he lit and steadied the candle a faint perfume arose.

EXERCISE

1. Invent one or two flashback scenes for Bel Kaufman's "Sunday in the Park."

2. Outline how you would restructure "Rhody's Path" so that the snakebite is the point of attack and you present most of the other material through exposition and flashback.

3. The constant task of the fiction writer is to move characters through time and space while getting a number of other tasks done simultaneously. Imagine a character you have developed in a character sketch getting ready to meet his new girlfriend's, or her boyfriend's, parents for the first time (or some similarly critical situation, such as getting ready for a job interview, a promotion review, or a trip to the doctor). Move your character through a believable landscape (or cityscape) and into the building and room where he or she will wait to meet the others. The character is apprehensive. Since this episode is your reader's introduction to the character (and the whole story), your writing must serve many functions at once without being too obvious. The character might be reminded of something in the past (which you could develop in a flashback), might notice certain details in the office building or home, might wish to escape the situation or else be eagerly looking forward to it. Keep the action moving. All aspects of fiction writing except dialogue can play a part here. If you use dialogue, keep it to a minimum. See Exercise 4 for some planning ideas.

4. Inspector A arrives at the home of Mr. and Mrs. X. He has come to interview them about their reported theft of a painting. Describe Inspector A's arrival at the X estate, his impressions of the owners from what his trained eye notices as he approaches the front of the house, enters, walks through the entrance hall or lobby, and is shown into the sitting room, where he waits for Mr. and Mrs. X to join him. Through physical details, the inspector is building an understanding of the people he is about to meet. You might as well have a butler answer the door. You might want to prepare a sketch such as the one on page 219 to help you visualize the situation.

SCENE AND SUMMARY

In *Writing Fiction*, R. V. Cassill tells us that **scenes** "bring the action and sometimes the dialogue of the characters before the reader with a fullness comparable to what a witness might observe or overhear." Summary passages, on the other hand, "condense action into its largest movements." They tend to telescope events rather than present them in dramatic detail as scenes do. Janet Burroway, in her book *Writing Fiction*, considers "*scene*" and "*summary*" as ways of treating time: "A summary covers a relatively long period of time in relatively short compass; a scene deals with a relatively short period of time at length."

SKETCH OF GROUND FLOOR LAYOUT; SITTING ROOM SCENE OF THEFT

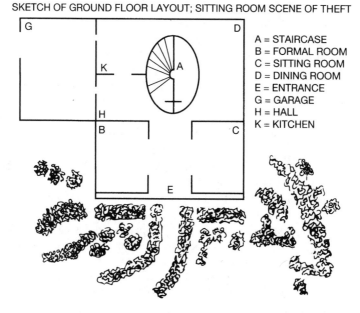

A = STAIRCASE
B = FORMAL ROOM
C = SITTING ROOM
D = DINING ROOM
E = ENTRANCE
G = GARAGE
H = HALL
K = KITCHEN

Burroway believes that while a summary is a useful device, scenes are absolutely necessary.

Scenes create the illusion of an unbroken stretch of time and action, usually in a single place. The business of summary passages is to stitch scenes together while performing expository work. In your scenes you make your work come alive.

A crucial task for the writer is to determine which material demands development in a scene and which requires only summary handling. The principle of economy operates here: scenes should be chosen to perform multiple tasks, and no plot should have more scenes than it needs.

On the pages that follow, we discuss the development of plot through scenes in three short stories: Joyce's "The Boarding House," Jones's "First Day," and Hemingway's "A Very Short Story." Though we mainly concentrate on the selection and juxtapositioning of scenes, we will pay attention as well to point of attack, exposition, flashback, summary, and characterization. The idea here is to help you look at these issues as a writer.

"The Boarding House" by James Joyce provides a clear example of economy in scene selection. In fact, Joyce has handled his story so economically and suggestively that, with no loss of impact, he has been able to leap over a scene that we would expect to be dramatized. He has also presented us with a summary telling of another potential scene.

"The Boarding House" is built out of four scenes in the ongoing present into which are embedded past scenes and some observations about past events. The story begins slowly, as Joyce takes a leisurely five paragraphs to give us a fairly detailed backgrounding of the situation in which Mrs. Mooney and her daughter Polly find themselves. However, if we study these expository paragraphs carefully, we see that Joyce has established a vivid personal situation inside a larger cultural one. The moral environment of the story is one of Joyce's main concerns, as it is throughout *Dubliners*, from which this story is taken.

Only after readers receive the background situation and the initial portraits of Polly and her mother does Joyce focus the story through dramatized scenes. The first scene establishes the time—Sunday morning—in which all of the unfolding action occurs. We see the respectable-looking churchgoers out on the street, while the fallen establishment that Mrs. Mooney runs is being aired out. We are given a close-up description of the breakfast remains, and we hear about the frugal measures taken by Mary under Mrs. Mooney's instruction. The images of propriety ("gloved hands") clash with the images of egg streaks and bacon fat, intensifying thematic concern with the distance between outward appearances and inner truths. So, too, the expansive gesture of the open windows and ballooning lace curtains conflict with the pettiness of putting "the sugar and butter safe under lock and key." Joyce's scene contains precise images that not only render the place concretely—materially—but also suggest the moral issues of his story.

Embedded in this scene is Mrs. Mooney's reconstruction of the previous night's conversation with Polly. *That* scene, however, is not dramatized: we get none of the conversation and only the barest summary of what transpired. Nonetheless, we know exactly what happened.

Scene 1 continues with Mrs. Mooney planning her attack on Mr. Doran. She knows that she holds all the cards of moral pressure. She and Polly have been silent accomplices in the pursuit of a proper marriage for Polly. Their plan is based on a reading of Mr. Doran's character and an intimate knowledge of how important reputation is in Dublin. The morally repugnant scheme depends on the concern for appearances, and it reinforces the superficiality of those appearances. Ironically, Joyce has Mrs. Mooney consider that she has just enough time to blackmail Mr. Doran and still make it to church by noon. She sees no inconsistency between the two acts.

We get to know Mr. Doran a bit through Mrs. Mooney's ruminations. The second scene presents Mr. Doran in his room puzzling over his fate. We learn that Polly had come to see him after discussing things with her mother the night before, and that she had told him about the mother and daughter conversation. He is remembering his confession to a priest, examining the overall situation, and retracing the steps of his involvement with Polly. Within this second scene is a flashback—Doran's vivid recollection of the night he succumbed to Polly's seductive behavior. The second scene concludes with Mary's arriving to summon him to see Mrs. Mooney.

The third scene, Mr. Doran's journey down the stairs, intensifies his anxiety, especially as he passes Polly's brother Jack, a man capable of violence who has threatened anyone who would jeopardize his sister's reputation. Jack, we gather, is the strong-arm version of his mother.

Between the third scene and the concluding scene, we know that Mrs. Mooney and Mr. Doran have had their little chat. However, Joyce chose not to present it, trusting the reader to feel the full weight of the inevitable through silence.

Instead of following Doran into the parlor for his confrontation with Mrs. Mooney, we visit Polly's room and enter Polly's thoughts. We see her preparing for the news that is bound to come. It is an emotional moment for her, but her complex imaginings of the future are left unspecified. Joyce leaves us to ponder the kind of relationship these two can have, given the questionable foundation on which it is built. Mrs. Mooney's voice breaks through Polly's reverie, announcing that Mr. Doran has something to speak to her about.

In conveying this story, Joyce has made a series of decisions about plot. These decisions have had to do, in part, with how to get the essential material to the reader. That is, Joyce lays out not only a series of events, but also—and more importantly—a series of experiences for the reader. The plot is not the story, but rather is the strategy by which the story is communicated: the selection of scenes for dramatization, the selection of perspectives from which to render those scenes, the selection of materials to summarize and "tell" about rather than present dramatically, and the decision to let the reader's imagination do some work— that is, the selection of those story ingredients only implied or briefly sketched.

QUESTIONS

1. Joyce uses dialogue sparingly in this story. What does he save it for?

2. Joyce allows access to the thoughts of each of his three main characters. How is this omniscient technique handled? Why is it necessary? (*Note*: The selected scenes do not show the characters interacting.)

3. How does Joyce make the initial five paragraphs of exposition count? In particular, what do readers gain from knowing about Polly's father?

EXERCISE

1. Rewrite "The Boarding House" beginning with the sixth paragraph, layering in the material Joyce has presented in the first five paragraphs.

2. Invent the two "missing" scenes: the conversation between Mrs. Mooney and Polly and the one between Mrs. Mooney and Mr. Doran.

3. Imagine Jack Mooney's perspective on what has been going on. Develop one or two scenes from his point of view.

Ed Jones chooses scenes in his story even more thriftily than Joyce. "The First Day" is built around six scenes, one of which is extremely brief:

1. Preparing for the first day of school.
2. Going to school.
3. Arriving at school and being told that it is the wrong one.
4. Going to the designated school.
5. Registering the child.
6. Leaving the child.

Preparing for the first day at school is really a flashback scene because at the point of attack, the opening sentence, they are already on their way. The effect is to get the characters in motion before slowing down to set the background. The narrator is the grown-up child who is looking back and trying to recapture the feel of that day as her younger and more naïve self might experience it. The narrator tells us that she "learned to be ashamed of her mother" as a young child. However, we come to understand that now she is proud of her mother's fierceness and courage. In fact, the central paradox of the story is pride coexisting with the shame. The detail in the preparation scene is rendered with loving care (colors, food, school box) which suggests that Jones thought carefully about what a little girl might remember and what would excite her. We learn also that the child is fatherless and that fact, as we read on, accounts for the mother's combination of sternness and indulgence. She has to be both parents. Mentioned in passing is the fact that the narrator has sisters, which tells us something of the difficulty this single parent family faces. Though Jones doesn't say this is an African-American family, the detail tells us it is (Dixie Peach hair grease and the plaits). When the mother slaps the child for using a street label (dykes?) for Miss Mary and Miss Blondelle, the speaker reveals that her mother wanted her to be proper and respectful.

The brief second scene, in which the child sees none of the children she knows on the way to school, suggests that something is amiss. We also get a hint that the mother chose Seaton Elementary because it was across from her church. In a later scene we will learn the reason for the assumption.

The scene at Seaton school opens with a sentence that is meant to establish another point about how the child looks at the world. She is keenly aware of and impressed by what she takes to be the fancy dress, "out of . . . *Ebony*," worn by the school administrators and teachers. At the same time, if we haven't figured it out previously, the writer lets us know again that this is an African-American mother and child in an African-American community. The later revelation about the mother being illiterate is foreshadowed in her tiff with the school administrator. Later, we will realize that the mother tries to cover up her failure to understand the concept of school districts (and, perhaps, inability to read notices sent to homes about where a child is to go) when she says: "If I'da wanted her someplace else, I'da took her there." She is a proud woman and that makes her later admission at the other school more powerful. We learn one other aspect of the mother's character: she may respect authority but she doesn't bend to it.

The next scene is so short one might think Jones could skip it. Why not jump to the new school and save the transition? Partly the scene shows the mother's decisiveness when she knows she is licked on what ultimately is a minor point. She hurries the child off to the correct school. The speech "One monkey don't stop no show" we take as a way of saying the bureaucracy will not defeat her and that there is more than one way to skin a cat. She is a woman who keeps the primary goal in mind and will not be distracted by trifling aggravation.

To this point the scenes serve the following dramatic purposes: (1) they tell us about the situation and key facts while revealing aspects of the mother's character; (2) they foreshadow complications, the details of which we will not understand until the fourth scene; and (3) they set up the block to the characters fulfilling their wants and needs. In the fourth scene we see the mother overcome the obstacles at a price. She has to admit that she can't read or write. She has to reveal her shame to her daughter. She has to beg someone for help. We notice that the narrator also reveals another quality of the mother. She is prepared with all the documents she might need and some that she doesn't need, like the public assistance payments—documents that, ironically, she cannot read. Also, instead of telling us that the family is on public assistance, Jones has us learn the information through the action of presenting the papers. Having overcome the blocks to achieving her goal caused by her illiteracy, the mother and child reach their goal.

The final scene, though apparently anticlimactic, actually adds to the immense ache one feels at the end. In the first place, when we hear that the mother will pick up the child at noon, it is borne out to us that this is only kindergarten and we understand the struggles the mother will have to go through for her children in the future. We also learn why and how the child learns to be ashamed of her mother and when the shame began. The women out of *Ebony* and her mother's darned socks and loud shoes, her coming understanding of her mother's illiteracy, and everything she will learn directly and indirectly at school combine to "learn" the daughter to be ashamed. This bitter irony, however, is softened by the story itself which tells us that the narrator adult has finally transcended her younger self and is intensely proud of her courageous mother. Otherwise, why tell the story as lovingly as she does?

EXERCISES

1. Why does the woman who fills out the form for the mother seem "so much happier" and why does she take the money? In the same scene, in what way does the other child's staring fit the narrator's understanding of how the first day experience affected her? What would happen to the story if the first sentence were left out?

2. Try to write a synopsis of this story in one paragraph. What elements would the reader who only looks at your summary miss?

3. As much as possible Jones keeps to the first person, present tense to communicate the immediacy of the events to the child. Several times, however, he has the narrator pull back and have an adult view. When, how, and why does he do this?

4. Expand the scene on the way to the second school. Keep in touch with Jones' characters and maintain the same narrative style.

Ernest Hemingway's "A Very Short Story" appears to violate some earlier practices we have suggested: the scenes are many and brief and the key characters are stock characters. However, we take the story to be a summary that relies on us knowing something about the events that render them typical. In parody, satire, and allegory, the characters exist to drive home a message and so we do not expect the writer to develop them in the same way as we might in another type of story. The story and the plot are simple. Boy meets girl; boy loses girl. The war-time setting provides the set, so to speak. The characters—a young, wounded soldier who falls in love with the young, healthy nurse—have been used in a thousand stories and movies, including Hemingway's. The events are quite what we might expect and the scenes are almost like a movie scenario (an art film, no doubt, because the heroes are not reunited), mostly narrated rather than shown. Here are a few of the scenes or presumed scenes:

1. An opening on the hospital roof with a wounded soldier and a young girl who have fallen in love (or, at least, fallen in sex) and who have sex.
2. The operation scene.
3. Settling into a type of hospital domesticity.
4. A scene in the church (the Duomo).
5. The letters arriving.
6. A scene in which they talk about their wedding plans and decide to hold the marriage after he has a job in the States.
7. A quarrel scene on the train.
8. A trip home.
9. Luz returns to hospital.
10. Luz is seduced by an Italian major (of course).
11. Luz writes a dear John letter.
12. The major dumps Luz.
13. Luz writes to America to tell the young soldier (now former) about the end of the affair.
14. The boy takes a ride through Lincoln park and makes love to a salesgirl who gives him gonorrhea.

In fact, Hemingway touches upon so many expandable scenes one could almost write a novel from "A Very Short Story."

Hemingway condenses a typical story into a small area to show us that it was a typical pattern during and after the First World War. He expects us to understand that war brings on feelings of impermanence, isolation, and separation that put people under intense pressure to seize the moment and rush into romantic relationships. The scenes that along rush, tumbling over one another, capture the intensity of a war-time romance. The plot is driven by the sequence of scenes but the readers have to supply the elaboration and connections from their experience with literature and life.

But, once the war is over, the romance is likely to cool. It's an old story. The assumed scene in which we are told that Luz and he agree to wait, linked to the scene when they have the fight, suggests that it is Luz who convinces him to go back to America without her. Because Hemingway reveals none of their back story, we don't know her motives. What he did before the war, what he will do in the future (except have some unfortunate sexual encounters) we know nothing of, nor need we. The characters don't need to be three dimensional because, in this story what counts is what they do, not why they do it out of their character. Luz has the affair with the major because she is lonely. What we don't know, though we may conjecture, is why she chooses this solution to her loneliness.

Despite the brevity of the scenes, Hemingway does dramatize those that are a bit longer. In the opening scene we learn that the affair has already begun, that the war is on (the search lights), and that they have been having some kind of party on the roof (the bottles which we assume are wine bottles). In a later scene, we see them in church where, we assume, they are praying for his safe return. Hemingway sketches the moment by letting us know that there are other people and that it was "dim and quiet." After the armistice, when he gets the letters, sorts them, and reads them, Hemingway neatly encapsulates their content in a sentence that, considering later events, becomes ironic: "They were all about the hospital, and how much she loved him, and how it was impossible to get along without him, and how terrible it was missing him at night." An experienced reader will intuit that a reversal is coming. In a later moment, after having been ditched by the major, Luz's unanswered letter to Chicago suggests that she is regretful but hopes to reopen communications and, perhaps, revivify their relationship.

The plot begins on the roof with a love affair and comes to an end in lust and venereal disease. The brief and suggested scenes allow us to see the curve of events over a longer period of time than one might expect in "A Very Short Story."

EXERCISES

1. How is "A Very Short Story" not short? Why might Hemingway decided to move the story along so rapidly? How does he indicate that the others have empathy for the couple? Why is the narrator omniscient? Are there any indications that Hemingway may have had his tongue in his cheek when he wrote this story?

2. Describe the transitions from event to event. What does Hemingway assume you know? Put in one or two such suggested but not stated transitions.

3. Every paragraph, in fact almost every sentence and sometimes part of a sentence, contains a scene. Choose one and expand it with detail. As much as you can, keep to the Hemingway voice.

ADDITIONAL EXERCISES

1. Examine the structure of scenes in Sagstetter's "The Thing With Willie." How many scenes are there? What does each accomplish? What kind of material is summarized? How are events handled that occur before the ongoing present time of the story?

2. Earley's "Just Married" is really one large scene surrounded by an opening and a short final scene. Why might Earley have structured his story that way?

3. Outline or make marginal notes on the methods of characterization in Bel Kaufman's "Sunday in the Park."

4. How would you describe the conflict in Kaufman's story? Is the ending a fortuitous surprise, or has the author built toward it carefully?

5. Return to the detective story set in motion in Exercise 4 on page 218. Imagine that some time has passed. The inspector has interviewed Mr. and Mrs. X, who are now left alone to respond to what has happened. Pick up the story with their interaction.

6. Recast Jeffrey Sweet's "Last Day of Camp" (Chapter 15) as a short story. Can you do so in one scene?

VERISIMILITUDE

We could have dealt with this topic in any of the previous sections because the writer's successful handling of characterization, plot, setting, and scene creates in the reader a feeling of **verisimilitude**—a sense that both individual elements and the whole fiction is *like the truth*. Of course, in creative nonfiction your story elements and overall story *are* the truth.

A historian or biographer has to report precisely literal reality, something that anyone else who has found the same evidence would report. (Differing interpretations, of course, are another matter.) Fiction writers have only to give the *impression* that their fictive history or biography follows the rules of evidence.

Therefore, while writers cannot be arbitrary, they need not prove that the facts can be tested in the chemistry lab or FBI files. Verisimilitude is like Nutrasweet: it needs to taste like sugar but not *be* sugar.

Inexperienced writers often waste energy trying to re-create literal reality rather than an impression of it. Experienced writers understand that, for the sake of a good story, readers are willing to suspend their disbelief in the "facts" of the fictive world. Thus readers already do half the job of producing a feeling of reality. For example: because we tell stories about our parents to others, we accept easily the appearance of storytelling that we find in Jones' "The First Day."

Readers don't task writers with explaining which chemical laws allow a prince to be turned into a flounder, or how a spaceship can go faster than light, or what motivates a white whale to go around eating legs, or exactly how a sudden coup managed to establish a patriarchal society in New England despite the Constitution and U.S. Army. Readers never ask how first-person narrators can remember verbatim conversations that happened two or ten or thirty years ago. We don't see how the young soldier gets to the front in "A Very Short Story." The "how" is unimportant for this story. *If the characters believe in the fictive world*, we'll believe.

In fact, when the writer goes about nervously matching the fictive world to the phenomenal world, the reader begins to question the fiction. It is best not to explain how it happens that your character can fly. Just let your hero fly early and late, have Lois Lane believe it, and we'll believe it so long as we are convinced that the unbelievable fact works in the story. Interestingly enough, a story will lack verisimilitude only if our flying character doesn't fly when, for example, abandoned on a lonely desert island (unless, of course, the writer has created a reason the character cannot fly in that particular circumstance).

Verisimilitude is maintained as long as the writer is careful about the following matters:

1. *The characters should behave consistently from scene to scene* (not just in one scene), or the reader must be prepared for a deviation from an expected behavior or trait. A personage who has been a coward throughout cannot suddenly save a child from a runaway horse just because the writer has discovered that the situation requires the child to be saved and grow up to invent the electric light bulb. Nor can the writer finesse the point by saying "something just came over him." If you haven't done it in the first place, you need to **foreshadow**—to find some way to suggest the possibility that the coward can be brave. In brief, a story begins to lack verisimilitude when the special identity of the character is ignored merely to satisfy the plot.

2. *Surprising plot elements shouldn't pop up merely to get out of a dead end.* The long-lost, rich uncle can't be made to appear just when the newlyweds are about to go down for the third time. (See **deus ex machina** in the Glossary.)

3. *All the props are planted before they are needed.* The gun doesn't just happen to be in the purse. Either we see it put into the purse, or we are convinced

by other means that it is likely to be there. (Incidentally, if we are shown a loaded gun in a purse, it had better go off sometime in the story.) This principle is a variation of number 2.

4. *The outside reality that the story calls on the reader to know is rendered accurately.* When a writer depends on the reader's knowledge of outside facts for some of the internal effects of the story, then the facts must (a) have verisimilitude in the story and (b) accurately reflect outside reality. A chase scene in New York City that has the pursuer's car traveling due east on Broadway (mostly a north-south street) is likely to offend the experienced reader's sense of reality with no gain for the fiction. Readers will more easily accept Superwoman deflecting bullets with her bracelets than they will accept that she did it on the border between Alabama and Arizona. The need for accuracy cannot be overstressed. If your readers catch you in a factual mistake, you may lose them.

5. *Your characters must interact with the environment or "set" you have created for them in credible ways.* If a scene occurs in a howling gale on the deck of a schooner, don't have them whisper to one another. If your characters are two recluses in a house full of cats, the cats will be rubbing up against the characters' legs, scratching at the Victorian sofa, and sniffing around the hamburger. One of your recluses will be forever shooing the cats away. For more on how characters interact with their world, see the drama section. The essential point is that we believe in characters who see, hear, taste, touch, and smell the world in which the writer has placed them.

Creating verisimilitude requires that you plot (or replot) so the "equipment" necessary to move the story—straw, caves, knowledge, experience, ray guns—does not magically or awkwardly appear in the scene just at the moment needed. If you don't plan (or go back and fix up), the sudden appearance of the new element will unpleasantly surprise the reader: "How did that get there? Did I miss something? Why would George kill Andrea? I think the writer got stuck." When you have destroyed verisimilitude in this way, readers begin to ask the kinds of questions that destroy belief in your story.

As you can see, foreshadowing in both a limited sense (getting the gun into the purse) and a more profound sense (suggesting changes in relationships) is at the heart of creating a sense that the story is like reality.

Unsophisticated writers often try to justify an event—a coincidence, for example—that is not convincing *in the story* by saying, "But that's the way it happened." Strange though it seems, some things, like coincidence, happen more in "real" life than they can in fiction or, to put the issue another way, coincidence happens differently in life than it can in fiction.

For example, in real life you might be broke and alone in a big city, let's say Chicago. Night is coming on. Your family can't be reached because they've gone to Nepal on vacation. Besides, you don't even have enough money to make a call. You are getting frightened as you walk the Loop in the crowd of homeward-bound people. Suddenly a hundred-dollar bill swirls down in the stiff breeze off Lake Michigan and lands right at your feet. Saved! Once in a billion times you have won the lottery of life. In real life, the chance may be a billion to one, but there is room in reality for that statistical *one*.

In plotting, there are no statistics. Everything that happens, even a coincidence, is part of the writer's plan. It is the writer who is dealing out the fifty-dollar bills for the character. The reader of a story would feel that the happy coincidence just described occurs only because the writer could not think of another, more logical solution to the character's dilemma. The wind-blown inheritance, no matter how well disguised, is a cop-out, a way of rescuing the character that does not grow from the situation (except that Chicago is windy) or from the character's identity. Because the writer has not plotted well, the surprise that has been sprung on us is not satisfying: no amount of foresight could have predicted it *in this story*.

In contrast, the surprise that grows from an inevitable but unanticipated event at the climax of the story is one of the pleasures you provide your reader, who says, "I should have realized that." Some stories are aimed directly at this pleasure—for example, O. Henry-type short stories or James Bond novels. But the surprise that is not inevitable, the surprise that readers cannot kick themselves for having missed because it was foreshadowed, the surprise that seems to exist only to keep the action going or to get the characters offstage—that kind of surprise destroys verisimilitude.

EXERCISE

1. Can you think of ways to use such an unexpected event as the windblown money without injuring the reader's sense of verisimilitude? For example, what if you did not use the event at the end of a story but at the beginning? Work out the first paragraph of a story that has the event as its central incident. Can you think of any other ways to give the event verisimilitude?

2. List the ways in which the authors convince (or fail to convince) the reader that the following potentially unlikely circumstances are in fact like reality (obviously, don't worry about the ones you haven't read).

   a. Mr. Doran's accepting the trap set for him rather than just moving out of the boarding house to avoid marrying Polly.
   b. The snake's escaping in "Rhody's Path" and Rhody's being the one whom it bites.
   c. The mother's becoming the bully at the end of "Sunday in the Park."
   d. That a young boy goes to Wizard School and learns spells rather than to junior high school and learns math.
   e. Lilliputians.

3. What techniques does Hemingway use in "A Very Short Story" so that we accept his story's reversals? Can you find elements of foreshadowing?

4. As a fiction or for that matter any other kind of writing, you will need to find the answers to questions like the following. Can you? How?

    a. Turn over a Toyota truck with a hand grenade?
    b. What are beer brands from Argentina?
    c. Will a typical college library have many windows or few?
    d. What were the hit songs in January 1980?

PROBLEMS

In this section we discuss some typical problems of beginning writers. Some of these are illustrated here. Some would take perhaps an entire story to illustrate, so we have merely described the problem. In a sense, we are protecting the guilty and saving you from reading too much ineffective prose.

Needless Complication

A misguided sense of what makes for verisimilitude, or a desire to surprise the reader, can lead a writer to give a character an unconvincing action. In the following opening passage, the student writer is so intent on piling up details and creating suspense that he fails to build the character and situation in a truly plausible way.

> Brian brushed his long blond hair out of his eyes, then quietly opened the door to his bedroom. He was tall and rather thin. As he gently closed the door, he thought himself lucky that his parents hadn't heard him come in two hours late from his date. The room was consumed by darkness except for the narrow streak of light along the bottom of the door. He turned and tip-toed over to his desk.
>
> He opened the drawer slowly and began to carefully sort through the disarray. It was hopeless, groping about in the darkness, so he reached over and drew the curtains open slightly. Moonlight shown in illuminating the scene. Bending over to look into the drawer, he spied them—a small bottle of pills in the back right hand corner. He pulled the pills out of the drawer and set them on his nightstand.

Of course, you can spot any number of problems in style, diction, and even grammar and spelling. But the conceptual failure would remain even after you smoothed out the rough spots. Here it is: Brian is searching for drugs. When the reader learns this, the elaboration of the search becomes unconvincing. Who would "hide" drugs so carelessly? Brian should know just how to get his hands on the bottle. All the business about a hopeless disarray and letting in the moonlight rings false once we discover what he is actually doing.

Misuse of Dialogue

Too often in premise or adventure fiction, characterization is given no attention. As a result, dialogue serves only obvious expository purposes. Because the
writer of the following material is so concerned that the reader understand the
situation, the characters seem to exist only for that purpose.

> "Colonel Yeshnick, I refuse to sign this visa for Donnis to defect to
> the United States," responded General Alexeev in a rejecting manner.
> Colonel Yeshnick replied placatingly, "Sir, he will be immigrating,
> not defecting to the United States, and you are the only one left from
> the Premier on down who has to approve it. Sir, with all due respect,
> you promised him that he would be allowed to leave if he would not
> retire from athletics until after the Olympic Games. Not only did he
> compete, but he won the silver medal, and also set a new. . . ."

The dialogue seems forced and artificial because it is. It is in the service of exposition that could be handled more smoothly in another way. In fact, the entire
story is told primarily through conversations between these two officers, while
Donnis, the character whose fate is at stake, hardly gets any attention. Even
though we are always hearing voices, we are never getting in touch with characters. They are doing the narrator's work. Note also the awkward, heavy-handed
use of designators.

Here is a shorter example of dialogue being used, obviously and clumsily,
to do the work of exposition.

> "You must be that Penny fellow from Bangor. I'm Mrs. Johnson.
> We're the caretakers. The Cables are expecting you. Come with me."

This passage can also serve to illustrate another ineffective use of dialogue: the
attempt at verisimilitude that comes from trying to detail the most trivial kinds
of "actual" speech. In this category we include those interchanges of "hello"
and "goodbye" that have no emotion or characterizing energy. Just because it is
easy to make these exchanges sound authentic is no reason to use them in a
piece of fiction. Better a few instances of **indirect discourse**—the narrator's
"after saying hello" or "after stating his business" or "the introductions having
been made"—than a tedious reproduction of speech. Rarely would we need to
belabor this part of a scene or transition, and even more rarely would we need
to have it dramatized. (See Chapter 14, "Dialogue and Its Problems.")

Sudden Comfort

Beginning writers often call too much attention to the contrivances that their
stories depend upon. We have read too many stories in which, within the course
of seven or eight pages, morose lovers or spouses become suicidal, and when

they need a weapon to blast them out of their misery, the author conveniently provides one—all this just as the story is about to end.

Case in point: Bill's wife has left him. He regrets that he has been a drunk and a bully, often forcing himself on her in brutal ways. But now, seeing that she has moved out, he convinces himself that all is lost. His tortured mind leads him to set up a romantic dinner for himself and an imaginary version of his wife. Just before he brings that special bottle of wine to the table, something draws him to a nightstand: "Bill reached under the drawer and pulled off an object that had been obviously concealed." Well, of course, this mysterious object is identified a few sentences later as the "small 38 caliber pistol" that he fires into his temple. How convenient for Bill and for the author.

The sudden appearance of a gun or any other fortuitous plot saver happens, in part, because the story is weak and skeletal to begin with. However, only in first drafts, when the flow of events is taking on a shape, are such conveniences forgivable. Then it's time to recognize the problem and do something about it.

1. To revamp the whole story because it is hackneyed.
2. To create a plausible reason, long before it is needed, for a gun to be available, and to build that reason into the story with some subtlety.
3. To avoid depending on the gun gimmick altogether.

Sudden Omniscience

Once you have established a perspective from which events and information are revealed, you must stick to it. One student writer made his main character, Connor, the central intelligence. We go where he goes, see what he sees, and have access to his thoughts and feelings. Connor, who runs a bar, has decided to walk Katherine, one of his waitresses, to her car. It's late at night:

> As he walked her to where she had parked her rental car, he could see from her face that she was still upset over the night's events.

But wait! Nothing that comes earlier in the story allows Connor to know that she is driving a rented car. The narrator has moved too far outside of the limited perspective chosen for this story. We wonder whether this information has special importance (it doesn't) or is simply an attempt at verisimilitude—a fortuitous fact that backfires.

Ping-Pong

Shifting the point of view too rapidly, especially without any clear reason for breaking the convention of maintaining a single point of view throughout a scene (if not an entire work), disorients the reader and strains credibility.

In one student work, we are asked to follow the path of a mysterious killer, taking things in through his perspective: "The night sounds were a calming friend to him" and "he noticed a car light stop on the bridge above him" and "his adrenaline began to flow freely" establish the reader's means of access to the story. When the author writes "After the killer had ascended the sloping hill up to the bridge, his form became visible to the stranger . . . ," we are momentarily jolted by the shift in perspective, and to no good end.

In a story about Michael Locklear, whose thoughts about a coming confrontation with the Soviet Union are generously provided, we suddenly encounter the following after Michael's conversation with Admiral Pete Mitchell: "Mitchell returned to his chair and levelled his gaze at the President. Damn it, he thought, there was no alternative." And then, in the next paragraph, "Locklear shifted in his seat." Nothing justifies this convenient presentation of Mitchell's thoughts, which fractures our illusion of *being with* Locklear throughout the story. Furthermore, "Mitchell" is too easily confused with "Michael"— the main character's first name.

The same mistake occurs in the following scene, in which a policeman, Bob Bryant, is questioning Miss Lee about the death of her boyfriend. Bryant is the story's central intelligence whose perspective the reader shares.

> Boy, you're losing your touch and your sensitivity, Bob told himself. "I'm sorry to bother you, but we need to ask you some more questions. Can you think of any reason why someone would have wanted Wayne dead?"
> Miss Lee seemed calmer now, but she never got over her agitation during the half hour she spent with Bryant.

Unless Miss Lee's agitation is shown outwardly (and it isn't) or is somehow perceived by Bryant, we shouldn't be told about it.

Wrong Technique

In the same story treated in the "Sudden Omniscience" section, the author has attempted to reproduce Connor's thoughts rather than simply characterize them:

> "God it's hot," thought Connor, "maybe I should think about investing in an air conditioner for the joint. Yeah, and I oughtta set the temperature *way* low. The girls wouldn't be wild about it, but I bet business would triple. Hah—I'm a damn funny guy."

These thoughts read too much like self-conscious speech; even Connor's habits of pronunciation are reproduced. Better to simplify:

> Connor wondered if he should buy an air conditioner. If he had one, he would set it way low. The girls wouldn't be wild about it, but business would probably triple. Connor was amazed at his own cleverness.

Notice how the revised second and third sentences come across clearly as Connor's thoughts even though they aren't given designators, quotation marks, or verbal quirks. The narrator has slid quietly in and out of Connor's mind.

Pogo Stick

Beginning writers often feel the need to sketch many short scenes, presenting some bit of information in each but not developing any of them fully enough to further the plot or deepen the character. This quick jumping around from scene to scene without any clear direction being established only confuses the reader.

In the Bob Bryant story discussed earlier, an early scene in the station house contains a celebration of Bob's successful "sting" operation in which a major narcotics organization was put out of business and the leader shot. The scene does nothing for the story at hand; none of its details have any relevance later on. All it establishes is that Bryant is a policeman, something the first mention of his current case would make clear anyway.

Descriptive Clutter

Sometimes the search for verisimilitude ends in amassed details that only slow the story down while the reader is forced to pay attention to "realistic" trivia. Here is an example:

> He went back to the van. The door on the driver's side was slightly rusting near the bottom front corner. He opened the door, climbed in, and closed the door. The sound of vibrating steel resounded throughout the car.

For this story, we don't need to know the degree or exact placement of the rust, nor the three steps the character takes to get behind the wheel. Essentially, the writer's job is to get him moving again. So, "He got back in the van and winced as the rusty door slammed shut" would do it.

Another kind of clutter comes from trying to introduce too many characters at once. Here is the opening of a novel that causes more confusion than clarification, especially since some of the characters mentioned here are never heard of again.

> Dolly McKee's timing was less than perfect. Sam Parker was just getting to the part of his meeting with the president that Ken Meyers had been patiently waiting to hear about.
>
> "I'm sorry to break in," Dolly said, her hand on the doorknob, little more than her birdlike face visible as she leaned into the room. "Levi says he's got to talk to Ken. He's upset about something. It sounds important. Can you handle it, or should I call Simpson?"

Sonofabitch, Meyers thought. What a time for a housekeeping problem. Just when Parker might say something about whether Babcock was
planning to reappoint him. He told Dolly to show the black man into
his office.

Even though one could argue that these characters are real to one another, such
a barrage of names, labels, and pronouns will raise any reader's anxiety level—
and for no good reason.

Other Problems

We have no space to illustrate the story in which one action follows another and
yet nothing happens. That is, the events don't reveal character or shape an
understanding of some issue. Nor will we ask you to consider the other extreme:
the story that constantly screams out its meaning by glossing every action and
every physical detail as if the writer felt obliged to present both the story and its
interpretation. Nor the kind in which the author has gone back and disguised all
the evidence we need to make any sense out of what's going on, believing that
bewildering the reader is a worthy goal if one can later show how cleverly the
obscuring had been done. These and other problems take whole stories to illustrate. In any case, a reader, classmate, teacher, or editor will be quick to point out
the myriad of difficulties that interfere with effective storytelling, especially in
your work.

It is easy to go wrong in telling stories because so many demands come to
bear at the same moment—character development, plot, exposition, description, narration. You can't let down your guard and cruise for a while, because
what is said on page 20 has to connect with page 6 and both with page 23. You
need constantly to anticipate, recognize, and then solve the problem. The pay-
off is an effective story.

11

Creative Nonfiction

THE NATURE OF CREATIVE NONFICTION

"Creative nonfiction," a relatively new term, describes a host of familiar sub-genres including essay, personal essay, letter, memoir, anecdote, and journal entry. In one sense, the term identifies an old bias, the attitude some people have that writing nonfiction is somehow a lesser creative activity than writing poetry, fiction, or drama. However, if we go back less than three centuries, we discover that English writers like Daniel Defoe and Henry Fielding were borrowing the prestige of nonfiction for the new form, the novel, that they were developing. *Tom Jones* purports to be biography, while *Moll Flanders* comes to us in the guise of a slightly edited memoir by an untutored woman. The form in which the fiction is cast immediately confers reality—verisimilitude—on the fiction. After all, people do keep diaries, write history, and exchange e-mails.

The term "creative nonfiction" reminds us once more that all writing can be creative and that the barriers between one genre and another is porous, as Tony Early suggests in his postscript to the short story "Just Married" (p. 275). Nonfiction can involve just as much problem solving, selection, and invention as do any of the other genres. From this point of view, a more useful term would be "literary nonfiction." This term suggests that the distinction is not between creativity and noncreativity but between nonfiction written primarily to pass on information and nonfiction in which information serves other purposes. Look, for example, at the following two paragraphs, both describing the same hotel in Spain:

> 1. For those of you on a tight budget, I suggest you consider the Hotel Comercio for $25.00 per person. The exterior is unprepossessing, but the rooms are clean, if a bit old-fashioned, and the proprietors are extremely pleasant. For a few more dollars, ask for a room with a balcony so that you may observe the life of the city. I give it one star.

> 2. Below my balcony the life of the city flowed past. In the early morning a team of mules with tinkling bells pulled the trash wagon along the street. Housewives carried fruit and vegetables home from the indoor market. Two blind lottery vendors and bootblacks called out for clients. A herd of goats trotted by, surrounding a black-robed priest. A truck driver sounded his horn at a slowly walking burro overloaded with sacks of grain. Across the street, boys looked into a shopwindow full of athletic shirts with the names of American universities on them, and a small boy pushed a wheelbarrow of onions up the street.

> from Merrill F. McLane, *East from Granada: Hidden Andalusia and Its People*

Despite the first person, example number one is intended to pass on the facts about the hotel and the balcony. The second example is meant to allow us to share the writer's excitement about what he saw from the balcony. Such literary travel writing, a subgenre of the memoir, is invested with personality and with a sense of place that goes beyond mileage tables, directions, types of accommodations, and price. The writer is allowing us to share an experience.

Often such pieces read like adventure stories or quests during which the author reports discoveries that have emotional power as well as universal meaning. As in fiction, the author evokes the feel of the place while passing on to you the population statistics or the price of a hotel or the latest research in animal sexual behavior. We don't mean to erect a brick wall between writing to report information and creative nonfiction. "How-to" subgenres can have a literary dimension even while their thrust is to provide the facts of the case. Many restaurant reviews, medical or exercise columns, and sports columns transcend—as reading experiences—the information and advice they give us.

The additional dimension can come from the entertainment the essay gives us, from the aesthetic satisfaction we receive because the piece is so well written, or from our sense that the facts may add up to more than appears on the surface. For example, Conniff's article, "Close Encounters of the Sneaky Kind" (pp. 281–285) on one level appears to be a summary of recent research on sexual behavior in fish, birds, snakes, and insects. One of the reading pleasures we experience in the article is its humorous language, comparisons, and double entendres. We enjoy the process of learning and Coninff has striven as creatively as any other writer to find ways that we might enjoy the information. But he has gone further. By the end of the article, we begin to suspect that the article adds up to something more than a report of the sex life of the dung beattle and the mating strategies of lizards told in the language of human sexual behavior. If nature shows us so much variety, who are we to judge that there is but one sexual behavior?

In obvious ways, creative nonfiction is likely to be the natural outgrowth of research, diaries, and journal work. In fact, your journal writing, if it is more than a flat record of events, *is* one kind of creative nonfiction. The very journal that Anaïs Nin kept (see pp. 21–22) in order to be, in part, a seedbed for stories and novels came in the end (with selection, revision, and polishing) to surpass her fiction; the journal is now considered her main literary achievement. We can imagine the number of interviews and amount of reading that Conniff had to do and notes he took. Unlike reading Nin's journals, of course, reading Conniff's notes would give us little literary pleasure.

Though creative nonfiction comes in many packages, today it is most frequently thought of as short, sometimes fragmentary writing offered up with some kind of insight or emotional charge. That is, it has much the flavor of a journal entry. Stephen Dunn's "Locker Room Talk" below may well have started as just such a journal entry, but it has been developed into an engaging meditation with a firm shape and focus. It has become the kind of memoir or personal essay, a counterpart to the short story, that we will have in mind when making further remarks about creative nonfiction in this chapter:

> Having been athletic most of my life, I've spent a fair amount of time in locker rooms and have overheard my share of "locker room talk." For reasons I couldn't understand for many years, I rarely participated in it and certainly never felt smug or superior about my lack of participation. In fact, I felt quite the opposite; I thought something was wrong with me. As a teenager and well into my twenties I'd hear someone recount his latest real or wishful conquest, there'd be a kind of general congratulatory laughter, tacit envy, but what I remember feeling most was wonderment and then embarrassment.
>
> There was of course little or no public information about sex when I was growing up in the forties and fifties. The first time I heard someone talk about having sex was in the school yard (the locker room without walls) when I was twelve or thirteen. Frankie Salvo, a big boy of sixteen. Frankie made it sound dirty, something great you do with a bad girl. It was my first real experience with pornography and it was thrilling, a little terrifying too. My mind conjured its pictures. Wonderment. Not wonderful.
>
> Some years later, after experience, wonderment gave way to embarrassment. I wasn't sure for whom I was embarrassed, the girl

spoken about, the story teller, or myself. Nevertheless, I understood the need to tell. I, too, wanted to tell my good friend, Alan, but for some reason I never told him very much. In retrospect, it was my first test with what Robert Frost calls knowing "the delicacy of when to stop short," a delicacy I took no pride in. I felt excessively private, cut off.

I began thinking about all of this recently because in the locker room at college a young man was telling his friend—loud enough for all of us to hear—what he did to this particular young woman the night before, and what she did to him. It was clear how important it was for him to impress his friend, far more important than the intimacy itself, as if the sexual act weren't complete until he had completed it among other men.

This time I knew something about the nature of my embarrassment. It wasn't just that he had cheapened himself in the telling, but like all things which embarrass us it had struck some part of me that was complicitous, to a degree guilty, the kind of guilt you feel every time there's a discrepancy between what you know you're supposed to feel (correct feelings) and what in fact you've thought of, if not done. But more than that, I was embarrassed by the young man's assumption—culturally correct for the most part—that we other men in the locker room were his natural audience. There were five or six of us, and we certainly didn't boo or hiss. Those of us who were silent (all of us except his friend) had given our quiet sanctions.

What did it all mean? That men, more often than not, in a very fundamental way prefer other men? Or was it all about power, an old story, success with women as a kind of badge, an accoutrement of power? Was the young man saying to the rest of us, "I'm powerful"? I thought so for a while, but then I thought that he seemed to be saying something different. He was saying out loud to himself and to the rest of us that he hadn't succumbed to the greatest loss of power, yielding to the attractiveness and power of women, which could mean admitting he felt something or, at the furthest extreme, had fallen in love.

From Samson, to the knight in Keats' poem "La Belle Dame Sans Merci," to countless examples in world literature, the warning is clear: women take away your power. To fall in love with one is to be distracted from the world of accomplishment and acquisitiveness. But to have sex and then to talk about it publicly is a kind of final protection, the ultimate prophylactic against the dangers of feeling.

"Love means always having to say you're sorry," a friend once said to me. The joke had its truth, and it implied—among other things—a mature love, a presumption of mutual respect and equality. On some level the young man in the locker room sensed and feared such a relationship. He had ventured into the dark and strange world of women and had come out unscathed, literally untouched. He was back with us, in the locker room which was the country he understood and lived in, with immunity. He thought we'd be happy for him.

EXERCISES

1. Base an essay on a specific or generalized scene in which women talk about men.

2. Dunn calls the locker-room talk "the ultimate prophylactic against the dangers of feeling." What other kinds of group behavior function in the same way? Develop a narrative illustration from your own experience.

A nonfiction counterpart to the novel is a work like Norman Mailer's *The Executioner's Song*, in which history is reimagined with a novelist's tools and techniques. Michael Herr's *Dispatches* (a series of highly stylized personal essays about the journalist's experiences in Vietnam); Ernest Hemingway's *Death in the Afternoon* (a mixture of narration and meditation on bullfighting); Annie Dillard's *Pilgrim at Tinker Creek* (a meditative journal with fine observations of natural processes); and William Warner's *Beautiful Swimmers* (a classic piece of nature-writing) represent different types of book-length creative nonfiction.

Contemporary creative nonfiction is most often—though, as we have seen, not always—told in the first person or with the strong sense of an "I" present. The unreality, if you will, of such nonfiction is that it purports to be literal, a "real" picture of what people did, feel, and think. The very neatness of a piece like Rita Dove's "Loose Ends," however, should expose its novelistic qualities of selection and shaping:

> For years the following scene would play daily at our house: Home from school, my daughter would heave her backpack off her shoulder and let it thud to the hall floor, then dump her jacket on top of the pile. My husband would tell her to pick it up—as he did every day—and hang it in the closet. Begrudgingly with a snort and a hrrumph, she would comply. The ritual interrogation began:
> "Hi, Aviva. How was school?"
> "Fine."
> "What did you do today?"
> "Nothing."
> And so it went, every day. We cajoled, we pleaded, we threatened with rationed ice cream sandwiches and new healthy vegetable casseroles, we attempted subterfuges such as: "What was Ms. Boyers wearing today?" or: "Any new pets in science class?" but her answer remained the same: I dunno.
> Asked, however, about the week's episodes of "MathNet," her favorite series on Public Television's "Square One," or asked for a quick gloss of a segment of "Lois and Clark" that we happened to miss, and she'd spew out the details of a complicated story, complete with character development, gestures, every twist and back-flip of the plot.

Is TV greater than reality? Are we to take as damning evidence the soap opera stars attacked in public by viewers who obstinately believe in the on-screen villainy of Erica or Jeannie's evil twin? Is an estrangement from real life the catalyst behind the escalating violence in our schools, where children imitate the gun-'em-down pyrotechnics of cop-and-robber shows?

Such a conclusion is too easy. Yes, the influence of public media on our perceptions is enormous, but the relationship of projected reality— i.e., TV—to imagined reality—i.e., an existential moment—is much more complex. It is not that we confuse TV with reality, but that we prefer it to reality—the manageable struggle resolved in twenty-six minutes, the witty repartee within the family circle instead of the grunts and silence common to most real families; the sharpened conflict and defined despair instead of vague anxiety and invisible enemies. "Life, my friends, is boring. We must not say so," wrote John Berryman, and many years and "Dream Songs" later he leapt from a bridge in Minneapolis. But there is a devastating corollary to that statement: Life, friends, is ragged. Loose ends are the rule.

What happens when my daughter tells the television's story better than her own is simply this: the TV offers an easier tale to tell. The salient points are there for the plucking—indeed, they're the only points presented—and all she has to do is to recall them. Instant Nostalgia! Life, on the other hand, slithers about and runs down blind alleys and sometimes just fizzles at the climax. "The world is ugly,/ And the people are sad," sings the country bumpkin in Wallace Stevens's "Gubinnal." Who isn't tempted to ignore the inexorable fact of our insignificance on a dying planet? We all yearn for our private patch of blue.

from Rita Dove, "A Handful of Inwardness," in The Poet's World

The opening anecdote about her daughter is the dramatic lever for Rita Dove's observation that television is attractive because it is so condensed and simple. Although everything in the piece is drawn from life, the elements are carefully selected to achieve the same effects of scene, tension, and character that a fiction writer wishes to create. As writers we are aware that the details, including the dialogue, are carefully distilled from dozens of such homecomings to make us experience the parent's sense of frustration.

Before reading on, take another look at "Loose Ends" and list all the elements that suggest we are dealing with an event transformed by memory, selectivity, imagination, and purpose.

Here is our list:

1. "For years" is obviously hyperbole, created for dramatic effect. Children don't behave the exact same way for years or watch the same programs for years.

2. Dove actually calls her anecdote a "scene" to signal us that she is creating a typical event, not an actual one.

3. "Thumped" and other words are chosen for dramatic effect.

4. The dialogue is offered as *habitual* or *representative* rather than as the perfectly remembered language of a specific conversation. This technique allows Dove to avoid the issue of whether an actual dialogue can be accurately remembered.

5. *Lois and Clark* is probably one of many television shows that Aviva enjoyed with members of her family. Dove chooses this one not only for the appeal of the specific but also to suggest something specific about her daughter's interests—beyond mathematics. Dove makes the anecdote convincing through such selection and specificity.

6. The diction and images ("life, on the other hand, slithers about . . . ") appear chosen for effect as they are in a poem.

EXERCISES

1. Use Dove's essay as a springboard for your own consideration, presented through a story, of how public media influence people's perceptions.

2. Write an essay about television like Conniff's, except compare television behavior to the behavior of animals.

While creative nonfiction uses many of the techniques we have come to associate with fiction—scene setting, character development, narration, and dialogue—these elements in nonfiction are more often (and more obviously) shaped in the service of the writer's message, as in Rita Dove's piece. Nonetheless, the reader must agree to believe that the events rendered actually happened exactly as the writer reports. We are not suggesting here that the writer violates the truth—which is the essential promise or contract of nonfiction—but rather that no writing that we would wish to read ever fully represents a slice of life. Selection and compression distort the reality of the minute by minute passage of time, the flow of sensation, and thought. Indeed, the conceptual level of a memoir may be a present-day overlay on a distant experience. The truth is the truth of memory and the truth of the revealed self.

In the following pieces notice how James Jones reveals his helplessness and despair in a "factual" report from Vietnam.

The Beggar Woman

I had seen her on the Sunday, when I was walking back to the hotel for lunch. It being Sunday, there was almost nobody on the street. That made her more noticeable. I was as inured to beggars as the next man. In fact, I had just turned down two ladies with credentials, begging for some Catholic orphanage. If you did not get hardened to the beggars, you would have no money left at all – and you still would not have made a dent in them. But this one was not begging. She was standing, leaning against a shuttered Sunday storefront. I was across the street from her.

Something about her posture caught me. I thought I had never seen anyone look so beat. She stood with her head against the grillwork of the closed store, her face in the corner angle the grill made with the masonry. And she didn't move.

She seemed vaguely familiar, as if I might have seen her up the street near the hotel or the Times office, where the beggars congregated. She was dressed like any Viet woman, a conical straw hat, black trousers, a ragged *ao-dai*. There was no way of telling how old she was. An old US Army musette bag stuffed with something hung from her left shoulder, and she had a bundle of what looked like rags in her other arm.

I watched her a full four minutes, I timed it, and she did not move. Then her shoulders heaved themselves up slowly and fell, as if she were drawing a breath, and she became motionless again.

I wondered if she could be dying, standing there. Instinctively, like some animal reacting, I took a thousand-piastre note out of my wallet and crossed the street and touched her on the shoulder.

Her hand came up. I put the bill in it and patted her on the shoulder. Only then did her head come up, and she looked at me with such a dumb, wordless despair that it was as if someone had thrown acid in my face. I have never seen such destroyed heart, such ravagement of spirit on a person's face. I turned and walked away, realizing belatedly that there had been a scrawny baby in the bundle.

I got as far as the corner before I could get myself stopped, or put my head in order. The baby didn't bother me. The baby didn't matter. It was the woman. I could not even put into thoughts what I was feeling. Most of us have defenses in our personalities. Usually, we have layer after layer of them. Even when we are dying, we can still put some last personality defense on our faces. This was a face from which the last, bottom layer of defense had been peeled away like an onion.

I took the rest of the money I had with me, four thousand piastres, and walked back to her and put that in her hand with the other note. She did not even look at it, and raised he face again, and he face did not change. However much money it was, it would not be enough. She knew it, and I knew it. It might keep her going for a week, maybe even longer, that was all. Somewhere under her defenselessness some part of her seemed to by trying to tell me she appreciated my concern.

I walked away, wondering what kind of hope I'd hoped to give. There wasn't enough money to help her. Not now. The United States had not helped her. Neither had the French. The South Viets hadn't helped her, the North Viets hadn't helped her, the VC had not helped her. And what any of them or all of them might do for future generations would not do her any good at all.

She was all of Vietnam to me.

From *Viet Journal*

The piece is more than a report that there are beggars in Vietnam. Jones transforms it in an indictment of the war.

EXERCISE

Write of a single contact with another human being in which the reader will see the pain or new awareness that the event caused you.

HOW THE WRITER CONVINCES THE READER

Exposure of Self

The "I" in a personal essay promises to be really you, not a character created to tell the story. You cannot say, "Hey, mom, it's a story I made up." She knows better. The "fictions" in creative nonfiction provide no distance between the actual you and the reader. To create a sense of authenticity, you have to look for the real feelings and beliefs and be willing to risk appearing foolish, ignorant, weak, mean spirited, or any other of the hundreds of human frailties to which we are prone. You, not your character will have the warts. For example, in "Locker Room Talk" Stephen Dunn is not only exposing his youthful sexual insecurity but also exposing himself to the accusation that, even now, he is an unmanly sexual wus. Of course, showing your warts may be also a way of verifying the truth element in your writing. Or, even more disturbing to some people, would be the following passage.

> I was twenty-five years old. He [Al] was thirty-eight. He was a black man, the son of a coal miner from Dolomite, Alabama. . . . I was a young white woman from Long Island working at Boston's anti-poverty agency. We had met ten months earlier, in June, and moved in together in October to an old Victorian house just past Brighton Square. I had a two-year-old daughter who couldn't say "Al." She transposed the consonant and vowel and called him "La." He got home from work first and would greet her upon her return from nursery school every day with a snack of Hawaiian punch and animal crackers. They cooked soul food, hooked rugs, and watched football together. He taught her to ride a bike and change the oil in the car.
>
> From Cecilia Cassidy, "Dialysis and the Art of Life Maintenance"

Though certainly not as scandalous as it once was, some blacks and whites will react negatively to this piece because it describes a mixed-race sexual relationship (among other things). But even if the writer could write the piece without the facts of race, she must take the risk of exposing herself to rejection, or even danger, in order to render the emotions truly.

If the personal essay is not honest, the reader will spy out inauthentic emotions and react negatively to easy truths, such as "this teaches us to respect good writing."

Testable Elements Hold Up to the Test

In presenting nonfiction to the public, you must make sure that your handling of events, dates, locations, and other people's attitudes stand up to scrutiny. In a work of fiction, readers may excuse a writer for creating a nonexistent intersection in a well-known urban neighborhood, but they will be far less tolerant in a work that purports to be rooted in fact. Similarly, don't have your character buying a new Studebaker after the company had ceased operation. "It was 1977, and the American Embassy in Saigon was making final plans for evacuation . . . " just won't do. The year should be 1975. And for someone to claim "well—I always remembered it as being 1977" does nothing to mend the broken contract between writer and reader. If a person you are writing about was born in Hoboken, don't relocate to Newark for effect. And just to make your point don't report in your article about the variety of sexual strategies (pp. 281–285) that Barry Sinervo claims humans behave sexually like California lizards (the animal kind) when he doesn't. And be sure to spell his name correctly. (For additional examples, review "Verisimilitude" in Chapter 10.)

Anecdotes Must Feel Universal

Though readers can be engaged in and entertained by the colors and textures of the unfamiliar, the writer must make a connection between the freshness of the material and the familiarity of the felt experience—the shareable human element. In Pablo Medina's "On the Beach," readers encounter specific and perhaps exotic details of the author's childhood in Cuba. However, what makes the memoir click is the universal recognition that this was a defining moment in Medina's life, a deeply felt image of perfection that changes Medina by setting in his mind an ideal of feminine beauty:

> On their day off, the maid Sagrada and her husband, Manolo, took me with them to a beach on the outskirts of the city. I was used to the clubs and resort beaches in Matanzas, particularly Varadero with its pearly sand and crystal waters. This particular beach, however, was different. For one thing it was very crowded and, unlike Varadero, the people there were dark skinned and rowdy. Few of them wore swimsuits, many going into the water fully clothed or, in some cases, in their underwear. The younger children wore nothing at all. I remember the smell of food, as the beach had been turned into a giant kitchen, with families gathered round big pots filled with *moros con cristianos* (rice and black beans) and roast pork. There was music, too—guitars and

the tat-tat-tat, ta-pum, tat-tat of bongos, and one naked girl, no older than four, doing the rumba to the accompaniment of her family's syncopated clapping.

It was an overcast day, and damp, so that the air was heavy and the sand cold and unpleasant to sit on. My physical discomfort was heightened by the awareness of not belonging—I was too white, too inhibited.

In order to pass the time, I occupied myself by building a medieval sand city. As I was giving shape to the large wall that surrounded the burg, a girl of fourteen or fifteen approached the water's edge. She wore a white cotton dress and walked lithely, sliding her feet and kicking up sand as she went. When she reached the waves she did not stop to test the water, nor did she make a face as people are prone to do when their toes first feel the cool sea. Rather, she kept going without missing a step as if the ocean was her element and she was returning to it after a brief foray onto solid ground. The girl reached waist-deep water then dove under. Her head surfaced a few yards away, eyes closed, and a smile parting her glazed lips. She rubbed her face with both hands and started back, her gait the same: casual, relaxed, like a tropical Nereid.

Out of the water, she paused by me to stretch her body, shake her matted hair, and comb it back with her fingers. The dress clung to her body delineating every dip and curve and swell. I was still kneeling, looking up at this beauty in white when she glanced in my direction with eyes like glinting coals. She offered a smile and disappeared into the crowd.

I could work no more. I returned to where Sagrada and Manolo were sitting and lay back on the sand to watch the gouache of clouds get darker and darker until the rain came and forced everyone off the beach.

To this day that girl is my picture of the feminine ideal and it is to her that I compare the women I know. I am the child building sand castles; she, the one braving the waves, coming back all the more beautiful for it. She smiles; she walks into the sea of bodies behind us; her interruption is a blessing on my labor.

from *Exiled Memories: A Cuban Childhood*

All of us have experienced moments that stick in the memory (a first smell or taste, a great catch, a brief conversation) that is forever evoked by later experiences. It is this evocative power of memory we recognize and share with Medina.

When readers feel that they are sharing an experience not as voyeurs but because something like it has happened or could happen to them, they feel enriched. Of course, tell-it-all stories of the famous—we suppose the ultimate in personal essays (frequently more fictional than nonfictional)—often describe lives that could hardly be our own. For most of us, however, the interest and pleasure of the reader comes from less pyrotechnic experiences. We are more likely to succeed because of honesty, close attention to the virtues of accuracy, and careful thought and selection of detail.

VIRTUES IN NONFICTION

If the entries in the following list sound like virtues of fiction as well as of non-fiction, of course the distinction is fuzzy around the edges. In fact, contemporary philosophers and critics would say that there is no pure fiction or nonfiction. That may be true on the cosmic level, but for writers, practical differences exist at the working level. Here is our list.

1. Creative nonfiction often tends to sound like conversation or musing, as in a journal entry or a letter. The style is closer to the colloquial or the familiar than in academic or business writing. However, we do accept the intrusion of more latinate diction and phrasing as well as a greater mix of diction levels than we are likely to be comfortable with in fiction. Rita Dove's "devastating corollary" is more formal than conversational, while the following sentence mixes levels effectively: "The salient points are there for the plucking." In "Chinese Medicine" (Chapter 12), Hilary Tham translates Chinese phrases into English, a convention that would be intrusive in a story but is perfectly acceptable in nonfiction of all types.

2. While fiction should "show not tell," creative nonfiction writers may specifically, though not always, state a thesis, a point they are trying to prove. Sometimes they will tell you exactly what it all means, as in the Dove piece. Still, the most effective creative nonfiction does a good deal of showing, re-creating the event(s).

3. As we have discussed in more detail earlier, despite a carefully limited use of fictional elements, the writer promises to be as honest as possible about the events, emotions, and beliefs that the piece reports. It takes courage to tell an audience of strangers that your father kept a mistress, as Hilary Tham does in her memoir.

4. The writer is almost always talking in the first person and, except for comic writers, tends not to wear a mask. In fact, of course, even the non-fiction writer creates a mask (persona), but the reader is not intended to feel that a mask exists. At the end of the piece, we feel we can say: Dove or Tham *believes* so and so. As an illustration of different effects of mask, look at Tham's prose portrait of her father in "Chinese Medicine" and then at her poem about him (p. 148). Notice how the personal anger is more diffused by the cooler tone Tham employs to tell about her father's desertion. This difference resides partly in the effect of the memoir's first person singular, which becomes the plural "our" and "us" late in the poem. In some ways, of course, the bitter final two lines of the poem and the understatement and control of that bitterness have more impact and tell a much different story to the reader than does the prose.

5. In most creative nonfiction, the writer often uses the storytelling to explore an idea, to meander through a great number of considerations

and reconsiderations, and to digress. In effective fiction, we feel that everything must fit the plot. In nonfiction, the writer might start in one place and end up in a completely different place with a new cast of characters. Often we are in the presence of a mind in the process of thinking, and a piece may feel unshaped (though the lack of shape should be a fiction and a disguise). The structure of much creative nonfiction, when it is not strictly narrative/chronological, is the structure of discovery. Notice how Tham's "Chinese Medicine" starts off as if it is to be about growing up in a Chinese household but changes into a piece about discovery, disappointment, and anger.

PROBLEMS IN CREATIVE NONFICTION

Among the many problems that can sink a piece of creative nonfiction, the following are most weighty (and often just like the problems one finds in fiction):

1. *Poor storytelling that grows from lack of detail, ineffective selection of events or detail, clunky dialogue, and too much explaining.* We have discussed these elements in Chapters 9 and 10.

2. *Factual elements that fail the truth or reality test as in the following sentence:* "While I drank my tea, I pressed the seashell to my ear as I anxiously opened one of mother's bibles to the first page." Try opening a book with one hand while drinking tea and pressing something to your ear. What is factually wrong with the following?

   > A silver-haired gentleman was rapping to attract my attention as he walked to the nearest bench. My attention was on the cane with the silver coat-of-arms engraved on the handle.

   Normally people hold on to the handle of a cane. How did the narrator see the coat-of-arms?

3. *Off-putting tone, especially mawkishness:* "I closed my eyes and urged my mind to wander back to those glorious summer days when I and the world was younger." "Urging" one's mind like one urges a horse appears rather a rough way to treat one's mind. Obvious attempts to impress the reader as in the following: "The strong scent of roses hindered my walking any farther in this old, well-trodden road in an ancient country. The teasing and the beckoning of this wild robust aroma captured my imagination." Not among the least of the problems in this prose is its failure to capture our imagination. (See also Chapter 4, "Language is Your Media.")

4. *The other side of that coin is flat writing, as in*:

> The main mystery of my friend's life centered around his daily routine and one could tell the time by his odyssey from the Red Line Metro to his domicile in the apartment complex on East West Highway which sat at the complex juncture defined by Wisconsin Avenue and Chevy Chase Section Four. (See Chapter 4 on style.)

Beyond the fact that "Odyssey" does not exactly conjure up the image of a "daily routine" (unless meant ironically), the language and sentence structure are more suitable to case histories or legal reports (and not very precise ones, at that).

5. *In order to create intensity or excitement, the writer may actually create a sense that the emotions are inauthentic—that is, false.* Consider the following:

> The dirty wooden box I carried into my house yesterday might have stayed at the estate auction if I'd known what it contained. I bid on it only because I had this weird sense of knowing its contents. Curiosity nearly got the best of me before I got it inside. I hurriedly opened the heavy domed lid.

Apart from any other difficulties in the passage, the author pretends to feelings that she could not have had, since the box turns out to contain memorabilia from her grandmother that proves the truth of a pleasant childhood memory. So, surely she would have bid on it. About her mystical sense of knowing its contents—another reason to bid on it—we also have some doubt. The sum is that the reader comes to sense in the prose an attempt to create excitement by creating an unreal report of the narrator's feelings at the time. Later on, the same writer reports that following the experience, "I heard the blood running through my head. . . ." How often has that experience happened to any of us?

6. *The story fails as a whole to connect to universals and so has a true aimlessness, like a friend walking in and telling us "Yesterday I got a dent in my fender."* We have neither the space nor the unkindness to print a long example, but the piece of nonfiction cited in number 5, about the box, goes on to reveal that her grandmother's stories were based on fact. Gosh! That's the type of "true" anecdote that reports the facts but leaves us saying "So?" A variation of this problem is a story so private that while it may be gripping for you, your family, and friends, it lacks a context that will grip a larger audience. Look at the following series:

a. My uncle Fred ran off to Arizona and married another woman without divorcing his first wife.

b. My mother never talked in front of us kids about Uncle Fred, who ran off to Arizona and married another woman without divorcing his first wife.

c. My mother never talked in front of us kids about Uncle Fred, her brother, who ran off to Arizona and married another woman without divorcing Aunt Sally, my father's sister. I knew it was wrong of me, but I kept in contact with him. However, I never told my parents.

The last in the series starts to have possibilities because it evokes the truths of family secrets and betrayals. For another example, look at Hilary Tham's anecdote about her threat to charge her husband for housework. Without the context of the other memories, it lacks power and becomes more of a cocktail party anecdote. Or, consider what would happen if you removed the last paragraph from Medina's piece. It would then be just a report of a day at the beach.

In a way, of course, what we are telling you here is a truth of all writing: you have to have something interesting to say, and you have to say it well. The prior condition for doing both is to do some serious observing and thinking about both the exterior and the interior worlds.

EXERCISE

Take a simple fact from your family history and, in three paragraphs, elaborate following the same process we did in number 6 in the preceding list of problems.

FINDING MATERIALS

Reading

The personal essay and related forms of creative nonfiction must be sampled and studied by the apprentice writer. Examine the classic models of Seneca, Plutarch, Montaigne, Addison and Steele, Lamb, Emerson, Thoreau, Orwell, and E. B. White. Attend to such contemporaries as Loren Eiseley, Annie Dillard, Peter Matthiessen, and Tom Wolfe. You must read not only to develop a wider sense of the possibilities of subject matter, form, and technique in creative nonfiction, but also to develop expertise in the areas of interest that you mean to pursue in your own writing as Richard Conniff has in the literature of sexual research. For further direction on this kind of exploration, see Chapters 5 and 17.

Exploring Yourself

In creative nonfiction, you can make an essential connection between your responses to experience and your reader's curiosity. If you handle the writing task well, this curiosity will lead to the reader's imaginative engagement with your responses. What do you have to share? Who are you? Think of all of the ways in which you interact with other people, the various roles you play as family member, friend, lover, student, political partisan, employee, leader, patient, client, shopper, borrower or lender, sportsperson, hobbyist, worshipper, and writer. In each of these roles, and in many others, you have particular stories to tell that can connect you with readers who have found themselves in similar roles.

What irks, pleases, or perplexes you? How do you celebrate holidays? Birthdays? What are your feelings and thoughts at weddings, anniversaries, or funerals? In what areas do your most passionate feelings lie? What pictures in the family album get you most upset or bring you the most joy? Why? This is the kind of work you can begin working on in your journal and later develop with greater attention to form and audience.

Exploring Others

Interviewing, observing, and researching other people will provide ample material for third-person nonfiction narratives. While you don't have to be as diligent as James Boswell was in following your subjects around, you should learn some of the basic techniques of the interview. With carefully recorded quotations, you can provide real voices that make the character portrait and the whole essay convincing.

Before you interview anyone, gather all the facts you can and determine just why it is important for you to get closer to this individual. Have a checklist of initial questions, but don't be a slave to them: be ready to follow up on provocative responses. Pay attention to your subject's anxiety level and body language. What is being said that isn't literally being said? Above all, be a good listener. Careful attention to responses will help you find out what your subject really cares about and thus help you shape further questions.

Research involves doing background reading on the individual, the business or profession, and the issues that you wish to probe. Don't let this research answer all your questions. Don't have your subject figured out ahead of time. Use your notes (or tape recording) and your memory to form opinions over time. Verify information offered as fact.

Personality profiles can be fascinating, especially the popular "day-in-the-life" kind of narrative that provides a mix of interview and other quotation sources with behavior and places that you can re-create for your readers.

EXERCISES

1. After reading the whole of "Close Encounters of the Sneaky Kind" (presented in Chapter 12), consider the balance of attention between the personal story and the presentation of information. Explore a subject about which you believe the public should be better informed. Connect those facts to the tissue of human experience. What's at stake?

2. Also in Chapter 12 you will find Hilary Tham's "Chinese Medicine." Use it as a springboard for your own tale of conflict between cultures or generations.

3. Reread Pablo Medina's "On the Beach." The latent power in the memory for the storyteller is an image of an ideal. Most of us carry similar images of perfection: perfect bliss, perfect confidence, perfect accomplishment, perfect kindness. Each is no doubt rooted in a personal story that can be shaped similarly to Medina's. Write one!

4. Reread Hilary Tham's piece and her poem "Father" (p. 148). Take an experience of disappointment that you have had in someone you love and write about the experience first as nonfiction, than as either fiction or poetry.

On the surface, creative nonfiction seems as open-ended as "free" verse. It appears that anything goes; all a writer has to do is put down a personal experience in any form whatsoever. However, to move an audience, a personal essay or journal piece requires the same old precisions of observation, language, and shaping that any other successful writing demands.

12

❦

Stories and Nonfiction

The Thing With Willie

KAREN SAGSTETTER

On a fishing trip with her father, Anna faced her first authentic test of faith. It was 1890, near Galveston, and the boat had skimmed over the water, out to sea, and his tanned face rocked toward her and away as he pulled oars forward and back, forward and back in a hard, sure rhythm. She later recalled sounds of waves slapping the sides of the boat, and his voice, telling her facts about the ocean, for instance, how a flounder lies flat on the bottom, two eyes on the same side of his head like a person, not like a fish.

They dropped lines; right away there was a yank on hers, and he helped her manage a snappy little trout. He'd packed sandwiches and cold tea, and he fed them to his child, talking about everything under the sun. When it got hot, he steered toward home, saying that the coast stretched like a lazy cat all the way to Mexico.

Twenty yards from shore, her father reached over the side of the boat and plunged his hand into the water; his sleeve was dark and wet, soaked to the shoulder. He pulled out, sand dribbling down his arm in rivulets, and unwound his fingers to show her: a craggy, pear-shaped shell. He rinsed it well in the sea water, taking his time, pushing mud from the crevices with his thumb, and with the force of his knife pried it open fast, like a man who knew what to do about things.

Inside the shell was a pecan-sized gray blob. Grinning, he caught it up in his fingers. "Sugar, open your mouth!" She opened up and a fat oyster swam down her throat, tasting like salt water. It was her first completely fresh morsel of seafood.

But in the 1930s people were fishing not for fun but for their lives. So many jobs had disappeared in Galveston, everywhere in the country. When the thing with Willie happened, Anna remembered her father's oyster. Probably that was the moment when she had first become so extremely particular about her seafood.

> Willie, clean me a half-dozen flounder, three or four croakers, and a couple of dozen crabs, will you?
> Yes ma'am.
> How's your wife? Okay?
> Yes ma'am.
> Your children? Gettin' big I'll bet.
> My little boy Raymond isn't too good.
> Oh sorry to hear that. What's wrong?
> He don't walk yet. Doctor don't know what to do.
> How old is he?
> He's four, ma'am.
> That must be a worry. Sometimes they take their time. How about the others?
> Oh they're mostly fine. Taller every day. Eat plenty.
> Don't I know it.
> Your boy okay, ma'am? Your girl?
> Yes, fine, okay. Lucy's fine. All grown up. Louie's a mess sometimes.

She almost said Can't stay still, but didn't so not to hurt his feelings about his own boy.

Willie was the colored man who worked at John's Seafood. He had a bunch of kids, and his wife Patti Ann kept chickens and a vegetable garden to help out. Because he was a true professional, he and Anna got along, but her husband Howard didn't like him.

> What's your problem with Willie?
> He's slow.
> He's not slow. He's fast when he cleans a crab.
> Doesn't answer sometimes. I don't like that. Not polite.
> He's busy. Tired.
> I couldn't do what he does. I hate fish guts.
> I don't mind. I'm thinking of what I'll make later.
> It's a good thing you have work to like, isn't it?

Howard had lost his job; his car dealership had folded. He wasn't all that prejudiced but he disliked the idea of a black man having work when he didn't. It came back to his wife making the money for the family, too. Willie was part of that. Anna Clinton was a very good cook, and she was a hit with farmers and fishermen, who paid to enjoy her thick sauces with the red pepper and garlic.

Scales and shells didn't bother her at all. She liked to watch Willie clean fish because she was looking forward to the money she'd make cooking those fish for the hospital or church. Willie tended his knives so they were sharp and shiny; a gleam ricocheted off the ceiling while he worked, his fish heads scuttled to the edge of the counter, scales showered upward, and you had a beautiful fillet in thirty seconds. The same with oysters—he shucked to beat the band. Where he paused was right at first—to prod the edges of the shell and find exactly the right spot for the oyster knife to go in. Then he pushed it hard and quick, the shell opened with the sound of a small belch, like a secret getting out, followed by a scrape of the knife that made her mouth water as the oyster tumbled into a jar.

Still, she could see Willie was exhausted. He was six feet tall, with short-cropped inky hair and a sweet expression. Bent over, like his shoulders were not carrying just him, but invisible weight, too. Sometimes he'd be moving a chaos of entrails into a heap, and he'd stop to prop himself with the broomstick and yawn. Sometimes he forgot to answer and would only nod, which a black man normally would never do in relation to a white lady. Unless he was swaying at the brink.

Anna had a big order coming up—the Valentine's benefit at the firehouse was two weeks away. As if she needed trouble, the teacher stopped by to discuss her son Louis. She commented that he had a decent mind. Could read well, so what was the problem with his math?

Howard talked with him man-to-man on the front porch. The end of that week was bingo night at St. Aloysius, the Catholic church, a new client. Meaning they needed to progress from mounds of okra, crabs, shrimp, onions, tomatoes, and rice, by virtue of elbow grease and correct calculations, nevermind inspiration, to gumbo. Anna said, Here's a recipe for twelve, and Howard said, You specify how much okra, how many crabs, how many onions we need to prepare dinner for forty salivating people who have Friday night appetites and want to win the jackpot, and write it down for your mother.

Louis reacted by looking bored and rolling his eyes, a very dangerous thing to do because that bored look always caused Howard's forehead to turn red and he wasn't going to put up with it for an instant. *Now!* he shouted.

Louis scrammed, leaping away like a hound, over the ottoman in the living room and around the side table with the recipe squashed inside his pant pocket. While his mother planted twenty caladiums in the front flower bed and ironed four shirts, Louis toiled in his room. When he emerged clutching a large

sheet of lined paper, the sass had subsided. He'd been stuck on okra because no one knew how many pods were in a bushel. But he'd written:
Gumbo for Forty

1. Okra: two-thirds of a bushel basket.
2. Crabs: 4.95 dozen.
3. Oysters: 33.
4. Onions: 19 and 4/5 @ four-inches in diameter.
5. Chopped parsley: sixteen and a half tablespoons.

Of course, Anna had never in her life used a precise recipe for stews. For her famous cakes, yes, and she had to be fussy about whether to add one teaspoon of vanilla or one and a half. But gumbo came about after an evening at the kitchen table chopping okra while you were sipping iced tea. The idea of 19 4/5 onions was amusing, but in the spirit of the math lesson, Anna followed it faithfully.

At John's Seafood, she and Louis shopped together. Anna told Willie that her son figured she needed 33 oysters and 59.4 crabs.

> That right, Mr. Louis?
> Yes, Willie, the way I calculate it.
> Well, you got it. You watch me.
> I'd like for Louis to practice his timekeeping, Anna added.
> Yes ma'am.
> You're so fast with the oyster knife, could he practice with the stopwatch right here?
> All right, Miz Clinton.

Louis observed that Willie shucked thirty-three oysters in four minutes and fifty-seven seconds flat. He made a note of this. Instead of .4 of a crab, Willie suggested they take half of a giant blue crab's body.

The rest of the week, Willie wouldn't prepare Anna's fish without asking: did your boy figure this for you, ma'am? If she said no, he'd say, well ma'am, won't he be disappointed if you don't check with him?

Before the '29 crash, Anna had been a professional baker. Now her business wasn't weddings and birthdays but Easter lunch at the hospital or fried fish for the city plumbers late shift. She usually prepared extra because in Galveston, like all over, there were people who if they didn't hook a flounder that day, they did not eat—regulars at her back porch who would sweep or rake in exchange for a bowl of soup.

After a long day cooking, she liked to go walking on the beach. Anna had never seen a mountain or even a hill. She'd never seen snow. But she'd been born to the Gulf of Mexico, and when she was young, all she wanted to be was wet. On the island, summer heat was treacherous, and her mother didn't object even back in the nineties when she waded into the surf in an old dress. She liked the mush of sand between her toes—hot sand on the beach, wet sand at the water's edge, cool water inching over her feet to her ankles—and she'd push at the tide as it was grabbing her stomach, her breasts, and rising up and over her back while she moved against the friendly resistance of the ocean, like rough-housing with her uncles, wild and safe at once, deeper and deeper until the water surmounted her shoulders, swells were nipping her cheeks, and her skirts were billowing to her hips. She walked slowly, savoring, and didn't mind the fish nibbling her ankles; they made her smile to herself. She'd plunge her face under, shaking her head from side to side and snorting out the salty water like a dog in a bath. Dogfish, her mother called her. And she'd swim and trot along, riding the current back, taking a long time for it. She wanted her hair soaked, dripping, wanted water to sink clear through her scalp, and whatever slab of worry was weighing on her chest, well, it dissolved.

No denying it was a nice break to be getting business from the fire-house—fifty chicken and dumplings suppers for the annual Valentine's benefit. Louis studied the situation and constructed the shopping list. This led to Anna's visiting a chicken farm to select thirteen and two-thirds pullets which, since she was purchasing them live, was going to be difficult. (Louis's fractions were the current family joke.) She'd arranged to have them dressed, so she left the birds squawking and scratching at the butcher's, and stopped in at John's. Anna and Johnny chatted about the mild February weather and the price of flounder, and then he mentioned that Willie's wife Patti Ann was pregnant with her seventh baby and that Willie hadn't shown up for work for two days. What's wrong, she thought. He needs the money. And who'll clean my fish for me? That was Wednesday morning.

Thursday was the day before the benefit. In the evening the whole family—Howard, Anna, Louis, and sister Lucy—were hacking chickens into stew-sized pieces and tossing skin, bones, and fat to the center of the kitchen table, when Willie knocked on the back door, a child in his arms.

The child had to be Raymond. He was small. Cocker spaniel sized. Not malnourished—his skin was a strong coffee color and he wasn't skinny—but he was limp. A bag of limbs. Bones bundled together, but not holding him up. His head rolled around on his neck, and he was drooling.

Evening, Miz Clinton, ma'am. Don't mean to intrude. This here's my boy Raymond.

Why hello Willie. We're cutting all these chickens up. There's a big mess in here and an awful smell.

Can't be as bad as fish.

I don't mind the fish smell.

Really she didn't. To see trout and redfish laid out fat and glistening on ice, begging her for butter, garlic, and lemon, was a pleasure.

The young son Raymond wasn't just slow or sick. He had something terribly wrong with him. He made a constant noise, whimpering and howling, and Willie couldn't shift him around frequently enough to quiet him. Raymond was four years old and had never uttered a single word. He was wearing a diaper.

> How is your wife, Willie?
> She's all right. Expecting her seventh. We just found out.
> Oh, well, that's nice.
> Yeah. I suppose. Listen Miz Clinton, I was wondering. It's Raymond's fifth birthday on Saturday. Patti Ann ain't feeling so good right now and I want a cake for my little boy here.

As Anna talked with Willie, she kept turning her ear toward her family. The kids and Howard were still at the chickens in the kitchen; the hammer of the cleaver and their chatter created a comforting stir in the background. She had a queasy feeling, watching the idiot child. Willie's shoulder was soaked, and she produced a towel.

> What sort of cake, Willie?
> I'd like to buy one of your great cakes I've heard about. Chocolate icing. And I want you to write Raymond's name on it. With icing
> Why sure, Willie. Of course, I'll make it. What color icing?
> You decide. You can make it pretty. I've heard.

Howard didn't like the interruption and snapped how did she think she was going to get everything done? Things were on his nerves.

Getting that cake baked in the midst of the chicken bones and biscuit dough with the fire chief's wife stopping in every hour to check on things—the idea got on Anna's nerves, too. But she determined to do it.

She labored over her broth, intensifying it with more and more bones, extra onions and green peppers, boiling it down, and down again. She and Lucy sauteed the chicken pieces, set them aside in bowls, kneaded biscuit dough for the dumplings, and around eleven, they put the house back together. With the big mop, Louis washed the kitchen, living room, and hall floors, and Lucy swept the back porch, where they'd been throwing chicken skin, onion peel, and celery ends onto spread-out newspapers. That is, when she wasn't leaning on the broom yawning. Anna was going to assemble and simmer the stews Friday morning and afternoon, and the event was at 7 p.m., so the only time for the cake was that very Thursday night, late, after the kids and Howard went to bed. Without exactly lying, she gave Howard the impression that she was contriving a treat for the fire chief.

> What's the cake for?
> I'll give some to people who help us get our dinners together or maybe to the fire chief, since he's trusting us with the job.
> Not a bad idea.

Since the crash, Anna had been working with chicken guts and fish parts and hadn't made many beautiful desserts. "Weddings by Anna" had become known because of a particular specialty: her four-layer spice cake with buttery almond frosting and on top, a burst of white sugar calla lilies with yellow stamens and pistils in a surround of blue asters. But now people who had been wealthy in the twenties were driving old Fords and dispatching their children to the justice of the peace to get married. So her longing for the finest lately was expressed with extra spices and sensational gravies.

In the good solitude of the dim kitchen, Anna sifted her best white cake flour twice, so it would be silky and light. She had always known, as if angels were whispering how, about creaming the butter and sugar thoroughly. About using sweet Ware's Dairy butter in the first place. About superior Mexican vanilla and fresh eggs. She still possessed a few bars of premium Swiss chocolate, which she grated and swirled into the batter for a marble cake effect. She whipped six egg whites and folded them in quickly so the cake would be airy, divine.

At two in the morning, aroma flowering from the oven, she took the risen cake out to cool. The frosting came easy. For that she used regular baker's chocolate, melted in the top of a double boiler, and then mixed into the already combined confectioner's sugar and butter. She spread the cake with the chocolate icing and divided the reserved, not-chocolate icing into three mounds, adding green coloring to one, pink to one, yellow to the other. With her French cake decorator she dripped pink sugar roses, the size of a baby's puckered mouth, in a circle on top of the chocolate frosting, and in the center she wrote, in looping script, *Raymond*. She crafted perfect green stems and leaves and added yellow centers to the roses. Then she removed her sapphire ring—her birthstone—licked the frosting from it, carefully rinsed and dried it, and put it back onto her right ring finger. She believed that something pretty could usually make you feel better and she felt inspired by its confident beauty, its perfection. "Clear minded" was what the sapphire stood for, and she always wore it while she worked.

Her fourth apron of the day was splattered with god knows what, and she smelled like ground up animals and plants. As she ran a dishrag around the drain boards, her arms cramped; she was dead on her feet; her feet were somewhere below, far away from the rest of her body.

Really, she thought, one more rose would make it look better but she stopped at six because it was the boy's fifth birthday: five and one to grow on. Finally, she arranged the cake in a covered cooler so the roses wouldn't subside. At 3:30 a.m. she fell into bed.

Late Friday afternoon, Anna and Lucy were packing serving utensils for the last run to the firehouse hall when Willie rapped at the back door, crumpling a dollar bill in his fist. He was alone.

But Anna had decided that this cake was not for sale. She told Willie that her husband was very strict about how she disposed of her cakes, and he had given her instructions that because Willie had helped so often when they needed a rush order of shrimp or oysters, the cake was to be a birthday gift to Willie and his family. Well, Willie would not have it.

> No ma'am. No way. I have the money right here and you have to take it.
> But you gave me a chance to show my stuff, Willie. Nobody's asking for pretty cakes these days. You did me a favor.
> Your cake is just beautiful. Beautiful. His name and all. I don't know how you do it, but it's just right.

Anna couldn't take cash from such a poor man. But there was no arguing with him (My feet are planted here till you take it.), and she didn't have time for a prolonged discussion. He insisted. Okay, she said, I'll take a nickel, and held out her jar of change. He kept dropping coins in until she retracted the jar, so he must've deposited two or three. For a long time after, the clink of his nickels stayed with her, like a deep shiver.

With the cake in the bakery box, Willie disappeared into the alley, and they got busy with the firehouse supper. Some time during the evening, Anna told Howard the cake had gone to Willie. She wanted to clear that up: she didn't like unfinished business. Howard was enjoying the cheer in the firehouse hall, so all he said was, why'd you give him the whole thing?—to show he could still question her decisions.

By 10 o'clock they must have wiped their hands on their aprons a hundred times, splashed gravy onto the floor fifty times, and said you're welcome two hundred times. But they would surely be hired to supply more benefit dinners, the fire chief's wife all but said so, and with four of them working, tidying the mess wouldn't be that bad.

Very early Saturday morning, while Anna and Howard, Lucy and Louis, were sleeping hard, Willie carried the pretty cake and his little boy Raymond to a jetty. There, tied to a piling, was an old but spacious rowboat, belonging to someone, he didn't know who. The weather was perfect: cool, clear, blue sky blooming with pink and orange clouds.

Willie tied his son's legs to the seat so he wouldn't be tossed over in a swell and joined him in the center of the boat. He rowed east toward the sunrise, passing shrimp boats, cotton ships, and fuel barges, and on and on they went straddling waves, jumping waves, bouncing, riding all the way with the Gulf. After they were beyond sight of the beaches, he aimed a pistol at Raymond's head, pulled the trigger, and then pointed it at himself.

By late Saturday afternoon, the boat had drifted back to shore. The cake was still in the bakery box, secured with ropes in the hold between the two bodies. It was intact—fragrant and colorful—except that it had been neatly cut. Two large slices were missing. All the pink sugar roses, with the perfect green leaves and yellow centers, were gone too.

Soon it grew hot again, and hotter still, March to July, and so on. Anna started going to the beach in the early mornings, walking ankle deep in the small waves. Howard found a job selling typewriters, and he and Louis were the ones who on Sundays delivered Anna's étouffées to Patti Ann. She had a baby girl at the end of the summer.

◦🐃

A Very Short Story

Ernest Hemingway

One hot evening in Padua they carried him up onto the roof and he could look out over the top of the town. There were chimney swifts in the sky. After a while it got dark and the searchlights came out. The others went down and took the bottles with them. He and Luz could hear them below on the balcony. Luz sat on the bed. She was cool and fresh in the hot night.

Luz stayed on night duty for three months. They were glad to let her. When they operated on him she prepared him for the operating table; and they had a joke about friend or enema. He went under the anesthetic holding tight on to himself so he would not blab about anything during the silly, talky time. After he got on crutches he used to take the temperatures so Luz would not have to get up from the bed. There were only a few patients, and they all knew about it. They all liked Luz. As he walked back along the halls he thought of Luz in his bed.

Before he went back to the front they went into the Duomo and prayed. It was dim and quiet, and there were other people praying. They wanted to get married, but there was not enough time for the banns, and neither of them had birth certificates. They felt as though they were married, but they wanted everyone to know about it, and to make it so they could not lose it.

Luz wrote him many letters that he never got until after the armistice. Fifteen came in a bunch to the front and he sorted them by the dates and read them all straight through. They were all about the hospital, and how much she loved him, and how it was impossible to get along without him, and how terrible it was missing him at night.

After the armistice they agreed he should go home to get a job so they might be married. Luz would not come home until he had a good job and could come to New York to meet her. It was understood he would not drink, and he did not want to see his friends or anyone in the States. Only to get a job and be married. On the train from Padua to Milan they quarreled about her not being willing to come home at once. When they had to say goodbye, in the station at Milan, they kissed goodbye, but were not finished with the quarrel. He felt sick about saying goodbye like that.

He went to America on a boat from Genoa. Luz went back to Pordenone to open a hospital. It was lonely and rainy there, and there was a battalion of arditi quartered in the town. Living in the muddy, rainy town in the winter, the major of the battalion made love to Luz, and she had never known Italians before, and finally wrote to the States that theirs had been only a boy and girl affair. She was sorry, and she knew he would probably not be able to under-stand, but might someday forgive her, and be grateful to her, and she expected, absolutely unexpectedly, to be married in the spring. She loved him as always, but she realized now it was only a boy and girl love. She hoped he would have a great career and believed in him absolutely. She knew it was for the best.

The major did not marry her in the spring, or any other time. Luz never got an answer to the letter to Chicago about it. A short time after he contracted gonorrhea from a salesgirl in a loop department store while riding in a taxicab through Lincoln Park.

<figure>❧</figure>

The Boarding House

James Joyce

Mrs. Mooney was a butcher's daughter. She was a woman who was quite able to keep things to herself: a determined woman. She had married her father's foreman and opened a butcher's shop near Spring Gardens. But as soon as his father-in-law was dead Mr. Mooney began to go to the devil. He drank, plun-dered the till, ran headlong into debt. It was no use making him take the pledge: he was sure to break out again a few days after. By fighting his wife in the pres-ence of customers and by buying bad meat he ruined his business. One night he went for his wife with the cleaver and she had to sleep in a neighbour's house.

After that they lived apart. She went to the priest and got a separation from him with care of the children. She would give him neither money nor food nor house-room; and so he was obliged to enlist himself as a sheriff's man. He was a shabby stooped little drunkard with a white face and a white moustache and white eyebrows, pencilled above his little eyes, which were pink-veined and raw; and all day long he sat in the bailiff's room, waiting to be put on a job. Mrs. Mooney, who had taken what remained of her money out of the butcher business and set up a boarding house in Hardwicke Street, was a big imposing woman. Her house had a floating population made up of tourists from Liver-pool and the Isle of Man and, occasionally, *artistes* from the music halls. Its res-ident population was made up of clerks from the city. She governed the house cunningly and firmly, knew when to give credit, when to be stern and when to let things pass. All the resident young men spoke of her as *The Madam*.

Mrs. Mooney's young men paid fifteen shillings a week for board and lodgings (beer or stout at dinner excluded). They shared in common tastes and occupations and for this reason they were very chummy with one another. They discussed with one another the chances of favourites and outsiders. Jack Mooney, the Madam's son, who was clerk to a commission agent in Fleet Street, had the reputation of being a hard case. He was fond of using soldiers' obscenities: usually he came home in the small hours. When he met his friends he had always a good one to tell them and he was always sure to be on to a good thing—that is to say, a likely horse or a likely *artiste*. He was also handy with the mits and sang comic songs. On Sunday nights there would often be a reunion in Mrs. Mooney's front drawing-room. The music-hall *artistes* would oblige; and Sheridan played waltzes and polkas and vamped accompaniments. Polly Mooney, the Madam's daughter, would also sing. She sang:

> *I'm a . . . naughty girl.*
> *You needn't sham:*
> *You know I am.*

Polly was a slim girl of nineteen; she had light soft hair and a small full mouth. Her eyes, which were grey with a shade of green through them, had a habit of glancing upwards when she spoke with anyone, which made her look like a little perverse madonna. Mrs. Mooney had first sent her daughter to be a typist in a corn-factor's office but, as a disreputable sheriff's man used to come every other day to the office, asking to be allowed to say a word to his daughter, she had taken her daughter home again and set her to do housework. As Polly was very lively the intention was to give her the run of the young men. Besides, young men like to feel that there is a young woman not very far away. Polly, of course, flirted with the young men but Mrs. Mooney, who was a shrewd judge, knew that the young men were only passing the time away: none of them meant business. Things went on so for a long time and Mrs. Mooney began to think of sending Polly back to typewriting when she noticed that something was going on between Polly and one of the young men. She watched the pair and kept her own counsel.

Polly knew that she was being watched, but still her mother's persistent silence could not be misunderstood. There had been no open complicity between mother and daughter, no open understanding but, though people in the house began to talk of the affair, still Mrs. Mooney did not intervene. Polly began to grow a little strange in her manner and the young man was evidently perturbed. At last, when she judged it to be the right moment, Mrs. Mooney intervened. She dealt with moral problems as a cleaver deals with meat: and in this case she had made up her mind.

It was a bright Sunday morning of early summer, promising heat, but with a fresh breeze blowing. All the windows of the boarding house were open and the lace curtains ballooned gently towards the street beneath the raised sashes. The belfry of George's Church sent out constant peals and worshippers, singly or in groups, traversed the little circus before the church, revealing their purpose by their self-contained demeanour no less than by the little volumes in their gloved hands. Breakfast was over in the boarding house and the table of the breakfast room was covered with plates on which lay yellow streaks of eggs with morsels of bacon-fat and bacon-rind. Mrs. Mooney sat in the straw armchair and watched the servant Mary remove the breakfast things. She made Mary collect the crusts and pieces of broken bread to help to make Tuesday's bread-pudding.

When the table was cleared, the broken bread collected, the sugar and butter safe under lock and key, she began to reconstruct the interview which she had had the night before with Polly. Things were as she had suspected: she had been frank in her questions and Polly had been frank in her answers. Both had been somewhat awkward, of course. She had been made awkward by her not wishing to receive the news in too cavalier a fashion or to seem to have connived and Polly had been made awkward not merely because allusions of that kind always made her awkward but also because she did not wish it to be thought that in her wise innocence she had divined the intention behind her mother's tolerance.

Mrs. Mooney glanced instinctively at the little gilt clock on the mantel-piece as soon as she had become aware through her revery that the bells of George's Church had stopped ringing. It was seventeen minutes past eleven: she would have lots of time to have the matter out with Mr. Doran and then catch short twelve at Marlborough Street. She was sure she would win. To begin with she had all the weight of social opinion on her side: she was an outraged mother. She had allowed him to live beneath her roof, assuming that he was a man of honour, and he had simply abused her hospitality. He was thirty-four or thirty-five years of age, so that youth could not be pleaded as his excuse; nor could ignorance be his excuse since he was a man who had seen something of the world. He had simply taken advantage of Polly's youth and inexperience: that was evident. The question was: What reparation would he make?

There must be reparation made in such case. It is all very well for the man: he can go his ways as if nothing had happened, having had his moment of pleasure, but the girl has to bear the brunt. Some mothers would be content to patch up such an affair for a sum of money; she had known cases of it. But she would not do so. For her only one reparation could make up for the loss of her daughter's honour: marriage.

She counted all her cards again before sending Mary up to Mr. Doran's room to say that she wished to speak with him. She felt sure she would win. He was a serious young man, not rakish or loud-voiced like the others. If it had been Mr. Sheridan or Mr. Meade or Bantam Lyons her task would have been much harder. She did not think he would face publicity. All the lodgers in the house knew something of the affair; details had been invented by some. Besides, he had been employed for thirteen years in a great Catholic winemerchant's office and publicity would mean for him, perhaps, the loss of his job. Whereas if he agreed all might be well. She knew he had a good screw for one thing and she suspected he had a bit of stuff put by.

Nearly the half-hour! She stood up and surveyed herself in the pierglass. The decisive expression of her great florid face satisfied her and she thought of some mothers she knew who could not get their daughters off their hands.

Mr. Doran was very anxious indeed this Sunday morning. He had made two attempts to shave but his hand had been so unsteady that he had been obliged to desist. Three days' reddish beard fringed his jaws and every two or three minutes a mist gathered on his glasses so that he had to take them off and polish them with his pocket-handkerchief. The recollection of his confession of the night before was a cause of acute pain to him; the priest had drawn out every ridiculous detail of the affair and in the end had so magnified his sin that he was almost thankful at being afforded a loophole of reparation. The harm was done. What could he do now but marry her or run away? He could not brazen it out. The affair would be sure to be talked of and his employer would be certain to hear of it. Dublin is such a small city: everyone knows everyone else's business. He felt his heart leap warmly in his throat as he heard in his excited imagination old Mr. Leonard calling out in his rasping voice: "Send Mr. Doran here, please."

All his long years of service gone for nothing! All his industry and diligence thrown away! As a young man he had sown his wild oats, of course; he had boasted of his free-thinking and denied the existence of God to his companions in public-houses. But that was all passed and done with . . . nearly. He still bought a copy of *Reynolds's Newspaper* every week but he attended to his religious duties and for nine-tenths of the year lived a regular life. He had money enough to settle down on; it was not that. But the family would look down on her. First of all there was her disreputable father and then her mother's boarding house was beginning to get a certain fame. He had a notion that he was being had. He could imagine his friends talking of the affair and laughing. She *was* a little vulgar; some times she said "I seen" and "If I had've known." But what would grammar matter if he really loved her? He could not make up his mind whether to like her or despise her for what she had done. Of course he had done it too. His instinct urged him to remain free, not to marry. Once you are married you are done for, it said.

While he was sitting helplessly on the side of the bed in shirt and trousers she tapped lightly at his door and entered. She told him all, that she had made a clean breast of it to her mother and that her mother would speak with him that morning. She cried and threw her arms round his neck, saying:

"Oh Bob! Bob! What am I to do? What am I to do at all?"

She would put an end to herself, she said.

He comforted her feebly, telling her not to cry, that it would be all right, never fear. He felt against his shirt the agitation of her bosom.

It was not altogether his fault that it had happened. He remembered well, with the curious patient memory of the celibate, the first casual caresses her dress, her breath, her fingers had given him. Then late one night as he was undressing for bed she had tapped at his door, timidly. She wanted to relight her candle at his for hers had been blown out by a gust. It was her bath night. She wore a loose open combing-jacket of printed flannel. Her white instep shone in the opening of her furry slippers and the blood glowed warmly behind her perfumed skin. From her hands and wrists too as she lit and steadied her candle a faint perfume arose.

On nights when he came in very late it was she who warmed up his dinner. He scarcely knew what he was eating feeling her beside him alone, at night, in the sleeping house. And her thoughtfulness! If the night was anyway cold or wet or windy there was sure to be a little tumbler of punch ready for him. Perhaps they could be happy together. . . .

They used to go upstairs together on tiptoe, each with a candle, and on the third landing exchange reluctant good-nights. They used to kiss. He remembered well her eyes, the touch of her hand and his delirium. . . .

But delirium passes. He echoed her phrase, applying it to himself: "*What am I to do?*" The instinct of the celibate warned him to hold back. But the sin was there; even his sense of honour told him that reparation must be made for such a sin.

While he was sitting with her on the side of the bed Mary came to the door and said that the missus wanted to see him in the parlour. He stood up to put on his coat and waistcoat, more helpless than ever. When he was dressed he went over to her to comfort her. It would be all right, never fear. He left her crying on the bed and moaning softly: "*O my God!*"

Going down the stairs his glasses became so dimmed with moisture that he had to take them off and polish them. He longed to ascend through the roof and fly away to another country where he would never hear again of his trouble, and yet a force pushed him downstairs step by step. The implacable faces of his employer and of the Madam stared upon his discomfiture. On the last flight of stairs he passed Jack Mooney who was coming up from the pantry nursing two bottles of *Bass*. They saluted coldly; and the lover's eyes rested for a second or two on a thick bulldog face and a pair of thick short arms. When he reached the foot of the staircase he glanced up and saw Jack regarding him from the door of the return-room.

Suddenly he remembered the night when one of the music-hall *artistes*, a little blond Londoner, had made a rather free allusion to Polly. The reunion had been almost broken up on account of Jack's violence. Everyone tried to quiet him. The music-hall *artiste*, a little paler than usual, kept smiling and saying that there was no harm meant: but Jack kept shouting at him that if any fellow tried that sort of a game on with his sister he'd bloody well put his teeth down his throat, so he would.

Polly sat for a little time on the side of the bed, crying. Then she dried her eyes and went over to the looking-glass. She dipped the end of the towel in the water-jug and refreshed her eyes with the cool water. She looked at herself in profile and readjusted a hairpin above her ear. Then she went back to the bed again and sat at the foot. She regarded the pillows for a long time and the sight of them awakened in her mind secret, amiable memories. She rested the nape of her neck against the cool iron bed-rail and fell into a reverie. There was no longer any perturbation visible on her face.

She waited on patiently, almost cheerfully, without alarm, her memories gradually giving place to hopes and visions of the future. Her hopes and visions were so intricate that she no longer saw the white pillows on which her gaze was fixed or remembered that she was waiting for anything.

At last she heard her mother calling. She started to her feet and ran to the banisters.

"Polly! Polly!"

"Yes, mamma?"

"Come down, dear. Mr. Doran wants to speak to you." Then she remembered what she had been waiting for.

⌒🐦

Sunday in the Park

BEL KAUFMAN

It was still warm in the late-afternoon sun, and the city noises came muffled through the trees in the park. She put her book down on the bench, removed her sunglasses, and sighed contentedly. Morton was reading the *Times Magazine* section, one arm flung around her shoulder; their three-year-old son, Larry, was playing in the sandbox: a faint breeze fanned her hair softly against her cheek. It was five-thirty of a Sunday afternoon, and the small playground, tucked away in a corner of the park, was all but deserted. The swings and see-saws stood motionless and abandoned, the slides were empty, and only in the sandbox two little boys squatted diligently side by side. *How good this is*, she thought, and almost smiled at her sense of well-being. They must go out in the sun more often; Morton was so city-pale, cooped up all week inside the gray factorylike university. She squeezed his arm affectionately and glanced at Larry, delighting in the pointed little face frowning in concentration over the tunnel he was digging. The other boy suddenly stood up and with a quick, deliberate swing of his chubby arm threw a spadeful of sand at Larry. It just missed his head. Larry continued digging; the boy remained standing, shovel raised, stolid and impassive.

"No, no, little boy." She shook her finger at him, her eyes searching for the child's mother or nurse. "We mustn't throw sand. It may get in someone's eyes and hurt. We must play nicely in the nice sandbox." The boy looked at her in unblinking expectancy. He was about Larry's age but perhaps ten pounds heavier, a husky little boy with none of Larry's quickness and sensitivity in his face. Where was his mother? The only other people left in the playground were two women and a little girl on roller skates leaving now through the gate, and a man on a bench a few feet away. He was a big man, and he seemed to be taking up the whole bench as he held the Sunday comics close to his face. She supposed he was the child's father. He did not look up from his comics, but spat once deftly out of the corner of his mouth. She turned her eyes away.

At that moment, as swiftly as before, the fat little boy threw another spadeful of sand at Larry. This time some of it landed on his hair and forehead. Larry looked up at his mother, his mouth tentative; her expression would tell him whether to cry or not.

Her first instinct was to rush to her son, brush the sand out of his hair, and punish the other child, but she controlled it. She always said that she wanted Larry to learn to fight his own battles.

"Don't *do* that, little boy," she said sharply, leaning forward on the bench. "You mustn't throw sand!"

The man on the bench moved his mouth as if to spit again, but instead he spoke. He did not look at her, but at the boy only.

"You go right ahead, Joe," he said loudly. "Throw all you want. This here is a *public* sandbox."

She felt a sudden weakness in her knees as she glanced at Morton. He had become aware of what was happening. He put his *Times* down carefully on his lap and turned his fine, lean face toward the man, smiling the shy, apologetic smile he might have offered a student in pointing out an error in his thinking. When he spoke to the man, it was with his usual reasonableness.

"You're quite right," he said pleasantly, "but just because this is a public place. . . ."

The man lowered his funnies and looked at Morton. He looked at him from nead to foot, slowly and deliberately. "Yeah?" His insolent voice was edged with menace. "My kid's got just as good right here as yours, and if he feels like throwing sand, he'll throw it, and if you don't like it, you can take your kid the hell out of here."

The children were listening, their eyes and mouths wide open, their spades forgotten in small fists. She noticed the muscle in Morton's jaw tighten. He was rarely angry; he seldom lost his temper. She was suffused with a tenderness for her husband and an impotent rage against the man for involving him in a situation so alien and so distasteful to him.

"Now, just a minute," Morton said courteously, "you must realize. . . ."

"Aw, shut up," said the man.

Her heart began to pound. Morton half rose; the *Times* slid to the ground. Slowly the other man stood up. He took a couple of steps toward Morton, then stopped. He flexed his great arms, waiting. She pressed her trembling knees together. Would there be violence, fighting? How dreadful, how incredible. . . . She must do something, stop them, call for help. She wanted to put her hand on her husband's sleeve, to pull him down, but for some reason she didn't.

Morton adjusted his glasses. He was very pale. "This is ridiculous," he said unevenly. "I must ask you. . . ."

"Oh, yeah?" said the man. He stood with his legs spread apart, rocking a little, looking at Morton with utter scorn. "You and who else?"

For a moment the two men looked at each other nakedly. Then Morton turned his back on the man and said quietly, "Come on, let's get out of here." He walked awkwardly, almost limping with self-consciousness, to the sandbox. He stooped and lifted Larry and his shovel out.

At once Larry came to life; his face lost its rapt expression and he began to kick and cry. "I don't *want* to go home, I want to play better, I don't *want* any supper, I don't *like* supper. . . ." It became a chant as they walked, pulling their child between them, his feet dragging on the ground. In order to get to the exit gate they had to pass the bench where the man sat sprawling again. She was careful not to look at him. With all the dignity she could summon, she pulled Larry's sandy, perspiring little hand, while Morton pulled the other. Slowly and with head high she walked with her husband and child out of the playground.

Her first feeling was one of relief that a fight had been avoided, that no one was hurt. Yet beneath it there was a layer of something else, something heavy and inescapable. She sensed that it was more than just an unpleasant incident, more than defeat of reason by force. She felt dimly it had something to do with her and Morton, something acutely personal, familiar, and important.

Suddenly Morton spoke. "It wouldn't have proved anything."

"What?" she asked.

"A fight. It wouldn't have proved anything beyond the fact that he's bigger than I am."

"Of course," she said.

"The only possible outcome," he continued reasonably, "would have been—what? My glasses broken, perhaps a tooth or two replaced, a couple of days' work missed—and for what? For justice? For truth?"

"Of course," she repeated. She quickened her step. She wanted only to get home and to busy herself with her familiar tasks; perhaps then the feeling, glued like heavy plaster on her heart, would be gone. *Of all the stupid, despicable bullies*, she thought, pulling harder on Larry's hand. The child was still crying. Always before she had felt a tender pity for his defenseless little body, the frail arms, the narrow shoulders with sharp, winglike shoulder blades, the thin and unsure legs, but now her mouth tightened in resentment.

"Stop crying," she said sharply. "I'm ashamed of you!" She felt as if all three of them were tracking mud along the street. The child cried louder.

If there had been an issue involved, she thought, *if there had been something to fight for. . . . But what else could he possibly have done? Allow himself to be beaten? Attempt to educate the man? Call a policeman? "Officer, there's a man in the park who won't stop his child from throwing sand on mine. . . ."* The whole thing was as silly as that, and not worth thinking about.

"Can't you keep him quiet, for Pete's sake?" Morton asked irritably.

"What do you suppose I've been trying to do?" she said.

Larry pulled back, dragging his feet.

"If you can't discipline this child, I will," Morton snapped, making a move toward the boy.

But her voice stopped him. She was shocked to hear it, thin and cold and penetrating with contempt. "Indeed?" she heard herself say. "You and who else?"

༻

The First Day

EDWARD JONES

In an otherwise unremarkable September morning, long before I learned to be ashamed of my mother, she takes my hand and we set off down New Jersey

Avenue to begin my very first day of school. I am wearing a checkeredlike blue-and-green cotton dress, and scattered about these colors are bits of yellow and white and brown. My mother has uncharacteristically spent nearly an hour on my hair that morning, plaiting and replaiting so that now my scalp tingles. Whenever I turn my head quickly, my nose fills with the faint smell of Dixie Peach hair grease. The smell is somehow a soothing one now and I will reach for it time and time again before the morning ends. All the plaits, each with a blue barrette near the tip and each twisted into an uncommon sturdiness, will last until I go to bed that night, something that has never happened before. My stomach is full of milk and oatmeal sweetened with brown sugar. Like everything else I have on, my pale green slip and underwear are new, the underwear having come three to a plastic package with a little girl on the front who appears to be dancing. Behind my ears, my mother, to stop my whining, has dabbed the stingiest bit of her gardenia perfume, the last present my father gave her before he disappeared into memory. Because I cannot smell it, I have only her word that the perfume is there. I am also wearing yellow socks trimmed with thin lines of black and white around the tops. My shoes are my greatest joy, black patent-leather miracles, and when one is nicked at the toe later that morning in class, my heart will break.

I am carrying a pencil, a pencil sharpener, and a small ten-cent tablet with a black-and-white speckled cover. My mother does not believe that a girl in kindergarten needs such things, so I am taking them only because of my insistent whining and because they are presents from our neighbors, Mary Keith and Blondelle Harris. Miss Mary and Miss Blondelle are watching my two younger sisters until my mother returns. The women are as precious to me as my mother and sisters. Out playing one day. I have overheard an older child, speaking to another child, call Miss Mary and Miss Blondelle a word that is brand new to me. This is my mother: When I say the word in fun to one of my sisters, my mother slaps me across the mouth and the word is lost for years and years.

All the way down New Jersey Avenue, the sidewalks are teeming with children. In my neighborhood, I have many friends, but I see none of them as my mother and I walk. We cross New York Avenue, we cross Pierce Street, and we cross L and K, and still I see no one who knows my name. At I Street, between New Jersey Avenue and Third Street, we enter Seaton Elementary School, a timeworn, sad-faced building across the street from my mother's church, Mt. Carmel Baptist.

Just inside the front door, women out of the advertisements in *Ebony* are greeting other parents and children. The woman who greets us has pearls thick as jumbo marbles that come down almost to her navel, and she acts as if she had known me all my life, touching my shoulder, cupping her hand under my chin. She is enveloped in a perfume that I only know is not gardenia. When, in answer to her question, my mother tells her that we live at 1227 New Jersey Avenue, the woman first seems to be picturing in her head where we live. Then she shakes her head and says that we are at the wrong school, that we should be at Walker-Jones.

My mother shakes her head vigorously. "I want her to go here," my mother says. "If I'da wanted her someplace else, I'da took her there." The woman continues to act as if she has known me all my life, but she tells my mother that we live beyond the area that Seaton serves. My mother is not convinced and for several more minutes she questions the woman about why I cannot attend Seaton. For as many Sundays as I can remember, perhaps even Sundays when I was in her womb, my mother has pointed across I Street to Seaton as we come and go to Mt. Carmel. "You gonna go there and learn about the whole world." But one of the guardians of that place is saying no, and no again. I am learning this about my mother: The higher up on the scale of respectability a person is—and teachers are rather high up in her eyes—the less she is liable to let them push her around. But finally, I see in her eyes the closing gate, and she takes my hand and we leave the building. On the steps, she stops as people move past us on either side.

"Mama, I can't go to school?"

She says nothing at first, then takes my hand again and we are down the steps quickly and nearing New Jersey Avenue before I can blink. This is my mother: She says, "One monkey don't stop no show."

Walker-Jones is a larger, newer school and I immediately like it because of that. But it is not across the street from my mother's church, her rock, one of her connections to God, and I sense her doubts as she absently rubs her thumb over the back of her hand. We find our way to the crowded auditorium where gray metal chairs are set up in the middle of the room. Along the wall to the left are tables and other chairs. Every chair seems occupied by a child or adult. Somewhere in the room a child is crying, a cry that rises above the buzz-talk of so many people. Strewn about the floor are dozens and dozens of pieces of white paper, and people are walking over them without any thought of picking them up. And seeing this lack of concern, I am all of a sudden afraid.

"Is this where they register for school?" my mother asks a woman at one of the tables.

The woman looks up slowly as if she has heard this question once too often. She nods. She is tiny, almost as small as the girl standing beside her. The woman's hair is set in a mass of curlers and all of those curlers are made of paper money, here a dollar bill, there a five-dollar bill. The girl's hair is arrayed in curls, but some of them are beginning to droop and this makes me happy. On the table beside the woman's pocketbook is a large notebook, worthy of someone in high school, and looking at me looking at the notebook, the girl places her hand possessively on it. In her other hand she holds several pencils with thick crowns of additional erasers.

"These the forms you gotta use?" my mother asks the woman, picking up a few pieces of the paper from the table. "Is this what you have to fill out?"

The woman tells her yes, but that she need fill out only one.

"I see," my mother says, looking about the room. Then: "Would you help me with this form? That is, if you don't mind."

The woman asks my mother what she means.

"This form. Would you mind helpin me fill it out?"

The woman still seems not to understand.

"I can't read it. I don't know how to read or write, and I'm askin you to help me." My mother looks at me, then looks away. I know almost all of her looks, but this one is brand new to me. "Would you help me, then?"

The woman says Why sure, and suddenly she appears happier, so much more satisfied with everything. She finishes the form for her daughter and my mother and I step aside to wait for her. We find two chairs nearby and sit. My mother is now diseased, according to the girl's eyes, and until the moment her mother takes her and the form to the front of the auditorium, the girl never stops looking at my mother. I stare back at her. "Don't stare," my mother says to me. "You know better than that."

Another woman out of the *Ebony* ads takes the woman's child away. Now, the woman says upon returning, let's see what we can do for you two.

My mother answers the questions the woman reads off the form. They start with my last name, and then on to the first and middle names. This is school, I think. This is going to school. My mother slowly enunciates each word of my name. This is my mother: As the questions go on, she takes from her pocketbook document after document, as if they will support my right to attend school, as if she has been saving them up for just this moment. Indeed, she takes out more papers than I have ever seen her do in other places: my birth certificate, my baptismal record, a doctor's letter concerning my bout with chicken pox, rent receipts, records of immunization, a letter about our public assistance payments, even her marriage license—every single paper that has anything even remotely to do with my five-year-old life. Few of the papers are needed here, but it does not matter and my mother continues to pull out the documents with the purposefulness of a magician pulling out a long string of scarves. She has learned that money is the beginning and end of everything in this world, and when the woman finishes, my mother offers her fifty cents, and the woman accepts it without hesitation. My mother and I are just about the last parent and child in the room.

My mother presents the form to a woman sitting in front of the stage, and the woman looks at it and writes something on a white card, which she gives to my mother. Before long, the woman who has taken the girl with the drooping curls appears from behind us, speaks to the sitting woman, and introduces herself to my mother and me. She's to be my teacher, she tells my mother. My mother stares.

We go into the hall, where my mother kneels down to me. Her lips are quivering. "I'll be back to pick you up at twelve o'clock. I don't want you to go nowhere. You just wait right here. And listen to every word she say." I touch her lips and press them together. It is an old, old game between us. She puts my hand down at my side, which is not part of the game. She stands and looks a second at the teacher, then she turns and walks away. I see where she has darned one of her socks the night before. Her shoes make loud sounds in the hall. She passes through the doors and I can still hear the loud sounds of her shoes. And even when the teacher turns me toward the classrooms and I hear what must be the singing and talking of all the children in the world I can still hear my mother's footsteps above it all.

Just Married

Tony Earley

Late one night, the summer my wife and I lived on the mountain, we saw a deer standing on the traffic island at the end of our street. We saw the headlights of a car coming up the highway. We saw the deer fidget and leap into the light.

By the time we made it to the wreck, the old woman had called 911 on the car phone. The old man held on to the wheel with both hands and stared straight ahead through the webbed glass of the windshield. On the old woman's knee was a large drop of blood shaped like an apostrophe.

"Well," said the old man.

"Well," said the old woman.

"I guess I wrecked your car."

"But it was just a car," she said. She patted his hand.

"We just got married," he said.

"Tonight," she said. "Six hours ago. In Huntsville. We stayed too long at the reception."

"Everybody was there."

"All the grandkids. His and mine. We didn't want to leave."

The old man almost smiled. "Well," he said. "We did and we didn't."

"That's true enough", she said. "But we had a grand time."

"We've been married for a hundred years," he said.

"Just not to each other."

"I was married forty-nine years. She was married fifty-one."

"That makes a hundred. Isn't that something?"

"We were high school sweethearts."

"We just didn't get married."

"Not until tonight, anyway."

"Because of the war."

"I was on a destroyer in the Pacific."

"That's why we didn't get married."

"I had to leave before we figured things out."

"We didn't get anything decided."

"And when I came back, she was married."

"Oh, you make me sound so bad. It wasn't like that. We just never decided anything."

"I didn't mean it like that. I knew Frank. We played ball together. Frank was a good man."

"And Nell was a good woman. I always liked Nell."

"I was always faithful to Nell."

"Of course you were. Of course you were faithful to Nell."

"We were married forty-nine years and I was always faithful."

"Nell and Frank died last year," she said.

"Within a week of each other."

"Isn't that odd?"

"Then one day I just up and wrote to her. And she wrote me back and said she had been thinking about writing to me."

"And I was. Isn't it funny the way things work out? Sometimes you can almost see the plan."

"I still have her letter. It's in my suitcase. In the trunk."

"I put his letter in my safety-deposit box."

"Oh, it's just a letter."

"Not to me."

The old man tapped the steering wheel once with his forefingers. "Let me tell you something," he said. "I always knew she was the one. I was married forty-nine years, and I loved my wife, but I always knew she was the one."

"And I felt the same way about him. I always knew that he was the man for me."

I saw my wife glance up at me. I could tell she was wondering if I was the right man, or if there was a better man, a different life, waiting out there somewhere. And I could tell she knew I was thinking the same thing.

"You just can't say those things," the old woman said.

When the ambulance came, we walked up the highway and looked at the deer. It had slid on its side maybe fifty yards up on the road. A sharp piece of bone stuck out of one of its legs. The eye staring up at us seemed made of dark stone. We stared at the deer, and we sneaked looks at each other. We didn't talk. In the woods beside the highway, we could hear small living things moving beneath the leaves. We could hear the cicadas and the crickets and the tree frogs and the night birds calling out, all the breathing creatures looking for something in the dark.

❧

The following commentary by Tony Early appears at the end of the story in the anthology *New Stories from the South*. It tells us a good deal about the relationship between fiction and nonfiction, about how easily they flow from one to the other. What do you make of his casting the "true" event as if it might not be genuine? See the exercise on p. 209.

Okay, suppose there was this writer, who, while living one summer on top of a mountain in Tennessee, was stricken in the middle of the night by a craving for a frozen burrito and a Diet Coke. And suppose this writer, as he approached the highway near his home, happened to see a car traveling at a high rate of speed strike a deer. What if inside the wrecked car the writer found a man and a woman, both in their seventies, who had been married earlier that evening and were on their way to their honeymoon? And what if these hypothetical newlyweds told this hypothetical writer a story much like the one in this anthology? If you found out that the writer appropriated the story of these strangers, added a fourth character to provide symmetry and dramatic tension, and sold it to a magazine as fiction, would you think less of him than if he had told you that the whole thing was a product of his imagination? What if the writer told you that he drove to the motel where the couple had reservations and made arrangements to pay for their breakfast? If such a writer existed—and I'm not saying he does—your opinion might determine whether or not he told you the truth.

⌖

Chinese Medicine

Hilary Tham

I learned about love from my parents. I learned that love was unstable as water, that fathers were heroes one day, taking you out to feast at restaurants or to the beach on an unexpected Sunday; that the next day, they will disown you and call you an unbearable burden. I accepted that fathers were to be waited upon, hand and foot, at the brief twilight hour when they were home for their bath and dinner, before they left again "for business." It was an unquestioned rite in our house that we boiled hot water for our father's bath, placed his towel and fresh boxer shorts ready to his hand. It was our way of life that fathers had to be catered to and pampered, for they were the earners of wages. I learned early that fathers had temper tantrums, that they smashed and broke things if they did not get their way, that they threatened to leave the family, something that mothers never do.

Mothers were the opposite of fathers: they were dull as walls and furniture. They nagged, they disciplined, they had a moral or proverb for every occasion. If I complained as a child about something being "not fair," she'd say, "*Hak gau dau sek, baak gau dong joi.* The black dog steals the food, the white dog gets punished." (The world is not always fair or just.)

"*Choi kar m'chip hak, chut lo mo kwai yan.* Refusing to receive guests at home, on the road, no hosts or patrons." (Do unto others as you would have them do unto you.)

On prudence and saving for a rainy day, she gave us this proverb: "*Sek gai daan, m'sek gai na.* Eat the eggs but not the mother hen."

She had worldly wisdom: "*San don yau chek shi, sai kai mo chek yan.* In the forest, there are straight trees; in the world, there are no straight persons." Do not be too trusting—*tai ngan sik yan.* Wear eyes when meeting people. On the other hand, we were to be sensitive to others' needs, and not to be *dhin dhang dham,* an electric lightbulb staying brightly lit when lovers wanted to be alone in the dark.

My mother had proverbs for love, too. Often, on seeing lovers hand in hand in the public gardens, she would shake her head and say with a tolerant smile, "*Yau ching yam seui baau.* With love, drinking water fills the belly."

I think she envied the euphoric time when lovers think they can be happy with love alone, though she'd warn us it was most unrealistic. One cannot live on love alone, echoing the English proverb "When poverty knocks at the door, love flies out the window."

My mother believed that one must make allowances, especially in a marriage. Since one was not perfect, one could not expect perfection or perfect happiness. She used to say, "*Daan ngan lou tai louh poh, yat ngan hoi, yat ngan mai.* The one-eyed man viewing his wife." (He keeps one eye blind to her faults.) She urged her children to study hard, for that was our only road out of poverty, a landscape she had grown too familiar with since her marriage. She stressed the need for a career, our own earning power, especially for us girls; she wanted us to avoid her fate, being chained to a loveless marriage, having to suffer a feckless husband. "Never stay with a man who hits you. The moment he lays a hand on you, you walk out the door. Or you are not my daughter."

My father never hit my mother, not because he did not want to. In some of their altercations, I have seen him poised with raised hand and voice to strike her. But he was prevented by her courage and reactions. She never flinched or cowered from him. She always grabbed a weapon, once a ceramic vase, once a large pair of scissors, and promised him she would harm him, she would spill his blood and his life, if he touched her. He believed her and shunted his violence aside, smashing many radios, gramophone records, once his brand-new TV set.

Until my early teen years, I believed they fought about money. I was not aware there were other conflicts underlying the fight over housekeeping money. When I was thirteen, my mother made me her confidante and shared with me her hopes and her betrayals. It was my stumbling accidentally onto one of the betrayals that thrust me into the role of secret sharer, and later, fierce champion that has been mine ever since.

I was thirteen the year I discovered there were dark secrets underlying the calm and easy rhythms of our very ordinary lives. I think this eventually led to my need to become a writer, to fill out the shapes and shadows beneath the surfaces people present to the world.

At thirteen, I wanted things and people to be what they seemed. Change bothered me. My body bothered me. It was changing, filling out. I was suddenly growing hair in strange places. My secret fear then was that I was changing into a beast, like Kafka's cockroach man. I asked my brother and he told me, from his vast experience of having lived two years more, that it was a natural thing; that even our parents had armpit and pubic hair.

Wanting confirmation, I asked Mother and she explained that I was not turning into an animal, just into a woman. She showed me how to crumple and pulverize cheap rice-chaff paper into coarse feminine napkins to catch the blood my body would begin to expel every month. She said rich women used soft, absorbent cotton napkins, Modess, instead of hard rice-chaff. I had naïvely assumed from the "Because . . ." ads that the elegant ladies were modeling dresses for that brand name.

I hated the physical process of becoming a woman. Month after month, I had "accidents" that mortified me, embarrassed me. It was made worse by the fact there would be no end to this process for the next forty years, an eternity to a teenager. At that time, a newspaper article brought me comfort. In Sweden, the first sex-change operations had been performed successfully. Though they were to change men into women, I felt cheered and confident that Western medicine would have achieved the ability to do the opposite operation by the time I grew up and saved enough money. I resolved to have my sex changed. This decision must have become embedded in my subconscious. Years later, when I was picking my baptismal name, I chose the uni-sexual name of Hilary.

Mother offered to let me have my hair permed. I think she sensed my difficult adjustment to puberty. Most of my friends had curly hair: the Malay girls came by theirs naturally, the Chinese girls artificially. Mongolian straight black hair is a dominant genetic trait and I had hair that stubbornly refused to curl, however much I braided it. We all wanted curly hair and despised what we had. Only when I came to America did I realize that our long, straight black hair was a thing of beauty to Western eyes. I had begged Mother for a permanent. She refused because we couldn't spare the money. I knew her offer was her "handful of raisins," the sop she used for getting us children to swallow bitter medicine.

In my experience, Chinese medicine always came in the form of a huge bowl of bitter black broth with stomach-turning ingredients like earthworms, cockroaches, scorpions, creepy-crawly things, fungi, and roots, simmered in a clay pot for hours to condense the bitterness. One almost had to get well fast to avoid another dose of the evil-smelling, evil-tasting liquid. Mother would give us a packet of sweet golden raisins as a treat after, but the raisins never quite erased the bitter aftertaste of the medicine.

My friend Swee Hoe recommended the Mei Wah Beauty Salon on Kapar Road. It was located above the Bata Shoe Store in a row of three-story shophouses by the market. I climbed the stairs and turned off the first landing. The stairs continued up to private apartments above; I could tell by the shoes parked by the stairwell. In Malaysia, you take off your shoes before entering a private home.

It was my first visit to a beauty salon and I was overwhelmed by the smell. It was as if someone had washed the floor with *eau de cologne* after a herd of cows had used the place as a bathroom. The salon assaulted the eyes as well: bright pink walls, bright pink linoleum floor, bright pink plastic seats, sinks, hair-dryers, rollers, brushes. Contrast was provided by snippets of black hair on the pink floor around each seat. The horror was amplified by mirror-covered walls.

There were two customers, both their heads and faces hidden by pink beehive hair-dryers and women's magazines. There were two girls in pink smocks, both Chinese. One had dyed her hair red and it looked most incongruous with her sallow complexion. The other girl smiled and asked me in Cantonese how I wanted my hair done. I showed her my pin-up of a magazine model, an English girl whose beauty I yearned for, the high nose, the deep large green eyes, the light brown hair; I hoped to achieve the look of her lustrous curls. The salon girl shook her head, not unkind. She must have been used to customers coming in with unrealistic dreams. She said my hair was not long enough for that style. I picked one she suggested from her folder. She told me her name was Su-lin and started to pin and clip my hair. Then she shampooed it, rolled it in tight curlers, and drenched the curlers with pink perm solution (the source of the cow urine smell). She seated me under a steel contraption with a mass of dangling black wires, clamped a wire to each roller, handed me a bundle of magazines, and told me it would take thirty minutes for my hair to be "electrified." The Chinese word for perming is to "electrify the hair." I looked at my reflection in the mirror and decided I looked like Medusa in an extreme state of shock.

A long time later, or so it seemed to me as I sat in an odor of burning hair and ammonia, Su-lin released me, rinsed my hair (still in rollers), and stuck my head inside a pink beehive blow-dryer. I watched the other women taken out of their beehive captivity and their transformation as their rollers were removed and their hair fluffed out and styled. I began to read my magazines.

Looking up from an irritatingly arch article on "What Men Like in Women," I saw Father in the doorway. Actually, I saw his reflection in the mirror as I was sitting with my back to the door. I returned to my magazine and decided to let him surprise me when I had achieved my transformation.

I was happy he had come to take me home. At the time, my father outshone all the storybook heroes in my eyes. He played the saxophone (self-taught) in the local band; he was a lead actor in the Amateur Chinese Opera Association. He told magnificent stories and took me on outings with his large group of friends in their beautiful cars. He was a leader in the group even though his only means of transportation was a bicycle. He spent money freely and bought presents for me on those outings. His friends were as lighthearted and always game for adventure as he was.

I was disappointed when Su-lin finished my hair. Reality did not match my hopes. I was doubly disappointed when I looked for Father and he was not there. Su-lin said no one had come in after me.

I told Mother about the curious appearance and disappearance of Father at the Mei Wah Beauty Salon. She became very still for a moment, then she continued to spoon rice into my bowl. When I pressed her for an explanation, she admitted that she had known for five years that he kept a mistress above the Mei Wah.

I was not ready for such adult knowledge, though I must have subconsciously picked up earlier hints so that her statement had the force of truth, the click of the final piece in the jigsaw puzzle fitting into place. I protested the impossibility of it, the unreason of it. I tried to make my adults fit the rules of my then simpler universe.

"Is she more beautiful? What's she got that you haven't got?" I couldn't understand my father's betrayal. Mother was beautiful by Chinese standards: she still had a lovely figure. (Later she became heavy after six pregnancies, too little exercise—housework drudgery is not exercise; it does not burn calories—and too much starch in the diet.) She waited on Father, trained us to wait on

Father hand and foot, and treated him as the most important person in the household (except when they had their fights). She kept the house neat and clean; she did not waste his money. What more, I argued, childish in my fear of change and loss, could a man want?

Mother showed me a photograph of Father's Badminton Club. Badminton is a serious sport in Malaysia. For us, the International Thomas Cup is as big a deal as the World Cup in England or the Superbowl in America. I'm still rather proud that I played for the varsity team in my first year in college. Whether we won or lost the season is a total fog to me. Strange, thinking back on it now. But I've realized and grown to accept this fact about myself: I am not a fiercely competitive person. I want to excel, to do well, to make the grade. But I am content at that level; it does not bother me that I am not the best; it does not bother me that there are others above me (as long as the number is not too many). I think this habit of being content was drilled into me by Mother's favorite proverb, "*San ko wan yow yat san ko.* Tall mountain, there's another mountain taller." (Do not be arrogant: you may be the best here, but somewhere, there is someone better than you.)

When Mother pointed out a woman in the Badminton Club photograph as my father's mistress living above the Mei Wah Beauty Salon, I stared. The woman was plain. She had a square face and a square body. Her eyebrows were bushy, her eyes too small, and her mouth too large.

"She's ugly. How can he prefer her to you?"

My mother must have asked herself this question many times. And worked her way to a painful, partially correct answer. "Men like change. Men like admiration. They need admiration and will choose it over devotion and a good housekeeper every time."

"You admire Father," I said. It seemed as obvious as mentioning that the sky was blue.

Her answer shocked me.

"I stopped admiring your father years ago. When Second Daughter died. When she was sick and he did not care enough to come home to take her to the doctor. It's hard to admire a selfish man who takes food from his children's mouths to take other women out for dinner. All these years, week in and week out, I am begging him for housekeeping money. Each time I beg, another piece of my heart turns to stone."

Years later, I would realize how this constant feeling of powerlessness in her life had embittered her. She was a woman whose intelligence, passion, and perceptions knew little outlet except secondhand, through her children. Surrounded by children and neighbors and relatives, my mother was essentially alone. She had to maintain the façade of a happy household to save the "face" of my father, of our family. My mother had a strong sense of integrity, of dignity. Until she turned to me as a receptive listener, there had been no one with whom she could share her hurt and shame at having an unsatisfactory husband; no one with whom she could speak the truth and not "lose face."

I sat while my rice grew cold and hard. I felt betrayed by both parents. My father in betraying my mother had betrayed me. I felt honored by my mother's telling me adult secrets. Yet the feeling was tinged with resentment. I felt burdened, weighed down, legs trembling like a colt carrying an overfed man. Looking back, I can name the thing I subconsciously grasped at the time. She made me grow up before I was ready.

"I would not stay after such betrayal," I said, quick to judge her. Thirteen is not an ideal confidante. At thirteen, there is only black and white, no varying shades of gray and compromise. Mother showed me a little of women's realities in 1959. Divorce was a social disgrace and rare. It was available for men whose wives cuckolded them, but few men wanted to "lose face" in such a drastic way. It was the social norm for men to have more than one woman. My father's lack of money was the only bar to his having concubines. A woman with little education and no children could become a house servant at subsistence pay. A woman who left her husband and children for such a position would be vulnerable to unwanted male attentions; she would have a full belly but she would have "no face" to meet the eyes of the world. My mother explained that she could not abandon us children to the hardships a second wife would inflict on us; she could not earn enough to take us with her. Women who were dependant on their husbands had to shut their eyes (and mouths) to things like mistresses. My mother was progressive in her outlook. She believed fervently that times were changing. She was determined on equality for her daughters—we were to have as much education as we could attain. She knew daughters needed it more. She had sworn her daughters would not suffer as she had to.

I had never thought much about Mother—she was just there, like the roof over our heads. She sheltered, she scolded when we were out of line, she controlled our lives. It jarred me to learn she was powerless in a man's world. Compared to Father, who could come and go as he pleased, love whom and where and when he pleased, she was like a household pet constricted by invisible fences, her power real only to her children and her pots and pans.

In my own marriage, I have had a tiny taste of her lifelong powerlessness and the rage that seeps up with being caged. After the birth of our daughters, I stopped working to stay home full-time. It was my choice to be with my babies, yet I had an underlying uneasiness at having no income, no career of my own. One day, I purchased a trash compactor to reduce the bags of trash I had to haul to the curb each Tuesday night. My husband was shocked at the price: three hundred dollars for an unnecessary luxury. He felt I should have asked his permission (which he would have refused) before buying the contraption. He said that in future, I was not to buy anything over two hundred dollars without his okay. My mother had sensitized me. I recognized the male power play: first, to demean what I did in our household as of little worth, not meriting a labor-saving device. My husband did not subscribe to the macho myth that the "Man of the House" takes out the trash. In this and many practical aspects, ours is a very Asian household. The second part of the power play demoted me from equal to subordinate, from spouse to child, someone who needed to ask permission before action. My reaction was to demand that he pay me a salary (retroactive, please) at the going rate for full-time housekeepers. "Fair's fair," I said, "if you are going to treat me like an underling, then I want my underling's pay to call my own; money I can use to buy trash, much less trash compactors, if I so desire." In fairness to my husband, he was not consciously seeking to belittle me or reduce my self-worth. He was thinking of being prudent with money, saving for the children's college educations. But if I had acceded to his restrictive proposition, my sense of self-worth would have been eroded and we would have stepped onto the slippery slope of resentment, of feeling betrayed and unloved, that is the beginning of the breakdown of many marriages. I have to thank my mother for the lessons she taught me, consciously and unconsciously.

That was the only time I had my hair permed. I decided I preferred having straight hair. I also gave up the idea of changing myself into a man. I stopped liking raisins; I was a grown woman, and could take my Chinese medicine in all its bitterness.

🦬

See also Tham's poem, "Father" on p. 148.

🦬

Close Encounters of the Sneaky Kind

RICHARD CONNIFF

SOMEWHERE IN A RAIN FOREST in Panama, a big bruiser of a dung beetle with a formidable horn on his snout stands ready to defend his turf. Let's call him Mr. Big. He is the beau ideal: not only tall, dark and handsome, but also ferocious in combat. What he's defending is, OK, howler monkey flop, but this is an insanely precious commodity for local dung beetles. They get to it 15 seconds after it hits the ground.

Under the monkey dropping, where Mr. Big stands guard, a female is sequestered in a tunnel. She's supposed to be busily packing up food for her offspring by Mr. Big. Instead, she's having sex with a dismal runt named Raoul.

What's wrong with this picture? Absolutely everything, according to our conventional notions about sexual behavior. The Mr. Bigs of the world—the beefy macho types—are supposed to get the girls. They also get to kick sand in the faces of the 98-pound Raouls. But recent research has starkly demonstrated that the conventional wisdom is all wrong. The natural world is full of what biologists call "satellite males" or "sneaker males." Many of them are relative weaklings, or lack the masculine ornamentation to dazzle choosy females. Some even practice unconventional strategies like cross-dressing. Yet surprisingly often, it's the 98-pound weakling who gets the girl.

Scientists have documented sneaker-male behavior in hundreds of species, from damselflies to Sumatran orangutans. Among red deer, for instance, a 12-point buck may be the apparent stud, defending a harem of 20 hinds. But young males with dinky little antlers loiter nearby, grabbing matings whenever they can. (British biologists refer to them as "sneaky rutters," or worse.) Similarly, an old horseshoe crab may no longer have what it takes to latch on to a female of his own. So instead, he waits to find a young couple already mating, then scrambles aboard and manages to fertilize about 40 percent of the female's eggs.

But let's go back to Raoul. Mr. Big is twice Raoul's size, with a horn that accounts for 15 percent of his body weight. Among male dung beetles, the horn is the main secondary sex characteristic and the chief weapon for headbutting combat. Raoul, by contrast, has no more than a pitiful nub where his horn's supposed to be. Having been malnourished at a crucial stage in his early development, he will never grow a respectable horn, nor ever be able to stand in the doorway of his own handsome pile defending his claim to a female. About half of all male dung beetles suffer the same sorry fate. In the old way of thinking, they could resign themselves to romantic and evolutionary oblivion.

"But nobody had looked at what goes on underground," says Douglas Emlen, a biologist at the University of Montana. He set out to change that 12 years ago, as a graduate student at the Smithsonian Tropical Research Institute in Panama. Emlen built glass-fronted ant farms, put the dung beetles inside and then watched what really happened. The smallest sneaker males, he says, relentlessly attempted to slip into the tunnel entrance while Mr. Big was looking the other way. Others, like Raoul, withdrew to a respectful distance and dug tunnels of their own. Once hidden safely underground, these sneakers veered sharply sideways to intersect the main tunnel and enjoy a tryst with Mrs. Big while Mr. Big himself stood stupidly at the door.

Emlen's supervisors were cautious. Maybe that's just something that happens when you put dung beetles in ant farms, they said. So Emlen went out and made latex casts of dung beetle tunnels in the wild. What he found was that after Raoul kisses Mrs. Big good-bye, he often continues digging sideways to intersect the tunnels of five or six other females similarly sequestered under that same dropping.

Up until the 1970s, it was scientific dogma that the males in every species—little boy dung beetles and damselflies alike—all wanted to grow up to be fighters. That is, they wanted to acquire and defend territories and harems. At least in theory, the combined forces of natural selection (getting killed by predators or disease) and sexual selection (getting killed by rivals or chosen by females) would ruthlessly weed out any sissy alternative lifestyles.

In fact, Charles Darwin himself noticed that alternative forms persist in many species. But biologists generally ignored this insight because they couldn't explain it—or they just didn't see it in the first place. Sneaky behaviors designed to fool other members of the same species often fooled outside observers too.

"Theory determines what you see," says University of Toronto biologist Mart Gross, who's studied mating strategies in fish. And in the open-minded political and scientific zeitgeist of the mid-1970s, evolutionary theorists started to look beyond the fighter stereotype. But it required a kind of collective gulp to face up to the question of how a male might actually benefit from being smaller, weaker and, well, more effeminate.

For instance, in bluegill sunfish a significant percentage of males actually impersonate females. They wear female striping, and their eyes darken to resemble the limpid black pools of a female bluegill. They also have heightened levels of the female hormone estradiol. Gross coined the term "satellite males" to describe the way these impersonators orbit the nests of conventional males.

The conventional males frequently get fooled and invite the cross-dressers into their nests. Gross carefully documented what happens next: when a female impersonator enters a nest, he dips down, turning on one side—moving as a real female would to release eggs for the resident male to fertilize. But—*vive la différence*—the cross-dresser is in fact secretly releasing his sperm onto eggs deposited by females.

This kind of transvestite mating tactic has turned out to be surprisingly common in other species. Take the giant cuttlefish, a voluptuous, three-foot-long relative of the squid. Conventional males are the Robert Goulets or Enrique Iglesiases of the marine world; they put on a lavish, romantic display for females. A courting male waves extended, banner-like webs on his arms and turns his body into an amorous light show with bright colors and pulsing zebra stripes.

So far, so good. But sometimes a small sneaker male accompanies the happy couple and, by assuming the shape and body patterns of a female, avoids attack. Sooner or later, Goulet/Iglesias will have to drive off some other big male. In the resulting confusion, says Australian biologist Mark Norman, the female impersonator "waltzes in, sneaks under the covers, grabs the female and starts passing sperm to her." When Goulet/Iglesias comes back, the sneaker male once again tags along, looking girlish and innocent.

Cross-dressing isn't just a way to get a mate. Some female damselflies, for example, appear to imitate males for the opposite reason—to avoid being sexually harassed. Most of the time, though, cross-dressing and other sneaky ploys have just one purpose: getting the girl. Which is why the big boys of the world spend so much time and energy on what biologists call "mate guarding." (Also known, to human females, as "desperate-male clinging.") Mr. Big, the dung beetle, for instance, regularly patrols his tunnel to check on Mrs. Big, and if he catches her in flagrante delicto, he throws the interloper out. Then he immediately has sex with Mrs. Big, to displace the interloper's sperm with his own. In fact, he may have sex with her ten times a day, just to be certain—or at least a little less uncertain—that he's the father of her offspring. Waterbugs are even more anxious about paternity. In one study, a male mated with the female 100 times in 36 hours.

The burden of mate guarding, whether by fighting or marathon lovemaking, can leave even the sturdiest male feeling weak-kneed. Among northern elephant seals, a big bull who wins bloody contests against other bulls gets to stake out a stretch of beach and wallow in lubricious splendor with his harem. He may mate with 50 females in a season, while many lesser males go celibate. But defending his harem also means not going back to the sea to eat, and he typically loses about 40 percent of his weight during the three-month breeding season.

This is why "success" as a conventional male is not always all it's cracked up to be. DNA testing in red-winged blackbirds, for instance, has revealed that the longer a resident male stays away from the nest gathering food, the greater the likelihood that his putative offspring will actually be fathered by someone else. In one Australian bird species, the superb fairy wren, fully two-thirds of the offspring get fathered by somebody other than the man of the house. If male animals could perform a cost-benefit analysis, they would almost certainly conclude that it's cheaper and easier to be a sneaker male. You don't need to keep up a large territory, court females, fight off rivals or provide parental care.

But is cheaper ever really better? In most species, females are the choosers when it comes to mating, and they usually seem to prefer the big boys. Northern elephant seal females, for instance, clearly regard the big beefy alpha as their best possible mate. They howl in protest when the alpha mounts them—but they howl louder and longer if a lesser male tries it, so the big bull will come thundering to the rescue.

Still, the strategy that's lord of the dance one season may be out on the street the next. Take the side-blotched lizards living among rocky outcrops in the coastal mountains of central California. They're about two and a half inches long, and conventional males typically display by doing push-ups while also puffing out the bright patch of color at their throats. Barry Sinervo, a biologist at the University of California at Santa Cruz, has identified three different, genetically determined mating tactics, each identified by a distinctive throat color.

The Big Boy orange-throats are the "ultradominants," patrolling large territories with lots of females. The Average Joe blue-throats are about 15 percent smaller, but still manage to maintain modest territories and diligently mate guard however many females they can round up. And then there are the Slacker yellow-throats, which mimic females, do no courtship push-ups and maintain no territories, but instead skulk in nooks and crannies among the rocks hoping to get lucky. It ought to be easy for everyone to spot the Slackers and make them disappear.

But is life ever that simple? If Average Joe blue-throats happen to predominate in a population, then the Slacker yellows are indeed out of luck. The blue-throats recognize them as rival males and evict them from their territories. But blue-throats never predominate for long, because the Big Boy orange-throats have the size and stamina to beat them up and take away their females. Thus orange-throats get more offspring in the next generation, and in a year or two, they supplant the blues.

Orange-throats apparently are not so bright. They don't recognize the Slacker yellow boys as rival males, so they tolerate them in the neighborhood.

This allows the yellows to make what Sinervo calls "little sperm strafing runs" through orange-throat territories. After a year or two, yellow Slackers actually outnumber orange-throats. Then it's time once again for the blue-throats to make their move. In fact, the three male types regularly displace one another in the reproductive hierarchy over a four- to five-year cycle.

In many other species, the sneaky approach seems to work best when picky females concentrate their favors on a relative handful of big brutish males (or when the big brutes corral females in harems). The alpha males do best with this kind of strong sexual selection, but the overwhelming majority of conventional males wind up as losers. So sneaker males in this scenario may actually do better on average than the ordinary Joes. "Any time you have a great imbalance between the haves and the have-nots," says Purdue University biologist Richard Howard, "the have-nots find a way around." Sneaking also works better in habitats with lots of places to hide when the big guy comes fe-fi-fo-ing onto the scene.

At the very least, sneaky mating tactics provide a way for weaker males to avoid being weeded out, but they may actually be much more than that. After his work on bluegill sunfish, biologist Mart Gross went on to study coho salmon. Some coho males, called jacks, mature early, at 2 years of age, and typically measure under 15 inches in length. Others delay maturity for an extra year and become big "hooknose" males 25 inches or more in length. Sports fishermen naturally regard the hooknoses as the trophy fish, the best of the bunch. But Gross says they are not. Both jacks and hooknoses mature in open ocean, but jacks spend much less time at sea, so the percentage of jacks surviving and making it home to the spawning grounds is more than double that of hooknoses. And once they get there, the jacks are adept at hiding and darting out after a spawning female to steal fertilizations from the lumbering hooknoses. In terms of genetic fitness, says Gross, the hooknoses are in fact the weaker members of the population.

So what does all this mean for humans? To risk scientific and pop-cultural heresy for a moment, is it possible the real love god is not, after all, Barry White ("I'm Qualified To Satisfy You"), but some sneaker male like 5-foot-2 Prince? Not Arnold Schwarzenegger but Danny DeVito?

Alas, scientists do not go there. They are properly cautious about extrapolating from the behavior of other animals to explain ours. They might look at the story of Princess Diana and her riding instructor, James Hewitt, and mutter to themselves, "sneaker male." But the most they will say out loud is that the mating strategies of people are at least as diverse as those being studied in the rest of the animal kingdom.

In any case, our old stereotypes are unlikely to vanish overnight. And the Raouls and Slacker yellow-throats probably like it better that way. The tendency of Big Boys to regard them as harmless is their best possible protection. It is their entrée, their invitation. So relax, Mr. Big. Put your feet up, Ben, Denzel and Brad. You should know that the little guys of the world wish you nothing but sweet dreams.

13

❧

The Elements of Drama

THE NATURE OF DRAMA

In a way, playwriting is only another aspect of the storytelling one also does while writing poetry or prose. All three have a foundation of the same techniques in narration, expression of emotions, character development, finding precise language, and more. Playwrights (who may become poets or prose writers on other days) also keep journals, read, and research. For the writer, the boundaries between genres may be faint. We have seen that a story can appear to be a memoir and that a poem may sound and look like prose (albeit very good prose). *The Glass Menagerie* is both poetic memoir and play. For the writer, the classroom categories are not very helpful.

What may be more useful is a grasp of how the technical mastery needed for each genre is different. Poets need to listen to sounds with extra attention and learn to manage line breaks dramatically. Prose writers have to learn to vary the density of the words on the page and what techniques will speed the readers on their way. For most playwrights the only way to master the technical advantages and limits of the stage (or camera) is to involve themselves on a working level in the theater (or film, or television, or radio).

In some capacity—acting or moving sets, directing or running a camera—you should become engaged in the production of dramatic work so as to experience its freedoms, conventions, energies, and limits. Working in the media, even as a gopher (go-for coffee, go-for a script, go-for a chair) or as a spear carrier, will make you more sensitive to the problems that your collaborators face. These collaborators are the artists who will design your living room, light it, and dress and direct the actors who, in turn, must kiss with convincing passion as if an audience were not watching. Once you have spoken lines that make no sense, or stood about in a scene with nothing to do, or changed a set for the third time in fifteen minutes—once you have been exposed to the *physical reality* of the media—you are more likely to be sensitive to such difficulties and to construct your plays to avoid them. You will begin to think performance.

Of course, you can argue that the reader of a poem or story performs your work mentally; however, the reader's performance does not have to be limited by talent, space, or material. This state of affairs is far different from having a director, sound technician, lighting technician, costumer, set designer, and actors among your host of ultimate collaborators. These other contributors literally and figuratively put on (embody) your words.

Consider the following action: "They walked into the living room and kissed passionately. Then they began to remove their clothes." Think of the difference between your response to this action (1) brought to your mind's eye through print and (2) brought to your senses as it *happens* on stage or screen.

As a reader, you can allow your imagination to build on the writer's material, you can decide to read more quickly to see if the couple will be interrupted or more slowly to savor the experience, and you can interrupt the experience by putting down the book and then picking it up again. Or you can skip it. Of course, you could close your eyes at the nudity in a play, but you need to know it is coming (though you could close your eyes immediately and reduce your time exposure). In any case, our reaction to actual nudity is bound to be different than to imagined nudity. In reading you have some degree of safety and control because you can easily put a distance between yourself and the potential impact of the writer's words. At some level, you are always conscious of holding a book or magazine and looking at the printed page.

In plays and films, the illusion of life-going-on is the result of other people doing something with the writer's words. As a member of an audience, you are confronted by something *happening.* You are a *witness* to the disrobing. Real people as well as characters are undressing before you. The pressure and the pace of the production absorb your attention. Images and voices from outside of you run at someone else's pace and create the particular illusion of life-going-on that is so different from the illusions of fiction.

One way to master the particular illusions of drama so as to exploit them is to have hands-on experience with the dramatic media. Another step is to read books intended for the other stage professionals—actors, directors, designers—in order to know their language and concerns. The more familiar you are with their world, the more you can do to ensure that your play will be produced and performed as you have conceived it.

In the sections that follow, we touch only lightly on matters discussed in the fiction chapters. If you have turned to this chapter first, you may want to refer back to those discussions of plot, character, point of attack, scene, and setting. Here we stress how these same elements need to be reconsidered for dramatic presentation. Our discussions refer to Joyce Carol Oates' *Procedure* and Jeffrey Sweet's *Last Day of Camp*, found in Chapter 15, and to some of the short stories in Chapter 12.

STORYTELLING WITH PEOPLE AND THINGS

The "drama" retains the force of its original meaning in Greek—*to do*. You write out your script to communicate with those who will *do* the play for still other persons (the audience). Though your script may end up printed because your play is a success, publication is a by-product of your collaboration. It is best, then, to think of your play as being similar to a musical score: signs placed on paper that show others how to play your work. You can't ask the musician to play notes or make sounds that the instrument can't produce.

Because fiction and drama use many of the same terms, you can easily fall into the trap of thinking that playwriting is simply telling stories on a different instrument and without having to type from margin to margin. It is certainly true that the story you want your collaborators to present for you contains many of the same elements discussed in the fiction chapters. Like fiction, a play has the following elements:

1. A *story* out of which you carve a *plot*
2. in which *characters*
3. are in *conflict*
4. because they want their *desires* to dominate about some object and/or idea and/or emotion.

The wants and needs of the characters are based on beliefs that the author and the audience may or may not share. Willy Loman in *Death of a Salesman* believes that personality—being well liked—can bring success and excuse lying and stealing, and that what people think of you is more important than what you know or what you can do. Arthur Miller's point of view appears to be that this kind of search for outward success—measured by money—prevents Willy from recognizing his real talents and needs. The struggle to achieve at any cost a materialistic version of the American Dream results in a tragically empty life. (We come to know Miller's point of view because of what happens to Willy Loman.)

Such a combination of (1) controlling ideas in the characters plus (2) a set of circumstances is called the **premise**. The dramatic premise triggers the actions in the play at the point of attack. Because Willy has followed his beliefs, he has—by his lights—failed. He no longer can go on as a salesman either emotionally, mentally, or physically. He is thinking of suicide. At that very moment his son Biff returns. In *Death of a Salesman* the combination of Willy's beliefs, his traits, and the circumstances is the seed from which grow the conflicts, the flashbacks, and all the other actions that, ironically, lead to Willy's suicide. The elements of the premise, then, can be seen as an opportunity, a potential, for something to happen.

Though we might find the basic concept of premise to be useful for any type of storytelling, the *dramatic* premise requires an especially intense combination of triggering forces at the point of attack. For example, it is much more critical in a dramatic presentation for the point of attack to be as close to the climax as possible. At most the playwright has only a few hours of audience attention for showing the story. In effect, most of the events and the development of essential character traits will have happened before the curtain rises. So late a point of attack creates great pressures. In an actual ten minutes or two hours, the playwright must have the characters (1) reveal all the information necessary for us to understand who they are and what they are doing (the exposition) and (2) do and say the things that will bring on the dramatic conclusion. The pressure of squeezing so much into a limited time has, as we shall see, both advantages and drawbacks.

Playwriting is so linked to the material presence of actual time, spaces, sounds, and people (actors)—life-going-on—that it has unique energies and limits. Many a writer successful in another genre (Henry James, for example) failed in playwriting by ignoring the particular life, effects, and affects of drama. What might be dismissed as merely mechanical differences are quite complex and can cause important changes in the writer's decisions about developing and presenting character and plot.

The following discussions about how one might adapt stories from fiction to drama will begin to illustrate this point. (We suggest you read the pieces of fiction before you read the discussion.)

I. *"Belling the Cat"* (page 187)

The fable is based on the following ideas: (1) If a solution to a problem cannot be put into effect, it is a foolish suggestion, and (2) an inexperienced individual (in this case, a young mouse) is more likely to propose a foolish solution than is an experienced individual. These ideas (whether correct or not) are dramatized through the "plot" which they control. The setting is minimal, as is the characterization. You can read the fable in a minute, absorb the "truth" of the premise (which is stated directly), and move on. It is the idea in the premise that dominates the characters and circumstances.

If you wanted to turn the fable into a dramatic work, keeping the same characters (mice and cat) and circumstances, what problems would you have? (Jot down a few ideas before going on.)

The most obvious problem, though not the most important, is that you would have to teach mice to talk. *Solution:* Make a cartoon and let real human voices substitute. *Or:* Dress human beings in mouse costumes. *Or:* Let the human beings simply think of themselves as mice. Such problems can be solved by dozens of conventional devices (as in *Peter Pan, Equus,* or *Cats*). A good principle to follow when trying to solve such mechanical problems is simply to borrow a convention the audience is used to.

The more difficult "dramatic" problem is how to activate the premise so that it can occupy the stage or screen for more than a minute or two. The typical solution would be to expand the number of scenes and develop the characters. For example, to show us the precise nature of the dilemma, the playwright might add a scene in which the Cat decimates a group of the mice as they are raiding the kitchen. Or, perhaps the dramatization will begin with Young Mouse and Old Mouse as father and son. Old Mouse tells Young Mouse not to make a fool of himself at the meeting. What has caused Old Mouse to do that? Young Mouse is fresh out of Rodent College, where he majored in conflict resolution and felines. He has returned, full of piss and vinegar, to put his academic training to practical and immediate use. Perhaps the first scene will begin just slightly before the meeting. The last scene will show the mice actually trying to bell the cat (as we see in one of the cartoon versions). Somehow, though, in the process of developing the material, we have changed a part of the premise. It's not just about wisdom, it has come to involve a conflict between education and experience, new ways and old ways, sons and fathers.

Inexorably, the move from a fictional premise to a dramatic premise will bring changes—additional actions, a reshaping of emphasis, and different ways of developing character. (*Note*: We are by no means suggesting that dramatizing a piece of fiction always requires expansion. It almost always requires contraction of some events and expansion of others. However, compare Hemingway's "The Killers" to the film.)

In the end, the experience we will receive from "*Belling the Cat*—the Movie" will be different from the experience we get from "*Belling the Cat*—the Fable" because the audience's expectation of the media has been met. We will see and hear the movement rather than imagining it. Also, because the Old Mouse and the Young Mouse will be present to us, we do not expect to be told one is older and one is younger. The director will make sure we can see that. In fact, the characters won't be telling us anything we can see for ourselves. We might, on the other hand, expect to see Young Mouse actually try to *do* the belling.

Ironically, then, it is no praise to say of the dramatic version that it is exactly like the original.

EXERCISE

One might argue that the premise of "Belling the Cat" is all wrong. How would you do so? Now devise a new premise. Can you think of a circumstance around which you could build a plot for your new premise?

II. *"Sunday in the Park" (pp. 267–270)*

The thematic element of Kaufman's premise is this: at bottom, no matter how much they may praise and encourage the civilized virtues of intellect and gentleness, some women really want a man to protect them (another way of saying to be "manly" or "macho"). Because Bel Kaufman has chosen to tell the story from the wife's point of view, we are as surprised as the wife is to find her more "primitive" nature surfacing after the bully faces down her husband, Morton. The insight—the epiphany—works in the short story because the woman's sudden *conscious* awareness *is the point.* In a way, the premise is not the revelation of her desire for a "manly" man, but the fact that she wasn't aware of the depths of her dissatisfaction.

Taking the same premise for a play, however, would require major changes and expansion. For example, the antagonist (the bully) in the story has a simple function; he forces Morton's choice of whether to fight for his family's right to share the sandbox in peace or to walk away. Once you put the bully into the flesh of an actor and the actor starts walking on stage or through the film, you need something more for him to do during that time than this single action. You might, of course, shape the action so that the bully comes on only toward the end of the scene but, for the purpose of this discussion, let's assume that the bully must be present for a longer period so that his action does not appear gratuitous—mere bullying for the sake of showing power.

In order for the character to be present to the audience for a longer period of time, the dramatist will have to increase the bully's active role. What would happen, for example, if instead of separate benches, as in the story, there was only one bench to share and the bully had entered and joined the couple? What kind of byplay would occur among them as they jostled for room? What are the emotions evoked when people have to share territory? Would the bully sit on Morton's *Times*? Might Morton and his wife try to placate the man? Might Morton offer him a section from his *Times*? Would the bully resent this offer because he senses both Morton's and Morton's wife's condescension? Is the bully (a construction worker) sick and tired of the "college boys" telling him that the concrete isn't mixed properly? Perhaps, after all, he isn't merely a bully; he has a grievance. Are Morton and his wife regentrifying the construction worker's neighborhood and slowly driving out the working class? Notice how the very fact that the bully will be physically present generates questions that begin to affect the premise.

In a ten-minute skit or a comedy show, such elaboration probably would not be needed, but the presence of a character who is more than a functionary increases the playwright's obligation to account for that character.

More important, if the premise has to do with the woman's sudden recognition of her more "primitive" desires, a way has to be found to let the reader directly experience what the narrator only reports: "It was more than just an unpleasant incident, more than defeat of reason by force . . . it had something to do with her and Morton, something acutely personal, familiar, and important." At the very same time the playwright must (1) find ways to reveal how the woman is hiding her true desires beneath what she believes she ought to desire, and (2) convince the spectators to accept that, with the same evidence they have, she can fail to draw the same conclusion until the very end. (For the audience, seeing what she doesn't see increases the dramatic tension. When is she going to find out what is so clear to us?)

It might appear, then, that the playwright needs only to organize and expand the events in preparation for the wife's moment of realization, ignoring (as the narrator of the story can) the husband's wants and presence. Because Bel Kaufman focuses the events through the woman's point of view, the reader is not concerned about the husband. Since a play normally has no narrator to focus the point of view, the husband will be *present to the audience*, and his presence must be fulfilled. The playwright shouldn't suddenly throw a spotlight on the wife and filter out his presence. The audience won't forget the husband's reality as quickly as a reader would.

Since the bully creates an occasion for the wife to realize her true feelings but is not directly involved in the important developments in the marriage, the playwright may feel there is no problem getting him off stage. But surely the husband cannot be treated like a functionary. He is directly involved in the conditions that lead to the wife's recognition. To dramatize the wife's dissatisfaction, to put it into action, the playwright is going to have to show us the relationship. The husband's wants will become important, if only to make us interested in the conflict. Perhaps he and the wife will need a scene before the bully enters to give the audience a sense of the prior relationship. And once the husband's prior set of circumstances are revealed, he acquires importance in the dramatic presentation. Inevitably his importance will lead to adjustments in the premise and in the resolution, because he shares the audience's attention with the wife. How is he going to react to her self-realization? Would he say: "I'm signing up for refresher karate lessons. I would have done it long ago if you'd have let me. I should never have let myself get out of shape." In that case, to the premise must be added new ideas and circumstances: sometimes a man's civilized behavior merely reflects a woman's overt desires; given a chance he'll revert to "manliness."

Here is the principle: the playwright must account for *all the characters who have been involved in the conflict that springs from the premise*. Servants, spear carriers, and other beings who function in the plot only as mechanisms do not, of course, need to be accounted for, because they don't have a unique identity in relationship to the premise. In the process of accounting for the major characters, however, other aspects of the premise will begin to change.

EXERCISE

Since the wife's recognition alone is not likely to suffice for the ending, we will have to create something that gives the husband an "ending" in relationship to her new premise: I want a *man*. He might have a recognition: You got what you created and I'm comfortable being a wimp. Or, he might throw her over his shoulder and take her off the stage. Plan an ending for a dramatic version of "Sunday in the Park." Be sure to work up what the husband *wants*. Try to keep the play to one set.

III. *"The Boarding House"* (pp. 262–267)

The premise in "The Boarding House" is complex: marriage is seen as a form of "reparation," a payment to the woman for the satisfaction of the male's sexual desire, which the woman may in fact arouse to trap the man. Because men don't want to be married, they must be trapped into it. Manipulation of men through the power of social convention (and their fear of it) is often the way they are brought to heel. The subtle relationships between sex, marriage, family, church, and society are a replay of a very old premise: "In Adam's fall we sinned all," and how ironic it is that we keep on paying for it. It is a rather dreary view that, at best, is lightened by Joyce's wry sense of just how this particular marriage comes to happen.

The unexpressed desires that motivate the major characters (Mrs. Mooney, Mr. Doran, and Polly Mooney) would be difficult to dramatize because Joyce deliberately wants to show the passions as internal and inexpressible. Mrs. Mooney desires for her daughter a good marriage—at least a better one than she had; Polly desires sex and marriage; Doran desires to escape the trap but is too guilty and fearful (of violence, of losing his job, of what others will say) to flee. The technique of the story allows us to see that these desires cannot be expressed to others because one can hardly acknowledge them to oneself.

As a result, a good deal of this story's power comes from what we imagine is floating in the characters' minds. Among the images are the run-down boarding house and Dublin itself—Victorian, morally oppressive, and dreary. These are part of the circumstances in which the characters have developed. We assume that Mrs. Mooney's disappointing marriage is what motivates her—a history told, not shown. Doran's weakness (his mental and physical cowardice) we deduce from many small hints. Even the events that are shown, such as Polly's waiting for her proposal, tend to be internal; while she is waiting, Polly's visions of the future are described as amorphous. The scenes not shown—the sex scene, Doran's confession, Mrs. Mooney's confrontation with Doran—have the most potential for action and conflict, the lifeblood of the dramatic genres. Joyce filters out those in order to stress the results. He exploits the possibilities in narrative fiction for *showing* the rich interiority of the characters. He relies on the reader to imagine the scenes and the motives that the dramatist would be sweating to *show* in a different sense of the word—show so that an audience could literally see and hear the action.

For the dramatist, "The Boarding House" contains no end of scenes which invite such showing:

- A scene at Doran's job (to show his fearfulness).
- A scene of women going to mass (including Mrs. Mooney).
- A visit from Mr. Mooney (the former husband).
- A dinner scene with all the boarders.
- A scene in which Doran confesses.

And on and on. While the interiority of the story would be lost in the requirement for showing, for example, why Doran is quite right to fear the brutality of Polly's brother, new possibilities emerge. The playwright could show Polly's brother unfiltered through Doran's fearful imagination, exploiting a hint in the narrator's ironic presentation that the brother is a blowhard. Such a comic bully might well create a different sense of Doran's cowardice. Has Mrs. Mooney put her son up to scaring Mr. Doran?

However, to capture Joyce's internal world, the playwright would have to expand on the external world because the emotions that Joyce has rendered subtly could be recreated in the audience only by an accretion of many scenes, if at all.

Here is the principle: *though the ultimate effects may be quite subtle, drama requires presentation to the senses.* Therefore, when the writer imagines a premise requiring an internalized presentation and immense amounts of exposition, the material *as imagined* may not be suitable for a play. The very nature of drama—people witnessing actions and things—requires that the playwright create circumstances in which the motives and emotions of the characters can be swiftly and easily apprehended and felt.

Note: A producer or director might believe it worthwhile to try to recreate the mood of Dublin in the 1890s. In such a circumstance Joyce's story would be an occasion for a different creative motive, a desire to produce *spectacle*—the pleasure the audience derives from setting and extraordinary action (like acrobatics). Spectacle is one of the arts of the dramatist's collaborators. When the pleasures from spectacle dominate the drama, the playwright's premise becomes subordinate to the pleasures derived from those collaborators' arts. In other words, the play becomes an aspect of the spectacle and not the reverse. Such spectacle for spectacle's sake is outside the concern of this book.

EXERCISES

1. Write Doran's confession scene with the priest so that he reveals his inner terrors about marriage (and, of course, his sin of fornicating with Polly). Or write the scene in which Mrs. Mooney gets out of Polly what has happened with Mr. Doran. Is Polly pregnant?

2. Create a **treatment** (a scene-by-scene outline) for a movie version of "The Boarding House." As you select your scenes, keep in mind that you are trying to suggest in another medium the effects of Joyce's short story. For a model, read Joyce's "The Dead" and see John Huston's film rendition of the story.

☙

Adaptation, of course, is but one way to find a subject for a play; often you will start with your own combination of premise, situation, and characters. The principles will be the same: you will need to develop a premise suitable for the demands of a presentation, not of a printed page. The essential elements of story construction will remain the same as in fiction (see Chapter 9), but the pressures of dramatic presentation will determine how you go about developing the plot.

By this point it should be clear that when you intend to tell stories with real people and things, you must constantly be alert to the impact of the visual. The illumination of characters and plot in dramatic media is more than a matter of transferring your narrative into dialogue and stage directions.

MORE EXERCISES

1. Choose a popular fairy tale ("Little Red Riding Hood," for example). What is the premise? What is your point of attack? Why? Briefly describe what scenes you would need and list the events in those scenes.

2. Assume that "The Boarding House" characters live today—let us say at an exclusive but small and seedy college dedicated to the arts and overrun with mice, not donors. What kind of premise might you come up with that captures the spirit of the original if Mrs. Mooney runs some kind of off-campus establishment (small apartment house in a former mansion) and Mr. Doran is an assistant professor who is coming up for tenure? Outline your version of the play.

A Final Note

The point of attack in a dramatic presentation, as in fiction (see the discussion in Chapter 9), is generally as close to the climax of the story as the playwright can make it. Try to structure the events so that as much of the story as possible has happened before the curtain rises or credits end. The less that needs to be shown, the less time the production will take and the fewer actors and sets will be required. The drawback is that you have to find dramatic ways to provide the back story (the exposition) to the audience.

CHARACTERS

As we have already discussed, a character is the sum of "characteristics" that create for an audience some sense that the personages in stories, narrative or dramatic, are present and distinct. (See Chapter 9 for more about this aspect of character.) Just as a fiction writer does, the playwright builds a sense of the characters' reality by having them behave in a manner consistent with their development in the plot. In Ibsen's *Hedda Gabler*, Hedda behaves in a self-centered, independent way, reflecting characteristics attributable to her upbringing as a general's only child. In part, her suicide is understandable as an outcome of (1) that independence and her refusal to allow another man to dominate her, and (2) her fear of public exposure. These characteristics are seen in actions before her suicide.

A flesh-and-blood person will play Hedda. This special condition—actor plus the role the actor plays—creates for the playwright special opportunities and problems. Unless something about a character's physical appearance is extremely important, the playwright need only sketch it in. The director will choose the actors for gross distinctiveness (sex, age, looks) in accordance with the plot. Obviously, except in a radio presentation, the audience will not have to visualize these elements. The actor will provide the accent and the details (makeup, costume, sex, stature, and mannerisms) that a narrator constantly has to supply in fiction. Nor does the dramatist have to provide details to help the spectators visualize actions. The actor (and the other collaborators) present them directly to the senses. On the surface, then, it might appear that since half the job is done, all sensible writers would become playwrights.

The freedoms from some tasks actually create terrible responsibilities because, for most dramatic presentations, the characters have to carry forward in what they say and do almost all the elements of both the premise and the plot. Everything is compressed into the showing—characteristics, relationships, and conflicts. In some ways, condensation for effective dramatic presentation is closer emotionally and artistically to the demands of poetry than to fiction.

In small compass, the following radio advertisement (a playlet) shows how much is compressed into the characters and the situation that unfolds through them, all in a continuous time. We have decided to call it "The Teeth of the Problem."

(TIME: *The present*
SCENE: *A restaurant. Sounds of dishes clattering and other restaurant noises in the background.*)
   MAN: Hi. Sorry I'm late.
   WOMAN: Oh, that's O.K. This is a nice place.
   MAN: Speaking of nice places—
   WOMAN: Uh-huh?

MAN: I got the brochures. Here's Jamaica, the Virgin Islands, Martinique.

WOMAN: I have a [pause] "brochure" for you, too.

MAN: (*reading*) "When Your Child Needs Braces?" What is this?

WOMAN: Your child needs braces.

MAN: Eric?

WOMAN: That's what Dr. Marshall says.

MAN: Darn. What's that going to cost?

WOMAN: Oh, the price of a nice cruise.

MAN: Which means—

WOMAN: Right.

MAN: Diane, we need this trip.

WOMAN: Uh-huh.

MAN: We've waited five years for it.

WOMAN: Eric isn't too happy about this either.

MAN: I know. Is there any way we could swing both?

WOMAN: I don't see how, honey.

VOICEOVER: *For anyone who has ever said there isn't enough money, now there is. Sovran has half a billion dollars to lend.*

In traditional terms, we could analyze the elements of the playlet as follows:

Situation: A couple have been planning for a Caribbean cruise for some time and have saved money for it. They have sacrificed to raise their children (or child), and they may need this trip for the health of their marriage and their own mental health. The husband has gone to the travel bureau and picked up information; the wife has taken their son to the dentist. Previously they had planned to meet for lunch and discuss the trip.

Complication: Their son needs braces.

Crisis: They don't have enough money to meet their responsibility and also to take the trip they have worked for.

Conflict: Do they give up their trip or have their son grow up with crooked teeth?

Climax (and resolution): A **deus ex machina**—the bank—arrives to say there is enough money because the bank is willing to make loans.

Premises: (1) You can fulfill your responsibilities to others and yourself if you have enough money. (2) Some pleasures, such as a vacation, may actually be responsibilities. (3) If you are responsible, you are rewarded with pleasures.

It is not fanciful to say that the "plot" of the play we experience here grows from the attributes of the characters. Both are responsible people (they have saved for their trip and take good care of Eric). The husband appears to be the less responsible. He is the one who picks up the brochure, and he also seems, at least for a moment, to be the one less willing to give up the trip. So we have a potential dramatic conflict. The wife is the one who takes Eric to the dentist, she arrives on time, and she has apparently already determined that the money is to be spent on Eric. Their need for a vacation comes from the very fact that they are married (rather a stock situation which may reflect the audience's understanding of reality). Their dilemma, paying for the braces, comes from the fact that they have had Eric and are responsible enough to take him to a dentist. "Plot" and "character" are related.

The message from the bank fulfills their needs in terms of their character traits. Anybody as responsible as they have already shown themselves to be can have a slice of the half billion. Such people pay their debts. The principles on which the bank operates—the subtext of the message announced to the audience—is obvious and neatly self-fulfilling.

Note how much of the couple's past, present, and future is condensed into a single minute of presentation, some twenty lines of dialogue. For the playwright to get all this into such short compass requires a sense of how to create for the audience the images that it can instantly understand. As we will see, the dramatic presentation does not (usually) contain a narrative point of view to provide additional comments, to filter out accidental impressions, or to focus the audience's attention. Essentially, the whole task of storytelling has to be done with what the characters say and do. Notice how much faster the advertisement plays than it took you to read the analysis. Speed intensifies dramatic tension.

EXERCISE

1. Continue the scene after the bank's message, showing what would happen if the wife decided it would be irresponsible to take out a loan. (Consider what situations and premises would make her decide this, and be sure to keep to the characteristics already established, though you may, of course, add to them.)

2. At what point do you grasp that Lillian has a different meaning for "like you" than does Craig in Sweet's "Last Day of Camp" (Chapter 15). Imagine they meet in New York at some party (perhaps a camp reunion). Given that they know the evening at the camp, write a scene in which Craig tries to come on to Lillian.

PRESENTING CHARACTER

Beginning playwrights often forget how much the revelation of character traits can be condensed through exploiting opportunities already provided by the character's physical presence in the actor. The actor interacts with the environment while speaking dialogue. Indeed, the playwright is responsible for preparing conditions that will give the actors opportunities for **stage business**—something to *do*. The stage business need not be spelled out for the actor or director but should be inherent in one or more of the following:

1. The physical habits and condition of the characters. (Has one of them a cold and is the other a hypochondriac?)
2. The physical action called for at a particular point. (Might one play the guitar?)
3. The place in which the characters find themselves. (Is it a hospital waiting room?)
4. The relationships among the characters. (Are they married or just living together?)

The more physical the action, the less "business" the actors will have to think up for themselves (and the less they have to say because we see what they are doing). In a screenplay set in Montana, the actors hunting on horseback for wild buffalo will have little difficulty finding things to do when the cameras are rolling.

If your play occurs in a palace, however, and the issue is whether the king will abdicate or not, the actors might find the stage business less obvious. Granted that what the characters say to one another will be a kind of doing, their talking for two hours about the problem is likely to put a strain on the director's and actors' ingenuity for creating visual effects as well as an audience's ability to stay awake. Now give the king a cold (almost too obviously symbolic) and a large briefcase into which he is placing papers from his desk. A servant (let's make him a wise fool) comes and goes, bringing handkerchiefs (a king does not use Kleenex), drinks, and news.

> SERVANT: These are the last clean ones, your highness.
> KING: I suppose I should get used to using Kleenex. Bring me the ashtray.
> SERVANT: You should get used to fetching your own.

The king's habit of command is revealed, as is the changing situation to which he must soon become accustomed. The servant's "forgetting" to say "your highness" in the second speech indicates his realization that the situation is changing. Might not the king's posture stiffen also? Does he touch the crown he is wearing? Suddenly, there are things for the actors to do whether or not they are speaking—objective realities for what are inward attitudes. Remember, though, that these outward manifestations of the plot and character ought not be mechanical. Don't say that the queen pulls at her nose unless you know why she does it and how the other characters might react to it.

Obviously, stage business is most effective when it is the result of clearly thinking through the character's inner cast of mind. In *The Caine Mutiny*

Court Martial, Captain Queeg's disturbance is expressed by the business of rolling the two ball bearings in his hand; the same action suggests psychosexual disturbance. His uncontrolled manipulation of the bearings triggers the past for him. Both what he says and what he does reveal to the military jury that Queeg is mentally ill, leading to the acquittal of the mutineers. In this case, stage business that grows from character leads to revelation and resolution.

EXERCISE

1. Create a scene in which a student is trying to get a better grade from a teacher. Let us see within the first five lines of dialogue the student's need (or needs) but not the reasons for it. The teacher does not want to give the student a passing grade but does not wish to *say* so. You may reveal this fact at any point. Now create things for the characters to handle and do that will indicate their inner natures. Bring us to a point at which the teacher can convincingly tell the student about the "F" because now he or she wishes to.

2. Imagine that you are directing a television version of the radio ad on pp. 296–297. Write out directions for how you want the actors to appear and what you want them to do. Include directions for a scene to be shot in a restaurant, their kitchen, or their bedroom. Change the dialogue as necessary (remember we can see what's happening). Try to keep to the same performance time.

STOCK CHARACTERS AND CHARACTER DEVELOPMENT

Stage business often is what creates the audience's sense of a distinctive trait in what is really a stock character, a stereotype from life or literature. (For more on stock character, see pp. 205–206.) The shy, awkward maid whose role is to serve tea becomes a presence when she invariably spills it. If she is not fired (or put to other activities), the audience makes judgments about the people who pay her salary. One bit of business starts to create a potential for more stage business revealing even more characteristics. The playwright is continually shuttling between the character's business, the internal state that the business indicates, how the other characters react, their internal state, and on and on. In the course of a play's development, a stock character, like Shakespeare's Falstaff (the stock bragging soldier), may acquire a sharper identity because while inventing stage business the playwright delves further into the traits behind the visible effects.

In fact, even those characters you originally conceive of as having complex attributes need to be revealed first through their stock attributes, moving from the type to the individual. The actors will be dressed as kings, servants, slatterns, hippies—something that categorizes them. They will be washing dishes, driving a BMW to work, jogging, sleeping, carrying a load of books. In the first few moments the audience will judge the characters by their dress, their looks, what they are doing, what is around them. In the same few moments the audience will be trying to absorb the environment (set) and to figure out what the issues are. Things easily and quickly recognizable—the stock characteristics—orient the audience, just as they would in daily life. The beginning of the play is no time to present the "To be or not to be" soliloquy. The revelations about Hamlet's interior landscape are so complex that they would be lost until we are comfortable with his exterior.

In *Last Day of Camp*, for another example, all the characters are seen in their expected role—they are camp counselors, young and green. Because it is the last day of camp, we expect them to be a bit nostalgic. Fiona comes on as the jaded, experienced sexpot. Still, when Craig invites her to smoke pot with the suggestion that they'll end up making love, she doesn't accept the offer. The audience realizes that Fiona is more talk than action. Craig appears to us at first as the sensitive dreamer but we see that he is actually insensitive. Lillian seems to be the stock Goody Two Shoes. However, in the end we sense that she might be the one who would swing if Craig asked her. Even in a short play like *Last Day of Camp*, the dramatist starts us in familiar territory and moves us into unfamiliar territory.

Since the audience has no narrative filter to explain characteristics, nor can it flip back the pages and control the display of information, the playwright has to reveal the characteristics in stages. You might want to think of this gradual revelation as similar to how an image slowly emerges on Polaroid film. The image is already there; it must be developed. Of course, sometimes the revelation we have is a horrifying ratification of our first perception as the characters do more. Nurse A, the experienced nurse in *Procedure*, appears to be totally cool and almost inhumanly mechanical. Her chilly personality, almost unbelievably chilly, is revealed when we learn that the dead man is her father. The dramatic process is fairly typical; the unfolding of the events creates an opportunity to see aspects of a character that can attract or repel us. Putting it another way, we can say that the playwright's plot creates opportunities for the audience's understanding to develop and change.

Of course, the characters may "change" in the sense that events they have experienced will or will not modify their perceptions of past events, the other characters, their own condition, or the decisions they should make. We learn why Nurse A can be so "professional." Her father is not beloved. Nurse A will always be an iceberg. The one who might change is Nurse B who, having gone through the experience once, may herself become more professional. This will be a change of behavior, not of characteristics since we are likely to feel that she'll always be more sympathetic and emotional than Nurse A. Shakespeare's King Lear, on the other hand, does appear to undergo a basic change. He appears to soften and become more capable of love and pity. But does he change, or do we see hidden traits revealed? The role that Lear has had to play as a king has disguised his loving nature (a softness that his two wicked daughters understand). When the "king" is beaten out of him, Lear's loving side stands revealed.

EXERCISE

Take two of the stock characters in the list on page 206. Put them in a laundromat, waiting to use the only working dryer. Both their wash loads are finished at the same time. *Problem*: Who is going to use the dryer first?

1. Create dialogue based on what the audience might expect such characters to do and say.

2. Now assume that after a while, one of the characters realizes that he or she is behaving like a stock character. Give that character something to say or do that indicates this realization.

3. Go back to the dialogue you wrote for number 1 and revise it to indicate the character's potential for having such a realization.

Some Final Points

One of the reasons a play appears so raw when you read it, perhaps even emotionally crude, is that the attributes of the characters, like musical notes in a score, can gain timbre—that is, subtlety—only from the player and the context of the presentation. In Ibsen's *A Doll's House*, Nora's slamming the door after she leaves her husband appears **melodramatic**, overdone, when we read it. When we experience the actual sound, it appears almost understated. This strange alchemy is in part the result of the fact that we can see her husband react to the sound. The playwright who attempts to show a character with the same narrative subtlety as one would in fiction is attempting to provide what the medium is not intended to carry. In a playscript, the writer needs to paint with a much broader brush.

The playwright should not expect that an important element of character slipped in subtly at the beginning of a play and never reinforced is going to enable the audience to understand another element of character or plot at the end of the play. Remember, the audience does not have the luxury of stopping the film or play to say, "Let's see that again because my attention slipped and I missed what happened." Or, "I see what happened, but what does it mean?" Or, "Now that we've gotten to this point of the play, I appear to have missed something. Let me flip back to see what it was." Of course, you could see the play or film on a DVD which will afford you an opportunity to move back and forth to shed light on an action or character. However, it is highly unlikely that you would because you would then destroy your pleasure in the ongoing action.

Finally, characters on a page will ultimately have to be turned into actors on a stage or in film. As a practical matter, you cannot multiply characters in a play with the same degree of freedom as you can in fiction. The cast of thousands is not possible on the stage and seldom is in film. For one thing, budgets are not likely to be big enough. More important, unless the "characters" are merely part of the scenery, the audience cannot meet too many in such a short period of time and keep them all in mind. (Think of what happens when you meet ten new people at a party.) Certainly it is easier to keep track of four characters than of forty. Many theaters with an interest in new plays suggest that the play require no more than eight to ten actors. While this fact has little to do with the artistic considerations that ideally should concern the writer, in the less than ideal world another character means another actor to pay and costume. Remember, a very late point of attack often avoids the necessity of multiplying characters.

CHARACTERS IN PLACE AND TIME

SHEILA: There are a lot of memories in this room.
BEN: There certainly are. Remember when we bought that piece?
SHEILA: Oh, Ben, we need to talk now.

For condensation and characterization, a playwright exploits the fact that an actor "puts on" the character and moves in real space and real time. Imagine, for example, a character coming home determined to tell her husband that she is leaving him. She enters the living room that contains all the objects they have collected during six years of marriage. The actor *sees* those objects that the designer has placed on the set. (Remember that to the actor in the role of a character, it is a living room, not a set.) If the playwright remembers the small statue the couple bought on their last trip to Stockholm, the actor playing Sheila may have something to pick up and handle lovingly to indicate a state of mind. Her remembrance may well be revealed not in precise terms but as a re*action* that suggests her emotion—and then her immediately conflicting emotions as she replaces the statue on the mantle, turning off Ben's efforts to re-create the past.

The awareness of physical place and objects has to be matched by the playwright's awareness of time. At the simplest level, if an actor goes off to change a costume (to the character it is a change of *clothes*), the other actors must have something to do that advances the plot or the audience will grow restive in the real time that it takes to make the costume change. A planned silence that the playwright uses to reveal character, advance plot, or create tension is different from silences imposed by the fact that the characters have nothing to do or must cross space without something to say. A real minute can appear to be hours to an audience (or actor) unless the dramatic minute has something in it that advances the plot.

Sometimes the very fact of "real" versus "stage" time can be used for the creation of exciting effects. In the following scene, the climax of Christopher

Marlowe's *The Tragicall History of Dr. Faustus*, Faustus is about to pay with his soul for the bargain with the Devil, a bargain that has given Faustus wealth, power, sex, and knowledge. As we pick up the action, his friends are leaving:

> ALL: Faustus, farewell!
>   *Exit* Scholars. *The clock strikes eleven.*
>   FAUST: Ah, Faustus,
> Now has thou but one bare hour to live,
> And then thou must be damn'd perpetually!
> Stand still, you ever-moving spheres of Heaven,
> That time may cease, and midnight never come;
> Fair Nature's eye, rise, rise again and make
> Perpetual day; or let this hour be but
> A year, a month, a week, a natural day,
> That Faustus may repent and save his soul!
> *O lente, lente, currite noctis equi*
> (Run slowly, slowly steeds of the night.)
> The stars move still, time runs, the clock will strike,
> The Devil will come, and Faustus must be damn'd.

After twenty-one more lines, at most another two to five minutes, we (and Faustus) hear the clock strike again:

> Ah, half the hour is past! 'T will all be past anon!

And, then after another eighteen lines—perhaps one minute of acting—we hear the clock strike midnight. We are told that an hour has gone by, but only ten minutes or so have gone by in real time. The difference creates a sense of speed that fits the situation.

The next part of the action manipulates the opposite effect of time. Keep in mind during the following scene that the clock will be tolling steadily but with greater intervals between each strike than in real time.

> *The Clock striketh twelve.*
> O, it strikes, it strikes! Now, body, turn to air,
> Or Lucifer will bear thee quick to hell!
>   *Thunder and lightning*
> O soul, be chang'd into little water-drops,
> And fall into the ocean—ne're be found!—
> My God, my God, look not so fierce on me!
>   *Enter* Devils
> Adders and serpents, let me breathe awhile!—
> Ugly hell, gape not!—Come not, Lucifer!—
> I'll burn my books!—Ah, Mephistophilis!
>   *Exit* Devil *with him.*

The director will stretch out this speech so it will take as long as possible, dragging out Faustus's final moments.

In a production, the manipulation of the difference between stage time and real time creates tension in the audience that is equivalent to the tension in Faustus. The speeding up of time is an enactment of his desire to hold time back. On the other hand, dragging out the time that it would actually take to strike twelve from thirty seconds into two or three minutes increases the tension unbearably. Just as Faustus fearfully waits for Mephistopheles, the great forecloser on souls, so do we. The device that Marlowe uses so effectively is a rather standard technique in many films, particularly the ones in which a bomb is about to go off.

EXERCISE

1. Plan a five-minute scene in which the devil is waiting for Faustus. Faustus will come in at the end. The devil's concern is that Faustus will beg God to forgive him and so be saved. Aside from his desire to have Faustus's soul, try to give the devil a personal reason for concern. We will hear the clock that Faustus hears, but we will hear it at a tempo you decide on. Invent other characters if you need to.

BEATS

On stage and in film you can signal the passage of time through a variety of conventional devices. On the stage, the lights or the curtain can be lowered and raised (as between scenes or acts); in film, fades or cuts serve the same purpose. The breaks in the flow of the action work much as a chapter break might, allowing us to focus on key elements in the plot rather than the transitions. The fact that the audience accepts such devices is useful in two ways: (1) The few minutes of a curtain's dropping and raising is accepted as the hours it would take for a character to go from New York to Chicago or the years it takes for a character's hair to grow white; and (2) it allows the writer to account for the time it might take a character's traits to modify. In effect, the audience accepts that, during the break in the time flow signaled by the convention, people have gotten from one place to another and hours, days, or years have gone by. Such devices allow you to compress twenty years of story events into a few hours of performance.

Such conventional devices work as a kind of gravitational force holding scenes and acts, the large conventional units, firmly to the needs of the plot. The **beat**, a smaller unit of stage time, is, from the playwright's point of view, the essential working unit of the play. It is like the line in poetry and the sentence in fiction.

Directors often speak of a play as if it were a piece of music made up of chords or "beats." The sum of the beats is the play. Each beat contains a revelation of a mood, relationship, or an action that advances our understanding of the whole plot. Each beat resolves some tension and leads to another beat until the end. Let us say, for example, that you are writing a car chase scene for a film. The villains are after the heroes, who are trying to rendezvous with a helicopter that will fly them to safety.

Beat 1. The Blues (the villains) are chasing the Greens (our heroes). The Greens approach a railroad crossing. A train is coming. The Blues are catching up and one of the villains is just raising the M-16. The Greens cross the tracks and The Blues screech to a halt.

Beat 2. The Greens' car develops a flat. The heroes frantically work to change the tire. The Blues are under way again and rapidly closing. Just as they round the curve, the tire is fixed and the heroes are back on the road.

Beat 3. The chase continues and the villains are catching up. In the distance we see the helicopter. One of the heroes carefully aims and shoots out the front tires of the villains' car, which overturns. Just ahead now is safety.

Beat 4. The heroes' car squeals to a halt next to the helicopter. With happy smiles on their faces they start to run to the cabin. In the helicopter we see the head villain raise a submachine gun.

And so on.

Constructing by beats is equally necessary in less action-filled playscripts, as in the following scene from Harold Pinter's *The Collection*. Note how rapidly the beats follow on one another. The beats are punctuated with a pause.

Situation: Harry enters his apartment and goes to a phone, which we have heard ringing. It is late at night.

HARRY: Hello.
VOICE: Is that you, Bill?
HARRY: No, he's in bed. Who's this?
VOICE: In bed?
HARRY: Who is this?
VOICE: What's he doing in bed?
(*Pause*)
HARRY: Do you know it's four o'clock in the morning?
VOICE: Well, give him a nudge. Tell him I want a word with him.
(*Pause*)
HARRY: Who is this?
VOICE: Go and wake him up, there's a good boy.
(*Pause*)
HARRY: Are you a friend of his?

VOICE: He'll know me when he sees me.
HARRY: Oh yes?
(*Pause*)
VOICE: Aren't you going to wake him?
HARRY: No, I'm not.
(*Pause*)
VOICE: Tell him I'll be in touch.
(*The telephone cuts off.*)

In the first beat, by not answering Harry, the Voice fails to give Harry what he wants. In the second beat, Harry is forced into the unreasonable position of having to respond to the Voice's questions without having received an answer to his. In a sense, he is defeated. The beat ends when the Voice treats Harry as a servant by asking Harry to wake Bill. Harry, quite understandably, tries to establish equality but is again defeated when the Voice does not answer the question; instead, the Voice reasserts his position of authority. Harry is not a "boy." In the next beat Harry again tries to establish his equality, but his question receives an unexpectedly indirect answer—an answer that is almost threatening. Harry's last speech in this beat is a question because he has not really been given an answer. But "Oh yes?" also has in it an assertion of its own—that is, you had better tell me more. In the next to last beat, the Voice refuses to give that information and Harry reestablishes his equality by refusing the Voice's request. In the final beat the Voice wins by cutting Harry off after making a demand that Harry cannot fulfill. Since the Voice has never given his name, who can Harry say called? We end with a feeling that *something* bad is going to happen.

As the Pinter excerpt demonstrates, a beat is like the clenching and unclenching of a hand. Sometimes the struggle between the characters is obvious, ending with violent gestures and actions; sometimes the struggle is simply for a mastery of the situation. Each time the beat unclenches we see a momentary restoration of some type of balance, a relaxation of tension. This relaxation is a small instance of the large resolution we expect at the end of the play. In the Pinter play, the hanging up of the phone literally disconnects the characters and releases the immediate tension. The playwright will, of course, vary the degree of tension in each beat, trying to reach the most intense beat (the climax) as close as possible to the resolution, the final unclenching.

EXERCISE

1. Think of a game whose rules you know well (Trivial Pursuit, Monopoly, Scrabble, Chess). Now take two or three characters who are in conflict about something (for example, whether or not to divorce, whether or not to rob a bank, whether or not to sell their business, whether or not to kill their hostage). Write a scene in which your characters are playing the game or kibitzing. You might also have your characters waiting for someone to arrive or waiting for a phone call with important information that in the actual world would create tension.

2. Describe the beats—struggle–balance, struggle–balance—between the characters.

3. What would happen in your scene if one of the characters did not know the game or did not play it well?

4. If you haven't done so already, add a third character who is making something (a cake, a house of cards, a bookshelf, a bomb). *Note*: You should know how to make or do whatever you have your character making or doing.

SETTING

We already discussed in Chapter 9 the idea of setting or place for your scenes. You may wish to review that section before continuing here. From your characters' point of view, the setting is not a series of words, it is a real place with real temperatures, light (or dark), furniture or grass, sirens or crickets. The setting in the story becomes a "set" in the play, a workplace prepared for the actors who will assume the fictive roles. (Film allows for actual places to become sets.)

In printed versions of plays, you might see the following description of a set:

> SCENE: *A court apartment in Los Angeles in the West Adams district. The room is done in white—white ceiling, white walls, white overly elaborate furniture—but a red wall-to-wall carpet covers the floor. A wall bed is raised. Upstairs, two doorless entrances stand on each side of the head of the bed. The right entrance is to the kitchen; the backstage area that represents the kitchen is shielded by a filmy curtain and the actors' dim silhouettes are seen when the area is lighted. The left entrance will be raised and offstage right at the head of a short flight of stairs and a platform which leads into the combination bedroom—dressingroom—closet.*
>
> from Ed Bullins, *Goin' a Buffalo*

You may even have seen more elaborate descriptions using words such as "stage left," "curtain," and "scrim." What you are reading in such cases is most likely the playwright's description of the set from the first production of the play. It is unlikely that Ed Bullins had that specific a set in mind when he was first writing the play. Most likely, he thought of his play as happening in a "court apartment." Perhaps he also had in mind that the rooms would be painted totally in white, have a red carpet, and contain ornate furniture.

In many cases, the playwright has a much sketchier notion, a notion more related to a sense of the place in which the action occurs rather than a theatrical set:

> *Galileo's scantily furnished study. Morning.* GALILEO *is washing himself. A barefooted boy,* ANDREA, *son of his housekeeper,* MRS. SARTI, *enters with a big astronomical model.*
>
> from Bertolt Brecht, Galileo

From this description, a set designer may well build a set just as detailed as the one we see described in Bullins's play.

When you are drafting, you probably are wasting energy if you spend large amounts of time working up a set, though you need to be highly conscious of the place your characters are in because they will be conscious of the place whether it be a mountaintop or their living room. Some playwrights, like some novelists, actually draw out rough designs of the place, but they do so to give themselves a sense of what the character is seeing, not in order to become set designers. Though the matter is not the playwright's primary concern, producers do worry about a play's meeting the needs of the available space and money.

Beth Henley's *Crimes of the Heart* might well have first caught someone's eye because the entire play takes place in an old-fashioned kitchen:

> MEG: What's the cot doing in the kitchen?
> LENNY [Meg's sister]: Well, I rolled it out when Old Granddaddy got sick. So I could be close and hear him at night if he needed something.
> MEG (*glancing toward the door leading to the downstairs bedroom*): Is Old Granddaddy here?
> LENNY: Why, no. Old Granddaddy's at the hospital.

The door, of course, actually leads offstage. And, if we are experienced with theatrical reality, we also assume that the cot is in the kitchen to provide a place on which several people can sit at once, saving perhaps a set change to a living room. By the end of the beat, however, from the audience's point of view the door leads to a bedroom and the cot is there for the reason stated. Grandfather's presence is established and so is the cot. (In fact, Grandfather never actually appears in the play.) From a producer's point of view, *Crimes of the Heart* focuses the whole world of the characters in a relatively simple, inexpensive set.

Many theaters specifically request that the plays submitted to them be doable in simple sets (unit sets). Playwrights who make sets too specific ignore the reality that stages will vary enormously both in shape and size. All these variables suggest that you can waste a good deal of energy being too specific about details of setting that are not absolutely relevant to the particular actions of the characters.

Imagine yourself, for example, as a producer for a local small theater faced with the following description of a set:

> The scene is set in William Hurt's study. At stage left is a small Queen Anne writing table, two by three feet, and next to it is a Chippendale chair with pettipoint seat done in subtle shades of blue and rose. The pattern is a fleur-de-lis in the manner of Rogette. The carpet is a Bengali with dominant mauve colors. Stage right is a large bookcase containing the complete works of Dickens with Dore woodcuts. Upstage is a padded door, the type that one sees in libraries and music halls. It is the only exit from the room. Stage front are two large matching leather chairs with an end table between them. On the table is an ivory chess set with the pieces spread on the inlaid board. The game in progress is a repeat of the famous Spassky/Fisher "Indian Defense" played during the Tunisian challenge. . . .

While one might argue that the playwright needs to think of the setting in such detail, almost as a novelist might, writing it out is largely a waste of time. In any case, the director and set designer will probably ignore the elaborate detail.

The following notation will be sufficient for your purposes:

> SCENE: William Hurt's study. A small antique desk and chair, a bookcase filled with a matched set of books, other bookcases and two large chairs separated by a low table on which a chess game is in progress.

Finally, keep in mind that the setting for the play is more than a visual environment. It influences how the characters are feeling, what they say and do. Possibilities for characterizing may grow from the fact that the environment may contain smells; it may be hot or cold, light or dark. The playwright can exploit the fact that the characters can react to all the physical elements even when they are not talking about them. (In fiction, the writer has to remind the reader continually that such physical elements are operating.)

EXERCISE

Return to one of the scenes you wrote for the television version of the radio advertisement. Write dialogue for the husband and wife that will be a response to the following facts: it is twelve degrees out and the wife is wearing a new perfume. Remember, these facts are known to them before the scene opens.

14

❧

Dialogue and Its Problems

DIALOGUE: THE ESSENCE OF DRAMA

When you write a play, most of what you are going to write is dialogue. Here is what your dialogue must do:

1. Contain all the necessary exposition, including what happened before the point of attack, between scenes and acts, and offstage (though the audience can be told some things through sounds, such as a gunshot offstage).
2. Reveal everything about the characters' feelings, beliefs, and wants.

In other words, the dialogue is both exposition and action.

From the playwright's point of view, dialogue is not "talk," although the actor is, of course, "talking" the character's words. In fact, transcriptions of how people actually talk are difficult to follow because most of our talk lacks shape, that is, purpose in relationship to a plot. While one may suppose there can be idle *talk*, *dialogue* must be idle only for a purpose. Every line of dialogue must serve (or appear to serve) one or more of the following dramatic purposes:

◆ To reveal the character's nature.
◆ To reveal the character's needs and intentions.
◆ To have impact on another character or characters.

Dialogue means, literally, the *words through*; a stage play will happen mostly through what the characters say. Much of the playwright's work goes into shaping the plot in such a manner that the dialogue is what the characters will *do* to each other. If the dialogue contains information that the audience needs for understanding the situation, that information usually will be a by-product of the interaction among the characters. Even in a screenplay, in which the characters' action can be more physical, the dialogue must be treated as a type of action.

Ideally each speech a character makes will contain both a **text**—an intended message directed at the other character(s)—and a **subtext**—which conveys the characters' real feelings, needs, and attitudes.

> SON: Can I do the dishes after I talk with Joanne about the test tomorrow?
> MOTHER: Do you want to borrow my car on Saturday?

The visible messages—the text—are requests for information. Clearly, however, the son is also trying to put off a task by suggesting that doing the dishes is not as important as doing homework. His real intention (talking with Joanne) is the subtext. The mother's subtext is so clear that it needs no analysis. The questions, as it turns out, are not questions at all.

Even if the other characters do not catch the subtext, the audience will, consciously or unconsciously. As we saw earlier, each character has an agenda, and this agenda will be reflected in both text and subtext. Just as the surface of what we say to others is only the window into what we really mean, so too for what characters say to other characters.

The opening scene from a traditional "well-made" play, Noel Coward's *Blithe Spirit*, illustrates the idea. In the play, Charles Condomine, a writer, is talking to his second wife, Ruth, while they have cocktails before guests arrive. Their previous dialogue has been about how Charles got the idea for an interesting character in his last novel. Elvira, Charles's first wife, is dead.

1. RUTH: Used Elvira to help you—when you were thinking something out, I mean?
2. CHARLES: Every now and then—when she concentrated—but she didn't concentrate very often.
3. RUTH: I do wish I'd known her.
4. CHARLES: I wonder if you'd have liked her.
5. RUTH: I'm sure I should—as you talk of her she sounds enchanting—yes, I'm sure I should have liked her because you know I have never for an instant felt in the least jealous of her—that's a good sign.
6. CHARLES: Poor Elvira.
7. RUTH: Does it still hurt—when you think of her?

Before you go on, think about what this beat is establishing. Of course, the overt purpose (text) is simply that Ruth is asking for information about her predecessor, information that the audience learns also. But we sense other, complex messages. A director and an actor preparing the beat for a rehearsal might analyze the subtext as follows:

1. Ruth is really asking if Elvira had the same importance as she does as Charles's creative helper. In a way, Ruth is indicating her concern about something in their relationship. Perhaps she wants to or needs to be told that she is not simply a "second" wife but someone unique.

2. Charles does not catch the subtext at first, and so answers unthinkingly. If he does not modify or correct what he has begun to say, he will have answered "yes" to Ruth's question. That answer would indicate there is nothing unique in their relationship. He realizes immediately that he has been insensitive (does he see a *look* in Ruth's face or a sudden stiffening of her posture?) and in midsentence modifies his statement. The problem is that he can't really correct what has already been said. In any case, he has to either be unfaithful to the memory of his first wife or lie to his second wife.

3. Ruth tries to appear merely inquisitive, as if she is not jealous. Obviously, however, she is thinking about her dead "competition."

4. Charles's question responds to Ruth, but the word "wonder" tells us that something has flashed across his mind about the differences between his wives.

5. Ruth indicates her jealousy precisely because she raises an issue that no one has raised, and the audience will tend to doubt people who deny an emotion no one has accused them of feeling. In short, we don't believe the text of someone who "protesteth too much."

6. Charles appears not to be responding to what Ruth has said but to the train of thought set off by his previous statement. In fact, we might feel that Ruth has started a chain reaction different from the one she expected. (*Note*: Charles responds to what he is thinking, not to the other character's dialogue. He is starting to say what he *has* to say, not what the logic of the dialogue appears to call for.)

7. Ruth has recognized that she has set off a chain of associations in Charles. The text tells us that she is thinking of his well-being. The subtext tells us that she wants some kind of assurance for herself.

Without anyone telling us what they are like, the text and subtext in the speeches between Charles and Ruth allow the audience to see that the characters are debonair, intelligent, and witty. The subtext also creates a sense of mystery revealed rather than stated. Something is going on that has brought Ruth to push the conversation in this direction. The information that is communicated also creates tension because

1. We wonder what the characters really mean, what they may be hiding in the way of feelings or facts.
2. Or we wonder when another character will catch on to what we know is really being said.
3. Or we wonder when characters will realize something about themselves that we have already figured out.

At one and the same time, the most effective dialogue does all the above. In sum, creating the subtext—suggesting without telling—is a large part of the playwright's work. Effective dialogue will show not tell.

EXERCISE

1. Before reading the following passage from the same play, review the preceding passage and ask yourself: What is the first word that Charles should say in his answer to Ruth? Now read on:

> CHARLES: No, not really—sometimes I almost wish it did—I feel rather guilty—
> RUTH: I wonder if I died before you'd grown tired of me if you'd forget me so soon?
> CHARLES: What a horrible thing to say . . .
> RUTH: No—I think it's interesting.
> CHARLES: Well, to begin with I *haven't* forgotten Elvira—I *remember* her very distinctly indeed—I remember how fascinating she was, and how maddening—I remember how badly she played all games and how cross she got when she didn't win—I remember her gay charm when she had achieved her own way over something and her extreme acidity when she didn't—I remember her physical attractiveness, which was tremendous—and her spiritual integrity which was nil . . .
> RUTH: You can't remember something that was nil.
> CHARLES: I remember how morally untidy she was . . .
> RUTH: Was she more physically attractive than I am?
> CHARLES: That was a very tiresome question, dear, and fully deserves the wrong answer.
> RUTH: You really are very sweet.
> CHARLES: Thank you.
> RUTH: And a little naive, too.

2. Analyze the preceding speeches as we have done for the previous passage. Note that Ruth's question ("I wonder . . . ?") really contains two questions. Is Charles's answer a dramatically effective one? Has anything about their

emotional relationship been established? Who, if anyone, has "won" points during the beat? How do you know?

3. Assume that Charles says, "Yes, Elvira was more physically attractive." Write a beat for that answer.

4. Take the following situation and write dialogue for the characters. The scene is a dorm room or shared apartment. The situation is that roommate A is trying to get roommate B to leave the room for the evening but does not want to say why. Remember that the audience at some point has to be let into the reasons for A's action and B's response.

5. Tape-record a real conversation—at the dinner table, for example—and transcribe it (or get a raw transcription of a legislative hearing). As you will see, most of it will be boring, and some of it will be incomprehensible and repetitious. Try to carve a dramatic beat from your transcription.

PRINCIPLES AND COMMON ERRORS

Your Exposition Is Showing

The characters should not tell each other expository information simply to transfer that information to the audience. Unless you have a character who has just come into the story and therefore is ignorant of the facts and needs to know them, you must remember that the characters are usually aware of what has happened to them and to each other. Nothing is so absurd as one character telling another:

> John, do you remember when we had our children—Annabelle, Hermes, and Philo?

Nothing destroys an audience's sense of verisimilitude more than characters' telling each other about what they obviously must know. The audience suddenly becomes aware of itself: "Oh, I'm watching a play, and the characters are telling me stuff I have to know." Instead of following the characters, as if following real people, the audience becomes conscious of the exposition because the playwright has failed to find a reason in plot and character for slipping in this necessary information. The audience begins to *think about* the play instead of emotionally participating *in* it.

Look at the following scene, for example, in which a couple are having an argument about moving to the town where the wife's parents live.

> JOAN: You are not being fair, Mike.
> MIKE: Joan, the issue of fair has nothing to do with it. Your parents do not have a single socially redeeming quality between the two of them.
> JOAN: What do you mean my parents do not have any redeeming qualities? Why do you try to hurt my self-esteem like that?

MIKE: That is easy, your father is loud and obnoxious. Your mother, on the other hand, cannot stick to a subject. She comes totally out of the blue with ideas.

JOAN: Mike, you are being totally unreasonable. The last time my parents were over you had a great time.

MIKE: Joan, do you remember the last time we were with your parents? It was at our wedding reception and that was almost six months ago.

JOAN: Is that so?

MIKE: Do you remember how your dad's Polish jokes almost caused my Uncle Joe to throw him through a window? And Uncle Joe had come all the way from New Zealand to be with us. Aunt Sylvia was not any happier.

Aside from any other problems you may have noticed with the dialogue, Mike's speeches are clearly addressed to the audience, since Joan would surely remember the last time they saw her parents. And if she does not, we have to know why.

One way of communicating such expository information naturally is to imbed the information in the dialogue as part of the tension between the characters. Assume Mike and Joan have often talked about the wedding and that it always comes up in their spats.

MIKE: I still feel like hiding when I think about it.

JOAN: It was six months ago, Mike. I am tired of hearing about it.

MIKE: Your dad had to know my mother was Polish.

JOAN: He was just trying to be friendly.

MIKE: If it was not our wedding, I think my Uncle Joe would have thrown him out the window.

JOAN: It was only a Polish joke, Mike.

MIKE: Poles are not dumb. Chopin. Milosc.

JOAN: You tell them yourself.

MIKE: It's different.

JOAN: You just do not like my dad.

MIKE: My uncle did *not* come all the way from New Zealand to be insulted.

JOAN: Do not change the topic.

MIKE: We're not moving to Urbana. I do not like your mother either.

Though the dialogue still needs work, in the rewritten version the audience is beginning to overhear characters who know what their situation is. The information is now within a dramatic beat; it doesn't seem to be directed to the audience but feels like an outgrowth of Joan and Mike's psychological situation.

In short, dialogue must appear to be talk for the characters' purposes, not for the benefit of the audience. When they create dialogue, most playwrights adhere to a primary dramatic convention: *there is a wall between the characters and audience.* The space inside that wall is the real, the only world. Each time the dialogue lapses into obvious exposition, a crack appears in the wall. Too many cracks and the audience will begin to wonder why the playwright didn't try to write a novel instead of promising a play.

Note: The limits of dialogue as a tool for revealing the exposition have led modern dramatists to bring back the chorus as a device for revealing opinions and information. But the chorus in a modern play is usually one person, a kind of "stage manager." If your plot involves long stretches of time (as in a history play) or a great deal of exposition (as in a thriller), you may wish to construct the plot so as to use a narrator. For examples, see *A View from a Bridge*, *Equus*, or *Amadeus*. Such a device appears less clumsy than long stretches in which the characters simply tell the plot to each other. Remember, though, that such stage narrators should not simply provide the narrative bridges for the plot's sake; they should be characters who belong to the play's structure. This convenient device can be a burden since the playwright will also have to account for the narrator. In drama, as in the other genres, there are no free rides.

Contractions and Formality

You do not want your characters to speak as if they are delivering dedications or eulogies. Unless you deliberately intend that your characters demonstrate formal traits, they will elide their speech. In any case, if the playwright doesn't do it for them, the actors will change "it is" to "it's" and "cannot" to "can't," especially if the formality appears merely to be the playwright's adhering slavishly to the absurd rule that one should never use a contraction in writing. In Mike and Joan's dialogue, not using contractions gives their speech a formal quality; it sounds more like a debate than an argument between lovers. Note how stiff even the revised dialogue sounds if you read it aloud.

With the contractions in, their speeches still often sound curiously formal, as if they are reading from a prepared script. Mike's use of the phrase "single socially redeeming quality" (in the first version) is stiff and intellectual, to say nothing of how difficult it is to speak. Though your characters may talk formally because of their natures or because the plot has reached a point that requires a formal address (see "Long Speeches," page 321), the playwright must prepare the dialogue so it appears to have come from that character at the moment. In other words, the playwright has to plan the dialogue so it seems unplanned.

EXERCISE

Assuming that Joan is not stuffy, rewrite the first version of her dialogue. Now assume that Mike tends to be stuffy and rigid because he thinks that formal speech is a sign of education and class. Rewrite Mike's dialogue to let the audience know that his formality is a bone of contention between them. (You may want to assume that Mike is self-educated.)

Interruptions and Other Ways of Creating Verisimilitude

Dialogue is usually most effective when it follows the *patterns* rather than the content of conversation. Your dialogue is felt as "real" not because it reports what people actually say but because it follows the *way* people talk, the structures of conversation. Just as in actual conversation, your characters' dialogue may be interrupted, may fail to follow from what others have just said, or may appear to be illogical and unreasonable. One reason Mike and Joan sound so stilted is that they are skipping no steps in what they are saying to each other. Notice how one word is echoed in each speech as if they had to prove they were listening. (Go back and circle the repeated words in the first version.)

The devices for achieving an appearance of spontaneity are taken from the conversational patterns of real life:

- ◆ People interrupt each other.
- ◆ People trail off.
- ◆ People do not directly answer the question asked.
- ◆ People say things that are the result of a line of thinking not directly related to the conversation.
- ◆ People use contractions.
- ◆ People use pronouns, that is, they are aware of what is present to them.
- ◆ People respond to a look on another's face or to something the other does.

Let's apply some of these patterns to part of Mike and Joan's dialogue:

> JOAN: It was six months ago, Mike. I'm tired of hearing—
> MIKE: Your dad had to know my mother was Polish.
> JOAN: He was just trying to be friendly. He doesn't mean—
> MIKE: If it weren't . . . wasn't our wedding, I think my Uncle Joe would have thrown him out the window.
> JOAN: It was only a Polish joke, Mike. You know my—
> MIKE: Poles are not dumb. Chopin. Milosc. And . . . and . . . hundreds of other people.
> JOAN: You tell them yourself.
> MIKE: Copernicus.

Because interruptions are so typical of our actual conversational habits, they are the most obvious way of creating verisimilitude and of making your dialogue less formal. However, beware of overusing the technique. And be sure that *what* the character was about to say is clear before the next character interrupts.

> ROBIN: What if we get caught?
> THADEUS: That's—
> ROBIN: If the police take me home my father is going—
> THADEUS: Police? What are—
> ROBIN: Are you sure it will be O.K.?

Though it is clear that Robin is frightened, it is never clear to the audience what Thadeus was about to say. In fact, the actor who plays Thadeus will look like a fool if Robin's timing is a bit off, because he'll have to drag out the word being interrupted. Notice, however, that when Thadeus interrupts Robin, we understand how the rest of the sentence will go: "to give me hell" or some such thing. Be sure to give the character enough words before being interrupted so that the actors playing both the interrupter and interruptee can establish a natural timing.

Beginning playwrights, particularly those who have worked in fiction, often give their characters dialogue that would be used only if the characters were blind. The characters continually use one another's names, mention objects that the audience can see, and name actions as well as respond to them.

> JACK: Here's your martini, Barbara.
> BARBARA: I wanted an onion in the martini, Jack.
> JACK: Try the martini first, Barbara.
> BARBARA (*sips*): Now that I've tried it, what?
> JACK: What do you think, Barbara.
> BARBARA: I still want an onion in my martini.
> JACK (*knocks the martini from her hand*): You ungrateful bitch.
> BARBARA: Why did you knock the martini from my hand?

This dialogue sounds as if it were written for a novel without a narrator (not a particularly good idea) rather than a play with an audience who would see the events. Such dialogue is a sure sign of inexperience with stage or film.

Fake Dialogue or the Dialogue Dummy

Everything that characters say must serve their needs. When a character says a line of dialogue only to break up a long speech or when a character simply sets up another character's speeches, the playwright is committing two fatal errors in one: the poor actor who serves up the gopher ball feels like a fool ("Why am I saying this?"), and the audience begins to wonder whether they are observing a ventriloquist's dummy or a character with needs and wants of his or her own.

Ask yourself why Beth is saying the italicized speeches in the following dialogue:

> BETH: The pitcher has my goldfish in it. You'll have to use a mixing bowl.
> KEVIN: Looks like one of them has gone to paradise.
> BETH: *Paradise?*
> KEVIN: He is a floater.
> BETH: *Floater?*
> KEVIN: Dead.

Not only has the writer taken too long to establish a small point, but Beth appears simply to be feeding Kevin lines. Now add the following to Kevin's last bit of dialogue before the word "dead": "Are you listening to me?" At this point Beth's denseness begins to make sense.

EXERCISE

Go back to Beth's second speech. It also appears to be merely a placeholder. Write something for her to say that will give us a sense of her needs and advance the scene. If necessary, rewrite Kevin's speeches.

Designators, or Stealing the Actors' and Director's Jobs

The words the characters say should indicate their emotional state. Being overly elaborate in designating how the speech should be said is an error. The director or actor will ignore the designator unless the playwright's command for a special tone of voice is absolutely necessary. Observe the following:

> BARBARA (*concerned*): What do you want to do tonight?
> SAM (*only half listening*): How about us going to Seaside tonight, Diane?
> BARBARA (*shocked by what she hears*): Diane?
> SAM (*embarrassed and placatingly*): I can't believe I said that.
> BARBARA (*angry and puzzled*): What can't you believe you said?
> SAM (*in a squirming voice*): What I just said.
> BARBARA (*questioning*): Who's Diane?
> SAM (*whining because he knows he's trapped*): Diane is a friend.
> BARBARA (*incredulous*): A friend?

Many of the designators merely sound ridiculous; how does someone say something in an "angry but puzzled" voice?

The rule of thumb is never to use a designator unless the dialogue you write for a character normally would be said in a different tone of voice:

SAM (*softly*): Help.

In fact, a good discipline is to avoid designators altogether, especially when you are creating the playscript. Often writers use elaborate designators to avoid the work needed to ensure that what the characters *say* indicates their emotion. This principle also should be observed in writing dialogue for narrative fiction.

Long Speeches

Usually you will avoid long speeches. However, there are circumstances in which characters may talk on for some time:

1. A character has asked the other characters a question that calls for a long answer.
2. They are making a formal speech as part of the plot (as in a play that contains a trial).
3. Part of their nature is to be long-winded.

Most of the time, however, your characters will be interrupted, challenged, or simply waiting for responses. As a result, most of the individual speeches will be relatively brief alternating lines, what the Greeks called *stichomythia*. For a classical example look at Creon's and his son Heman's argument in *Antigone*. If you find your characters simply giving large blocks of information, it is likely that the dialogue is dialogue only in form.

Grunting and Pausing

Since the actors will create any extra sounds they need (1) for pacing, (2) for transitions, (3) for laughing or crying, or (4) for responding to the action and dialogue, you should avoid indicating grunts and wheezes, conversational placeholders. *Uhh, ohhh, ehh, ahh, er, ahhhh,* and other self-interrupters are not needed and look absurd on the page. If you wish an actor to pause, write "(*Pause*)" at the proper point; don't try to imitate the pause in the script with blank spaces, periods, or other visual means.

In the following dialogue, the writer appears amateurish, forcing effects on the actor or reader typographically. In this scene, Barbara and Sam are at the beach. Obviously, Sam is horsing around.

BARBARA: So where, *uhhhhh*, did we, *ha-ha*, decide to go tonight, Mike?
SAM: *YUK! YUK!* very funny.

> BARBARA: I'm *soooooo* sorry, *ha! ha!* . . . . hey cut that out you, don't you dare throw me in the water. I've got my contacts in! Ok, ok, I love you too, I said I love *yogloggglober glub glub gurgle gurgle!*

It would have been sufficient for the writer simply to let the actors know what is happening and allow them to supply the sounds to fit the action. (*Note*: Also avoid representing nonword sounds in fiction; it's a sign of amateurishness.)

Accents, Dialect, and Verbal Tics

The one area in which dialogue should be like conversation is in its imitation of social, regional, or national speech habits. It hardly needs saying that characters should have intonations, accents, grammar, diction, and syntax appropriate to their general background, the circumstances in which they find themselves, and their intentions. Without good reason, a waiter with a seventh-grade education is not likely to speak like a Harvard graduate.

When you give a character an accent that is merely a matter of pronunciation, you need only indicate in the description of the character what accent is necessary:

> FORSYTH P. WILLOWBY, a cadaverous-looking man of about forty who speaks with a Boston accent.
> PRISCILLA HESTER GARARD, a thirtyish blond who affects a southern accent. Nonetheless, one can detect her Brooklyn accent.

Presumably, you have given this information to the director because the characters' particular accents are important. The information will be sufficient and the playwright does not need to indicate the pronunciation through phonetic spelling. In fact, the playwright should not do so. For the following speech, for example, the actor will work out the proper accent according to the playwright's directions about where the character is from (Boston, Alabama, or Russia):

> ROSALINDA: After we have finished this game, I intend to leave and never come back.

It is the director's job to cast an actor who can produce the desired accent.

The writer's task becomes more difficult if the character's origins require a dialect. Unlike an accent (how the words are pronounced), a dialect involves different vocabulary, grammar, syntax, and elisions, which will have to be provided for the actor.

Swearing

One way contemporary playwrights create verisimilitude is by reflecting *the words* people use in real life. Words that were once forbidden are now staples for naturalistic plays; in fact, they are almost conventions for creating a feeling of reality. As with all other diction decisions, the type of swearing, if any, your characters will do depends on what they are like and how they would respond verbally to the situations in which they find themselves. You have to take your chances on your audience's reaction. The producer will not choose to do your play if strong sexual language is inappropriate for the audience (e.g. an audience composed of the school board in a small Missouri town). On the other hand, if the audience feels your characters should react to misfortune with contemporary swearing and you have them saying "gee whizzes" when a hammer strikes a finger, then you may unintentionally cause laughter. The audience expects something stronger.

Never have your characters swear just because *you* wish to shock or to create the impression that your play is realistic. The audience will hear the author swearing, not the character. Of course, your character may be the type who unconsciously or unknowingly uses non-drawing-room diction or uses it deliberately for effect. That's part of his character. A good rule of tongue is to ask yourself why this particular character is swearing at this time. As with accents and dialects, don't use swear words unless you have an ear for their natural, idiomatic use—a wag might say "their proper use."

Locker Room Raillery

Though in real life we often chatter at one another in a mocking but friendly way, on paper—and on the stage—this type of wisecracking appears forced, though an individual character may deliver wisecracks as an aspect of his or her personality (as Hawkeye does in *M * A * S * H*). Effective humor occurs when (1) the characters seriously make statements that the audience finds absurd or (2) the character is truly witty, as Algernon is in Oscar Wilde's *The Importance of Being Earnest*:

> JACK: I am in love with Gwendolen. I have come up to town expressly to propose to her.
> ALGERNON: I thought you had come up for pleasure? . . . I call that business.
> JACK: How utterly unromantic you are!
> ALGERNON: I really don't see anything romantic in proposing. It is very romantic to be in love. But there is nothing romantic about a definite proposal. Why, one may be accepted. One usually is, I believe. Then the excitement is all over. The very essence of romance is uncertainty. If ever I get married, I'll certainly try to forget the fact.

Algernon intends the humor of his absurd statement as a comment on attitudes toward love. He means to be witty, and his wit is rewarded with our laughter. At the same time, of course, his trivial characteristics are revealed.

That kind of wit and humor is a far cry from the following rather crude locker room raillery:

KEVIN: Hey, asshole. Have you seen my Kleenex?
SPARKY: Up yours, Kev. You wanna go to Eben's for a couple of brews. The broads are easy.
KEVIN: You're so dumb you can't even get easy.
SPARKY: Who struck out with Lena the Hyena? A nerd can make it with her. Face it, you got the sex appeal of a dustball. . . .

The author of this dialogue might want to argue that the characters are meant to sound embarrassingly crude. As walk-on, walk-off characters, Kevin and Sparky could produce a mild discomfort, the embarrassed laughter that characters who are making fools of themselves produce. However, if the audience had to spend much time in their company, they would soon be more irritated than interested or concerned, just as if they met such people in real life.

In any case, the appeal to reality is not convincing. The mere fact that people really speak exactly as you report does not make the fictional or dramatic dialogue effective. A character who is meant to be boring must still be interesting in a way that does not bore the audience.

EXERCISES

1. Read the following scene from *The Day They Shot John Lennon.*

The Day They Shot John Lennon

JAMES McLURE

The date is December 9, 1980, the day John Lennon was shot. Shortly after the shooting was announced people began to gather across the street from his apartment house on Seventy-second Street in New York City. Some were fans; some were merely curious. They stood around for hours; they talked to strangers who stood near them; some cried.

One of those gathered that fateful day was Fran Lowenstein, whom the author describes as thirty-five years old, "a native New Yorker and all that implies. Tough, sensitive, a feminist and a member of the Woodstock generation who is also looking for a meaningful relationship." She works as a secretary.

Fran strikes up a conversation with Brian Murphy, who is "in advertising." The author tells us he is "given to quick opinions and stances of self-confidence (though) he is basically a confused individual looking for love." He is thirty-three.

By the time the scene below begins, among the topics Fran and Brian have talked about are Lennon's music, their jobs, the bars they frequent, politics, and modern painting. Their conversation continues:

FRAN: It's like spirals within spirals y'know. I mean I see images tumbling by. I see myself as a little girl on a visit to my grandmother's in Queens and we go to the park. And it's green and beautiful and my father's with me. Big, and young and strong. And whenever I think of that I think of "Penny Lane," it's like, that's the way it felt. (*Pause.*)

BRIAN: I know. It's like background music for our lives. I remember at my first high school dance and I was all sweaty and scared and I was gonna walk across the room to ask Richie Woodall to dance with me. And they started playing "Hey Jude" over the P.A. system. It was a Catholic dance. I think the nuns thought it was about St. Jude. The saint of lost causes.

FRAN: (*Passionately.*) Maybe that's what all this is. A lost cause. The sixties. The peace movement. Look what's happenin' now in the Middle East. El Salvador. Are we any closer? Are we getting there? Take a look at the E.R.A.? Are we getting there? Three-Mile Island. Are we getting there? How can we say we're civilized when we continue to hold people back. Because of sex, because of race. Is that getting us anywhere? Increased military spending, weapons for defense. (*Laughing.*) And the joke is we're all afraid of the bomb! We blame everything on "They." The Pentagon— "They"! The CIA—"They." But we all have to take responsibility for the society in which we live. All America wants to do is go to the movies! Is that getting us there? Where's the leadership? Where's the dialogue? We're not talking. We're not listening. We're missing the whole point. It's not the sixties. People are just burying their heads in the sand. People will do *anything* rather than be here now. (*Pause.*) Are we getting there? No. People are just going to the office and making money . . . People suck.

BRIAN: (*impressed*) Wow. You know, you're a very passionate woman.

FRAN: Well, what did you expect? Someone dumb?

BRIAN: No, it's just that women—

FRAN: Oh brother, here we go. It's just that women what?

BRIAN: Just that women that you meet in bars—

FRAN: Hey! You didn't meet *me* in a bar! Right? Get it?

BRIAN: But you said you *go* to bars.

FRAN: I go to bars. I wasn't born in a bar. Right?

BRIAN: It's just that I think you're very smart and very passionate and very attractive. And I don't meet women like that.

FRAN: Where do you meet your "woman," Brian?

BRIAN: Bars. I meet my women in bars.

FRAN: Well, then maybe that's *your* problem, Brian. Maybe you're meeting those kind of women—the passionate, attractive, intelligent kind of women but since you're just living for the night, maybe you don't see them for what they are.

BRIAN: Hey. Who're you kidding? You go to bars. You have drinks. You meet guys.

FRAN: That's right, Brian. And I'm the passionate, attractive, intelligent kind. (*He touches her arm.*)

BRIAN: Look babe, I didn't mean to—

FRAN: Don't touch me.

BRIAN: O.k. I won't touch you.

FRAN: Boy I hate your kind.

BRIAN: My *kind*? My *kind*? Boy if that isn't sexual stereotyping I don't know what is.

FRAN: Granted. Sexual stereotyping. But in your case, it works.

BRIAN: Oh yeah? And what is my type?

FRAN: You're—the button-down-collar-junior-executive-climbing-the-ladder-of-success-but-I'm-really-the-sensitive-young-man type. That's your type. I'll bet you haven't been to a museum in a million years.

BRIAN: For your information just last week I went to the Museum of Modern Art.

FRAN: Oh yeah. What did you see?

BRIAN: Paintings.

FRAN: What kind of paintings?

BRIAN: Modern paintings.

FRAN: Oh Jesus. What a fake. What a liar. I bet you weren't even at Woodstock.

BRIAN: I was too!

FRAN: Everybody has their little scheme don't they? Tell me, does this line work a lot? This I-like-art line? Does that work on everybody?

BRIAN: No. Just you.

FRAN: Well, it wasn't working on me. I can assure you of that.

BRIAN: Yeah, come to think of it, now, I've seen you before. Sure yeah. I see you all the time in the bars.

FRAN: You don't see me at bars.

BRIAN: Sure I do.

FRAN: You do not.

BRIAN: The Adams Apple, Michaels, Maxwells, The Meat Place, Martys, The Satyre, Pegasus, sure you're there all the time. You're not special. I thought you were but you're not. You're like all the rest.

FRAN: Fuck you.

BRIAN: My pleasure.

FRAN: One thing though.

BRIAN: Huh.

FRAN: If I'm like all the rest . . . so are you. (*Pause.*)

BRIAN: Look, I'm sorry . . . I don't know what we got so excited about . . . I mean . . . You're a nice girl.

FRAN: Woman.

BRIAN: Woman! Woman! Woman! (*Pause.*) Look . . . wanna smoke . . . I've got some gum . . . spearmint . . . Look I'm not like this . . . maybe I am. I didn't used to be. I don't meet women like you. I felt alive in the sixties. That's why I came here. I wanted . . . I wanted . . . then I met you. I mean. Something. In common. I don't know. Maybe not. I didn't want to go to work. I wanted to talk. (*She accepts cigarette. He lights it.*) I mean. Life goes on.

a. Assume you are the director and that you are discussing the intention behind each speech with the actors who play Fran and Brian. They have asked the following questions that you have to answer.

BRIAN: In the speech beginning "I know" why do I tell Fran who St. Jude is? Since I know who St. Jude is am I only setting up her speech? Or is something happening that makes me say that? Or should the writer redo the dialogue?

FRAN: In my long speech, do I really know what I'm talking about or am I simply spewing out words that I've heard?

BRIAN: What was Brian going to say when he starts talking about women? When Fran breaks me off and I start again, have I changed what I was going to say the first time?

FRAN: Why is Fran so uptight after her long speech? Up to that time she seems to have been getting along all right with Brian. In fact, Brian appears to be trying hard to please.

BRIAN: When Brian gets angry back starting with "My *kind*," is he serious or is that part of his come-on? And when Fran asks him about the museum, is he putting her on or has she caught him in a lie?

FRAN: Is this attacking and putting down of men one of the reasons that she doesn't get her man? Are her politics always so much up front—perhaps as a defense—that they cut off innocent conversation? Or is there *no* relaxing with her?

BRIAN: When he says he saw her in bars, it's clear that he's striking back because he feels put down. But why does he mention all the bars? And what does he mean when he says "You're like all the rest"?

FRAN: Is she the kind of person who says "fuck you"?

BRIAN: Sure she is, but something more important. His answer just feels like a place holder, a setup. I don't know why he says it from his point of view.

b. In this scene, Fran and Brian have been struggling over something. What is it? How is it resolved?

c. Why is Brian's last speech so chopped up and so illogical?

d. Picking up on Brian's last speech above, write a beat for the time it will take them to smoke the cigarette. Don't forget that they are holding a vigil outside John Lennon's apartment house.

2. Each of the short stories in Chapter 12 has a dramatic core; in some, that core is more readily apparent than in others.

  a. If you had to choose between doing a dramatic adaptation of "Sunday in the Park" or "First Day" which would you choose? Why?
  b. Develop a scenario (a play outline) for the story you chose.

3. We have a new way of conversing, the Internet. Chat goes back and forth, perhaps hovering between real speech and dialogue (shaped speech). Create an internet dialogue of two pages or so between two characters. One of their frustrations might be trying to talk and yet feeling limited by the time it takes to keyboard and send a message and then receive a reply. Think of a situation in which at least one of the parties wants something and the other does not want to give it.

4. Your character is in a restaurant with a significant other. They have not been getting along well before dinner. In fact they have gone out to neutral ground to hash out the situation. They are receiving exceptionally slow service. The waiter has finally given them a basket of rolls. Five in fact. They each have eaten two and then one says to the other: "Do you want the last one?" Write the dialogue that ensues.

A CHECKLIST FOR CREATING NATURAL OR FLOWING DIALOGUE:

1. Allow characters to interrupt or finish each other's speeches.
2. Stop a thought in mid-sentence.
3. Not respond to the other character.
4. Search for better word.
5. Respond to the look on the other's face or something the other does.
6. Give the speaker some business that concerns them while they are speaking.
7. Use indirect discourse as useful for avoiding dialogue dummy or create character who needs the information (i.e. detective, someone who has been away, just moved into the neighborhood).
8. Keep designators simple.
9. Avoid step dialogue in which characters constantly pick up a word from the previous speech or repeat part of the previous speech before going on.
10. Beware of long passages in which characters recite to other characters information—including information about feelings or social attitudes.
11. Remember that each character comes from a position so that his or her response should be in character.

Finally, to prepare yourself for writing effective dialogue, listen to the pattern of the way people speak rather than to their exact words. Dialogue is artful use of these patterns to indicate what characters do to each other.

15

❧

Plays and Screenplays

Joyce Carol Oates's *Procedure* and Jeffrey Sweet's *Last Day of Camp* are called "ten-minute plays." Even if they take longer to present, the phrase is used for very short plays that are now popular in theater circles, particularly the types of theaters that are most likely to put on dramas by beginners. Such plays are the equivalent of the short-short-story you find represented by "Sunday In the Park" (pp. 267–270) or "Just Married" (pp. 273–274). For the plays we present here, the technical demands are the same as those for their longer brothers. Both of the short plays in this section present (1) the pressure of an intense dramatic moment (2) containing the exposition of a past. Before each play we will discuss aspects of playwriting that you will find illustrated by the play itself. We follow each play with an expanded discussion of techniques and with several exercises. We introduce each play with some brief comments to heighten your awareness of its key features.

PROCEDURE

In *Procedure* the immediate need to prepare the deceased for the morgue is also the occasion for revealing the special past relationship between the deceased and one of the nurses. The exposition is simple. We find out that:

1. The place is a hospital.
2. The characters are nurses preparing a body prior to the "family" coming to see it.
3. One experienced nurse is training an inexperienced nurse.
4. The experienced nurse is apparently cold and indifferent; the inexperienced nurse is emotional.
5. The procedures are not simple and must be done in a certain order.

However, the stage business that goes on during the play is not like dusting a room or pouring drinks. The detailed preparation of the corpse is appalling work. Oates's careful exposition is the occasion for an even more appalling denouement (don't worry, the corpse is really dead). *Note*: How the director would represent a corpse and some of the procedures on stage is of no more concern to the playwright than how a sword fight should be choreographed. The body may be an actual nude person or a dummy or a nude person partly hidden behind a screen. Or the body may be imaginary and the actions mimed.

PROCEDURE

JOYCE CAROL OATES

CHARACTERS

A.—late twenties or early thirties
B.—younger and less assured

TIME & PLACE

The present.
A hospital room, and a nurses' lounge.

LIGHTS up. In a hospital bed, motionless, lies the BODY of a man. He is not elderly; perhaps in his sixties. An IV tube is attached to one of his nostrils: another tube snakes beneath the bedclothes, in the region of his groin. There may be a white screen partly enclosing the bed. A bedside table, with a minimum of items on it. From stage right enter two nurses' aides—A. and B. A. is in her late twenties or early thirties; brisk, self-assured, practiced in her movements. B. is not only younger but less assured; her movements are occasionally faltering and timid, but not excessively. B. is in every sense the apprentice, determined to learn PROCEDURE, and eager to acquit herself well. Both A. and B. are healthy, even husky young women, and both exhibit near-faultless posture.

Between them THEY are carrying the "Death Pack" equipment—a kit
out of which items (see below) will be taken, plus a small laundry hamper,
a large paper bag, two white sheets, a stretcher and litter straps.
The predominating color of the set is white: stark, dazzling white. The nurses'
uniforms, stockings, shoes; the dead patient's gown; the bedclothes. A
penumbra of darkness surrounds.
A. and B. approach the bed, B. just perceptibly hesitant.

A. (*Sharp, clear, mechanical voice.*) PROCEDURE. Open the Death
Pack. (*B. opens the Death Pack.*) Take out the DO NOT ENTER sign.
(*B. does so.*) Affix to outside of patient's door.

(*B. takes out the sign, which measures about 12″ by 8″, "DO NOT ENTER"*
in bold black letters; hangs from the outside doorknob of a door at the rear.)

B. (*Nervous smile, breathless laugh.*) I guess—anybody out in the hall,
they'd sure know what we were doing.
A. (*Freezing B. out by continuing, in the same voice.*) PROCEDURE.
Remove the contents of the Death Pack and set on available surface in
patient unit.

(*B. follows A's instructions, fumbling now and then; conspicuously not looking*
at the dead man.)

A. One wrapping sheet. Absorbent cotton. Padding. Bandage rolls.
Safety pins. Death tags.
B. (*Softly, as if dead man might overhear.*) This is—my first time. My
first—(*Gestures awkwardly, abashedly.*)

(*A. gives B. a look of reproof. A beat.*)

A. PROCEDURE. Remove treatment equipment, if any, from
patient unit.

(*B. detaches IV tube, etc., with A.'s assistance; pushes equipment to the side.*)

A. Lower the head rest, leaving a single pillow.

(*B. lowers head rest, fumbling a bit. Forgets to remove a pillow.*)

A. LEAVING A SINGLE PILLOW.
B. (*Quickly.*) Oh yes—sorry!

(*B. places one pillow on the floor; the dead man's head lolls, which alarms her.*
As A. gestures impatiently, B. adjusts the head. Her facial expression is taut,
but does not betray distaste.)

B. Poor guy—wonder who he was!
A. (*Continuing, perhaps more forcibly; in an incantatory, ritual-like*
manner.) PROCEDURE. Place the body of the deceased in as natural a

position as possible—arms at sides (*A. and B. do this. B. a bit timidly.*); palms turned toward thighs. (*B. does this.*)

    B. (*Breathlessly.*) Wonder *why*—"palms toward thighs."

    A. (*Coolly.*) PROCEDURE. (*A beat.*) Close eyelids gently.

    B. (*Nervous laugh.*) Gee—whyn't they have us do this *first?*—so, y'know, the—, the—, *he* isn't looking at us, like! (*Tries to close eyelids, without success.*) Oh my God—they won't *close.*

    A. (*As before.*) Close eyelids gently.

    B. (*Tries again.*) Oh mister, I wish you'd c-cooperate, I'm just kind of, kind of—NERVOUS. (*SHE succeeds in shutting both eyelids.*) Hey— O.K.! Thank God.

(*B. holds out her hands, for A. to see how they are shaking. But A. is indifferent.*)

    A. PROCEDURE. If the deceased has dentures—

    B. (*Pointing, frightened; as one eyelid opens slowly.*) Oh—he's waking up!

(*A., though exasperated with B., says nothing. In a quick, fluid, decisive manner SHE draws her fingertips down over both the dead man's eyelids; this time both eyelids remain shut.*)

    B. Oh!—how'd you do that? (*Pause; abashed.*) Well—I guess I'll learn.

    A. If the deceased has dentures, these should be cleaned and—

    B. (*Nervous attempt at humor.*) They *all* have dentures, seems like!

    A. (*Continuing, without inflection.*)—cleaned and replaced in mouth.

    B. (*Misunderstanding, leans over to peer at dead man's mouth preparatory to timidly poking her fingers into it.*) Oh—mister! You're gonna have to ex-cuse me—

    A. (*Irritated, but maintaining decorum.*) Dentures should be cleaned and REPLACED. (*As if in an aside, now that she is not repeating instructions from the handbook.*) You must know—dentures are not *in* the patient's mouth. (*Points to bedside table.*)

    B. Oh! Sorry! (*B. locates dentures in a glass on the table. Picks them up hesitantly. Holds to light.*) They look O.K. to me. I mean—clean. (*Peering; with a shivery laugh.*) Must be weird, wearing 'em. False teeth!

    A. (*Coolly, as if making a pronouncement.*) Nothing is "weird" in this place.

    B. (*Approaching patient.*) Well, excuse me, mister, gotta put these back *in.* So that your folks, coming to see you in the—the—downstairs—

    A. In the morgue.

    B. —so they'll see you at your best.

(*B. mimes replacing dentures in mouth. [Specific action may be hidden, or disguised, by portable bed screen.] Has difficulties, murmuring to herself.*)

B. Oh—damn—I just don't know *how*. Like, in real life, this guy'd do it *himself*. (*To A., pleading.*) Y'know—he's still warm. His mouth, I mean. Inside. Wet too—saliva. (*A pause. B. backs away, suddenly frightened.*) Oh God—that's a dead man!

A. (*In official voice.*) Sometimes, with the dead, dentures cannot be replaced. (*Looking on as B. tries gamely again.*) DO NOT FORCE.

(*B. fumbles dentures, drops to floor.*)

B. (*Aghast.*) Oh God! I'm sorry!

A. (*Picking up dentures, setting on table, continuing as before.*) PROCEDURE. Replace top bedding with draping sheet.

(*B. covers body awkwardly with large sheet, removes other sheet. The next several steps are done under the sheet, with some difficulty, and distaste, by B.*)

A. Remove patient's pajamas. (*B. does so, folding and thrusting them into a laundry hamper as quickly as possible.*) Press bladder gently to expel accumulated urine. (*B. does so.*) Remove catheter. (*B. does so.*) Place cotton pads over rectum and genitalia to absorb feces and urine which will be expelled as sphincters relax.

B. (*As she is doing this.*) Oh!—oh dear. I guess we had a little accident.

(*A. tosses B. a towel or more absorbent cotton. B. wipes, under the sheet.*)

B. (*Trying not to appear repelled.*) It's just so—oh geez what can you *say*. You start out life soiling your diapers and you end—

A. Clean old adhesive markings from skin, if any.

B. (*Peering under sheet.*) Poor guy—he's got 'em. (*B. busies herself with this task.*)

A. Prop sagging jaw with folded pads.

B. That's how *my* mouth comes open, if I sleep on my back! I hear this wet-sort-of noise, y'know, in my sleep, it wakes me up sometimes, or, a minute later, I'm *snoring*—(*As SHE props up dead man's jaw, with some initial difficulty.*) I'm gonna be so worried someday, when—if—

A. Pad ankles with cotton and tie together with bandage.

B. (*As SHE does this.*)—I'm married, or something. (*Pause.*) My father, he snores so you can hear it through the whole—

A. (*Making out tags, deftly.*) PROCEDURE. Tie one signed tag to right great toe (*Gives B. the tag.*)—tie one signed tag to left wrist.

B. Why *two*? The toe and the wrist aren't gonna get separated, are they?

A. Roll body gently to side of bed. (*A. helps B. do this.*) Place one clean sheet diagonally under body. (*Pause.*) DIAGONALLY under body. (*Pause.*) Roll body back to center of sheet.

B. (*Shivering.*) He's still warm—some places. Just his fingers and toes, and his face, are *real* cold. (*Pause.*) Looks like kind of a nice guy, don't he?—'course any man, no matter how cruel, he's gonna look nice, peaceful, sort of, in a weird way, like a *woman*, at a time like this. Y'know what I mean—?

A. (*Freezing* B. *out.*) Fold upper corner of sheet loosely over the head and face—(*As THEY do so.*)—the lower corner over the feet (*Etc.*)

B. (*Almost giddy with strain, waving to patient.*) Bye-bye!

A. Secure the arms at the sides by bringing the right and left corners of the sheet over to complete the wrapping.

B. (*Performs this action swiftly, keeping pace with* A.'s *words.*) Yeah! Right!

A. Fasten sheet with safety pins. (*Tosses pins to* B.) Fasten additional signed tag to outside of sheet. (*Etc.*) If dentures could not be replaced, wrap in gauze, identify, pin dentures next to tag. (*Etc.*)

B. He could be anybody now . . .

A. Lift wrapped body to stretcher.

B. Here's the hard part, huh? (A. *and* B. *lift body, lay on stretcher, which is on the floor; THEY have less difficulty than might be expected.*)— Geeze he's *light* isn't he!

A. Fasten litter straps at chest—(*THEY do so.*)—and just above the knees. (*Etc.*) Cover body with additional sheet.

B. (*Immense sigh.*) Well—that's that.

A. (*Continuing as before, with perhaps the slightest suggestion of sharing* B.'s *relief.*) PROCEDURE. Transfer body quietly and with dignity to the morgue, avoiding if possible public entrances and lobbies—

B. (*As* A. *and* B. *pick up ends of the stretcher, in a loud, somewhat giddy voice.*)—"QUIETLY and with DIGNITY to the morgue—avoiding PUBLIC ENTRANCES AND LOBBIES." Yeah! You bet!

(*LIGHTS down as A. and B. exit with stretcher.*

LIGHTS up. A. and B. are alone, apparently in a nurses' lounge; both have cans of soda which THEY open, and drink from; A. lights a cigarette, and offers one to B.)

B. (*Still shaky.*) I—uh, thanks but I—I'm not smoking now. I mean, I'm trying not to. (*Wipes face with tissue.*) Well. Sure glad I don't work in the *morgue.*

A. (*Imperturbably.*) It's quiet in the morgue.

B. I'll say!

A. (*Regarding her quizzically; almost friendly.*) It wasn't so bad, was it?

B. (*Laughing.*) To tell the truth, yes.

A. Just following procedure.

B. Procedure—! (*Shudders.*)

A. Not the first time you saw a dead patient, was it?

B. No, not exactly. But the first time I . . . touched one.

A. (*Clinical interest.*) And how was it?

B. (*Staring at A., perplexed.*) How was it? (*Pause.*) It was—something I won't forget.

A. You won't?

B. I sure *won't*.

(*A beat or two. A. regards B. as if bemused. BOTH sip from cans.*)

A. (*Casually.*) That man—dead man I mean—he was my father. (*Picking tobacco off tongue, as B. stares at her.*) I mean—that man, when living, had been my father.

B. (*Staring, blinking.*)—What?

A. Him. Just now. My father.

B. You're—joking!

A. Why would I joke? (*Half-smile.*) It isn't my practice to joke.

B. But—I don't believe it. Him—(*Points vaguely offstage.*)—us—you—

A. (*Matter-of-factly.*) I should explain—I hadn't seen him in a while. We weren't close.

B. Oh! You weren't "close."

A. He left us when I was sixteen. Didn't remarry or anything, just left. He lived in the city—I'd run into him sometimes—we'd talk, sort of. Sometimes, he'd avoid me. (*Pause.*) Or I'd avoid him.

B. Did you know he was here in the hospital?

A. Sure.

B. Did you know he was—dying?

A. More or less.

B. And you didn't tell anyone?

A. (*As if genuinely baffled.*) Didn't tell anyone—?

B. Oh—any of the nurses, or—

A. Why should I?—I'm a professional. I do my job.

B. And it didn't upset you to, to—

A. I said, I'm a professional. He wasn't *my* first.

B. (*Slight attack of dizziness.*) Oh—!

(*A. helps B., as B. leans forward, touching forehead to knees.*)

A. You're all right.

B. (*Recovering.*) I'm—all right. (*Pause.*) C'n I have a—?

(*A. passes the package of cigarettes to B., who takes one, lights it, exhales smoke gratefully.*)

B. (*Emphatically.*) My God, I'm so—embarrassed. Here I was thinking of myself, mainly. My first—death. (*Pause.*) I wish I could go through it again, now. See how you did it. Knowing what you told me . . .

A. (*Moving off.*) Sorry! It's a scene that can't quite be repeated.

(*LIGHTS out.*)

THE END

Discussion

The key devices Oates uses are ones we have discussed before. Carefully shaped repetition of the "one, two, three . . ." sort draws the audience into any work (whether it is a poem, prose, or drama). The process of preparing the corpse builds tension. Where will all this end and what will be the upshot? What also builds tension is the triangle—A, B, and the body. Not every play, of course, is built on the pressures inherent in situations in which three or more characters rather than two or one occupy the stage. Most are. (For a classic work using more than one triangular situation see Henrik Ibsen's *Hedda Gabbler.*)

Notice that Oates starts the play *in medias res.* Nurse A's father is already dead, they have been given the assignment of preparing the body, and they have gathered the "Death Pack." All this occurs before the point of attack. Other key pieces of information are contained in A's and B's first speeches. Oates establishes that A is matter-of-fact, experienced, and in charge. B is an apprentice and nervous, and her discomfort and inexperience is dramatized by her fumbling of some preparations. B's inexperience and ineptitude injects some humor that relieves the awful circumstances and punctuates the beats. Though it may appear that the revelation about the relationship between A and the corpse in the second scene is spur-of-the-moment, the audience will remember that A does appear almost too impatient, too cool, and too wedded to the procedures. Later, despite what she says about her indifference to her father, we sense that deeper emotions are operating. Notice how, as dramatists often do, Oates follows the dramatic revelation at the climax with another, lesser climax. B has been so focused on her own emotions that she hasn't learned the procedures.

EXERCISES

1. Write the scene for A's last talk with her father.

2. Write a scene in which B is training a new nurse to prepare a corpse for the morgue.

3. Write a scene in which Nurse A is assigned the task of preparing the body.

LAST DAY OF CAMP

Jeffrey Sweet's *Last Day of Camp* is a quiet play, almost the dramatic equivalent of an epiphany in which the denouement is a character's or an audience's sudden awareness of the true situation. The exposition or "back story" is simple. We find out that:

1. The children have left the camp.
2. It's night.
3. The camp is in the country.
4. Camp counselors receive tips from parents, not all of which are in cash.
5. A counselor was fired for smoking marijuana and also giving it to the children.
6. Craig has been carrying a torch for Fiona.
7. Lillian has been carrying a torch for Craig.

As you read, think about how much more the audience understands the situation than the characters do. What is the key structural element that creates the tension?

LAST DAY OF CAMP

JEFFREY SWEET

CHARACTERS

CRAIG
LILLIAN
FIONA

TIME & PLACE

The play takes place outside, at a camp, near the end of summer.

LILLIAN and CRAIG relaxing.

CRAIG. They do twinkle.
LILLIAN. Isn't that amazing? They really do.
CRAIG. You didn't know that?
LILLIAN. Not really.
CRAIG. Come on, you must know the song. Everybody knows the song.
LILLIAN. Which?
CRAIG. "Twinkle, Twinkle, Little Star." You don't know that?
LILLIAN. Sure.

CRAIG. Where do you think they got that from? I mean, art imitates life, right?

LILLIAN. I don't know. There's a lot of bullshit in songs. The only stars I ever saw twinkle were in Disney cartoons or Christmas pageants. Till this summer. I guess it's pretty hard to twinkle through all that guck in the city.

CRAIG. So you've had an educational summer, hunh?

LILLIAN. You're laughing at me.

CRAIG. Not really.

LILLIAN. That's OK.

CRAIG. I'm not laughing.

LILLIAN. You aren't?

CRAIG. No.

LILLIAN. I'm glad. But it would have been OK if you were. I mean, I like you.

CRAIG. Well, that goes both ways. And I wasn't laughing at you.

LILLIAN. (*Pretending to be embarrassed.*) Well, gosh and shucks, Craig. (*A beat.*) So quiet now. I've gotten so used to hearing kids' voices. Now they're gone, it all sounds sort of naked.

CRAIG. You packed?

LILLIAN. I'm putting it off.

CRAIG. I know, it's a drag, isn't it?

LILLIAN. No, it's not that. I think I just don't want to admit that it's over.

(*FIONA enters.*)

FIONA. Well, Lucy Bernell's mother finally showed up.

CRAIG. About time.

LILLIAN. What's this about?

FIONA. One of my little monsters in cabin three. Her mother was supposed to pick her up and she was late or something.

CRAIG. The mother or the kid?

FIONA. Who cares? They're both gone and out of our hair. They're all gone, thank God.

LILLIAN. You really like kids, don't you?

FIONA. Let's just say that when it comes to Hansel and Gretel, my sympathies are with the witch.

LILLIAN. Which is why of course you took a job in a summer camp.

FIONA. I heard there was a lake here. Thought with luck I might see one drown.

CRAIG. What a pleasant thought.

FIONA. I'm a meanie, didn't you know that?

CRAIG. Sure.

FIONA. I am.

CRAIG. I believe you.

FIONA. OK, don't say I didn't warn you.

CRAIG. Guess what I got for a tip?

FIONA. Most I got was a twenty.

LILLIAN. That's not bad.

FIONA. It's OK, but nothing spectacular. Divide that down by the hours I spent making sure they didn't break an ankle or get eaten by a bear, comes to pretty cheap babysitting.

LILLIAN. What were you saying, Craig?

CRAIG. This guy hands me an envelope and right away I can feel there's something other than money in it. I open it up and it's maybe an ounce of grass.

LILLIAN. Whose daddy was that?

CRAIG. You know Dave Greenberg?

FIONA. The little freak?

CRAIG. A clear case of like son, like father.

FIONA. OK, let's see.

CRAIG. See what?

FIONA. Isn't he cute when he plays innocent? Your tip.

CRAIG. I'll show you mine if you show me yours.

FIONA. You know what I'll bet, I'll bet it's some of that anemic home-grown stuff.

CRAIG. Only one way to find out.

FIONA. All right then, break it out and let's put it to the test.

CRAIG. Don't have it with me.

FIONA. Where is it?

CRAIG. Back in my cabin, in my secret hiding place.

FIONA. I'll bet.

LILLIAN. You'll want to be careful.

CRAIG. What about?

LILLIAN. Remember what happened to Leonard.

CRAIG. Leonard was a different case entirely.

LILLIAN. They caught him with dope.

CRAIG. They caught him turning on the kids in his cabin. That was Leonard's fatal mistake.

FIONA. Yeah, but till they kicked him out, he was the most popular counselor in the camp.

CRAIG. I think what tipped them off was the water pipe one of his kids made in arts and crafts.

LILLIAN. I'm just saying be careful.

CRAIG. I appreciate your concern. But we're leaving tomorrow, so it's not like there's any great danger.

FIONA. You going to turn him in, Lillian?

LILLIAN. Of course not. Why would you say a thing like that?

FIONA. Maybe you don't approve.

LILLIAN. It's not a matter of my approving or disapproving . . .

FIONA. She said disapprovingly.

LILLIAN. It's not. Just because I don't do it, I'm not laying anything on anyone else.

CRAIG. You've never smoked?

LILLIAN. Sure, I've smoked, but not anymore.

FIONA. Got to protect those chromosomes.

LILLIAN. No, it's just I didn't enjoy it.

CRAIG. You're kidding.

LILLIAN. Why am I kidding?

CRAIG. You didn't enjoy it at all?

LILLIAN. What, is this the new taboo—you don't admit you don't enjoy dope? You say it like it's something I should be ashamed of.

CRAIG. No.

LILLIAN. If you enjoy it, terrific.

CRAIG. Well, I do.

LILLIAN. Terrific. It's not often you find something you really enjoy. Only we all enjoy different things. If we didn't, what would be the point of being different people?

FIONA. Bet you I know why you don't like dope.

LILLIAN. I just don't.

FIONA. It scares you.

LILLIAN. No.

FIONA. You feel those inhibitions slipping away, you're afraid of what you might do. What wild, disgraceful things you might do. Maybe dance or tell dirty jokes or take you clothes off.

LILLIAN. I can do all those things without smoking.

FIONA. Yeah, but *do* you?

LILLIAN. Is that what you think of me—that I'm some virginal square hard-ass?

FIONA. What I think is you're a lady who hasn't investigated her full potential for having a good time.

LILLIAN. OK, yeah, right. There you have me nailed into one pithy sentence.

FIONA. Just telling you what I see.

LILLIAN. Thank you very much.

FIONA. OK, take it the wrong way if you want to.

LILLIAN. Don't you worry about what kind of time I'm having.

FIONA. OK.

LILLIAN. I'm having a fine time.

FIONA. If you say so.

(*A beat.*)

CRAIG. So what about it?

FIONA. What?

CRAIG. You want to sample a little of my tip?

FIONA. I thought you said you didn't have it with you.

CRAIG. Not with me, but back at my cabin.

FIONA. Back at your cabin, hunh?

CRAIG. Well, that's where it is.

FIONA. In your secret hiding place.

CRAIG. Yes.

FIONA. Back in your cabin.

CRAIG. Right.

FIONA. Well, it's a tempting offer, but no, I don't think so.

CRAIG. No, hunh?

FIONA. Mind you I'm flattered . . .

CRAIG. Nothing to be flattered. Just had a little, thought I might share with an appreciative colleague.

FIONA. I see.

CRAIG. That's all that was on my mind. Honest.

FIONA. You're getting cute again.

CRAIG. Well then, maybe back in the city, hunh?

FIONA. You're almost irresistible when you're cute.

CRAIG. So?

FIONA. I said "almost."

CRAIG. You're a cruel woman, Fiona.

FIONA. I told you I was. You thought I was lying, didn't you?

CRAIG. Oh well, guess I'll just have to smoke it myself.

FIONA. You could always look up Leonard. I'm sure he'd be glad to help you out.

CRAIG. Cruel.

FIONA. Goodnight.

LILLIAN. Night.

(*FIONA exits.*)

CRAIG. See how nuts she is about me?

LILLIAN. No accounting for taste.

CRAIG. Meaning me or her?

LILLIAN. Meaning nothing in particular really.

CRAIG. No, what, do you think I'm crazy?

LILLIAN. I don't know what to think.

CRAIG. Come on, Lill, we're friends. You can call me an asshole if you think I am one.

LILLIAN. I just don't think there's much potential there. For all of her talk about relaxing inhibitions and stuff. I don't think she . . .

CRAIG. What?

LILLIAN. No, I feel stupid talking about her like this.

CRAIG. What were you going to say?

LILLIAN. Just I don't think there's much action behind the talk.

CRAIG. Well, it isn't all talk.

LILLIAN. No?

CRAIG. No.

LILLIAN. How do you know?

CRAIG. Well, it happens I do know.

LILLIAN. You and she?

CRAIG. Once.

LILLIAN. Oh.

CRAIG. A couple weeks ago.

LILLIAN. How about that?

CRAIG. You don't mind me talking about this?

LILLIAN. Why should I mind?

CRAIG. It's just . . .

LILLIAN. You're pretty stuck on her, hunh?

CRAIG. Yeah, and I sort of got the impression that night that it was mutual. Or maybe I was reading something into it. Seeing what I wanted to see.

LILLIAN. That can happen.

CRAIG. Oh well, I guess I'll get over it. I mean, I was still in the infatuation stage. It really hadn't taken root.

LILLIAN. Not enough time.

CRAIG. Probably. Though this switch on her part, I guess it's got me a little off-balance. I mean, if she wasn't interested, then what was that night all about?

LILLIAN. Maybe she just wanted a good piece of ass.

CRAIG. (*Laughs.*) Anything's possible.

(*THEY lean back a minute.*)

LILLIAN. (*Sings.*)
    "Twinkle, twinkle, little bat,
    How I wonder what you're at."

CRAIG. Where'd you hear that?

LILLIAN. I think it's out of Lewis Carroll. That or *Pogo*. I'm not sure.
(*Sings.*)
"Up above the world so high,
Like a tea-tray in the sky."
(*Speaks.*) Lewis Carroll.

(*A beat.*)

CRAIG. Hey.

LILLIAN. What?

CRAIG. What do you say, in five years, if you aren't married and I'm not married, we get together and talk about it?

LILLIAN. What?

CRAIG. I'm not saying do it necessarily. But talk about it. And who knows, maybe do it. We could both probably do a lot worse, and probably will. So, what do you say? Five years?

(*A beat.*)

LILLIAN. (*Trying to hide how upset SHE is.*) You can be very cruel, you know that?
CRAIG. What? What did I say?
LILLIAN. Never mind. (*SHE gets up.*)
CRAIG. Where you going?
LILLIAN. I really ought to pack.
CRAIG. No, wait, hold on.

(*HE reaches out for her. SHE moves away from him, begins to cry.*)

CRAIG. What is it? Please.
LILLIAN. You stupid asshole.
CRAIG. (*Now HE understands.*) I'm sorry.
LILLIAN. You stupid, stupid asshole. (*SHE runs off.*)

THE END

Discussion

The late point of attack is indicated by the title. In fact, the action occurs not just on the last day but on the last evening. That these potential summer romances have been simmering for weeks increases the pressure on Lillian to let Craig know just how much she is taken with him and thus increases the dramatic tension. If not now, when?

Sweet extends the natural tension of the late opening by structuring his play around the triangular relationships—Craig is attracted to Fiona, Lillian is attracted to Craig, and Fiona is attracted to neither but stands between them. Craig says that Fiona has slept with him, but all the signs are that he is, to put it kindly, exaggerating. Sweet creates more dramatic tension by using a basic literary device in any form of storytelling—a character's lack of perception. In this case, the audience knows more than Craig does and wonders when or if he'll understand the true situation. (*Oedipus* is the most famous play using that device. Oedipus is similarly blind to reality but, in that play, the stakes are much higher.) One of the beats that helps us to understand Craig's insensitivity is his rather sophomoric talk about Fiona to Lillian. Genuinely adult men don't tell tales about sexual conquests to other men, much less to women.

Sweet uses a common technique to imply that the characters inhabit a shared world. When Fiona makes her entrance she mentions a camper as if Craig and Lillian know to whom she is referring, as they do. The audience needs not know anything about Lucy Bernell beyond the fact that she exists and that all of the characters know that she exists. They talk knowingly about other people. Lillian and Craig also see the stars together and talk about them. The sense that a world exists beyond the three characters suggests that they are not simply actors on a stage. To them, they are in a world they can see and know.

Last Day of Camp is a slim play but, like most effective plays, it contains more subtext than text. The childhood song "Twinkle, twinkle little star" is not only a response to what they are looking at but also a reflection of their adolescence, as is Fiona's cynicism, Craig's pot smoking and jejune sexual bragging, and Lillian's puppy love. Indeed, what they say is a mask for what they mean or who they really are or how they feel. Lillian's response to Fiona's "Goodnight" and Craig's line—"See how nuts she is about me?"—after Fiona leaves are filled with subtext. Lillian shows that she is relieved and, at the same time, dismissive of Fiona. Craig is covering up with braggadocio and feigned indifference just how put down he feels.

EXERCISES

1. Toward the end of the play, Craig insensitively suggests that they get together in five years. Write that scene with or without Fiona.

2. Assume the Fiona goes with Craig to his hut. Write that scene so as to reveal how much their talk is just talk.

3. Write a play using the characters and situation in "Just Married" (Chapter 12).

A WORD ON PLAYS FOR FILM AND TELEVISION

If you want to write playscripts for film (whether to be presented in a movie theater or on television), you need to master special techniques and jargon. You must read about the media, see the media, and work in the media. Special subgenre, dramatic programs such as *NYPD Blue* or sitcoms, require specialized knowledge about the television business. You are wasting your time writing a script for *Friends* when the producers use only contract writers or the network intends to cancel the program for the next year. That is, you are wasting your time unless you are simply practicing TV script-writing.

For those of you who do wish to try a filmscript, we have a brief list of suggestions that will be useful for all the subgenres. Please keep in mind that these are rules-of-thumb to which there are exceptions. Before reading on, you may wish to look at the sample pages from a filmscript by Marc Lapadula reproduced at the end of this section.

1. Read as many complete original *filmscripts* as you can, particularly of films that you can rent and study at home on your VCR or DVD. When we say "filmscript," we are not speaking of "shooting scripts" that include detailed instructions for the cinematographer nor of those scripts you may find printed in magazines. These often do not follow the author's original format. As you compare the writer's script with the final product, notice how short most "scenes" in a film script will be. A film "scene" is defined as any change in place or time. Put a stopwatch on the film and compare the time with the pages in your script. You will notice that a page of script is almost equal to a minute on the screen. In fact, a long scene (say three minutes or three pages long) in a film will usually be followed by several short scenes. Filmscripts that the producer can't scan at jet speed are likely to land quickly in the return basket. Reading the scene will take the same amount of time as viewing it. In the sample script, how long do you think the director would spend on Monica's staring out the window at the clouds?

2. In a stage play, the dialogue tends to be the action that the characters are performing, or it triggers an action that the characters will perform. In a film, the action triggers the dialogue. That is, someone does something and that causes a verbal response. Humphrey Bogart starts walking down the runway with Claude Raines and then says, "Louis, I think this is the beginning of a beautiful friendship." Or Dorothy lands in Oz and after looking around says, "Toto, I don't think we're in Kansas anymore." What she says is a reaction to both what she and we witness as part of the action. Not vice versa. In the sample script, the ticket agent responds to the numbers on his computer screen when he says the price will be high for the ticket.

3. Remember that the camera can and will see details of actions and gestures in ways that a theater audience cannot see them. Therefore, not as much dialogue will be needed. In fact, what the camera can see, the characters will seldom discuss. A student gets his paper back. He turns it over. The camera shows a *C*. When the student pulls a long face as he looks at his grade, the teacher won't say, "Are you unhappy with your *C*, Mr. Wanagrade?" Rather, she'll frown and say, "You didn't even deserve that grade." Student rips paper in half. Teacher picks up gradebook and changes grade to *F*. In the sample script, Meg does not say to Monica, "I'll send you the proofs because you are going on a trip." We see the airport and understand that Monica is going on a trip. The line of dialogue refers to a work task.

4. While novelists and playwrights often discover in the process of writing how the plot will turn out for the characters (remember that the characters are thinking of the "plot" as their lives), it is best in a screenplay to know exactly what choices the characters will have to make at the end. In other words, you should begin your writing with a relatively clear notion of the plot and write rather mathematically toward the conclusion. Most films are driven by time. Because of limited audience endurance, they usually have to be no more than two hours long. You have to fit everything

that needs to be shown in order to understand the plot and characters within that time. Unlike books, movies are made to be experienced in one sitting; if you watch them in pieces, you lose the intended effect. The minute in a film is a minute in the viewer's life. When you have a clear picture of the plot, you will not tend to meander.

5. They call them "movies" because people move. Audience do not expect characters to stand around and talk. They expect car chases and kisses (sometimes quite long car chases and kisses); and swinging, climbing, eating, and other actions (the verbs). Just as in a play, however, you do not have to worry about describing the details of the set or characters (the nouns). You have collaborators (set, costume designers, choreographers, explosives experts) and others who will provide the details. You should simply mention the place and get on with the action. In the sample script, notice how little Marc Lapadula says about the airport or the restaurant. He doesn't have to re-create the atmosphere for a reader's imagination. He simply has to let the director know where to take the cameras.

6. In the sample script, you will notice that Lapadula did not say "favoring shot," "close two shot," "camera dissolves to," or tell the actors how to say the dialogue ("whispering" or "with a whine in her voice"). Of course, on occasion you will want to suggest some details related to the action or acting but use such technical and directorial terms sparingly. One of the surest ways of having your script placed in your SASE and dropped off at the nearest mailbox is for the writer to usurp the tasks of the directors, actors, and the host of other collaborators who will spring into action when the producer chooses the screenplay. However, you will have to know the conventions about describing places, times, and the movement of characters; the general placement of dialogue and description; and such matters as when to use capital letters and when not.

Put your efforts into making a good story about the characters, one that exploits the possibilities within the medium. Your characters and their needs and desires will be no different from those in fiction or a play. Just how you let the viewer experience the story will be different because, just as in any other dramatic medium, you are providing a framework for others to perform.

EXERCISES

1. Using as a model the pages from the script by Marc Lapadula, try to "write" the script for a film as you watch it on your VCR or DVD. Notice how every change of location is a new "scene." Notice how little dialogue there is compared with a stage play.

2. Generally speaking, a film script will be about 120 pages long for a film that will run between 90 and 120 minutes. It will have about 120 "scenes." Of course, you don't write to that measure. The measure is the result of the medium's demand for movement through space and time. And, as you know, many films are adaptations from previous works. An adaptation exploits the audience's familiarity with the plot and the characters; however, the chief reason for the frequency of adaptations is that the scriptwriter (or producer) knows what will happen and so can concentrate on constructing the script. If you wish to gain experience constructing filmscripts, one useful place to start would be by adapting a published story. Try a filmscript of the first ten "scenes" of a story from Chapter 12 or of a novel you have recently read.

What follows is an excerpt from the filmscript *Night Bloom* by Marc Lapadula:

EXT—DRUGSTORE

Newspapers sit in stacks on a table outside. Rocks on the top papers keep them from blowing away. Hank picks one up. He leafs through, looking for something. It's clear he's not finding it.

A MAN steps up next to him.

> MAN
> Excuse me.

Hank looks up. The MAN reaches down and selects a paper. Hank tosses his back on the pile.

> HANK
> Which way is the bus station?

> MAN
> Straight down, turn left, then right.
> But I wouldn't waste too much time
> waiting there.

> HANK
> Why not?

> MAN
> Bus service stopped coming through four
> years ago.

> HANK
> So how does a person get out of this place?

The Man Laughs.

MAN

Close your eyes and make a wish.

The Man laughs again and heads inside.

Hank looks after him, his lips sliding into a slightly bemused smile.

EXT—CHICAGO O'HARE AIRPORT TERMINAL—DAY

A car drives up. The passenger door opens before the car comes to a complete stop. Meg is driving. Monica steps out.

MEG

Are you sure you're going to be okay?

Monica exhales deeply.

MEG

Be sure to call me if there's anything
I can do. I'll mail you the proofs.

MONICA

Thanks.

Monica quickly gets her bag out of the back and heads into the terminal.

INT.—TERMINAL—DAY

Monica walks through the streams of PEOPLE, her expression dazed and blank.

INT.—TICKET WINDOW—DAY

Monica stands before the male TICKET AGENT.

TICKET AGENT

That will require a change of plane in Kansas
City. The closest we can get you to Ulysses
from there is Wichita, a good two hundred
miles away.

MONICA

That far?

TERMINAL AGENT

Without advance purchase, you're looking at a
pretty steep fare.

Monica becomes momentarily distracted, her eyes beginning to tear.

TICKET AGENT

Ma'am?

> MONICA
> Just put me on the next flight.

INT.—AIRPLANE—DAY

Monica stares out the window at the swirls of white clouds.

INT.—JILL's RESTAURANT—DAY

Jill calls to the young girl, Annie.

> JILL
> Annie, honey, take these burgers over to
> the men at booth seven. You've been a real
> help today.

> ANNIE
> You look so sad, Mrs. Combs. Are you okay?

Jill smiles, her hand gently touching Annie's cheek.

> JILL
> Just bring the burgers over.

☞

SUMMARY

A playscript is an occasion for a performance. The most effective playscripts are those written with an appreciation of both the freedoms and limitations of the medium's conventions. On the one hand, the playwright has only to indicate the presence of a chair, not describe it; on the other hand, the detail of the pettipoint will not be visible to most spectators and so it cannot be as important as it might be in a work of fiction. Because a performance is unstoppable, the effects cannot be as subtle as those in poetry and fiction. Character and circumstance must be quickly grasped by the audience. The premise needs to be shaped so that the point of attack is late in the story. Above all, the playwright must master the craft of presenting both text and subtext in dialogue, the primary vehicle of character and plot.

The pleasure of playwriting is that in no other genre can you have so much immediate impact on an audience.

16

❦

From Revision to Submission

Revision

To **revise** means literally to "see again." To **edit** means to bring into conformity with established standards. Though these two terms are often used interchangeably, they point to different concerns. We will shift back and forth, sometimes focusing on one term, sometimes the other. Paradoxically, taking another look and honoring conventions become part of a single process as the author searches for ways to improve his or her work.

When to Revise

Most writers agree that writing and revising by wholes leads to the best results. It makes sense to begin revising and editing your work only when you have a complete draft in front of you. After all, if a successful literary work is a web of interrelated parts, then changes cannot be made in isolation. A revision in one place almost invariably demands a revision somewhere else. Revising a work that is only partly completed is better than doing nothing at all, but it is inefficient. You can revise Chapter 1 more effectively once you know which materials coming later in the work will affect Chapter 1.

However you should not completely ignore problems along the way. At the end of each writing session, take informal notes for future revision. Or, if you create on the computer, leave yourself notes as you go along. Then, when you have in front of you a draft of the whole work, or major portions of it, review those notes and determine what kind of revisions will satisfy your new concerns. For example, if you write your way into a situation that demands "backloading" of information, make yourself a revision note, but don't stop to do the actual revision: push on.

How to Revise

Revising means taking a critical stance toward what you have done. Many writers need to get away from their work for a while in order to see it clearly and objectively. Whether dealing with large-scale structural issues or consistent spelling of a nickname, we see things more clearly when we have reduced the emotional charge that is part of the creative impulse. In a way, you have to take on another personality. You have to become someone who can read and evaluate what you actually wrote, not what you wanted to write or hoped you wrote.

We can consider three levels of rewriting:

1. For literary quality.
2. For the conventions of mechanics, grammar, and manuscript form.
3. For factual accuracy.

When assessing the literary effectiveness of the work, we consider its impact on the reader, its focus, its handling of the conventions of genre, and its diction. Whatever feeds the aesthetic and conceptual dimensions of the work is considered here—including that elusive thing called **style**. Working with checklists will help you go through the process with greater thoroughness and efficiency than just "looking for things." A checklist is no more than a guide, however. Begin with the lists provided here, and then go on to develop your own based on your experience and work habits.

CHECKLIST FOR POETRY

1. Can the line breaks be justified?
2. Is the speaker's voice consistent?
3. Are the sounds and rhythms of language used expressively?
4. Do figures of speech (or any other devices) call too much attention to themselves at the expense of their function?
5. Have you eliminated stale language—especially clichés and unnecessary trite expressions?
6. Are the parts of the poem subordinated to an overall effect?
7. Are the parts (lines, images, stages, events) in the best possible order?
8. Have you let suggestivity and ambiguity turn into vagueness and unintelligibility?

9. If the poem is in sections, should it be?

10. Do you feel that each section has a proper relationship to the others and to the whole?

11. Do the visual and auditory levels of the poem complement each other?

CHECKLIST FOR FICTION

1. Is your point of attack effective? That is, have you begun the story too early (quite likely) or too late (not likely)? A properly chosen point of attack will allow you to give exactly what the reader needs in order to follow the story through its climax and resolution.

2. Is the structure effective? Do you have the scenes you need (and only the scenes you need) to develop your material? Are the scenes in the best order? Is there a sense of inevitability about the ending that grows naturally out of the flow of events and information without sending out obvious signals?

3. Are the transitions between scenes clean and clear?

4. Are the sections of summary and exposition adequate? Are they overdone? Have you struck an effective balance between showing and telling?

5. Is the narrator's perspective, the point of view, the best choice for this story? Is the perspective consistently maintained?

6. Are the main characters developed sufficiently? Do they become more than mere types? Do they have sufficient interest as rounded or shaded individuals? Are their actions consistent without being overly predictable?

7. Are minor characters and walk-ons kept to a minimum and kept within the bounds of their functions in the story?

8. Is the dialogue natural? Is it plausible? Does it do more than merely impart information? Are the dialogue tags kept simple? Is it always clear who is speaking?

9. Do you have an energetic mix of the various storytelling elements? Generally, it is wise to avoid long stretches of anything—description, exposition, dialogue. Keep the story moving forward and engage the reader on many levels.

10. Is there an overall unity of effect—a controlling idea, mood, emotion, or thematic thrust that the various ingredients support?

CHECKLIST FOR PLAYS

1. All of the items for fiction, plus . . .

2. Have you given your characters things to do while they are talking (and thereby given your actors something to do)? This is another way of ensuring that the play is visual.

3. Does each beat exist to advance the plot? Even if a beat or moment is interesting in itself, if it does not fit into the plot, you must remove it.

4. Have you removed or revised every beat that exists *only* for the purpose of giving exposition?

5. Does each character have an apparent want? Within moments after each character has appeared, something of his or her approach to life should be visible to the audience (even if the judgment will be modified later).

6. Are the character's wants in conflict with the other characters' wants? In most plays, meaningful conflict grows from these personal wants, not from ideas about how best to run the railroad.

7. Have you removed all stretches of dialogue that can be cut without the audience's missing anything of the plot? This type of revision requires line-by-line effort. If you sense that the dialogue (therefore the plot) is dragging, go back to where the drag began and try deleting until the play begins to feel alive again.

8. Is the environment built into the characters' actions, beliefs, and dialogue? The characters can see, and the audience can see what the characters can see. Exploit the possibilities.

9. Have you eliminated all unnecessary designators and stage directions?

10. Check to see that you have changed or eliminated elements that depended on scenes or characters you excised in the process of developing the script.

MECHANICS

Editing for mechanics requires that you refer to your dictionary and style manual and pay attention to the conventions of manuscript form.

Checking for Correctness

If some of the terms in this checklist cause you to draw a blank, go back to your style manual and give yourself a quick refresher course in mechanics.

Usage: Consult a dictionary whenever in doubt. Trust any anxieties you feel about a word choice or expression and make sure you are in control of your decisions. Check any idiomatic constructions that you're not sure of as well as regionalisms that you have appropriated for your work. Read your work aloud (slowly) to test what you have against your inner ear. If it doesn't "sound" right to your ear, don't let a problem go just because you are eager to get the manuscript into a publisher's or director's hands.

Spelling: There are no excuses here. Don't guess.

Punctuation: Stick to the conventions whenever you can. Variations for effect can be useful, but they can also be annoying. For example, multiple exclamation points, ampersands instead of "and," & ellipses that leave the reader . . . lost in the dots!!!!! In poetry, special conventions adopted for a particular work should be used consistently so the reader can become comfortable with how they are meant to operate. Be careful about what goes inside and what goes outside quotation marks. Remember that punctuation is an opportunity to shape how the reader sees relationships among words. Don't use punctuation mechanically. On the other hand, don't break conventions of punctuation except for a significant creative purpose.

Grammatical constructions: Avoid the common sins of the dangling modifier, the incomplete comparison, the run-on sentence, or the sentence fragment. Again, break with conventions for a good purpose, not out of ignorance or carelessness.

Agreement/consistency: Check for consistencies in tense and number. Make sure nouns and pronouns clearly agree.

Clarity of pronoun references: Avoid vague uses of "this," "which," "it," "she," "he," and other pronouns. Keep the distance between pronouns and their antecedents minimal. Make sure a pronoun does, in fact, refer to a noun or to a clause or phrase functioning as a noun.

Placement of modifiers: Keep modifiers near what they modify. Avoid "squinters" that point in two directions.

Economy/directness of expression: Choose precise, concrete nouns and verbs that will require minimal modification. Reduce modifying phrases to single words. Avoid circumlocutions.

Sentence style: Don't become a slave to a certain sentence construction or length. Mix complex and simple, long and short. Don't overuse parallelism. Keep your prose moving through sentence variety, and be alert to sounds and rhythms.

Finally, *read the work aloud and have others read it aloud to you*. Doing this gives you new perspective on the work's effectiveness and also gives you the opportunity to catch errors that are often missed in silent reading.

FACTS

Be able to verify all factual information, such as dates, place names, product features, holiday observances—even handgun calibers. Will that law school course your character is taking actually be given in the first year?

A DESK ON YOUR DISK

Almost every resource that sits on a writer's desk is available in electronic form. Dictionary programs allow you to check individual words or whole textfiles for spelling errors. Since all of these dictionaries are limited, and since they don't list proper names and certain word variations, the programs allow you to compile a personal dictionary so you won't keep being told that "Faulkner" is a possible error. Once you put an entry in the personal dictionary, the program knows that that sequence of letters is legitimate. These dictionaries are not, in fact, really dictionaries at all. They are spelling checkers. Whenever they come across an unknown configuration, the writer is asked to do something: either ignore the signal, change that instance, or change that pattern throughout the document.

These programs are useful for catching typographical errors. However, they do not take the place of your own careful proofreading. No spelling checker will question the word "their" when you mean "there" or "to" when you mean "too." Typographical errors that result in legitimate words—"place" instead of "plate"— will have to be discovered through the diligence of the responsible author.

An electronic thesaurus is available with many word processing packages. When you enter the thesaurus command, you will be given alternatives for the word at the cursor. Given what we have said elsewhere about there being no true synonyms, we won't elaborate here on the dangers of instant word lists. Remember that such a resource is best used to jog your memory. The responsible writer can use this resource wisely and clear the desk of one more reference volume. As with the spelling checker, the range of the computer thesaurus is limited. However, the speed and convenience of these devices is remarkable. No more turning pages to find something. Push one or two keys and what you want to know is on the screen, ready to be placed automatically in your textfile.

Can you put away your style manual? Maybe not. The style analysis programs tend to mark as errors too many formulations that are in fact legitimate and intentional. Still, running an analysis with one of these programs may help you catch some blunder you might otherwise miss. We tend to be skeptical about these programs, but see for yourself. And remember, it's *your* job to edit your work properly. There is no sense in blaming your software for your mistakes.

Even without such programs, you can perform basic checks on your work if you are aware of your worst tendencies. Do you tend to overuse forms of "to be" at the expense of active verbs? Use the "find" feature to locate instances of "is" and "are" in your draft; then decide whether substitutions are desirable. Do you use coordination when subordination might be appropriate? Run the "find" command for "and" and "but," and then revise accordingly.

You will need to experiment and talk to other writers before deciding which word processing programs and auxiliary programs will be best for you. With experience, you will find the combination that allows you to feel comfortable while taking maximum advantage of computer technology.

Because of the conveniences just described, the word processor can change the way you go about your business. Any writer inhibited by the printed word may find the ephemeral signs on the monitor screen easier to push around than the immovable figures printed on the page. The trial and error process that is essential to composing and revising becomes much less of a trial and more of a game. Word processing intensifies or even re-establishes the play aspects of creative writing that are so much a part of its delight.

SOME POSSIBLE PROBLEMS

There are some drawbacks to writing with a word processor. The monitor (screen) shows you only a fraction of a page at a time, usually somewhere between a third and a half. This limitation leads to tunnel vision: the tendency to pay too much attention to the limited amount of material glowing before your eyes and not enough to the larger flow of content and style. Even as you flip back and forth among screens full of text, you lose continuity.

To compensate for this difficulty, we recommend that you print out your work often and do much of your revising and editing on the printed copy. It is much easier to work with whole sheets of text, especially since you can then lay three or four next to each other to get a feel for the flow of your work. This practice will cost only a little of the time saved by using a word processor in the first place. With a mildly sophisticated system, you can be printing out one file (or a portion of one) while composing or outlining or revising another. Also, today's printers crank out high-quality copy many times faster than anyone can type. Working on printouts of successive revisions allows you to refine your work efficiently and effectively. Remember, you do little retyping; you only enter *changes* on the keyboard.

Some writers get around the tunnel vision problem by single-spacing when they draft, so they can see twice as much material. Then, depending on their word processor, they either reformat to double-spacing before printing or command the printer to double-space. At best, we find this a partial solution, especially since it is very difficult to read single-spaced material on the screen for a long time. Another partial solution is employing the "page preview" feature, which also crowds the screen. You'll have to discover what works best for you.

Proofreading in particular is best done on printed text. Staring at the monitor—any monitor—is more wearing on the eyes than is scrutinizing printed text. We find that our proofreading is less accurate when we read from the screen. Perhaps it's just a matter of an old habit dying hard, but most writers have had the same experience. Another advantage is the portability of the printed copy; you can work on it wherever you want to.

Frequent printouts are also a safeguard against the vulnerability of electronic text. Materials in memory only (not "saved" to a disk) are susceptible to voltage variations or accidents (such as someone's tripping over your power cord and unplugging it). Even saved textfiles can be ruined by keyboard mistakes or electromagnetic damage. Not only should you save and back up your files regularly, but also you should print out hard copy as a final defense against computer or disk failure. Although these failures are infrequent, it takes only one to make you wish you had taken simple precautions.

Another potential problem is the distraction caused by the very powerful features we have been discussing. Writing and saving textfiles is one thing; editing is another; and page formatting is still another. The gadgetry of the word processor tempts writers to move too quickly to editing or designing the page layout when they should be drafting. Sometimes playing around with margins, typefaces, and various commands affecting the appearance of the finished manuscript substitutes for creative working time in which new ideas and passages are generated. *Our advice*: Stay with the *process* of composition as long as possible. Enjoy the editing features only when you have something to edit. Enjoy the page design features only when everything else is done and you're ready to print out final copy.

SOME WORDS ABOUT PROOFREADING

Technically, **proofreading** means checking galleys or page proofs against the original manuscript from which the typesetting was done. The marking of proofs involves using a standard set of symbols that are illustrated on the next page. We also include a checklist at the end of the section that you may want to re-read before beginning the proofreading task.

Proofing can be done with two people, one reading the "copy" and the other reading the author's original. One person reads aloud, usually from back to front, including punctuation. (For example, for the preceding sentence, "period/punctuation/including/comma/front/to/back. . . .") Homonyms ("too," "two," "to") are spelled out. The other person reads along silently, searching for discrepancies between what is heard and what is seen. The goal is to ensure that the printed version of a work conforms to the author's intention, as recorded in the manuscript, in every way.

In preparing a work for submission to a teacher or an editor, you must take the same kind of care. The copy you present should be as close as possible to your ideal. From your reader's point of view, you are invisible. All the reader sees is the finished page. Errors that interrupt the activity of reading will annoy and confuse the very persons you are trying to reach. From the reader's point of view, a careless error is still an error. Careless copy tends to be carried forward even beyond the most careful copy editor and ends up in print.

Many writers find it helpful to proofread a number of times, concentrating on different potential problems each time through. You might read through once, using the "Checklist for Fiction," then again using the section "Checking for Correctness." A third time through, scan the right margin to check for proper hyphenation. Finally, read each sentence (or line) separately, beginning at the end of the work. By reading things out of order, you are less likely to have your objective examination foiled by anticipating and imagining what comes next.

Use the appropriate proofreading symbols as you prepare a draft for retyping. Familiarity with this system will be useful when your work has been accepted for publication and you are ready to check proofs. These symbols are also useful for editing your drafts.

Other marks are used specifically for typesetting problems. You will find a list of these in your dictionary. Also, your publisher will give you a style manual to follow when your manuscript is returned for further revision.

_ℓ_ delete; take it out out

⌒ close up; print as one word

_ℓ_ delete and close up

∧ caret; insert here /text

insert a space

stet let marked text stand as set

tr transpose; change order the

/ (used to separate two or more marks)

¶ begin a new paragraph

no¶ no paragraph

sp spell out; change 15 to fifteen

cap set in capitals

lc set in lower case

_H_ hyphen

_M_ dash

⌃, comma

⌄ apostrophe

⊙ period

: colon

; semicolon

❝❞ quotation marks

(/) parentheses

[/] brackets

Q ? or Q   Is this really correct (content or form)

PROOFREADING CHECKLIST

1. Do not rush through the proofing task.

2. Proofread for different elements—spelling, grammar, punctuation, typography. One time through, start from the end (last sentence, next to last sentence, and so on). You will pick up more spelling and agreement errors. Proofread from a paper copy.

3. Don't trust your computer tools to discover problems.

4. Read the work out loud with someone else who is following along on another copy of your text. You will both pick up mistakes and awkward phrasing. Proofread once looking only for your most common mistakes. For example, "to" for "too" or "it's" for the possessive pronoun. Proofread all over again if you start making changes in the text.

5. Don't speed up after catching an error. Errors often come in groups and the next word or sentence may contain one.

6. Use a reading guide (like a ruler or three by five card) to lead your eye to each word and sentence.

7. Having someone else proofread your material does not release you from proofreading. Another reader may miss errors because she is interested in the content. Don't proofread while watching television.

8. If you take a rest from proofing, clearly mark where you stopped so you won't skip text when you begin again.

9. Proofread under good light. (Florescent lighting tends to flicker and may cause you to miss errors.)

FINDING A HOME FOR YOUR WORK

Like most writers, you will want your work to be published or produced. However, you will discover that finding a proper outlet for your writing is often a frustrating endeavor that requires the skills and energy of a salesperson. The effort appears to be antithetical to the creative process, and it may well be. However, marketing your work is a reality, and you need to get to it rather than moaning about the soul-destroying effort. Even relatively successful writers have to face up to the submission process—and frequently the rejection slip. If that is so for them, then what for writers just starting to submit work for publication?

Many beginning writers have unrealistic expectations. They send their work only to the most prestigious magazines, forgetting that such outlets can publish only a tiny percentage of the thousands of manuscripts they receive. No beginning athlete would expect to go from a college course in golf to making the cut in the U.S. Open; that athlete would first try to make the golf team, then play in local and regional competitions.

In a sense, writing for publication is a form of competition. There are only so many available markets and many more writers seeking homes for their work. Sending manuscripts to inappropriate places only strains the system and lessens your chances of reaching an audience. It is important to send your work to those magazines and journals that are likely to give it a sympathetic reading. Marketing your poems, stories, or plays requires researching the literary or dramatic marketplace and honestly assessing what you have to offer.

At the beginning of this book, we argued that you shouldn't call yourself a writer unless you are a reader. As you become more and more concerned with publishing your work, your reading should also include a survey of the current literary marketplace. Discover the wide range of periodicals that publish literary writing and become familiar with the standards and tastes of the editors. Your starting place can be the entries on "Markets" that we provide in Chapter 17. The short paragraphs that these directories offer tell you what someone else— the magazine editor or list compiler—thinks you need to know. You can make a somewhat informed decision by carefully studying these lists. Check websites such as the ones we list in Chapter 17. And, if the publication has its own website, be sure to look there for the editors' interests and requirements.

For a more fully informed decision, you have to look at the publications. Use the market lists to select periodicals for direct examination. Subscribe to two or three at a time (changing your subscription list from year to year) and write for sample copies of others. Find out whether any bookstores in your area stock issues of these periodicals. Most importantly, scour the libraries, especially the college and university libraries. The best place to find literary periodicals is in the library of a university that has a creative writing program. Also pool your resources: exchange copies of magazines with others who are involved in the same search.

The noncommercial literary periodical, privately or institutionally supported, is the most likely place for you or anyone else to publish. These forums are the incubators, hatcheries, and country fairs of literature and literary reputations. They are not interchangeable, however, and some are less distinctive than others. Your task as a writer looking for markets is to read for a match between the editorial character of a periodical and your own work. In a way, you are learning to put yourself in the editor's place: if I were editor of *The Seven Bridges Quarterly*, would my story be considered worthy of publication there?

Your survey efforts will make you familiar with many writers who appear with some regularity in the periodicals you are reading. If your work has something in common with theirs, find out where else they are being published. Contributors' notes often provide such information, as well as a way of gleaning something about the achievement and status of the writers appearing in these pages. Is this periodical *really* open to previously unpublished writers?

Many of the magazines aimed at writers (we list the most important ones in Chapter 17) provide information in a more timely manner than the annual market surveys. Often you can find out about a recently announced contest, a special issue of an established literary magazine, or a call for submissions by a magazine just getting started. This last category is a reasonable place for a beginning writer to send work. You and the magazine have something in common. There are many internet market sources—and even internet magazines.

A useful and businesslike way to research the market for your poems and stories is to examine the acknowledgments pages of collections by writers whose work you admire, especially those whose style has some affinity with your own. Here you will find credited those periodicals that first published the individual stories or poems. Now you have a short list of possible markets for your own work. Get your hands on those magazines and target your submissions carefully.

Finally, there is nothing like the company of other writers to help you find your way into print. While literary friendships can be sought and exploited in unhealthy ways, there is something quite natural about being among people who share your interests and goals. Many of them will have that bit of information or that suggestion without which your work either will remain unpublished or will be published in a periodical of lesser merit than it deserves.

We have said nothing about marketing books. In the careers of most writers, publication in periodicals precedes book publication. Writers find their first congenial editors and their first audiences through submission to magazines, especially the noncommercial literary magazines whose main purpose is to nurture writers who have not yet captured a public large enough to warrant investment on the scale of the commercial publishing houses. The publication credits earned in these periodicals can win you the attention of a university or commercial press. What has happened, in effect, is that by meeting the standards and pleasing the tastes of many periodical editors, you have made a case for yourself.

Book publishers depend on such credits to help them sift through the thousands of manuscripts that come their way.

Though it is possible to break through with a first novel, most novelists begin by getting "samples" of their work published in periodicals. These samples, presented as short stories, are often relatively self-contained chapters of novels in progress.

Drama presents (if you will excuse the pun) a special case, since "publication" of a play is most often the residual of success in the theater (or on film). Be involved in theater (or with film), even if on a volunteer basis. Work with educational television, small acting groups, experimental theaters, and college and university theaters. Go to conferences and participate in programs at which you might have an opportunity to meet producers and directors. Enter contests for new plays (they'll *have* to read the playscript). The truth is that there is a good deal of "who-do-you-know" in the theater world, though, ultimately, the play has to satisfy also. Look for opportunities to have your play heard—at a staged reading, for example, or in a workshop group.

Just as we recommend that you not look to publish first in those few places in which everyone wants to appear, so we recommend that you have realistic expectations and not search for a Broadway production first time out. When you do submit to a theatrical company, be sure you have researched its requirements. There's no use wasting postage sending a play to a theater that either hasn't the means to produce it or is not interested in the premise. You will notice that many companies now ask for a query letter, a synopsis, and dialogue samples. *Don't send more than they ask for* if you want an unbiased reading.

Note: Beware of contests that charge excessive reading fees or that require the purchase of the "prize anthology" before a final decision can be made on your work. Too often these publishing ventures prey on naive authors who will succumb to their tricks. Your work will appear in print, but no exercise of editorial judgment has taken place: just the exercise of the author writing a check. The following excerpted article provides guidelines to steer you around swindles.

BEFORE YOU WRITE THAT CHECK

"The easy path to publication is paved with your dollars."

Essentially, scams fall into three categories:

1. services to writers—from editing, through organizations, to agenting
2. education for writers—including correspondence schools
3. publication—including contest and "prizes."

Sometimes the three categories can run together. All these categories, of course, reflect legitimate concerns that the confidence man/woman exploits. It would not be a confidence game if the attempt to rip-off the writer or would-be writer did not have the aura of truth. Sometimes, in fact, the confidence game is run by people who have confidence only in themselves. They fool themselves as much as they fool their customers. And sometimes, the legitimate shades into the doubtful before it enters the outright rip-off.

It is in the nature of the pure racket that the minute it's found, its name changes. Many rip-offs are around for so little time that, rather than develop an ever-changing list of their names, we've developed the following Test Kit for Scams.

TEST KIT FOR SCAMS

[Adapted from The Writer's Center Scam Kit]

Note: No single test necessarily damns the product. Two or more ought to make you pause before writing a check. Three or more probably calls for contacting the Better Business Bureau or the Criminal Complaints division of the Post Office. The tests are simple common sense in any situation where someone asks you for money. Beware of:

1. Any agent or publisher who asks for money, no matter how little. Pay entry or reading fees (no matter how small) only after carefully checking the publication and agent.

2. Any literary activity or service that asks for money *after* you have responded to its ad, but did not indicate a charge in that ad. In brief, beware of advertisements for free services.

3. Anything that sounds like another well-known literary activity but isn't. For example, suspect a publication called *Prairie Schoonover* or Mcgrew-Hille.

4. Any organization (educational or professional), publication, editor, or publisher that only has a post office box number, no phone and/or personal name.

5. Any publications and organizations that clearly are one-person operations.

6. Any mail request for money or membership put out on flyers that appear to have come off a poor dot matrix printer and sick copier. (However, fancy brochures do not a legitimate operation make.)

7. Any organizations, organizers, publications, publishers, instructors, judges—none of whom appear in any standard reference works. (However, just because it has a "name" does not mean it is quality or legitimate. We know of organizations that use names without permission. And remember, the reference listings do not necessarily check bonafides.)

8. Any claims to be non-profit that lack the IRS 501(c)(3) non-profit status.

9. Any out-of-towners coming to give a service (a course, or editing) who are not associated with a local organization. (However, even organizations you know about can be victims of scams.)

10. Anything that smacks of vanity publication. One warning sign that a magazine or anthology is a vanity press is if it does not give contributor's copies. That is, it expects you to buy copies and, sometimes, to sell them.

11. Any "publisher" who advertises for authors. They want authors all right. And their money.

The con artist plays on our lack of confidence in our work and, at the same time, our self-deception, perhaps even the con-person in us. Paying someone else to say we are writers or to make us published or to make out work publishable is—at some atavistic level—a wish for magic to do away with work. Abracadabras cost dollars and you still haven't paid your dues. Re-read "The Emperor's New Clothes."

Dr. Allan Lefcowitz from *The Writer's Carousel*

MANUSCRIPT FORM

The first principle of manuscript presentation is consistency. This is also the second. The third principle is to do everything in your power to make the task of reading and handling your manuscript as simple as possible.

If you take your writing seriously and want others to do so, then you will give your work every chance to succeed with editors. A sloppy manuscript suggests that the author has little regard for the work or for the editor. Your manuscript should have few—if any—hand corrections, and these should be done neatly and unobtrusively. It is a boon to be able to insert page numbers with the help of a word processing program. Don't forget them.

Prose should be double-spaced. Most editors accept single-spaced poetry manuscripts because this format will approximate the printed appearance of the poem, but some prefer that poetry be double-spaced (check market sources). Use standard margins: a 1 1/2-inch margin at top and left, an inch at right and bottom. Use the same margins for successive pages of your manuscript. Make sure that your printer is producing crisp, clear copy and that you use a good quality 8 1/2-by-11-inch bond paper manufactured for your type of printer. Avoid continuous tractor-feed computer paper. Use standard fonts (Times or Century) rather than any of the flashy, but distracting, alternatives. If you have a color printer, resist the temptation to use its capabilities. Basic black will do. Don't try to make your manuscript look like a printed page (no different sized type sizes and justified margins). Be wary of putting words in italic or bold. The pages will look too busy and are likely to turn off an editor.

Always be certain that your work is clearly identified. For multipage works, your name, address, phone number and e-mail address should appear at the top left side of the first page. The title of your story is given in capital letters, centered, about one-third of the way down the page. One custom, though it is hardly a requirement, is to provide an approximate word count at the upper right, along with an identification of the kind of work. Thus the first page of your manuscript will begin something like this:

```
Ima Writer
141 Dos Passos Lane                          Short story
Centerville, IA 52240                        3500 Words




[Start your story one-third of the way down]

              JAGUARS IN THE SNOW

And now the story begins. . . .
```

Number successive pages—the upper right corner is a convenient place—and give a short identifying tag, like your last name, in case the pages of your submission become scattered about the editor's office. For example, "Writer/2." Don't staple the pages together. If you must use a fastener, choose a clip that will hold your pages together securely without defacing the paper.

Poetry manuscripts can be handled more simply, especially since the appearance of the work tells us what kind it is. If the typed poem fits on one page, use the upper left corner for your address only and place your name after the poem, on a separate line and introduced by a dash. Nothing need go in the upper right corner. Do not begin more than one poem on a page. Do not number the page or the successive pages that hold separate works. If you like, a wider left margin—2 inches or even a bit more—can be used to bring the poem closer to the center of the page. Keep the title in caps, centered above the poem or flush with its leftmost margin.

In the case of longer, multipage poems, additional care is needed. Since your byline can't follow the partial poem that appears on the first page, put your name above your address as you would for a fiction submission. Use the upper right corner to indicate how long the poem is *in lines*. Type the word "continued" on the bottom right of the first and successive pages as necessary. At the upper right of the following pages, provide a short title along with page number ("Wheelchair-7"). This system is more useful than your name when you are submitting a number of poems at once. To be even more cautious, you might give your last name at the upper left of successive pages.

If you double-space your poetry manuscript, be sure to quadruple for divisions between sections (stanzas).

Most important, indicate whether the last line on a page does or does not coincide with a stanza break. Don't leave it to the editor or typesetter to guess about this important dimension of your work.

A one-page poetry manuscript might look like the sample shown below.

```
14 Stanza Turn
Petrarch, IN 12345


        MAKING THINGS FIT

        Sonnets are very hard to write.
        You shouldn't try one if you're too laid back
        Even if you've got the skill--or knack.
        It's best if you're a bit up-tight.
        Some people write them just for spite!
        They don't care if they're out of whack
        Just as long as they're on the right track.
        These people never see the light.

        Me, I've given up on verse
        That makes me twist my thoughts around.
        My lines and images get worse and worse,
        And rhythmic glitches do abound.
        Thus I do fume and fret and curse
        And swear to seek no more rhyme sounds.

                                --Wyatt Surrey
```

Since you usually send a play to a contest or theater, you need to follow the conventions for production scripts, which differ from the printed appearance of plays in books. Here are some guidelines:

1. Obviously everything that we have mentioned about neatness, paper size and weight, and general professional appearance holds as well for playscripts.

2. Unless you are told differently, firmly secure your play in some type of binder so pages need to be dynamited before they come loose (this procedure is contrary to the rule for submitting other manuscripts).

3. Be sure you send the following with your manuscript:

   a. A brief résumé about your experience with the theater and any staged readings or productions the play has had.

   b. A cast page. Producers don't want to be halfway into a play and find out they will need more actors than they have seats for the audience.

    c. A plot synopsis (two pages at most) that tells what happens, *not* "what it all means."

    d. Contact information *in the lower left of the title page*:
    Phyllis Player
    7803 Indian Road
    Flagstaff, AZ 29073
    (777) 652-0839
    e-mail: *pplay@production.com* (if you have email)
    Copyright or registration information.

    e. A brief cover letter (see "Cover Letters," p. 270)

The typing format for a playscript is as follows:

1. Single-spaced, but double-spaced between speeches.
2. The name of the character speaking is centered on the page. Some playwrights capitalize the whole name.
3. The speech runs across the page.
4. Stage directions are indented halfway across the page.
5. At the top right of every page, type the act-scene-page.

    Theater managers will not reject a manuscript just because it fails to follow exactly this or any other format, but generally speaking they expect a conventional presentation. Remember that manuscript form for playscripts is different from the printed version of the play. See the first pages of Oates' *Procedure* for an example of print publication format. On page 367 is a sample playscript prepared for submission to a producer, director, or theater company.

    The format for a screenplay is designed to provide the maximum amount of room for the visual effects. You will see that the dialogue (the heart of a stage play) is squeezed in. This format should tell you something about how much of the plot and characterization have to be "told" through *visualized* action and movement as filtered through the camera.

    Here are the basic rules:

1. Type the descriptions and directions (for cameras or actors) across the page.
2. Type dialogue in the middle of the page, each line no more than 3 inches wide. The character's name is centered.
3. Type designators for the speeches in parentheses centered below the character's name.
4. Single-space, but double-space between blocks of dialogue or directions.
5. Divisions of the action (such as FADE or CUT TO) are set apart on their own line, with double-spacing before and after. Some screenwriters put such directions at the right-hand margin.

Phyllis Player   I-i-1
The Mouse Bell

CAST :   Young Mouse - in his twenties (days)
         Sweet Mouse - just turning eighteen   (days)
         Grouch Mouse - seventy days if he's one but still spry
         Pal Mouse - in his twenties

Place: A comfortable nest between the walls. Pal Mouse, dressed
in jeans with Sweet Mouse who is laying out some crackers and
cheese.

                              Early Morning. Off-stage we hear a
                              terrible meeow, a shriek and
                              silence.

                              PAL
                    (rises up and sniffs the air.)
I thought they had let him out for the night.

                              SWEET
Who do you think he got?

                              PAL
Hey, not to worry. Young's too smart to be out--

                              SWEET
                    (Bites into the brie)
I know that but he does take chances sometimes. I do wish he'd
be more careful. I start to get nervous and eat too much.

                    (Grouch comes tottering in.)

                              PAL
Good morning, sir.

                              SWEET
Good morning, papa-mouse.

                              GROUCH
You haven't a right to call me that yet. Maybe never. Did you
hear?

                              SWEET
                    (Offers Grouch and Pal some crackers and cheese
                      but they refuse.)
He told us, papa-mouse that he was only going to scout out the
basement. They keep barrels of wheat in the basement, we heard.

and so on

6. The following elements are always typed in capital letters:

    a. CAMERA SHOTS AND DIRECTIONS
    b. INDICATIONS OF LOCALE AND TIME (when first mentioned)
    c. METHODS OF TRANSITION
    d. NAMES OF CHARACTERS (always capitalize above dialogue, but in
        descriptions only for first mention)

7. Leave almost 2 inches of margin on both left and right.

You will want to own a good text that gives you information about how to describe camera shots, transitions, and scenes. However, only direct experience will teach you how to avoid merely layering the technical on a story that might better be told in another medium. Or how to remake a story that you have not yet told for the camera.

You can see how screenplay format looks from the sample on the facing page and from Marc Lapadula's *Night Bloom* on pp. 347–349.

All work that you send out should be accompanied by a stamped, self-addressed envelope (**SASE**). If you fail to provide one, don't expect to receive your manuscript back. For short stories, short plays, and larger poetry sub-missions, send your work flat in a large manila envelope (with an *identical* one for return). If you are sending only five or six pages of poetry, a half-sized manila envelope that requires folding the manuscript once is sufficient. ("Thin" manuscripts often get bent and wrinkled in the mail; the double thickness stiffens the manuscript at the expense of one clean fold across the middle.) If you send out just a few pages, you can use a standard letter-size envelope and trifold the manuscript neatly.

Because a computer copy can be so easily created, many writers handle the SASE in the following way. In their cover letter, they say: "If the manuscript is not suitable, please destroy it and inform me of your decision in the enclosed SASE." It is often more expensive to send back a large man-uscript than it is to reprint it. If you are fortunate, a carefully prepared man-uscript sent in an appropriate envelope with an equally appropriate return envelope will survive both the postal system and the perusal of editors. If the manuscript still looks fresh when returned, you can send it out again. If it is beginning to look worn, then it's time to send out a fresh copy. Put yourself in an editor's place.

Most editors no longer mind photocopies, as long as they are crisp, clear reproductions. The old distinction between an "original" or "ribbon copy" and a reproduction has been lost to the technology of the word processor, which allows any number of copies to be prepared effortlessly. Moreover, a manuscript produced with a laser printer is easily confused with a first-rate photocopy.

For most editors, the concern about "simultaneous submissions" (send-ing to more than one market at the same time) still exists, in spite of the relaxed stance regarding the nature of the manuscript. Don't send a work to more than one place at a time unless you know that the publisher accepts this practice. Even then, you should always let editors know that a work is being considered elsewhere.

Book-length manuscripts should be sent unbound in a cardboard box, the kind of box that holds typing paper.

Finally, if they have one, always check the website of the publication, the-ater, or contest for any special directions.

Phyllis Player   1
The Mouse Bell

<u>FADE IN</u>:

INT. KITCHEN

AN OLD FASHIONED KITCHEN.   We see a MOUSE
running across the floor as if we were following
it.   In the distance looms a hole in a baseboard.
PANTING and CLAWS SCRATCHING.   The hole
looms larger.

NEW ANGLE

A HUGE PAW starts to descend.   SLOW MOTION.

                                        CUT TO:
INT. NEST

It's a typical farm mouse's home--sofa, rocking
chair, end tables, hooked rug. PAL is watching
SWEET MOUSE setting out a spread of crackers and
cheese. Pal is in his twenties, a pleasant but
weak-looking mouse, the type you think will be
a loyal friend but never will go far in life.
Sweet Mouse bustles about the room straightening,
putting out refreshments and moving things
around. MEEOW and SHRIEK. Pal stiffens and
begins to sniff the air.

CLOSE ANGLE ON SWEET

We see her shudder and then gain control.

                    PAL
           (His <u>voice is trembling</u>)
           I would have sworn they had let
           him out for the night.

TWO SHOTS

                  SWEET
           Do you think it's anyone we know?

She is immediately sorry she said it and begins
to bustle around as if she hadn't a care in the
world. Still, she looks at the hole every once
in a while. Pal gets off the couch and comes
toward her.

CLOSE ANGLE ON PAL

                    PAL
           (He <u>is going to put his paws around</u>

and so on

Cover Letters

Editors have conflicting things to say about the value of accompanying your submission with a cover letter, though all agree that if you send one, it should be brief. Essentially, a cover letter is a letter of transmittal: its job is to call attention to the manuscript as briefly and effectively as possible. A few sentences about yourself, a few about the manuscript, and a few about why you have sent it to this particular publication should do the job. Indeed, finding a way of showing your familiarity with the periodical certainly can't hurt. Don't get cute, abrasive, or overly humble.

Here is a sample cover letter accompanying a playscript:

```
                                           return address
                                           date
      addressee


      Dear _____:
            Please consider my play, "West of East," for production
      by Thespian Theatre.  SASE enclosed.
            Thank you for your time and consideration.


                              Sincerely yours,
                              Phyllis Player
```

You may be tempted to try to use the cover letter to "sell" the play, poem, or story. Not only is this tactic a waste of your writing energy, but also it will mark you as an amateur. Let your literary or dramatic work sell itself.

Don't send a manuscript out unless you keep a back-up copy on disk and/or in your files. Editors have been known to lose submissions, and the postal service has been known to fail.

A MANUSCRIPT CHECKLIST

Here are some additional considerations when submitting to a publisher or producer.

1. Don't be cute or impolite. Manuscripts with clever drawings (not associated with the story), elegant printing (yes, we know you have a word processor), calligraphy, or any of those other efforts to enhance the words by visual means will immediately mark you as an amateur.

2. Don't reverse pages to check whether or not your manuscript has been read. If your reader does not get far enough to read the reversed pages, they probably don't deserve reading or are not suitable for the publication

(or theater). The reader who does get that far will recognize the trick and be insulted.

3. Check your manuscript to see that all the pages are there. Copy machines do hiccup.

4. Make sure the manuscript will fit the SASE.

5. Don't call the editor(s). If you do, they will be sure to send the manuscript back, since they have better things to do than shepherd a Nervous Nelly.

6. Don't follow your submission with a revised manuscript. You should have sent the revision the first time!

7. Don't sit around waiting for the rejection slip or that beautiful letter saying they loved it. Keep writing.

WHAT ABOUT COPYRIGHT?

"Copyright is a form of protection provided by the laws of the United States . . . to the authors of 'original works of authorship' including literary, dramatic, musical, artistic, and certain other intellectual works. This protection is available to both published and unpublished works." (*Copyright Basics*, Library of Congress Copyright Office, Circular R1.)

Here are the important points for any writer to know:

1. Your work is automatically copyrighted when you get it into a fixed form—on paper, a rock, or a computer disk.

2. You cannot copyright an idea for a work.

3. You cannot copyright a title. (You can trademark one but the process is overkill 99.99% of the time.)

The key point about copyright is that you have to write something before you can claim copyright. And the minute you write it down (even a letter), you have copyrighted it.

If you want to *register* your copyright as evidence of when you wrote a work, request information and a form from the Copyright Office, Library of Congress, Washington, D.C. 20559. It has a website and you can download the forms and directions. Read the clearly written brochure, fill out the form, send it in with your check, and you are registered. Some writers are registering copyright these days because the penalty for violation of copyright increases when the work is registered. This step is probably useful only for non-fiction articles, books, and blockbuster novels like *Gone With the Wind* or *Harry Potter*.

In any case, copyright is usually premature for a beginning writer. Get your work out to publishers and forget copyright. You already have it. Get to work on your next piece.

Good luck.

17

Tools and Resources

This chapter lists books, periodicals, and organizations that will be most help-ful to the student of creative writing. The lists are organized according to the plan of this book, so you may think of each subdivision as "supplemental reading" for the individual chapters. Brief annotations follow most of the entries. Today's writer has enormously powerful tools and resources that weren't available to writers of past generations: these are the aids provided through electronic media. The Internet is filled with writer-oriented websites that offer advice on craft and marketing. There are also electronic versions of basic tools: dictionaries, writers' periodicals, copyright information, and reference databases of all kinds. The major sites developed for the writing community tend to be generous. They provide links to many other sites, which in turn send browsers on to additional information highways and byways. With all of these electronic resources so readily available, it's easy to get lost or to waste time that you need for your writing. Discover the handful of sites that offer the kind of information and advice that you seek most often, and stick to them until they begin to fail you. We will offer some suggestions later in this chapter.

WORKING LIKE A WRITER

Word Work: Surviving and Thriving as a Writer. Bruce Holland Rogers. Invisible Cities Press, 2002. A highly personal and immensely useful exploration of the writing life, its frustrations, and possible cures. Rogers' observations are not always comforting, but they are always tonic and promote a healthy attitude toward the life of the writer.

KEEPING A JOURNAL

At a Journal Workshop. Ira Progoff. Rev. ed. Tarcher/Putnam, 1992. An expanded version of Progoff's classic, this approach involves use of meditation techniques.

The New Diary. Tristine Rainer. Tarcher/St. Martins, 1978. Aimed at "self-guidance and expanded creativity," this guidebook is rooted in Rainer's appreciation of Anaïs Nin's famous diaries and in various schools of psychoanalysis and art.

Our Private Lives: Journals, Notebooks and Diaries. Daniel Halpern. Ecco, 1988. An excellent sampling of modern and contemporary writers' journals as well as journals by prominent people in other fields.

The Writer's Journal: 40 Contemporary Authors and Their Journals. Sheila Bender. Delta, 1997. Journal excerpts are set alongside authors' comments on how journal keeping helps their creativity. Often journal entries are works-in-progress.

Writing to Save Your Life: How to Honor Your Story Through Journaling. Michele Weldon. Hazelden, 2001. Though we are not usually fans of journal guidebooks that are rooted in journaling as therapy, this one has much more to offer than others in its category. Plenty of attention to the writing itself and to how your personal story or stories can be made meaningful to readers.

LANGUAGE IS YOUR MEDIUM

Dictionaries, Unabridged

American Heritage Dictionary of the English Language, 4th ed. Houghton Mifflin, 2002. Copiously illustrated. Contains reference material on language, history as well as maps, and usage notes. Thumb indexed. A good buy for a writer on a budget. Abridged version is called the *College Edition*. CD-ROM included.

Chambers Dictionary. Chambers Harrup, 1999. Perhaps the most comprehensive one-volume dictionary available, it is the official dictionary for U.K. Scrabble tournaments.

Compact Edition of the Oxford English Dictionary. 2nd ed. Oxford University Press, 1991. This small-type version, now miraculously found in one volume, comes with a magnifying glass at a fraction of the price of the standard set. Earlier editions are sometimes available at considerably lower prices. *Note*: Some book clubs offer special rates on this and other useful reference works.

Oxford English Dictionary. 2nd ed. 20 volumes. Oxford University Press, 1991. Latest edition of the most comprehensive English language dictionary available, though its price puts it far beyond the means of most writers. And who has space to store it? Make sure you find the closest library that holds this treasure. There is nothing better. The *OED* is notable for providing the historical development of words through usage examples. See description of *Compact Edition*.

Random House Compact Unabridged Dictionary, 2nd ed. Random House, 1996.

Dictionaries, Abridged

American Heritage Dictionary, College Edition, 4th ed. Houghton Mifflin, 2002.

Random House Webster's College Dictionary. 2nd ed. rev. Random House, 2001.

Merriam Webster's Collegiate Dictionary. 11th ed. Merriam-Webster, 2003. The standard for typesetters, proofreaders and copyeditors, this is the latest desk dictionary based on *Webster's Third New International Dictionary*. Includes excellent auxiliary material. While this popular dictionary has many competitors, we see no reason to prefer any of the others. Comes with CD-ROM and software for accessing online updates.

Dictionaries, Specialized

Concise Oxford Dictionary of English Etymology. Oxford University Press, 1993. Based on the comprehensive *Oxford Dictionary of English Etymology*, this handy writer's tool provides "succinct accounts of the origin, history, and development in meaning of a great many basic words and a wide selection of derivatives." A useful partner to your standard desktop dictionary.

Harper Dictionary of Contemporary Usage, 2nd ed. William and Mary Morris. Harper & Row, 1992. This valuable guide to the state of American English provides quick and authoritative opinions on what goes, what doesn't, and what shouldn't.

New Dictionary of American Slang, 3rd ed. Edited by Robert L. Chapman. Harper-Resource, 1998. A must for the writer of authentic dialogue. A joy for any writer. This collection has a tolerance for the ephemeral and the vulgar far beyond that of standard compilations.

NTC's Dictionary of American Slang and Colloquial Expressions. 3rd ed. Richard A. Spears. McGraw-Hill, 2000. This delightful phrase finder has an index to key words in idiomatic constructions.

Merriam-Webster's Rhyming Dictionary. Merriam Webster, 1999.

The Complete Rhyming Diction. Dell, 1992. Many consider this the best of its kind.

Thesauri

Roget's International Thesaurus, 6th ed. Revised by Robert L. Chapman and Barbara Ann Kipfer. Harper Collins, 2001. Latest update of the standard work. User begins by looking up word and closest meaning in the index, then turning to the main section entry indicated in the index. The main section is organized by broader and then narrow categories of ideas; that is, the largest headings are broad abstractions under which are found more concrete subdivisions and entries. Useful for zeroing in on the word choices needed to sharpen a general idea or impression.

Roget's II: The New Thesaurus. 3rd ed. Houghton Mifflin, 1995. A well-planned dictionary-style listing with convenient cross-references.

Roget's 21st Century Thesaurus. 2nd ed. Barbara Ann Kipfer. Delta, 1999. This thesaurus uses dictionary format and offers a concept index.

Synonym Finder. J. I. Rodale. Warner Books, 1986. An easy-to-use synonym list that is arranged in dictionary form rather than in the classic categories established by Roget. Originally published by Rodale Books (last rev. ed. 1978).

INVENTION AND RESEARCH

Reference

American Library Association Guide to Information Access. Sandy Whitely. Random House, 1994. Fine overview of research techniques and research tools with thirty-five chapters providing research sources classified by topic. Electronic sources included. Somewhat dated now but still valuable.

Catalog of Catalogs. Edward Palder. 5th ed. Woodbine House, 1997. An annotated list of free (or almost free) catalogs providing information on almost anything. Though this resource-source is not designed for writers, any writer with imagination can take advantage of this clever volume. Alphabetized by category.

The Craft of Research. Wayne C. Booth et al. 2nd ed. University of Chicago Press, 2003. Though focused on scholarly endeavors, this book will bring enormous benefits to any writer who needs a solid, scrupulous approach to research.

The Essential Researcher. Maureen Croteau and Wayne Worcester. Harper, 1993. An exciting and thorough sourcebook for all kind of fact-finding. Well-organized and reasonably priced.

New York Public Library Book of How and Where to Look It Up. 4th ed. Ellen Scordato. Hyperion, 2002. While countless facts are readily available in this resource, it is more useful for its alphabetical subject listing that leads to other references, collections, government agencies, and foundations.

Facts

Encyclopedia of American Facts and Dates. 10th ed. HarperResource, 1997. The ultimate resource for American history trivia, but also a quick way to check the facts alluded to in your historical novel. Organized in chronological columns with categories that include politics, the arts, business, religion, sports, fashion, and folkways. Wonderful suggestions for building "period" scenes and settings. (Aug. 6, 1890. The first electrocution took place at Auburn Prison, Auburn, NY.)

Facts on File Yearbook. Facts on File, published annually. Product of the Facts on File news reference service that summarizes, records, and indexes each week's news from major news sources. Fifty-two weekly news digests plus annual index. It's all here. Begun in 1941.

Time Almanac. Time, Inc. published annually. This "Atlas and Yearbook" covers a wide range of old and new information under scores of headings including awards, disasters, media, travel, weather, and climate. "Countries of the World" section useful for thumbnail sketches of history, geography, politics, demography, and so on. Formerly known as the *Information Please Almanac.*

The New York Public Library Desk Reference. 4th ed. Hyperion, 2002. An astonishing one-volume fact resource with information divided into useful categories ranging from weights and measures to the arts to health care.

People's Almanac. David Wallechinsky and Irving Wallace. Doubleday, 1975. Later versions by Morrow in hardback and Bantam in paper. Number 3 published in 1981, and various updates issued through the 1990s. The best browsing book for idea and fact stimulation. Inspirations for countless creative projects here. A spin-off publication by the same authors plus Amy Wallace is *The Books of Lists.* Morrow/Bantam, #3, 1983.

World Almanac and Book of Facts. Newspaper Enterprises Association, published annually (since 1868). More list oriented than its *Information Please* rival. Similar coverage. Comprehensive index up front.

Quotations

Bartlett's Familiar Quotations, 17th ed. Edited by John Bartlett and Justin Kaplan. Little, Brown, 2002. The classic of quotation books, and well deserving of its reputation. Reasonably priced even in hardback edition. A must for every writer's desktop reference collection. More than 25,000 quotations.

Concise Oxford Dictionary of Quotations. Oxford University Press. 3rd revised edition, 1997. A powerful resource drawn from the larger *Oxford Dictionary of Quotations.* Handy and inexpensive in paperback.

Facts on File Dictionary of Proverbs. Checkmark Books, 2002. Not only a handy compilation, but entertaining, too.

WRITING POETRY

In the Palm of Your Hand: The Poet's Portable Workshop. Steve Kowit. Tilbury House, 2003. Invigorating advice, exercises, and examples. Kowit strikes a conversational tone while presenting intelligent, practical advice. Plenty here to keep any writer working productively.

The Life of Poetry. Muriel Rukeyser. Paris Press, 1996. This reprint of a 1949 classic should find a wide audience. Both inspirational and practical, Rukeyser is properly appreciated in Jane Cooper's introduction.

New & Selected Essays. Denise Levertov. New Directions, 1992. There is more good sense on form, line-break, and the poetic process in this collection than in most how-to manuals.

On Being a Poet. Judson Jerome. Writer's Digest Books, 1984. While matters of craft are treated, Jerome is particularly concerned with the calling of poetry in both individual and societal terms. He describes the indispensable features of the poet's personality and the ways in which audiences can be reached. Largely a book about the attitudes and experiences of one who chooses to be a poet.

The Poem's Heartbeat: A Manual of Prosody. Alfred Corn. Story Line, 1997. Excellent expansion of principles that were outlined in Chapter 6.

Poetic Meter and Poetic Form, rev. ed. Paul Fussell. Random House, 1979. The very best discussion of the ways in which form communicates. Though not written for writers, every poet should be thoroughly familiar with this book. Relatively sketchy on free verse, Fussell's treatment of the older conventions is unparalleled.

A Poetry Handbook. Mary Oliver. Harcourt, 1994. Helps writers connect feelings to craft. Accessible and inspiring.

A Poet's Companion: A Guide to the Pleasures of Writing Poetry. Kim Addoniszio and Dorianne Laux. Norton, 1997. A very well-balanced treatment that attends to craft, process, and finding subject matter offering a healthy attitude toward the writer's life.

The Practice of Poetry. Robin Behn and Chase Twitchell. HarperCollins, 1993. A collection of exercises gathered from master poet-teachers that covers everything from inspiration to form to revision.

Rhyme's Reason, 3rd ed. John Hollander. Yale University Press, 2002. A witty, engaging, and most competent review of poetic conventions. The book contains many poems written by Hollander to illustrate his definitions.

Writing Poems, 5th ed. Robert Wallace. Pearson Longman, 1999. Copiously illustrated and very thorough on all aspects of poetic conventions, elements, and approaches to composition. A useful chapter on submitting poetry for publication. Always solid, rarely inspiring.

WRITING FICTION

The Elements of Storytelling. Peter Rubie. Wiley, 1996. Strong on how to pace information and on the relationship between character motivation and time shifting.

The Lie That Tells a Truth: A Guide to Writing Fiction. John Dufresne. Norton, 2003. Excellent presentation of the storytelling process, with an approach rooted at once in realism and method acting. Theory.

Making Shapely Fiction. Jerome Stern. Norton, 1991. Fascinating, conversational cook's tour of the possibilities and hazards of prose fiction. Always practical and always engaging.

On Becoming a Novelist. John Gardner. Harper & Row, 1983. Focuses on a writer's nature, education, and habits of mind. Not a craft book (thus unlike his *The Art of Fiction*), but an effective discussion of writerly attitudes.

On Writing the Short Story. Hallie Burnett. Harper & Row, 1983. A classic in the field.

Self-Editing for Fiction Writers. Renni Brown and Dave King. HarperCollins, 1993. A splendid manual for showing beginners and even more experienced hands how to polish a fiction manuscript for publication. Filled with useful examples and exercises.

The Passionate, Accurate Story. Carol Bly. Milkwee Editions, 1990. One of the most readable discussions, with important suggestions on how the successful writer must approach first drafts differently from later drafts.

Technique in Fiction, 2nd ed. Robie Macauley and George Lanning. St. Martin's, 1987. This major revision of the 1964 classic is thorough, clear, and well illustrated.

The chapter on "Narrative Style: Time and Pace in Fiction" provides excellent coverage of material that we have had no room to include in this book. An expert enumeration of problems and the way to avoid them, with examples from published work.

Writing Fiction: A Guide to Narrative Craft, 6th ed. Janet Burroway. Pearson Longman, 2002. Conceptually rich and generous treatment. Copious examples, including student work. Good on underscoring the many ways in which fiction is *not* like life.

WRITING CREATIVE NONFICTION

The Art of Creative Nonfiction. Lee Gutkind. Wiley, 1997. Useful on "levels of truth" and on the way to structure narratives.

The Art of the Personal Essay. Selected and introduced by Phillip Lopate. Anchor Books, 1995. Perhaps the best anthology of its type.

Creative Nonfiction. Philip Gerard. Story Press, 1996. A solid overview of types, techniques, and challenges. Especially strong on structural issues and on exploring the self for materials.

In Short: A Collection of Brief Creative Nonfiction. Edited by Judith Kitchen and Mary Paumier Jones. Norton, 1996. An excellent sampling of the range of creative nonfiction in short forms.

Writing Creative Nonfiction. Theodore A. Rees Cheney. Ten Speed Press, 2001. Especially good for showing how to incorporate research in order to amplify various dimensions of the personal story. Also, a fine discussion of ethical issues in nonfiction writing.

Writing the Memoir: From Truth to Art. Judith Barrington. Eighth Mountain Press, 1997. Clear, concise handling of writing principles, legal issues, and making the most of critical feedback.

Writing Personal Essays: How to Shape Your Life Experiences for the Page. Sheila Bender. Writer's Digest, 2002. An interesting mix of familiar classroom information on standard essay structure and provocative suggestions for enlivening one's personal story with imagination and style.

Your Life As Story: Writing the New Autobiography. Tristine Rainer. Tarcher/Putnam, 1997. Rainer writes with an eye to the recent explosion in memoir writing while discussing the transformative dimension of autobiography.

WRITING PLAYS

Art of Dramatic Writing. Lajos Egri. Simon & Schuster, 1960. This classic text works from character out to the other elements of drama. Explorations of characters' natures, motives, and relationships lead to the focusing of conflicts on which to build plays. Useful for fiction as well.

The Art & Craft of Playwriting. Jeffrey Hatcher. Story Press, 2000. One of the best of the new books by a working playwright who is also teaching the craft on the college level. He avoids formulas and focuses on process and technique.

Art of Screenwriting. William Packard. Thundermouth, 2001. Not only screenplay techniques, but also fundamental aspects of plotting and storytelling are covered. Includes a handy "Screenplay Format Glossary" that is illustrated with an actual screenplay.

Perfect 10: Writing and Producing the 10-Minute Play. Gary Garrison. Heinemann Publishing, 2001. A friendly introduction for those interested in trying the sub-genre. A short book with nut and bolts suggestions and sample plays.

The Screenwriter's Bible: A Complete Guide to Writing, Formatting, and Selling Your Script. David Trottier. Silman-James, 1998. An A–Z overview of all aspects of the craft, including marketing and resources.

Solving Your Script: Tools and Techniques for the Playwright. Jeffrey Sweet. Heinemann, 2001. By the author of a play presented in Chapter 15, this book is exactly what its title says. Good comments on student written scenes.

Television and Screen Writing: From Concept to Contract. Richard Blum. 4th ed. Focal Press, 1995. Excellent on script concepts and formats.

ADDITIONAL TEXTS ON CREATIVE WRITING

Three Genres, 7th ed. Stephen Minot. Prentice-Hall, 2002. Like the present volume, an attempt to cover all areas. Insightful throughout, but Minot does not provide as many exercises.

A Writer's Time: A Guide to the Creative Process, from Vision Through Revision. Kenneth Atchity. 2nd ed. Norton, 1995. An excellent application of time management principles for writers. Overcoming writer's anxieties, exploiting dreamwork, and working toward economies of effort are key issues.

Writing Down the Bones. Natalie Goldberg. Shambhala, 1986. Focused on freeing imagination and creativity. Not a craft or technique book, but a discussion of how to tap inner resources. In its relatively short life, this book has become a classic.

Writing in a New Convertible with the Top Down. Christi Killien and Sheila Bender. 2nd ed. Blue Heron, 1997. Shaped as correspondence, this lively discussion of the creative writing process stresses getting started, keeping going, and making your writing vivid.

FROM REVISION TO SUBMISSION

Chicago Manual of Style. University of Chicago Press, revised regularly (use most recent edition). This is the standard manual for manuscript form. Conventions for capitalization, hyphenation, and anything else you can think of are found here.

Revising Fiction: A Handbook for Writers. David Madden. Penguin/Plume, 1988. Contains 185 questions against which to measure your story or novel draft. Concrete illustrated suggestions for finding flaws and making improvements.

Marketing and General Market Lists

CLMP Directory of Literary Magazines and Presses. Manic D Press [publisher has varied over the years]. Updated annually. One of the better market sources, it features entries for independent publishers, literary magazines, and online literary journals, and includes submission guidelines, contact names and addresses, circulation figures, and payment policies. Recent edition lists over 500 well-selected literary publications.

International Directory of Little Magazines and Small Presses. Dustbooks, published annually. If you get no other market directory, get this one. It is the bible for marketing literary writing, though it excludes the commercial presses and periodicals that few beginning writers can hope to find space in. Of course, you know about these already: they're on every magazine stand. Specialized subsets of this reference are available, but we recommend getting this comprehensive version.

Writer's Market. Writer's Digest, published annually. Thorough coverage of the paying markets in all genres, but not as useful for the beginner or noncommercial writer as Dustbooks' *International Directory.* Includes information on greeting card companies and syndication publishers as well as the usual outlets for creative writing. Over 8,000 entries in 2004 edition. Writers' profiles are also included. Also marketed as Writer's Market Online which includes CD-ROM and software to online subscription service for market updates.

Markets, Poetry

Directory of Poetry Publishers. Len Fulton. Dustbooks, published annually. More than merely a subset of Fulton's remarkable *International Directory of Little Magazines and Small Presses,* this volume is well indexed and has detailed information on each of the listed markets. Gives data on submission policies, rights purchased, and so on.

Poet's Market. Writer's Digest, published annually. Lists 1,800 poetry publishers with information about publishers' needs, audience, remuneration, and so forth. Includes articles and "insider" reports.

Markets, Fiction

Novel & Short Story Writer's Market. Writer's Digest, published annually. The latest edition contains roughly 2,000 listings of magazines and book publishers hospitable to fiction. Articles on fiction writing as well as interviews with editors and authors are also included, as is information on e-publishing.

Markets, Plays

Dramatist's Sourcebook. Theatre Communications Group, Bi-annual. Where to send scripts for prize competitions, production, and publication. The latest volume includes information on script preparation, agents, fellowships, residencies, and service organizations.

GLOSSARIES

The Concise Oxford Dictionary of Literary Terms. Chris Baldick. Oxford University Press, 1990. A fine reference, especially good on the terminology associated with modern literary theory.

A Handbook to Literature, 4th ed. C. Hugh Holman. Bobbs-Merrill, 1980. One of the clearest and most complete handbooks of literary terms. This book, or something like it, should be in any writer's library.

PERIODICALS

American Theatre. Theatre Communications Group. 520 Eight Ave., 24th Floor, New York, NY 10018. Articles and information for playwrights. Published monthly. Keeps up on the opportunities for submissions as well as theater gossip.

AWP Chronicle. Associated Writing Programs. George Mason University, Fairfax, VA 22030. Articles and information for writers. Published four times a year. One or two solid pieces per issue, especially on the teaching of creative writing.

Poets & Writers Magazine. 72 Spring Street, New York, NY 10012. This is the flagship publication of Poets & Writers, Inc. (See Organizations section.) Published six times a year, this is our favorite way of keeping up with what's going on in the literary community. Highlights include provocative interviews and reports on regional literary activity. Articles are not craft oriented, but nonetheless valuable to any writer. Good market information on small and university press needs.

Small Press Review. Dustbooks. P.O. Box 100, Paradise, CA 95967. This monthly effort of the Dustbooks family includes news about small presses, notices from presses and magazines soliciting material, and reviews of small press books. A good way to find a sympathetic reading for your first book. www.dustbooks.com/sprinfo.htm.

The Writer. 120 Boylston Street, Boston, MA 02116. This monthly magazine features advice columns on craft and marketing in the various genres as well as updated market news.

Writer's Digest. 1507 Dana Avenue, Cincinnati, OH 45207. Content similar to *The Writer*, but this one has, in recent years, given readers more for their money. The status of contributors continues to be impressive. Published monthly.

ORGANIZATIONS

As well as the national organizations, you will find many local and state support organizations for writers. Some are what might be called "full-service" organizations offering everything from workshops to readings. Others focus on a particular genre or service, such as offering public readings or monthly get-togethers. What follows is a small sampling of the many national, regional, and local literary arts organizations. Your state arts council will be able to help you find a group in your area.

Associated Writing Programs, Tallwood House, George Mason University, Fairfax, VA 22030. (703) 993–4301. www.gmu.departments.awp. Associated Writing Programs is an umbrella organization serving undergraduate and graduate creative writing programs, their faculties, and their students. One can become a member through affiliation with a member institution or as an individual. AWP holds annual meetings at which sessions are conducted on aspects of creative writing pedagogy. The organization runs a placement service for writers and sponsors award series in various genres. AWP publishes its *Official Guide to Writing Programs* and also the *AWP Chronicle*.

Poets & Writers Inc., 72 Spring Street, New York, NY 10012. (212) 226–3586. www.pw.org. A full-scale service organization for writers and the literary community, Poets & Writers is primarily an information source. Its various publications include pamphlets on copyright and on organizations that sponsor readings, and the invaluable *Directory of American Poets and Fiction Writers*, which is updated regularly. See also *Poets & Writers Magazine*.

Theatre Communications Group, 355 Lexington Ave, New York, NY 10017. (212) 697–5230. www.tcg.org. The national service organization for playwrights. Publishes the invaluable *Dramatist's Sourcebook* and the monthly magazine *American Theatre* that comes with membership.

The Alabama Writers' Forum, Alabama State Council on the Arts, 201 Monroe Street, Montgomery, Alabama, 36130–1800. (334)242–4076. Ext. 233. awfl@arts.state.al.us.

Asian American Writers' Workshop, 16 West 32nd Street, Suite 10A, New York, NY 10001. (212) 494.0061. www.aaww.org.

Georgia Writers Association, 1266 West Paces Ferry Road, Suit 217, Atlanta, GA 30327. (678) 407–0703. www.georgiawriters.org.

Beyond Baroque, 681Venice Boulevard, Venice, CA 90291. (310) 822–3006. www.beyondbaroque.org.

Guild Complex, 1212 N. Ashland, ste 211, Chicago, IL 60622. (773) 227–6117. www.guildcomplex.com.

Hellgate Writers, Inc., 2210 North Higgins, P.O. Box 7131, Missoula, MT 59807. (406) 721–3620.

Hudson Valley Writers' Center, 300 Riverside Drive, Sleepy Hollow, New York 10591. (914) 332–5953. www.writerscenter.org.

just buffalo, 2495 Main Street, Suite 436, Buffalo, NY 14214. (716) 832–5400. www.justbuffalo.org.

The Loft Literary Center, Suite 200, 1011 Washington Avenue South, Minneapolis, MN 55415. (612–215–2575). www.loft.org.

The Log Cabin Literary Center, 801 S. Capitol Blvd., Boise, ID 83701, Suite 100. (208) 331–8000. www.logcablit.org.

Maine Writers & Publishers Alliance, Bath, Maine 04530. (207) 729–6333 www.mainewriters.org.

North Carolina Writer's Network, P.O. Box 954, Carrboro, NC 27510. (919) 967–9540. www.ncwriters.org.

Poetry Project at St. Mark's, Second Avenue and Tenth Street, New York, NY 10003. (212) 674–0910. www.poetryproject.com.

Richard Hugo House, 1122 E. Pike Street, Seattle, WA 98122. (205) 322–7030. www.hugohouse.org.

Unterberg Poetry Center, 92nd Street YW-YHMA, 1395 Lexington Avenue, New York, NY 10128. (212) 415–5755. www.92Y.org.

Walt Whitman Center, Second and Cooper Streets, Camden, NJ 08102. (609) 964–8300. www.waltwhitmancenter.org.

Woodland Pattern Book Center, P.O. Box 92081, Milwaukee, WI 53202. (414) 263–5001. www.woodlandpattern.org.

Writers & Books, 740 University Avenue, Rochester, NY 14607. (716) 473–2590. www.wab.org.

The Writer's Center, 4508 Walsh Street, Bethesda, MD 20815. (301) 654–8664. www.writer.org.

The Writer's Center of Greater Cleveland, P.O. Box 14277, Cleveland, OH 44114. (216) 321–2665. www.cleveland.com/ultrafolder/ litlife/writing/bio.htm.

Writer's Center of Indianapolis, P.O. Box 88386, Marian College, Indianapolis, IN 46208. (317) 929–0623. www.indianawriters.org.

Writers' League of Texas, 1501 W. 5th Street, Suite E–2, Austin, TX 78703. (512) 499–8914. www.writersleague.org.

The Writer's Place, 3607 Pennsylvania Avenue, Kansas City, MO 64111. (816) 753–1090. www.writersplace.org.

The Writer's Voice Project: YMCA, 5 West 63rd Street, New York, NY 10023. (212) 875–4124. This organization has branches in many cities. For a complete list, contact The Writer's Voice Project.

OTHER INTERNET RESOURCES

Zuzu's Petals Literary Resource. www.zuzu.com. This resource has over 10,000 entries, including everything from organizations to useful books.

Poets.org. The official website of the Academy of American Poets. A great source of establishment news.

Poetrysociety.org. The offficial website of the Poetry Society of America.

Writingclass.com. The official website of the Gotham Writers' Workshop. One of the oldest and best online workshop packages.

Glossary of Key Terms

ABSTRACT: Language is abstract when it refers to intangible attributes or qualities—love, freedom, ideas. *Abstract* does not point to the material, physical bases of experience. Abstractions appeal to the intellect rather than to the senses. See **concrete**.

ACCENT: In poetry, equivalent to *stress*. Accent occurs when a syllable receives greater emphasis in pronunciation than those around it.

ACCENTUAL-SYLLABIC VERSE: Equivalent to *metrical verse*. The poetic lines are based on counting units that in themselves systematically alternate stressed and unstressed syllables. See **meter**.

ACCENTUAL VERSE: Verse in which lines are defined by the number of stressed syllables, as in "iambic pentameter." See **meter**.

ACT: Major unit of a play containing a major division of the dramatic action. Acts are often marked by intermissions or a lowering of the curtain. Act divisions punctuate the emotional or logical development of the play. See **scene**.

ACTION: "What happens" in a literary or dramatic work. The events that constitute the **plot**.

ALLITERATION: Proximate repetition of identical consonant sounds at the beginning of words or emphasized syllables. Use with great care to avoid unintentionally comic effects and to avoid calling so much attention to the sound that the sense becomes submerged in the lilting lyrical lullabies of labial liquidities.

ALLUSION: **Figure of speech** making an implied reference to something, real or fictitious, outside the work. Effective allusions bring useful associations to the reader's mind. "She didn't exactly have his head brought in on a platter, but she might as well have," evokes in a short space a complex story from the Bible.

AMBIGUITY: In a word, passage, or complete text, ambiguity allows for multiple interpretations, none of which is allowed to prevail over the others. *Unintentional* ambiguity can result in confusion and distraction because the meaning is merely obscure. Purposeful ambiguity allows one meaning to enrich another or all plausible meanings to complicate an issue or observation. Ambiguity should arise because the subject and emotions are complex, not because the writer has failed to think deeply about the subject or express it well.

ANALOGY: Comparison, often figurative, that explains or describes an unfamiliar object or idea through characteristics it shares with a more familiar object or idea. "A dictator is like the captain of a ship who thinks his crew has no other purpose than to obey his commands."

ANAPEST: See **meter**.

ANAPHORA: Repetition of a word or phrase at the beginning of successive lines.

ANTAGONIST: Character representing an obstacle or blocking force to the **protagonist** or hero. Often the rival or adversary of the protagonist. Satan to God in *Paradise Lost*.

ANTICLIMAX: Sudden drop in dramatic tension or seriousness in a fiction or drama. Usually a falling off after the **climax**, allowing for a serene concluding note. Sometimes an unintentional failure to sustain interest, relevance, or power. It usually occurs because the writer wants to spell out what happened, leaving nothing to the reader's or viewer's imagination.

ARCHAIC: Relating to diction that is filled with obsolete words or word usage: "yore," "go thee hence." Archaisms in contemporary poetry are rarely tolerated, since they most often suggest the wish to receive unearned poetic status by a liberal sprinkling of terms and phrases from revered works of the past. Archaisms can be used successfully for special purposes, such as to capture the flavor of the past in a historical or fantasy narrative.

ARCHETYPE: Psychic strain or pattern, believed to be universal and stored in the unconscious mind, based on the typical experiences of humankind. An image, plot element, character type, or descriptive detail can be archetypal. These primordial patterns are found in dreams, fantasies, and folklore as well as in conscious artworks. See also **myth**.

ASSONANCE: Repetition of identical or similar vowel sounds in close proximity, as in "fetch the message."

ATMOSPHERE: Figuratively, the "air" or essential **mood** of a literary work: creepy, peaceful, gloomy, cheery. Related to the less tangible aspects of **setting**.

AWKWARD: The stylistic mistake without a better name. A clumsy relation of **diction** or **syntax**.

BALLAD STANZA: Popular quatrain in folk songs and poetry, in which the first and third lines are iambic tetrameter, and the second and fourth are iambic trimeter. The usual rhyme scheme is *abcb*.

BATHOS: Insincere or excessive **pathos**; a falling away from the sublime to the ridiculous or from the elevated to the banal or commonplace. Also, a miscalculation in which intended elevation is not attained.

BEAT: Working unit of dialogue in which a shift in the emotional dynamic between characters occurs.

BLANK VERSE: Unrhymed iambic pentameter. See **meter**.

CAESURA: Pause, usually punctuated, *within* a line of verse.

CATASTROPHE: See **denouement**.

CHARACTER: Imagined personage in a literary or dramatic work.

CHARACTERIZATION: Means used to create a **character**. Includes what the character says and does as well as what the narrator or another character is given to say (or think) about the character. Presentation of a character's thoughts, fancies, and dreams is also a means of characterization.

CHRONOLOGY: Relating of facts or events in the order of their occurrence. The temporal order of events, as distinguished from their rearrangement in memory or in a **plot**.

CLICHÉ: Stale phrase, usually figurative, that reveals the writer's unwillingness to work hard for something fresh. Such borrowed formulas of expression as "it takes two to tango" have lost their original strength through overuse (and even misuse). See also **dead metaphor**.

CLIMAX: Moment of greatest tension in a dramatic or narrative work; it is most often also the major turning point. The moment at which the reader or audience is moved to its highest pitch of excitement. See **crisis**.

CONCEIT: Particularly elaborate or striking **figure of speech**. Usually characterized by its quality of wit or intellectual sophistication.

CONCRETE: Concrete diction points to particulars, and most often to material objects, their qualities, and their motions. The concrete fastens upon palpable experience. See **abstract**.

CONFIDANT(E):   In drama, a character designed to receive the confidences of another (major) character. This device allows the pressured character to unburden his or her feelings, thoughts, and secrets—which now also reach the eavesdropping audience. Though to the same end, this device is thought to be more natural than the **soliloquy**.

CONFLICT: Actions and tensions resulting from opposing forces set loose in a **plot**. These forces may be external or internal. For example: Jill and Beth want the same man. Arthur is torn between honor and greed. The shipmates pit themselves against the storm.

CONNOTATION: Suggestions or associations provoked by a word. Though connotations are subjective, totally private ones cannot be communicated. Even though you may associate "pain" with ice cream on a hot day, it is unlikely your reader will. It is because of connotation that there are no synonyms. If "rug" and "carpet" mean the same thing (see your dictionary), how come no one advertises "wall-to-wall rugging"? Contrast with **denotation**.

CONSONANCE: Loosely, the echoing of terminal consonants in end words. More narrowly, a kind of *slant* **rhyme** in which patterns of consonants surround contrasting vowels: *blood/blade*.

CONVENTION: Literary or dramatic convention is any recognized and accepted means of expression within a particular form—or the form itself. When we speak of *convention*, we are usually addressing those features or devices that are particularly unrealistic: for example, Shakespeare's characters' speaking in **blank verse**, or a first-person narrator remembering a conversation word for word that happened twenty years before. The public's acceptance and expectation is what matters here. Often, conventions embody "rules": the conventions of the **sonnet**, of the well-made play, of indicating a change of speakers (in fiction dialogue) by beginning a new paragraph. The language system itself is a body of conventions dealing with how words and phrases may be related, spelled, and punctuated. Informational and artistic communication depends on the conventions shared by artist and audience, writer and reader.

CONVENTIONAL: According to **convention**. Sometimes used pejoratively to suggest a lack of inventiveness, but most often meaning the tried and true way of doing something.

COUPLET: In poetry, a two-line unit of composition (sometimes a **stanza**). Couplet lines are usually matched in length, meter, and rhyme.

CRISIS: See **climax**. That moment after which things must change for better or worse.

DACTYL: See **meter**.

DEAD METAPHOR: Overworked **metaphor** that has lost its figurative vividness and its image content. When we say "the constitution is the *bulwark* of the nation," we are using a dead metaphor because the meaning is now merely denotative. What was once concrete is in the process of becoming an abstraction. We no longer envision a wall or the side of a ship in a battle scene. A dead metaphor is often a **cliché**.

DENOTATION: Direct, specific meaning. Often called the "dictionary" meaning of a word, in contrast to **connotation**.

DENOUEMENT: Outcome of a dramatic work; the trailing or falling action that follows the climax and ties up loose ends. In tragic plays, the denouement is called the **catastrophe**.

DESIGNATOR: See **dialogue tag**.

DEUS EX MACHINA: Literally, a god out of a machine. The abrupt and improbable appearance of a solution to a problem. The use of such devices (as a miracle cure that saves the young wife because the story must end happily) almost always reveals a deficiency in plotting.

DIALECT: Regional or cultural variation (in pronunciation, **idiom**, grammar, or **syntax**) within a language: for example, the Yorkshire dialect in England or the Cajun dialect in Louisiana.

DIALOGUE: Representation of speech in a literary or dramatic work. More strictly, the representation of conversation between two or more characters.

DIALOGUE TAG: In fiction dialogue, the terminology that identifies the speaker and (sometimes) describes the tone of the speech. For example, "William said," "she screamed," "Jim answered haughtily." Avoid the excessive and unnecessary, as in the last two.

DICTION: Refers to the choice of words in a particular work. Writers must consider the aptness of their word choices to the occasion. Conventionally, there are four levels of diction: formal, informal, colloquial, and slang. We have argued that diction should be accurate, precise, concrete, appropriate, and idiomatic. How words are characteristically chosen and combined by an author constitutes that author's **style**.

DONNÉE: Literally, "the given," the raw material—**premise, character, theme, setting,** or idea—on which the writer works toward the development of the finished work. Also, the assumption, not necessarily made explicit, out of which the work develops.

DRAFT: Unless prefaced by "final," an early version or state of a work in progress. The preliminary work, in writing, that will be revised and edited into the completed and "finished" work. As a verb: to compose; to write tentatively; to explore in writing without stopping for refinements.

DRAMATIC MONOLOGUE: In poetry, a speech by a single character, usually to an implied listener or audience, that reveals the speaker's personality. The speaker is an imagined character, clearly distinguished from the poet.

DRAMATIS PERSONAE: Characters in a drama, usually as listed and described in the bill or program for a performance and in the printed version of the play.

DRAMATIZE: To create a **drama**. In **fiction**, to render a scene in detail, stressing what the characters are saying and doing. *Showing* in contrast to *telling* or *summarizing*.

EDIT: To refine a piece of writing by (1) bringing it into conformity with accepted standards (**conventions**) of usage and genre, and (2) making adjustments of the relationships between parts. See **revise**.

ELEGANT VARIATION: Comes from fear of repetition and often results in elaborate searches for another word when the best choice has already been made. Usually, the attempt is to impress the reader with the range of one's vocabulary rather than to communicate. "Scribe" or "maker" for "author."

END RHYME: **Rhyme** that occurs at the end of lines.

END-STOPPED LINES: Lines that terminate with some degree of grammatical completeness and with punctuation, causing a definite pause or break when read aloud or "heard" silently.

ENJAMBEMENT: Also, *ejambment* and **run-on** line. No pause at the end of a line. The grammatical structure (and sense) "runs on" from one line to the next.

EPIPHANY: Sudden insight or moment of illumination in which an important truth is understood by a character (or, additionally, by the reader). Often, the epiphany is the climactic moment of a short story.

EPISTOLARY: Poem that takes the form and tone of a letter. It is a cousin of the **dramatic monologue**. An epistolary novel is one in which the narrative is developed through an exchange of letters between characters.

EUPHONY: Pleasant combination of sounds.

EXPOSITION: Explanation. Presentation (by the narrator in fiction, through dialogue in drama) of essential information, especially what has happened prior to the ongoing present of the literary or dramatic work.

FABLE: Brief **narrative**, in prose or verse, composed to make a moral point. Fables often involve improbable or supernatural events and sometimes use animals as characters.

FARCE: In drama, a low form of comedy that depends on fast-paced, surprising twists of plot, physical frenzy, and misunderstandings. Farce aims at broad, unsubtle effects.

FICTION: Imagined happenings presented in the guise of history or biography—thus **narrative**—and usually in prose. The two principal types of fiction are the novel and the short story.

FIGURE OF SPEECH (FIGURATIVE LANGUAGE): Expressing one thing in terms of something else. Figurative language exploits words for more than their literal meanings. Major figures of speech include **metaphor, simile, personification**, and **allusion**.

FIXED FORM: Poem whose structure is defined by a set pattern of meter, rhyme, and sometimes repetition of line or phrase. The **sonnet, villanelle,** sestina, rondeau, triolet, and limerick are among the more popular fixed forms.

FLASHBACK: **Scene** that interrupts ongoing action with prior action, usually triggered by a present event that jogs a character's memory.

FOIL: A **character**, set in similar circumstances to the **protagonist**, whose nature or behavior sharply contrasts to that of the protagonist. Thus a foil is used for the **characterization** of the primary personage.

FOOT: In metrical poetry, a unit combining stressed and unstressed syllables in a set pattern. See **meter**. **Lines** are measured by the number of feet they contain.

FORESHADOWING: Manipulation of events and access to information so as to anticipate, without predicting, future events. Frequently the reader does not know that something has been foreshadowed until the events themselves happen. Foreshadowing is one way of creating **verisimilitude**. **Mood** is often used to foreshadow.

FORM: See **genre**. Also, the arrangement of component parts in a literary or dramatic work so as to ensure unity and coherence.

FORMAL: Following established custom, usage, or **convention**. Respecting decorums, especially of ceremonial occasions. Following the principles of the literary or dramatic type. In **diction**, serious or dignified.

FORMAT: General structure or plan; more specifically, the conventions of manuscript presentation or the layout of a page or book: the typographical design.

FREE VERSE: Lines that follow no fixed metrical pattern, though they are often loosely rhythmical. Free verse often employs parallel grammatical phrasing, verbal repetition, and typographical patterning as means of expression.

GENRE: Literary kind, species, or form. Each genre is defined and recognized by its **conventions**. **Novel**, **short story**, **poem**, and **play** are all such categories, as are subdivisions such as **sonnet** and **farce**.

HERO: Major character around whom the events occur. Loosely, a character held up for emulation because of his or her superior traits. See **protagonist**.

HEROIC COUPLET: Iambic pentameter rhymed **couplets**.

HYPERBOLE: **Figure of speech** in which exaggeration is used to make a point. Calling a prose style "hyperbolic" is usually a negative comment.

IAMB: See **meter**.

IDIOM: Particular usage peculiar to a language (or to a subgroup of a language) whose meaning does not logically grow out of the meanings of its parts. For example, when we say "the kettle is boiling," we are using an idiom we understand but that would not translate literally into another language. Indeed, the kettle is *not* boiling, though the water is. Most idioms have their roots in **metaphor**.

IDIOMATIC: Usage in accord with an **idiom**. Natural, vernacular, a normal expression of native speakers that may violate the school rules of the language. Write idiomatically.

IMAGE: **Concrete** representation of sensory reality. Thing or quality that can be experienced by one or more of the senses.

IMAGERY: Collective character of the **images** in a particular work: its sensory content and the suggestive nature of that content.

INDIRECT DISCOURSE: Paraphrase of dialogue without actually quoting.

IN MEDIAS RES: "In the middle of things." The strategy of beginning a literary or dramatic work in the midst of the action rather than at the beginning of the chronological sequence. See **point of attack**.

INTERIOR MONOLOGUE: Expression of a flow of thoughts through the mind of a single character, usually limited to a single event or occasion. A reproduction of interior experience. See also **stream of consciousness**.

INTERNAL RHYME: **Rhyme** words occurring *within* consecutive or proximate lines, rather than at the beginning (head rhyme) or at the end (**end rhyme**).

IRONY: Most forms of irony involve a contradiction (often only apparent) for what is at first taken to be true and then is discovered to be otherwise. *Verbal irony* contrasts statement and suggestion: Hemingway has Jake say "Isn't it pretty to think so," at the end of *The Sun Also Rises*, but it's really rather painful to think so. This form of irony fades into **sarcasm**. *Dramatic irony* involves a situation in which the truth is the tragic opposite of what the characters think it is, and the audience knows this truth before the character does. It is thought to be ironic when fate or luck pushes someone's life in an unexpected, undeserved direction (*cosmic irony*). Irony always involves an incongruity of some sort. It can be comic or tragic. Swift's *Modest Proposal* is ironic: his real intention is to make it clear that the English landlords are already, in effect, eating Irish children. The apparent prescription for a problem is really a description of the problem.

LINE: Unit of composition in poetry. Line as an expressive concern is one of the few absolute distinctions between poetry and prose.

LINE BREAK: Convention of how lines end in a particular poem or how a particular line ends. Line breaks may coincide with or counterpoint sense and syntax. They may be preset or unpredictable. They may or may not be reinforced by repeated sounds.

LITERAL: **Denotative**, without **figurative** suggestion or embellishment. "Jane looks like Mary" is a literal comparison; "Jane looks like a goddess" is figurative (**a simile**). In translation, a capturing of the exact meaning of the original: "Word for word."

LYRIC: Poem, usually brief, expressing subjective reality. Most often cast in the **first person**, lyric poetry is called the poetry of emotion.

MASK: See **persona**.

MEASURE: See **meter**.

MELODRAMA: Form of **drama** in which sensational incident and audience thrills dominate over characterization. Melodrama disdains probability and **motivation** while insisting on cheaply won justice for one-dimensional heroes, heroines, and villains. Thus, *melodramatic* is often used as a pejorative term.

METAPHOR: **Figure of speech** that depends on an unexpected area of likeness between two unlike things that are said to be identical. Metaphors tend to be literally impossible assertions: "The moon is a gold doubloon."

METER: In poetry, the recurrence of a pattern of syllables (**syllabic verse**), stressed syllables (**accentual verse**), or **feet** (**accentual-syllabic verse**). Most often used to describe the latter, in which **lines** are defined by type and number of feet. There are four basic feet in English meter. The **iamb** is an unstressed syllable followed by a stressed (˘/), the **trochee** is a stressed syllable followed by an unstressed (/˘), the **anapest** is two unstressed syllables followed by a stressed (˘˘/), and the **dactyl** is one stressed syllable followed by two unstressed (/˘˘). Two other feet are used only for variation within lines. These are the **pyrrhic**, of two unstressed syllables (˘˘), and the **spondee**, of two stressed syllables (//). Line length is labeled as follows: monometer, dimeter, trimeter, tetrameter, pentameter, hexameter, and heptameter. Thus a line of four dactyls would be called "dactylic tetrameter." *Meter* means **measure**. See **prosody** and **scansion**.

METONYMY: **Figure of speech** in which the name of one thing is substituted for another with which it is associated in some way. When we read "The White House announced," we know that, in fact, the White House represents a spokesperson for the president or the administrative branch of government.

***MISE-EN-SCÈNE*:**   (1) The scenery and properties used in a play to represent the **setting** (lights, costume, sound, and special effects), along with the positioning and gestures of the actors. Whatever is needed to stage a scene. (2) By extension, the surroundings in which something happens.

MIXED METAPHOR: **Metaphor** in which the terms of comparison are shifted, usually unintentionally. "I smell a rat, and I shall nip it in the bud."

MOOD: Emotional atmosphere of a literary or dramatic work. The state of mind produced in the reader or audience. See **tone** and **atmosphere**.

MOTIVATE/MOTIVATION: Causes, within a **character** and the circumstances surrounding the character, for the ensuing action. Literally, the character is *moved* to seek revenge because of some prior event or need. Without adequate motivation, the **action** will seem arbitrary and unconvincing.

MYTH: **Narrative**, usually communally developed and transmitted, often involving supernatural events and gods. Myths tend to be stories of origination: of the universe, of a river, of the seasons, of an animal, of a royal family, of a nation, of a ceremony. Myths are grounded in the folk beliefs and ritual practices of tribes, nations, and races.

NARRATE: Act of reporting a story or a scene in a story. The result is the **narrative**.

NARRATIVE: See **narrate**.

NARRATOR: Person who tells the story to the audience. The narrator may be a character in the story (first person) or someone the author makes up to tell the story more objectively (third person). To speak of the story's "narrator" or "speaker" allows us to speak about the manner in which the story is being told without confusing that manner with the author's. A "naive narrator," for example, may take quite a bit of sophistication to create.

OBJECTIVE NARRATOR: See **point of view**.

ODE: **Lyric** poem generally celebrating a person, place, or event and usually employing a complex stanzaic pattern (see **stanza**). More loosely, any poem of commemoration.

OFF-RHYME: See **rhyme**.

OMNISCIENT NARRATOR: See **point of view**.

ONE-DIMENSIONAL CHARACTER: Character who is presented without an explanation of the reasons for his or her behavior and who behaves in a relatively predictable way (see **stock character**). The term is often used negatively. However, a good deal of comic writing relies on one-dimensional characters, and even in noncomic writing, many of the characters who have simple tasks in the plot need only to be one-dimensional.

ONOMATOPOEIA: Imitation in the sound of a word (or word combination) of the sound connected to the action or thing named or described. "Slap," "swish," and "ping-pong" are examples, as is Poe's invention "*tintinabulation* of the bells. . . ."

ORGANIC (FORM): Idea that a work of art should be seamless. Ideally, the work would be so integrated that no word, scene, character, line—not a period—could be changed or deleted without destroying the effect of the work. When form is organic, it seems to grow out of its content, that is, to be inseparable from it. This is an ideal that the writer should aim for—though, ultimately, the work may be submitted without having reached the promised land.

OVERWRITING: Usually caused by excessive use of adjectives and adverbs in an attempt to impress the reader.

OXYMORON: Compressed **paradox** in which an apparent contradiction makes sense when one of the terms is reinterpreted, as in "the sound of silence." Most often an adjective-noun combination: "terrible beauty" or "fortunate fall" or (humorously) "jumbo shrimp."

PACE: Tempo of the unfolding action as it is felt by the reader. The writer controls pace through a careful blending of dialogue, narration, description, exposition, and other elements. Long, unbroken stretches of one or another method destroy pace in fiction. In plays, pace refers to the timing of emotional ebbs and flows.

PARADOX: Contradiction, as in "paradoxically Mary's humor, the virtue that attracted people to her, kept her in hot water with her friends." Paradox creates tension in a work because the human mind wants to resolve the contradiction. For example, in the **oxymoron** "hateful love," the contradiction leads us to see that love (a good) is hateful (a bad) when it is unrequited. Paradox is not necessarily effective *unless you have provided a resolution or potential for a resolution* of that paradox.

PARODY: Imitation of the **style** of a literary or dramatic work, usually treating a contrasting subject.

PASSIVE: Grammatical constructions in which the action is not given an immediate actor or agent: the verb has no subject (in the expected place). For example, "The ball was hit out of the park." Who hit it? "It was discovered that. . . ." Who discovered it? Passive constructions are often called weak because the energizing link of actor and action is either missing or weakly made: "The pail of water was fetched by Jack and Jill." Though legitimate for some purposes, passive constructions often give the impression of indecision, fuzzy thinking or imagining, or downright deceitfulness, as in bureaucratic and academic prose.

PATHOS: Evocation of pity and sympathy, particularly by the sufferings of blameless or helpless characters.

PERIPETEIA: Sudden, usually unexpected, change of circumstances or fortune.

PERSONA: In poetry and prose fiction, the speaker or **narrator** of a literary work, especially as distinguished from the author. A figurative *mask* the author wears in order to tell a story. In drama, more simply a **character**.

PERSONIFICATION: Giving human characteristics to inanimate objects: "the sleeping sea." In contemporary writing this figure of speech is used sparingly and with great care.

PETRARCHAN SONNET: See **sonnet**.

PLOT: Sequence in which an author arranges (narrates, dramatizes) events (actions). The order in which the reader or spectator receives information. Only when this sequence is chronological is plot equivalent to story. A *story* stresses the temporal connections among events; a *plot* stresses the causal connections, often by introducing causes after their effects (as in a **flashback**).

PLOT LINE: Metaphorical way of talking about a plot as if it were, for example, a clothesline on which the author hangs scenes.

POETIC DICTION: Refers to the belief that poetry is, in part, characterized by a special type of language composed of archaic grammar and diction ("thou," "erst," "yore," "finny prey") and the avoidance of common, unpoetic words ("fish," "toes," "sit," "crap"). Modern poetic practice is to avoid poetic diction as artificial and, therefore, unable to communicate real emotions.

POINT OF ATTACK: Moment in a literary or dramatic work at which the plot, but not necessarily the story, begins. See *in medias res*.

POINT OF VIEW: Vantage point from which the materials of a story are presented. See Chapter 3.

PREMISE: Combination of **character**, **setting**, and situation at the **point of attack**.

PROOF(READ):   To check your manuscript for grammatical, punctuation, and spelling errors. A manuscript with many proofing errors is unlikely to receive a favorable reading because the editor's attention is drawn to the manner rather than the matter.

PROSODY: Principle(s) of organization in a poem, especially those dealing with the **conventions** of **versification**: sound patterns, **rhyme**, **meter**, and **stanzas**. Also, the study of such principles. See also **scansion**.

PROTAGONIST: Main character in a work from whose destiny the plot develops. See **antagonist**.

PURPLE PROSE: Elaborately adjectival and adverbial descriptions torturing the reader's patience with high-sounding but often hollow verbiage. See **overwriting** and **hyperbole**.

PYRRHIC FOOT: See **meter**.

QUATRAIN: **Stanza** of four lines.

RESOLUTION: Moment at which the work's conflicting elements come together. See **denouement**.

REVISE/REVISION: To look at again. Of course, the idea is not to look at it but to make changes in what you look at. "Revision" is not the same as "proofing" or "editing." The word is meant to suggest a more radical act in which the author rearranges, eliminates, and adds elements to the work.

RHYME: *True* rhyme is the agreement in the last vowel and final consonant (if there is one) of two or more words: "Terence this is stupid st*uff*/You eat your victuals fast en*ough*" (A. E. Housman). Rhyme is no longer considered a sure sign that you are in the presence of poetry. Contemporary poets tend to avoid the blatancy of true rhyme in favor of less intense echoes, known collectively as **off-rhyme** or **slant rhyme**. These include consonant echoes ("leaf/chaff") and even the more subdued mating of similar but not identical sounds ("meat/lad"). For some poets, the occurrence of the same sound(s) anywhere in the last syllable (or word) represents a rhyme ("lass/slip"). One special kind of off-rhyme is **consonance**, in which a pattern of identical consonant sounds surrounds any vowel: "kiss/case."

RHYTHM: Flow of stressed and unstressed syllables, pauses, line breaks, and other devices the writer can control for musical effects. While we most frequently speak of "rhythm" or the lack thereof when considering poetry, prose also has rhythms that can add to or detract from your work. "Rhythm" can also be used more loosely to refer to how the parts of a work are patterned.

RUN-ON: See **enjambement**.

SARCASM: Type of bitter **irony** or cutting remark. It means literally "to tear flesh." A sarcastic tone in a character or narrator should be used with great care since it can easily be mistaken for mere nastiness.

SASE: Self-addressed, stamped envelope. To be included with all submissions to publishers.

SATIRE: Refers to those works (or parts of works) in which the actions or the statements of the characters ridicule contemporary behavior or fashion. Satiric writing relies for its effects on **irony**. Mishandled, satire falls off into mere **sarcasm**.

SCANSION: Analysis of the metrical features of a poem (accented and unaccented syllables, **feet, caesuras**). When we *scan*, we use graphic symbols to indicate and highlight the essential features. Scansion does not create these features, it only indicates what they are by conventional markings. Stressed syllables are indicated by slashes (/) placed over the syllables, unstressed syllables by hyphens (-) or breves (˘) over the syllables, feet by vertical lines between the syllables (|), and caesuras by doubled vertical lines (||) at the pauses. **Rhyme** schemes are described by equating the rhymed syllables to letter symbols. Thus a poem in rhymed **couplets**: *aa bb cc*, etc.; a poem in **terza rima**: *aba bcb cdc ded*, etc.

SCENARIO: In playwriting and screenwriting, an extended outline of the play's **action** used to convey (to a producer) what the completed script will contain. Less formal than **treatment**.

SCENE: Dramatic subdivision of a work, identified by a change of place or time. See **act**.

SENTIMENTAL (SENTIMENTALITY):   Not to be confused with "sentiment" (feeling), *sentimental* refers to the expression of inappropriately excessive emotions. One writes sentimentally when the language demands from the reader more intense responses than the occasion really demands. Unless meant humorously or to reveal the self-indulgence of a character, the writer of the following is sentimental: "Did my itty bitty kitty hurt its poor sweet tail?" A mature audience is likely to laugh at or throw aside sentimental writing.

SET (SETTING):   Physical place (and all the things in it) created for a play or film or parts of them in which the scene happens. It is the place the author mentions or describes in a story. See *mise-en-scène*.

SHIFTS: Normally, a work is told in one tense (past or present) and from a single **point of view**. Avoid unexplained, casual, or hectic changes from one tense or point of view to another.

SIMILE: Usually described as a comparison using "like" or "as," the simile is a type of analogy in which the quality of one thing is used to identify it with what is essentially a different thing: "A state is like a ship." "She is as beautiful as a rose." Effective similes give us a sense of an unknown through a known. See **figure of speech** and **metaphor**.

SLANT RHYME: See **rhyme**.

SOLILOQUY: Related to the **dramatic monologue**, this kind of poem or (in a play) speech represents the reflections or thoughts of a character, addressed to no one in particular. A speech to one's self.

SONNET: Poem in fourteen lines, usually iambic pentameter, rhyming in one or another of the major sonnet traditions or a variation thereof. The **Petrarchan** (Italian) sonnet rhymes *abbaabba/cdcdcd*. The first eight lines (octave) always use envelope rhymes on the same two sounds. The final six lines (sestet) have various schemes, including *cdecde* and *cddcdd*. The

Shakespearean (English) sonnet has three **quatrains** of alternating rhyme followed by a **couplet**: *ababcdcdefefgg*.

SPONDEE: See **meter**.

SPRUNG RHYTHM: System developed by Gerard Manley Hopkins in which a **foot** has one accented syllable followed by either no or varying numbers of unaccented syllables. Sprung rhythm forces an accumulation of stressed syllables, as in these lines from "The Windhover" by Hopkins:

> Brute beauty and valour and act, oh, air, pride, plume, here
> Buckle! AND the fire that breaks from thee then, a billion
> Times told lovelier, more dangerous, O my chevalier!

STAGE BUSINESS: Refers to the actions of an actor that are usually *suggested* by the script rather than *stated* in it. For example, if coffee is being served, the actor may sip from the cup for a needed pause or in order to do something while another character is speaking.

STANZA/STANZAIC: Group of lines defined by a space break from another, usually equivalent, group of lines. Stanzas are frequently organized around metrical (see **meter**) and **end rhyme** patterns that are repeated from stanza to stanza. See **strophe**. Though both *stanza* and *paragraph* are divisions that assume there is some type of internal organization, we do not use the word "paragraph" when speaking of a stanza.

STEREOTYPE: From the process that printers use to produce many copies from a casting, by analogy this refers to a character type continued or repeated without change from one work to another. Though the word is often used with a negative connotation, writers often rely on stereotypes. See **stock character** and **one-dimensional character**.

STICHIC: Continuous, unbroken poem. Browning's "My Last Duchess" is stichic.

STOCK CHARACTER: Such characters lack a unique set of traits, but they are immediately recognizable from their past appearances: "the good-hearted whore," "the wise-cracking Brooklyn street kid," "the deaf but spry grandmother."

STOCK SITUATION: Conventional situations found frequently in fiction and drama. Examples are (1) a boarding house (dorm, boat, hotel) filled with quirky people and managed by one relatively sane person, and (2) two girls—best friends—falling in love with the same guy.

STORY: See **plot**.

STREAM OF CONSCIOUSNESS: Type of **interior monologue** that pretends to imitate the unselected, chaotic, unorganized flow of real thought. Useful for writing works that invoke psychological realism.

STROPHE/STROPHIC: A strophe is a major division of a poem. A strophic poem is one that is divided into distinct, though not necessarily equivalent, units rather than being continuous (**stichic**). See **stanza**.

STYLE: Manner of expression typical of a writer or artist. Distinctive styles result from identifiable habits of **diction** and **syntax**. "Style" can also refer to typical choices of material or point of view. Everyone, of course, has a style, but that style may be dull or ineffective because the language is trite or inappropriate for poetry or storytelling.

SUBPLOT: Secondary series of actions that reflects and heightens the concerns of the main **plot**. Within a narrative that presents a group's struggle to survive a storm, a romance may spring up between two of the characters. The romance, as it complicates the survival plot, adds interest and point.

SUBTEXT: What is implied rather than stated in a communication. Whatever the words say on the surface, like an iceberg, most of the message lies beneath. At the simplest level, for example, "How did you like my poem?" contains a request for affirmation, a concern about your opinion, and an indication of insecurity (otherwise why ask?). It *is not* a request for an honest opinion, and the asker would be hurt if you gave a negative one. See **text**.

SYLLABIC VERSE: Verse in which lines are defined by the number of syllables.

SYMBOL: Concrete objects (or evocations of concrete objects through words) that stand for or evoke images of ideas, stories, or other things. *Natural symbols*, like water, may literally be life-giving and purifying, as well as suggesting spiritual purification. Both natural symbols and cultural symbols (the cross) or signs (a traffic light or these very words) can communicate relatively simple ideas (stop or you'll get a ticket) and extremely complex relationships (sacrifice, redemption, and salvation). Everyone, including writers, uses symbols for communication. For the most part it is a mistake to work consciously to create symbols for your works. In the process of creating precise images, symbols will naturally emerge. Usually people do not read or go to the theater for the symbolism.

SYNECDOCHE: Figure of speech in which a part refers to the whole: "Can I borrow your wheels tonight?"

SYNOPSIS: Summary of the plot. If you are asked for a synopsis, don't tell what the work is supposed to mean; tell what happens.

SYNTAX: *Order* in which you place the words. For example, in English syntax you normally place the modifier before the noun and the subject before the verb. (*Grammar* refers to how a word is changed to indicate number, time, and gender.) Unusual syntax in poetry or awkward syntax in prose tends to call attention to the order of the words and draws attention from their meaning.

TERCET: **Stanza** of three lines. A *triplet* rhymes *aaa*.

TERZA RIMA: Three-line stanza interlocked with adjoining **tercets** rhyming *aba bcb cdc* and so forth, as in Shelley's "Ode to the West Wind":

> Make me thy lyre, even as the forest is:
> What if my leaves are falling like its own!
> The tumult of thy mighty harmonies
> Will take from both a deep, autumnal tone,
> Sweet though in sadness. Be thou, Spirit fierce,
> My spirit! Be thou me, impetuous one!

TEXT: Either the written material under discussion ("Let's look at the text") or the surface meaning of the material. *Text* often refers to the **denotative** meaning, the vehicle for the **subtext**.

THEME: Paraphraseable *message* in a work. Literally "a proposition," the theme of a work is likely to involve the writer's view about society, nature, or some other system of relationships. A writer who has studied and thought most deeply about a subject and who has felt it most intensely is likely to have the most interesting things to say about it. Even if your wish to communicate a theme is the reason you start writing, your job is to write the work well. Don't push the theme; it will get in.

TONE: Refers to the narrator's (or speaker's) attitude toward the subject and/or the reader: haughty, playful, somber, nasty, or ironic, for example. Tone is related to **point of view** and **subtext** in that it results from choices in content and technique: images, symbols, rhythms, sentence structure, and so on. Metaphorically, "tone of voice." See also **mood**.

TREATMENT: Technical term for an extended synopsis that presents your idea for a film or television program. There are quite specific rules for doing a treatment, and you should read several treatments before trying your own. Compare **scenario**.

TRITE: Word for a figure of speech that no longer surprises because it is shopworn. Do not confuse trite ("that's the way the ball bounces") with idiomatic ("shopworn").

TROCHEE: See **meter**.

VERISIMILITUDE: *Like* reality. Distinguish between reporting real events and making up events that appear to be real. The creative writer's task is the latter, not the former.

VERSE/VERSIFICATION: Metrical aspect of poetry. Sometimes used synonymously for **line** or metrical, rhymed passages; for example, "in the following verses. . . ." Also used pejoratively, as in "that's merely verse," suggesting the work in question only wears the costume of poetry.

VILLANELLE: Nineteen-line poem in which the first and third lines of the first **tercet** are alternately the last lines of the following four tercets and also form the couplet that ends the concluding **quatrain**: $A_1bA_2\ abA_1\ abA_2\ abA_1\ abA_2\ abA_1A_2$. Thus there are only two rhyme sounds. Most often in iambic pentameter.

Acknowledgments

We wish to thank the following authors and publishers for permission to reprint or publish for the first time the following:

Lines from the poetry exercise "Hope" by Wilma A. Alcala, used by permission of the author.

A. R. Ammons, excerpt from "The Muse" from *Collected Poems 1951–1971* (New York: W. W. Norton & Company, 1972). Copyright © 1971 by A. R. Ammons. Reprinted with the permission of W. W. Norton & Company, Inc.

Roger Aplon. "In Those Days" from *Barcelona Diary*. American edition Barracuda Press © 2002. (Roger Aplon, 701 Kettner Blvd. N. 28. San Diego, CA 92101). Reprinted with the permission of the author.

Susan Astor, "The Poem Queen" from *Dame* (Athens: The University of Georgia Press, 1980). Copyright © 1980 by Susan Astor. Reprinted with the permission of the author.

Elizabeth Bennett, "Small Explosion" from *Poet Lore* (Fall 1986). Reprinted (along with an earlier draft) with the permission of the author.

"Beaufort Scale" from *Webster's Ninth New Collegiate Dictionary*. Copyright © 1987 by Merriam-Webster, Inc., publisher of the Merriam-Webster® dictionaries. Reprinted with the permission of the publishers.

Stephen Bluestone. "Isaac on the Altiplano" and "Moses Miamonides" from *The Laughing Monkeys of Gravity*. Mercer University Press ©1995 (Macon, Georgia, 31207). Reprinted with the permission of the publisher. Prose commentaries used by permission of the author.

Robert Bly, "Three Kinds of Pleasures" from *Silence in the Snowy Fields* (Middletown, Conn.: Wesleyan University Press, 1962). Copyright © 1962 by Robert Bly. Reprinted with the permission of the author.

James Boswell, excerpt from *The Heart of Boswell: Six Journals in One Volume*, edited by Mark Harris (New York: McGraw-Hill, 1981). Copyright © 1981 by Mark Harris. Reprinted with the permission of Editorial Committee of the Boswell Papers, Yale University.

Cecilia Cassidy, excerpt from "Dialysis and the Art of Life Maintenance" from *GW Forum* 42 (Spring 1994). Copyright © 1994 by Cecilia Cassidy. Reprinted with the permission of the author.

Siv Cedering, "Figure Eights" from *Letters from the Floating World: New and Selected Poems*. Copyright © 1984 by Siv Cedering. Reprinted with the permission of the author and the University of Pittsburgh Press.

Poetry exercise "January Thunder" by Sally Cheney, used by permission of the author.

John Ciardi, excerpt from "At My Father's Grave." Copyright © 1966 by John Ciardi. Reprinted with the permission of the Literary Executor of the Estate.

Richard Conniff, "Close Encounters of the Sneaky Kind" in Smithsonian (July 2003). Reprinted with the permission of the author.

Noel Coward, excerpts from *Blithe Spirit* (New York: Doubleday, 1942). Copyright 1942 by Noel Coward. Reprinted with the permission of Michael Imison Playwrights, Ltd.

Sandy Daniels, "Inside Out." Reprinted with the permission of the author.

Don Delillo, excerpt from *Underworld* (Scribner, 1997).

James J. Dorbin, "Dreams." Reprinted with the permission of the author.

Rita Dove, "Loose Ends" from Judith Kitchen and Mary Paumier Jones, eds., *In Short: A Collection of Brief Creative Nonfiction* (New York: W. W. Norton & Company, 1996). Adapted from "A Handful of Inwardness" from *The Poet's World* (Washington: The Library of Congress, 1995). Copyright © 1995 by Rita Dove. Reprinted with the permission of the author.

Stephen Dunn, "Locker Room Talk" from Judith Kitchen and Mary Paumier Jones, eds., *In Short: A Collection of Brief Creative Nonfiction* (New York: W. W. Norton & Company, 1996). Copyright © 1996 by Stephen Dunn. Reprinted with the permission of the author.

Cornelius Eady, "The Dance" from *Victims of the Latest Dance Craze*. Copyright © 1985 by Cornelius Eady. Reprinted with the permission of Omnation Press.

Tony Earley, "Just Married" in *New Stories from the South: 2000*. Reprinted with the permission of Regal Literary, Inc. as agent for the author.

Denise Edson, "Anatomy of Melancholy." Reprinted with the permission of the author.

Poetry exercises beginning "Summer came on slow" and "Kirk burned for a while" by Bruce Fleming, used by permission of the author.

Stanley Elkin, selection from *The MacGuffin* (Simon and Schuster, 1991).

Annie Finch. "Thanksgiving" from *Eve*. Story Line Press © 1997. (Three Oaks Farm, Brownsville, OR 97327). Reprinted with the permission of the publisher.

Roland Flint, "Earthworm" and "August from My Desk" from *Resuming Green: Selected Poems 1965–1982*. Copyright © 1965, 1968, 1972, 1973, 1974, 1975, 1976, 1978, 1980, 1983 by Roland Flint. Reprinted with the permission of Doubleday, a division of Bantam Doubleday Dell Publishing Group, Inc.

Brendan Galvin, "Fog Township" from *Seals in the Inner Harbor*. Copyright © 1986 by Brendan Galvin. Reprinted with the permission of Carnegie Mellon University Press.

Charles Ghigna, "An Alabama Request" from *Southern Poetry Review* 23, no. 2 (Fall 1983). Copyright © 1983 by Charles Ghigna. Reprinted with the permission of the author.

Margaret Gibson, excerpt from "Affirmations" from *Long Walks in the Afternoon*. Copyright © 1983 by Margaret Gibson. Reprinted with the permission of Louisiana State University Press.

William Goyen, "Rhody's Path" from *The Collected Stories of William Goyen* (New York: Doubleday, 1975). Copyright © 1960 by William Goyen, renewed 1988 by Doris Roberts and Curtis William Goyen Family Trust. Reprinted with the permission of Weiser and Weiser, Inc.

Lines from the poetry exercise "Island" by Kirsten Benson Hampton, used by permission of the author.

Ernest Hemingway, "A Very Short Story" from *In Our Time*. Copyright 1925 by Charles Scribner's Sons, renewed © 1955 by Ernest Hemingway. Reprinted with the permission of Scribner's, a division of Simon & Schuster, Inc.

Ernest Hemingway, from *The Sun Also Rises* (Simon & Schuster, 1982).

William Heyen, "The Return" from *Long Island Light: Poems and a Memoir* (New York: Vanguard, 1979). Copyright © 1977 by William Heyen. Reprinted with the permission of the author.

A. E. Housman, ["From the wash the laundress sends"] from *The Collected Poems of A. E. Housman*. Copyright 1936 by Barclays Bank, Ltd. Copyright © 1964, 1967 by Robert E. Symons. Copyright 1939, 1940, © 1965 by Henry Holt and Company, Inc. Reprinted with the permission of Henry Holt and Company, Inc.

Richard Hugo, "Letter to Kathy from Wisdom" (excerpt) from *Making Certain It Goes On: The Collected Poems of Richard Hugo*. Copyright © 1977 by W. W. Norton & Company, Inc. Reprinted with the permission of the publishers.

Lines from the poetry exercise "Desert Rain Poem" by Alice S. James, used by permission of the author.

Philip K. Jason, "Meeting the Day" from *Near the Fire* (Washington: Dyrad Press, 1983). Copyright © 1983 by Philip K. Jason. Reprinted (with earlier drafts) with the permission of the author.

Edward P. Jones, "The First Day" from *Lost in the City* (William Morrow, 1992). Reprinted with the permission of the author.

James Jones. "Sandbags" and "The Beggar Woman" from *Viet Journal*. © 1974. Dell Publishing. Reprinted with the permission of Random House, Inc.

Ward Just, selection from *Echo House* (Houghton Mifflin, 1997).

Rod Jellema, "Because I Never Learned the Names of Flowers" from *The Eighth Day: New and Selected Poems*. Copyright © 1984. Reprinted with the permission of Dyrad Press.

Bel Kaufman, "Sunday in the Park" from *The Available Press/PEN Short Story Collection* (New York: Ballantine Books, 1985). Copyright © 1985 by Bel Kaufman. Reprinted with the permission of the author.

Maxine Kumin, "Stopped Time in Blue and Yellow" from *Our Ground Time Here Will Be Brief* (New York: Viking Penguin, 1982). Copyright © 1982 by Maxine Kumin. Reprinted with the permission of the author.

Marc Lapadula, "Night Bloom" (excerpt) (previously unpublished). Copyright © 1995 by Marc Lapadula. Reprinted with the permission of the author.

Philip Levine, "For Fran" (first stanza only) from *New and Selected Poems*. Copyright © 1963, 1984, 1991 by Philip Levine. Reprinted with the permission of Alfred A. Knopf, Inc.

Audre Lorde, excerpt from "A Litany for Survival" from *The Collected Poems of Audre Lorde.* Copyright © 1978 by Audre Lorde. Reprinted with the permission of W. W. Norton & Company, Inc.

Poetry exercise "Teen Mall Rats Die in Suicide Pact" by Rose MacMurray, used by permission of the author.

Karen Malloy, "Bagged Air." Reprinted with the permission of the author.

Excerpt from the short story exercise "GP" by Jerome Marr, used by permission of the author.

William Matthews, "Hope" from *Selected Poems and Translations 1969–1991.* Copyright © 1987, 1992 by William Matthews. Previously published in *Foreseeable Futures* (1987). Reprinted with the permission of Houghton Mifflin Company. All rights reserved.

Merrill F. McLane, excerpt from "Hotel Comercio" from *East From Granada: Hidden Andalusia and Its People* (Cabin John, Maryland: Carderock Press, 1996). Copyright © 1996 by Merrill F. McLane. Reprinted with the permission of the author.

James McLure, excerpt from *The Day They Shot John Lennon* (New York: Dramatists Play Service, 1984). Copyright © 1984 by James McLure. Reprinted with the permission of Bret Adams Ltd. Artists Agency.

Pablo Medina, "On the Beach" from *Exiled Memories: A Cuban Childhood.* Copyright © 1990 by the University of Texas Press. Reprinted with the permission of the publishers.

Peter Meinke, "Goalfish" from *Scars* (Pittsburgh: University of Pittsburgh Press, 1996). Copyright © 1996 by Peter Meinke. Reprinted by permission of the publisher.

Marianne Moore, excerpt from "The Fish" from *The Complete Poems of Marianne Moore.* Copyright 1935 by Marianne Moore, renewed © 1963 by Marianne Moore and T. S. Eliot. Reprinted with the permission of Simon & Schuster, Inc.

Anaïs Nin, excerpt from *The Diary of Anaïs Nin, Volume VI: 1931–1934.* Copyright © 1966 by Anaïs Nin. Reprinted with the permission of Harcourt Brace & Company.

"9 Bodies Found in Fort Myers Storage Unit" *Daily News.* Reprinted with the permission of the publisher. [This might not be true. I find no evidence of a permission.]

Jean Nordhaus, "Gloves" from *A Language of Hands* (Adelphi, Maryland: SCOP Publications, 1982). Copyright © 1982 by Jean Nordhaus. Reprinted with the permission of the author.

Joyce Carol Oates, "The Procedure" in *More Ten Minute Plays* (Samuel French, 1992). Reprinted with the permission of Rosenstone Wender as agent for the author.

Mary Oliver, "The Waves" from *Dream Work.* Copyright © 1986 by Mary Oliver. Reprinted with the permission of Grove/Atlantic, Inc.

Dan Pagis, "Written in Pencil in the Sealed Railway-Car" from *The Selected Poetry of Dan Pagis.* Copyright © 1989 by Dan Pagis. Copyright © 1996 by The Regents of the University of California. Reprinted with the permission of University of California Press.

Robert Peters, "On Capturing Ducks" from *Kane* (Greensboro, North Carolina: Unicorn Press, 1986). Copyright © 1986 by Robert Peters. Reprinted with the permission of the author.

Harold Pinter, excerpt from "The Collection" from *Complete Works: Two.* Copyright © 1963, 1964 by H. Pinter, Ltd. Reprinted with the permission of Grove/Atlantic, Inc.

Interview with Annie Proulx on Amazon.com accompanying order information for *The Shipping News.*

Wyatt Prunty, excerpt from "What Doesn't Go Away" from *What Women Know, What Men Believe.* Copyright © 1986 by The Johns Hopkins University Press. Reprinted with the permission of the publishers.

Poetry exercise beginning "The old man sits" by Linda Replogle, used by permission of the author.

John M. Richardson, "Lifeguards." Reprinted with the permission of the author.

Theodore Roethke, "The Moment" from *The Collected Poems of Theodore Roethke.* Copyright © 1963 by Beatrice Roethke, Administratrix of the Estate of Theodore Roethke. Reprinted with the permission of Doubleday, a division of Bantam Doubleday Dell Publishing Group, Inc.

Jay Rogoff, "Murder Mystery 1" and "Murder Mystery 2" from *Shaping: New Poems in Traditional Prosodies,* edited by Philip K. Jason (Washinton: Dyrad Press, 1978). Copyright © by Jay Rogoff. Reprinted with the permission of the author.

Poetry exercise "Departure" by Pedro J. Saavedra, used by permission of the author.

Poetry exercise "Sunday Evening Matisse" by Lisa A. Schenkel, used by permission of the author.

J.K. Rowling, excerpt from *Harry Potter.*

John Godfrey Saxe, excerpt from "The Blind Men and the Elephant: A Hindoo Fable" from the Preface to *Cultural Awareness Teaching Techniques* by Jan Gaston (Brattleboro, Vermont: Pro Lingua Associates, 1984). Reprinted with the permission of the publishers.

Karen Sagstetter, "The Thing with Willie" from *Glimmer train.* Reprinted with the permission of the Author.

Peter M. Scheufele, "Jazz Sundae." Reprinted with the permission of the author.

George Seferis, excerpt from *Days of 1945–1951: A Poet's Journal,* translated by Athan Anagnostopoulos. Copyright © 1974 by the President and Fellows of Harvard College. Reprinted with the permission of Harvard University Press.

Karl Shapiro, "A Cut Flower" from *Collected Poems 1940–1978.* Copyright 1942 and renewed © 1970 by Karl Shapiro. Reprinted with the permission of Weiser and Weiser, Inc.

Pat Shelly, "French Movie" from *Bogg* #56 (1986). Copyright © 1986 by Pat Shelly. Reprinted with the permission of the author.

Myra Sklarew, "Leaving" from *The Science of Goodbyes* (Athens: The University of Georgia Press, 1982). Copyright © 1982 by Myra Sklarew. Reprinted with the permission of the author.

Dave Smith, "Night Fishing for Blues" (excerpt) from *Cumberland Station* (Champaign: University of Illinois Press, 1976). Copyright © 1973, 1974, 1975, 1976 by Dave Smith. Reprinted with the permission of the author.

"Sovran Bank Advertisement." Copyright © by Sovran Financial Corporation and Lawlor Advertising. Reprinted with the permission of Sovran Financial Corporation.

Sharon Spencer and Dennis Toner, excerpt from *Ellis Island: Then and Now* (Franklin Lakes, New Jersey: Lincoln Springs Press, 1988). Material as published in *Paintbrush* 11/12 (1984–1985). Reprinted with the permission of the authors.

Sue Standing, "A Women Disappears Inside Her Own Life" from *Deception Pass* (Cambridge: alicejames books, 1984). Copyright © 1984. Reprinted by permission of the publishers.

John Steinbeck, excerpt from *Working Days: The Journals of The Grapes of Wrath, 1938–1941*. Copyright © 1989 by Elaine Steinbeck. Reprinted with the permission of Viking Penguin, a division of Penguin Books USA Inc.

Adrien Stoutenburg, excerpt from "A Short History of the Fur Trade" from *Land of Superior Mirages: New and Selected Poems*. Copyright © 1986 by The Johns Hopkins University Press. Reprinted with the permission of the publishers.

Jeffrey Sweet, "Last Day of Camp" in *More Ten Minute Plays* (Samuel French, 1992). Reprinted with the permission of the author.

Karen Swenson. "Time and the Perfume River" from *The Landlady in Bangkok*. Copper Canyon Press © 1944. (P O Box 271, Port Townsend, WA 98368). Reprinted with the permission of the publisher.

May Swenson, "The Blindman" from *New and Selected Things Taking Place* (Boston: Little, Brown and Company, 1978). Copyright © 1978 by May Swenson. Reprinted with the permission of Little, Brown and Company.

Adaptation of "Gun and Bible: Ritual Poem" exercise from *Creative Writing Exercises* by Ross Talarico, Associated Creative Writers, Publisher, 1982. Used by permission of the author.

Peter Taylor, excerpt from "In the Miro District" from *The Miro District and Other Stories*. Copyright © 1974, 1975, 1976, 1977 by Peter Taylor. Reprinted with the permission of Alfred A. Knopf, Inc.

Hilary Tham, "Chinese Medicine" and "Father" from *Lane With No Name*. Copyright © 1997 by Hilary Tham. Reprinted with the permission of Lynne Rienner Publishers, Inc.

Dylan Thomas, excerpt from "Do Not Go Gentle Into That Good Night" and "The Hand That Signed the Paper" from *The Poems of Dylan Thomas*. Copyright 1939 by New Directions Publishing Corporation. Reprinted with the permission of New Directions Publishing Corporation and David Higham Associates, London as agents for the Trustees of the Copyrights of Dylan Thomas.

Poetry exercise "Land Lord Dharma" by Jerry Webster, used by permission of the author.

William Carlos Williams, "The Dance" ("In Brueghel's great picture") from *The Collected Poems of William Carlos Williams, Volume II, 1939–1962*, edited by Christopher MacGowan. Copyright © 1955 by William Carlos Williams. Reprinted with the permission of New Directions Publishing Corporation.

Baron Wormser, "Soap Opera" from *Good Trembling* (New York: Houghton Mifflin Company, 1985). Copyright © 1985 by Baron Wormser. Reprinted with the permission of the author.

Paul Zimmer, "Eli and the Coal Strippers" from *With Wanda: Town and Country Poems*. Copyright © 1980 by Paul Zimmer. Reprinted with the permission of Dyrad Press.

Index